Security Without War

Security Without War

A Post–Cold War Foreign Policy

Michael H. Shuman and
Hal Harvey

with a Foreword by Senator Paul Simon

Westview Press
Boulder • San Francisco • Oxford

Copyright © 1993 by Westview Press, Inc.

Published in 1993 in the United States of America by Westview Press, Inc., 5500 Central Avenue, Boulder, Colorado 80301-2877, and in the United Kingdom by Westview Press, 36 Lonsdale Road, Summertown, Oxford OX2 7EW

Library of Congress Cataloging-in-Publication Data
Shuman, Michael H.
    Security without war : a post–Cold War foreign policy / Michael H. Shuman and Hal Harvey
        p. cm.
    Includes bibliographical references and index.
    ISBN 0-8133-1883-1 (hard). — ISBN 0-8133-1884-X (pbk.)
    1. United States—Foreign relations—1989– . I. Harvey, Hal.
II. Title.
E840.S48   1993
327.73—dc20   93-28625
                                                                                      CIP

Printed and bound in the United States of America

The paper used in this publication meets the requirements
of the American National Standard for Permanence of Paper
for Printed Library Materials Z39.48-1984.

10   9   8   7   6   5   4   3   2   1

To Ping and Carol

You will say at once that although the abolition of war has been the dream of man for centuries, every proposition to that end has been promptly discarded as impossible and fantastic. Every cynic, every pessimist, every adventurer, every swashbuckler in the world has always disclaimed its feasibility. . . . But now the tremendous and present evolution of nuclear and other potentials of destruction has suddenly taken the problem away from its primary consideration as a moral and spiritual question and brought it abreast of scientific realism. It is no longer an ethical equation to be pondered solely by learned philosophers and ecclesiastics but a hard core one for the decision of the masses whose survival is the issue.

—*General Douglas MacArthur, 1955*

Contents

Foreword, Senator Paul Simon   xiii
Acknowledgments   xvii

Introduction   1

    Cold War Policies in a Post–Cold War World, 3
    Toward a New View of Security, 10
    Organization of the Book, 21

Part One
Redefining Security

  1 New Security Threats   25

    Military Threats, 26
    Political Threats, 31
    Economic Threats, 33
    Environmental Threats, 35
    A Comprehensive Security Policy, 38

  2 The Limits to Force   41

    The Folly of U.S. Intervention, 41
    The Recent Record for Other Users of Force, 51
    Force as a Last Resort, 53

  3 The Dangers of Arms Races   55

    The Controlled Arms Race, 55
    The War Risks of the Controlled Arms Race, 58
    Political Insecurity, 66
    Economic Insecurity, 68

Environmental Insecurity, 73
Security Without Arms Races, 76

Part Two
Preventing and Resolving Conflicts

4   The Political Roots of Conflict   81

Strong Democracy and Interstate Peace, 82
Strong Democracy and Intrastate Peace, 85
Promoting Strong Democracy Abroad, 90
Promoting Strong Democracy at Home, 96
Perpetual Peace, 103

5   The Resource Roots of Conflict   105

The Connections Between Resources and Conflict, 105
Alternative Resource Policies, 112
Security Through Sustainability, 119

6   The Economic Roots of Conflict   123

The Bretton Woods Economic Order, 124
The Insecurities of Cold War Liberalism, 125
Security Through Development, 133
Conversion Planning, 140

7   Conflict Resolution   143

Bilateral Cooperation, 145
International Norms, 148
International Regimes, 151
Global Institutions, 156
The End of History? 161

Part Three
Military Defense Against Aggression

8   Nonprovocative Defense   165

The European Offensive Arms Race, 165
The Advantages of NPD, 168

Components of NPD, 171
Criticisms of NPD, 175
NPD Today, 178

9   Collective Security   181

UN Collective Security, 183
Defensive Collective Security, 187

10   Control of Nuclear Weapons   193

Deep Arms Control, 194
Denuclearization, 205
Making Disarmament Possible, 211

Part Four
Implementation

11   Grassroots Participation   219

What Citizens Can Do for Peace, 219
Municipal Foreign Policies, 224

12   A Genuine New World Order   233

A Practical Vision, 233
A Resilient Security System, 235
National and International Savings, 242
Other Security Threats, 245
Choices for the Future, 251

Notes   255
Annotated Bibliography   297
List of Acronyms   303
About the Book and Authors   305
Index   307

Foreword

Security Without War is an ambitious book, but I would expect no less from Michael Shuman and Hal Harvey. They have done an admirable job exploring a future they believe can unfold without military conflict. Whether that future can be realized depends on how we reorder our thinking about the possibilities of the post–Cold War world.

With the dissolution of the Soviet Union, we now have new opportunities and new challenges. We're still sorting through the wreckage of the Cold War to come up with a new way of viewing international security. While I don't agree with everything in this book, I am pleased that a serious policy and academic debate has been joined in the authors' effort.

What are the future security threats that our planning must consider? The authors' holistic approach to security expands the traditional definition beyond military threats to include environmental, political, and economic threats as well. I agree with them that we ignore any one of these threats at our peril.

The thorny question of when to use force has plagued us since the beginning of the Republic. Despite the progress in arms control, we continually have to strive toward nonviolent conflict resolution. This is not always an easy task, but it is nevertheless more and more important as growing numbers of nations, despite our best efforts, build and acquire nuclear, chemical, and biological weapons.

In recent times, we have been fortunate that the wars we have fought have not been against adversaries possessing weapons of mass destruction. But as time passes, it becomes increasingly foolhardy to count on such good fortune. Strengthening international institutions like the United Nations and the International Atomic Energy Agency is in the best interests of international stability.

This volume also presents a third view with which I have long agreed, the view that the costs of an out-of-control arms race outweigh any potential benefits. While expanding our arsenal costs a great deal in dollar terms, the authors correctly assess the more frequently overlooked costs—the environmental costs of dumping nuclear waste, for example, or the national security costs of pressing other countries to engage in an arms race for their own sense of security. The challenge of this decade is to learn how to make other countries feel more secure, especially those nations that have not been our allies.

But perhaps the aspect of this book that I agree with most strongly is the premise that a foreign policy based on spreading democracy will work to prevent future conflicts. Not only does a democratic system of checks and balances act as a barrier to aggressive war, but these same checks and balances work to limit the civil wars that ring the globe. Investing in democratic institution-building is money well spent.

The authors also call for a new approach to international economic development, an approach that goes beyond doling out funds. Their approach includes fostering domestic compacts that mandate environmental protection standards, workers' rights, and minimum wages and improving corporate behavior, especially with regard to consumer protection. Attacking social ills through such compacts is a common-sense approach to forestall the inequities that can lead to war.

Enforcing international norms and laws through foreign policy will, in the long run, reduce conflict. I have supported the formation of an international criminal court to hold leaders responsible for their actions when those actions violate international law. If those who start aggressive wars and engage in war crimes are held accountable for their actions, other leaders will think twice before engaging in force to resolve disputes.

I especially appreciate the stress placed on nuclear disarmament and stopping the spread of nuclear weapons. The current trend dictates that many countries in time will have the requisite level of technology to build nuclear weapons. While the authors' conclusions in this area will be challenged—and I myself reach a different conclusion on this—the issues raised are important and provocative and demand serious study, consideration, and debate.

Ultimately, we have to move beyond theory into the practical world of action, and action by peoples, not just governments. Individuals will increasingly contribute more to building a peaceful world than they ever have in the past. This book shows us how to build on the new opportunity presented by the end of the bipolar world. *Security Without War* gives us a blueprint for moving into a new era of worldwide security while leaving behind the age-old horrors of war.

Senator Paul Simon

Acknowledgments

What should U.S. security policies look like in the twenty-first century?

When the two of us came together in the summer of 1986 to address this question, we were struck by the persistence of Cold War thinking. Even though a new, dynamic leader in the Kremlin was beginning to speak about disengagement from Afghanistan, demilitarization of Europe, deep cuts in nuclear weapons arsenals, and a new openness in Soviet life, U.S. security planners continued to assume that the Soviet Union was an expansionist "evil empire" bent on exploiting the Third World and conquering Western Europe. The Cold War was on the verge of ending, and yet the architects of U.S. foreign policy were completely unprepared for change. We set out to examine what this new world might look like.

This book was originally scheduled for publication in early 1990. Neither of us, however, foresaw the fall of the Berlin Wall and the rapid toppling of Communist dictators in Eastern Europe. By the time the book was about to go to press, our first four chapters had become obsolete.

Over the following two years, we reworked, reorganized, and updated the manuscript—not an easy task given the dizzying rate of global change. Germany reunified. The Warsaw Pact dissolved. Iraq took over Kuwait but was ejected by a U.S.-led multinational force. The Soviet Union fragmented into fifteen new nations. Old conflicts in El Salvador, Mozambique, and Cambodia neared settlement, while new wars engulfed Somalia and the former Yugoslavia.

Today, one fact is finally settled: The Cold War is over. The United States now has no choice but to formulate a security policy that takes full account of the changed circumstances. What follows are recommendations for a fundamentally new set of principles and policies for U.S. security planners.

Many people helped make this book possible. We wish to thank first Daniel Arbess, who participated in our initial discussions and writing sessions and helped frame many of our arguments. Arbess wrote the first drafts of our chapters concerning nuclear weapons and provided input at all stages of the project.

We owe special thanks to members of the staff and the board of the Rocky Mountain Institute (RMI) for sponsoring this endeavor long past its initial deadline, for critiquing our work in several invaluable roundtables, and for overseeing the accounting, fund-raising, and other logistics. We are particularly grateful to Amory Lovins, director of RMI, for two careful readings, each of which produced detailed suggestions and questions.

We also thank the staff and board of the Center for Innovative Diplomacy for allowing Michael Shuman to spend more than a year transforming the second draft into the completed book and the Institute for Policy Studies for providing him with office space and collegial support during this period.

We have been fortunate to receive comments and suggestions from dozens of readers. Foremost among them was Ronnie Dugger, publisher of *The Texas Observer*, who helped to harmonize our disparate writing styles. Dugger's incisive but polite manner continually helped us sharpen our arguments without compromising our views. Others who provided especially valuable comments were Len Ackland, Gina Adams, Ruth Adams, Larry Agran, Richard Barnet, John Cavanagh, Daniel Deudney, Daniel Ellsberg, Gordon Feller, Dietrich Fischer, Paul Golob, Mark Harvey, Richard Healey, John Holdren, Gregory Kats, Dominic Kulik, Michael Nagler, Averill Powers, Marcus Raskin, Wendy Silverman, Mark Sommer, Will Swaim, Betsy Taylor, Yevgeni Velikov, Frank von Hippel, Victor Wallis, Barbara Wien, and David Yaskulka.

Some of the research for this book would have been impossible without the skilled assistance of William Keepin, Richard Heede, and Terry Sabonis-Chafee. Victoria Baecher, Jennifer Kassan, Lynda Liu, Michelle Rinker, Leslie Rose, Sam Natapoff, and Anne Wilkas each provided several weeks of essential copy editing and cite-checking. Ginni Galicinao overcame computer breakdowns, deciphered our hieroglyphic handwritings, and integrated several rounds of changes into the evolving manuscript.

Funding for our work was generously provided by the CS Fund (Marty Teitel), the Mertz-Gilmore Foundation (Larry Condon and

Robert Crane), the Rockefeller Brothers Fund (William Deitel), the General Service Foundation (Marcie and Robert Musser), the Ploughshares Fund (Sally Lilienthal, Wayne Jaquith, and Michael McCally), Alan Kay, Ira Wallach, and Steven Hyde. During the workshops in Aspen, Connie Harvey also generously donated working space and provided comments well beyond the call of her duties as our host.

We are grateful for the unwavering support of Jennifer Knerr at Westview Press and for the skillful editing of Deborah Lynes and Richard Kalmanash.

Our deepest thanks go to Carol Bernstein Ferry and W. H. Ferry, to whom we have dedicated our book. When we began this book, we were in our twenties; Carol and Ping convinced us to set aside doubts caused by our relative youthfulness and take our idealism seriously enough to produce this book. At critical moments, they provided encouragement, sponsored a review forum for our New York funders, and goaded us to wrap up our work and publish it.

We have been privileged over the years to share our ideas and engage in sharp dialogues with hundreds of scholars, military analysts, politicians, journalists, and activists, many of whom we cite in the endnotes. We thank them for providing the threads of this tapestry, and we of course absolve them of any responsibility for our own shortfalls or oversights.

Michael H. Shuman
Hal Harvey

Introduction

For a brief moment in the late 1980s the world seemed to be on the verge of abolishing war. The Soviet Union withdrew its troops from Afghanistan and allowed one Communist regime after another to collapse in Poland, Czechoslovakia, East Germany, and Romania, prompting even hardliners like President Ronald Reagan to pronounce the Cold War over.[1] The U.S. Congress cut off military aid to the Contra rebels in Nicaragua and gave the Central American peace plan organized by President Oscar Arias of Costa Rica a chance to work. Soviet General Secretary Mikhail Gorbachev and President Reagan struck an agreement with South Africa and Cuba to remove all foreign troops from Namibia and Angola. Vietnam announced its intentions to withdraw from neighboring Kampuchea, and the United Nations began sponsoring peace talks with the Khmer Rouge, Prince Sihanouk, and the provisional government in Phnom Penh. As a euphoria of peace swept across the planet, State Department analyst Francis Fukuyama wrote a widely discussed article proclaiming the "end of history."[2]

But the celebration was short-lived. On August 2, 1990, Saddam Hussein, the iron-fisted dictator of Iraq, ordered his tanks to roll into the tiny kingdom of Kuwait. Within days the million-man Iraqi army crushed the emir's resistance and established undisputed control over Kuwait's people and territory.

Prior to August few Americans even knew where Kuwait was, let alone understood its geostrategic importance. Having a land mass smaller than the state of Massachusetts and a population the size of Houston, Kuwait hardly seemed to be a country worthy of a major war. But Kuwait had one resource other nations desperately wanted—oil. With a single military maneuver Saddam Hussein had virtually doubled his petroleum reserves and seized control over a fifth of the total global capacity for oil production.[3] And many feared that he would not stop at Kuwait. If his troops continued marching southward for another day or two, Hussein would capture the oil-rich kingdom of Saudi Arabia. We must defend Saudi Arabia, implored a *Wall Street Journal* editorial, "to protect the integrity of the world's oil supply."[4]

After emergency meetings with King Fahd of Saudi Arabia, President George Bush drew "a line in the sand" and immediately dispatched 100,000 U.S. troops to the Saudi-Kuwaiti border. He saw the crisis as an opportunity for the United States to build a "new world order." "In the life of a nation," Bush exhorted, "there comes a moment when we are called to define who we are and what we believe."[5] He convince Syria, Egypt, Britain, France, and thirty other nations to join in the defense of Saudi Arabia by sending troops, ships, weapons, and financial assistance. To win the support at the United Nations of once hostile nations such as the Soviet Union, China, and Zimbabwe, he offered loans, debt forgiveness, and upgraded relations. By the time the Security Council voted on whether to impose an economic embargo on Iraq, all five permanent members endorsed what became known as Operation Desert Shield, a mission dedicated to protecting Saudi Arabia.

In November, with congressional elections safely behind, President Bush declared his impatience with the embargo, doubled the number of U.S. troops in Saudi Arabia, and changed the objective of the assembled forces from defense to offense. The Security Council, under strong pressure from the United States, gave the coalition permission to wage war if Saddam Hussein did not withdraw from Kuwait by January 15, 1991. The day after the deadline expired, the United States announced Operation Desert Storm and began bombing Baghdad.

It took less than two months for the United States to achieve a lopsided military victory over Iraq, but the triumph was not without cost. Iraqi forces set more than half of the oil wells in Kuwait ablaze, executed or tortured thousands of Kuwaitis, and looted and vandalized tens of billions of dollars worth of Kuwaiti property. The three largest oil spills in history ravaged the fragile ecosystem of the Persian Gulf, a vital source of fish for millions of people in six countries. The dazzling array of high-tech weapons killed between 1,500 and 70,000 Iraqi soldiers and between 1,000 and 3,000 civilians.[6] Several months after the end of the war a team of medical and law students from Harvard University estimated "conservatively" that

170,000 Iraqi civilians died from shortages of food, medicine, and other supplies caused by the destruction of water, sewage, and electric power systems during the war and by the continuing UN embargo of the country.[7]

Perhaps the most tragic cost of the war was the squandered opportunity for the United States to help build a genuine new world order. Almost nothing about Desert Storm was "new" or "orderly." Instead of examining the crisis with a fresh dose of self-criticism and admitting to any U.S. culpability in precipitating it—such as the U.S. ambassador to Iraq, April Glaspie, telling Saddam Hussein a week before the invasion that "we have no opinion on the Arab-Arab conflicts, like your dispute with Kuwait"—President Bush singled out the Iraqis for all the blame.[8] Instead of establishing a new way to respond to aggression with nonviolent pressures, the United States abandoned economic sanctions long before they had a reasonable chance to work (most experts said one to two years would have been necessary). Instead of attempting to discuss Iraq's grievances through an orderly process of negotiations, U.S. officials insisted that short of Hussein's unconditional withdrawal from Kuwait there was nothing to talk about. And instead of creating a new UN military force capable of handling this crisis and preventing future ones, the Pentagon decided to mount the military operation itself, with only a fig leaf of approval from the Security Council. A more reflective, nonviolent, preventive, and multilateral response could have laid the foundation for a very different kind of world order. But the United States preferred to follow the familiar foreign policy script it had been using since the end of World War II.

Cold War Policies in a Post–Cold War World

For forty-five years the centerpiece of U.S. security policy was the Cold War. Proclaiming the need to deter a nuclear attack by the Soviet Union, the United States built a "holy triad" of weapons systems—land-based intercontinental missiles, submarine-based missiles, and strategic bombers. To contain the threat of a Soviet invasion sweeping across Western Europe, it joined with the nations of this region to form the North Atlantic Treaty Organization (NATO) and mobilized troops, tanks, aircraft, and "tactical" nuclear weapons along the East-West divide. Sounding alarms over the dangers of

Soviet subversion in the Third World, it sent troops to such far-flung places as Korea and Vietnam and supported counterrevolutionary forces in dozens of other countries.

By late 1988, however, the Cold War was beginning to come to an end. In a remarkable polling series sponsored by Americans Talk Security (ATS), a majority of Americans said—for the first time since World War II—that they regarded the Soviet Union as either a minor threat or no threat at all.[9] That President Reagan, a conservative with unimpeachable anti-Communist credentials, could laud Mikhail Gorbachev's policies of glasnost (openness) and perestroika (restructuring), could declare that the Soviets no longer felt "an obligation to expand" and conquer the world,[10] and could enter into an arms control agreement as significant as the Intermediate-range Nuclear Forces (INF) accord, prompted many Americans to reevaluate the Soviet threat. The facts were clear. Contrary to four decades of behavior during the Cold War, the Soviets were withdrawing their troops from Afghanistan, distancing themselves from revolutionary clients in the Third World, encouraging independent and reformist policies in Eastern Europe, and casting aside offensive military strategies and weapons developments.

Yet by August 1990, when Saddam Hussein invaded Kuwait, the United States was not prepared to discard its old security policies. Rather than recognize that Saddam Hussein was a fundamentally different kind of threat in a fundamentally different kind of world, U.S. security planners clung to the same five principles that undergirded the Cold War:

1. Gauge threats to security by focusing on military adversaries.
2. Respond to these adversaries by intimidating them through the acquisition and, if necessary, the use of fearsome weapons.
3. Emphasize tough military action ahead of "soft" alternatives to prevent and resolve conflicts without the use of force.
4. Organize security policies unilaterally so that the United States can guarantee that international affairs are consistent with its own interests.
5. Rely exclusively on foreign policy experts in the executive branch of government to craft security policies—and leave Congress, state and local governments, and the rest of the public on the sidelines.

These principles helped the United States achieve a victory of sorts in the Cold War, but they proved inadequate as the nation dealt with the first post–Cold War crisis.

Focus on Military Threats

Just as security planners had fixated on the Soviet military threat for forty-five years while downplaying other dangers in the world (such as growing poverty, resentment, and weapons proliferation in the Third World), they fixated on the military threat posed by Saddam Hussein. The initial deployment of U.S. troops in August clearly had deterred the Iraqi leader from invading Saudi Arabia and threatening other countries in the region. Nevertheless, President Bush branded Hussein as "worse than Hitler," warned against "appeasement," and rallied U.S. allies, the United Nations, and the American people to support full-scale war against Iraq. All other urgencies for U.S. foreign policy—assisting the new democracies in Eastern Europe, supporting the Soviet Union's transition from totalitarianism, strengthening U.S. competitiveness in the world economy—were given secondary status.

Finding a convenient villain was nothing new for U.S. security policy. A few years earlier it was the focus on the Iranian leader Ayatollah Khomeini that helped to create the Iraqi threat in the first place. Despite the plain evidence that Saddam Hussein had transformed Iraq into a brutal police state, poisoned thousands of indigenous Kurds with nerve gas, and launched an unprovoked attack on Iran in 1980, U.S. leaders praised him for being a secular, reasonable leader and tilted toward him during the eight-year Iran-Iraq War. Thanks in part to U.S. reluctance to regulate the international arms trade, Western munitions merchants eagerly sold Hussein tanks, fighters, and missiles that would later be aimed at U.S. troops. Technically, U.S. businessmen were not allowed to sell weapons to Hussein, but they nevertheless assisted the Iraqi war machine by selling components, machines, and tools that could then be used to produce advanced weaponry. The United States also provided Hussein with billions of dollars in loans and food credits, freeing up Iraqi resources for more arms spending.[11] The Atlanta branch of the Rome-based Banca Nazionale del Lavoro loaned more than $2 billion to Iraq, which, according to *Financial Times* correspondent Alan Friedman, "helped to finance Saddam's nuclear and chemical weapons, cluster bombs, SCUD missiles, and ballistic missiles"—possibly with White House approval.[12] When Iraq attacked the USS *Stark* in 1987, President Reagan wrote it off as a regrettable accident. Most Western governments looked the other way as Iraq worked assiduously to build factories for intermediate-range missiles, chemical and biological weapons, and nuclear bombs. Even in the weeks prior to Iraq's invasion, the Bush administration was fighting efforts by congressional Democrats to cut off economic assistance to Iraq.

Americans celebrated the end of the Persian Gulf War with yellow ribbons, fireworks displays, and victory parades, but many analysts quietly began to wonder how the new fixation on Saddam Hussein might come back to haunt the country. Did it make sense in early January 1991 to mute criticism of the Soviet crackdown on the Lithuanian independence movement because the United States was afraid of a Kremlin defection from the allied coalition a week before the start of Desert Storm? How smart was it to bully Bonn into contributing billions of dollars to the war effort after worrying just a few months earlier about resurgent militarism in a reunified Germany?[13] What new dangers had the United States created in the Middle East by providing billions of dollars in arms to Saudi Arabia, allying with Syria, or strengthening the relative power of fundamentalist Iran?[14] How many of the weapons shipped to the Middle East would inadvertently wind up in the hands of terrorists? Was it wise to exhaust foreign policy resources on a war in the Persian Gulf while dozens of other critical tasks remained unaddressed, such as preventing wars among ethnic groups in Eastern Europe, cutting nuclear-weapons stockpiles, and lowering the trade imbalance with Japan?

Intimidate Enemies

Another Cold War habit that the United States could not shake during the Persian Gulf War was to be provocative—to take a hard line in negotiations, to match offensive forces with terrifying counteroffensive forces, and to back up these threats, if necessary, by going to war. For four decades NATO threatened to transform the cities of the Soviet Union and Eastern Europe into smouldering ruins if the Warsaw Pact ever invaded Western Europe. Likewise, the principal tools the Bush administration used in the Persian Gulf were threats.

Leave Kuwait unconditionally, Iraq was told, or the West will strangle your economy and bomb your cities into the Stone Age.

Force, however, is inevitably a blunt instrument that rarely achieves the specific security policy objectives sought. Once Hussein's forces began retreating, President Bush realized that continuation of the melee would plunge Iraq into a long, uncontrollable civil war, with Shiite Muslims in the south and Kurds in the north vying to carve out new nations—and with Iran eagerly waiting on the eastern border to take advantage of the new power vacuum. Bush ordered his military commanders to halt the attack and to let "internal politics" in Iraq take their course. Saddam Hussein quickly reestablished control, routed the Shiites, and sent 1.5 million Kurds fleeing to the Turkish border for protection. The use of force enabled the United States to return Kuwait to the emir—but little more.

When the smoke from the conflagration cleared, nearly all the basic security problems of the Middle East remained as they had been before August 2. The memory of Iraqi Scud missile attacks strengthened the resolve of the hardliners running the Israeli government not to negotiate the critical question of a Palestinian homeland (though ultimately the conservative Likud Party was voted out of office in the summer of 1992). Much of the Iraqi military machine either was destroyed during the war or disarmed by the UN after the war, but Saddam Hussein remained in power to fight another day, outlasting his nemesis, President George Bush. Impressed by the performance of U.S. weapons, Israel, Syria, Saudi Arabia, and other nations in the region all raced to acquire more arms. The Bush administration used its new clout in the region to bring Israel, Syria, Jordan, Egypt, and the Palestinians to the negotiating table, but by the time it left office in January 1993 it had failed to get the parties to soften their bargaining positions and to agree to a long-term peace.

Even while holding an olive branch in peace talks, the United States was quietly dispensing weapons throughout the region. Rather than seriously contemplate how to increase the security of *every* nation in the Middle East and halt the upward spiral of armed terror, the United States provided billions of dollars worth of new advanced weapons to Israel and Saudi Arabia.[15] These arms buildups, of course, undermined the security of neighboring nations like Egypt, Iran, Jordan, and Syria and drove them to buy more arms from other suppliers. As most Middle East experts acknowledge, neither armaments nor war can resolve the deep, historic divisions between Arabs and

Jews and among various Arab nationalities, factions, and tribes. What is needed are serious negotiations and compromise.

Winning Wars Is Better than Preventing Them

A third habit of U.S. security policy since World War II, also evidenced during the Persian Gulf War, has been to emphasize winning violent conflicts over preventing them in the first place. During the Cold War the United States spent trillions of dollars to contain and deter Soviet military might, but almost nothing to undo the possible causes of Soviet expansionism (such as shortages of oil). Likewise, the United States never evaluated how it could have prevented or resolved the conflict with Saddam Hussein before violence erupted. Consider some of the policies for conflict prevention the United States could have undertaken throughout the 1980s:

- □ Had the United States embarked on a concerted program of cost-effective energy conservation, it could have rendered itself independent of imports of Persian Gulf oil and eliminated much of Saddam Hussein's leverage over the West.
- □ Had the United States initiated a Marshall Plan to develop the countries of the Middle East, Iraq might have perceived the benefits of cooperating with the West as outweighing the possible advantages to be gained from invading Kuwait.
- □ Had the nations of the West actively promoted the democratization of Iraq, perhaps by supporting human rights groups in Baghdad or by providing dissidents with decentralized information technologies like copier and fax machines, Hussein's adventurism might have been undercut by internal opposition.

U.S. military action against Iraq did little more than treat the symptoms of aggression. The underlying causes of war—dependency, poverty, and authoritarianism—remained wholly unaddressed and may have even been worsened by the conflict.

Take Unilateral Actions

Another habit of U.S. security policy during the Cold War was unilateralism. When the United States emerged victorious from World War II with the most powerful economy and military forces on the planet, it could afford single-handedly to rebuild wartorn Germany and Japan, to underwrite Europe's defense, and to fight communism in Korea and Vietnam. The United States led the charge against Saddam Hussein, using the same unilateralist game plan that worked so well against North Korea in 1950. In both cases the United States convinced the UN Security Council to meet aggression, not with a multilateral military force as envisioned in the UN Charter, but with a U.S.-led military coalition flying the UN flag in which two out of three soldiers were American.[16]

The advantage of unilateralism is that, when it works, the United States can shape the world to serve its own interests. But unilateralism also means that the United States must single-handedly bear the costs. In Korea, which was considered a victory for U.S. unilateralism, more than 54,000 Americans died, 103,000 were wounded, and the price tag was $278 billion (in 1990 dollars).[17] In Vietnam, 58,000 Americans died and 153,000 were wounded, at a cost of $595 billion (in 1990 dollars) and the loss of much of the world's respect. U.S. casualties from the Persian Gulf War were remarkably light—about 300—but the total bill, according to the Pentagon, was $61 billion.[18] (The United States was able to keep its costs down by strong-arming its allies into contributing $52 billion.) A truly multilateral approach, arranged through the UN or appropriate regional organizations, could have reduced the hemorrhage of American blood and treasure.

Leave Security Policy to the Experts

A final habit of U.S. security policy exhibited during both the Cold War and the Persian Gulf War was to exclude the American people and their elected representatives from the decisionmaking process. Contrary to the express demands of the U.S. Constitution that members of the Senate and House carefully weigh the benefits and costs of armed conflict before committing troops, all of the Pentagon's major operations during the Cold War—in Korea, the Dominican Republic, Vietnam, Cambodia, Grenada, Nicaragua, and Panama—were waged without congressional declarations of war. President Bush unsuccessfully tried to bypass Congress to fight Desert Storm, but he did manage to delay debate on Capitol Hill until the eleventh hour. By the time Congress weighed in, 500,000 U.S. troops had been flown halfway around the world, a coalition of fighting partners had been

recruited, the battle plans had been laid, and the administration intimated that the war would proceed even if Congress voted against it.
A majority of congressional members, fearful of "backing down,"
"losing resolve," and "abandoning the troops," overcame widespread
public skepticism (one out of two Americans wanted to give the embargo more time to work) and voted to permit the president to use
force (without actually declaring war). After the bombs started to fall
and the United States racked up one easy victory after another, most
Americans rallied around the flag and supported the war effort.

But the long-term will of the American people to fight wars thousands of miles away remains unclear. The Bush administration rushed
to battle against Panama and Iraq and fought those wars quickly
because it understood that the American people would have little
stomach to watch mangled Panamanians or Iraqis on television or to
see a steady stream of American coffins and crippled veterans coming
home. Two weeks after the resounding victory over Iraq, 60 percent
of Americans said they did not believe the United States should resort
to force more often.[19] Americans still apparently prefer the peaceful
resolution of conflicts to thousands of body bags.

Toward a New View of Security

The habits of U.S. foreign policymaking during the Cold War—
fixating on a single armed villain, relying on provocative threats, un-
dervaluing conflict prevention and resolution, acting unilaterally,
and keeping the U.S. public out of foreign policymaking—may have
helped the country outlast the Soviet Union, but they also carried
tremendous costs. Today, after spending several trillion dollars to defend the world, an exhausted United States must cope with unprecedented problems at home, including a gigantic national debt, 3 million homeless, 23,000 annual murders, an adult illiteracy rate of 20
percent, crumbling bridges and roads, a declining base of manufacturing, and spiritual malaise.

Whatever the value of the five Cold War principles for foreign policymaking in the past, they have become obsolete. They did not serve
the nation's interests particularly well during the Persian Gulf War.
Yes, the United States won the war with miraculously low casualties,
but its long-term security interests in the Middle East and elsewhere
were not strengthened. Moreover, future threats to world peace will
not be as easy to defeat.

Few U.S. security planners interpreted victory in the Persian Gulf

War as the end of the "Vietnam syndrome" and the beginning of a new era of sending U.S. troops to police every corner of the globe. Henry Kissinger, the architect of President Richard Nixon's foreign policy, stressed that the U.S.-led coalition was a "special case" for several reasons: The Soviet Union, "wracked by domestic crises and needing foreign economic assistance, had no stomach for conflict with the United States"; "Beijing considers Washington an important partner in China's determination to resist either Soviet or Japanese hegemony in Asia"; "the Gulf states and Saudi Arabia saw their very survival at stake"; and Syria's antagonism with Iraq "is only 2,000 years old." "Nor," added Kissinger, "can the American economy indefinitely sustain a policy of essentially unilateral global interventionism—indeed, we had to seek a foreign subsidy of at least $50 billion to sustain this crisis."[20]

President Bush was politically fortunate that heady national feelings of victory obscured a more sober assessment of the Persian Gulf War. But ultimately even he came to grips with the limits to U.S. military power. Despite growing public outrage in 1992 over Serbia's brutal aggression against Slovenia, Croatia, and Bosnia and its Nazi-like war crimes of "ethnic cleansing," the Bush administration resisted sending in U.S. troops to end the conflict. In Somalia, where millions were at risk of starving because of a protracted civil war, Bush sent the minimum number of troops necessary to protect convoys of food—but little more. There is a growing recognition that the United States no longer can prevent wars or resolve conflicts merely by selling weapons or dispatching troops on its own. Just as a mechanic equipped only with plumbing tools cannot fix a television set, security planners who continue to embrace Cold War principles and policies will find themselves ill equipped to deal with the foreign policy demands of the twenty-first century.

Today, the Soviet Union is gone, split into fifteen new nations, and with it has gone the raison d'être of the U.S. security system since World War II. Soviet nuclear forces, which security analysts once feared could wipe out the U.S. nuclear deterrent in a surprise attack, have been shorn of their most threatening capabilities. The Warsaw Pact, which the Cold Warriors warned could threaten blitzkrieg across Western Europe, has dissolved. Soviet adventurism in the Third World, which once justified the United States investing hundreds of billions of dollars for bases, arms sales, cooperative agreements, and other foreign commitments, has been discontinued.

The national security experts who were most responsible for

perpetuating the Cold War in the 1970s and 1980s now concede that the world is changing radically. Zbigniew Brzezinski, who as President Carter's national security adviser played a decisive role in sounding the alarm about the Soviet threat and launching a renewed arms race with the Soviet Union, says, "We are quite literally in the early phases of what might be called the post-communist period. This is a massive, monumental transformation."[21] Henry Kissinger argues, "The one thing that cannot occur is a continuation of the status quo. It will either disintegrate under the pressure of events or it will be reshaped by a constructive American policy."[22]

For the first time in two generations, foreign policy experts, politicians, and citizens are posing basic questions about U.S. national security: What are the real threats to security? How can the United States meet these threats effectively and control the costs of doing so? What are viable alternatives to the use of force? How can the United States escape the burdens of unilateralism? Who in the United States should decide and carry out security policy?

In the following pages we attempt to answer these questions. Our thesis is simple: If the United States is to be secure from foreign threats, it must assess *all* these threats and address them with policies that emphasize nonprovocation, conflict prevention, multilateralism, and democracy. We specifically propose that U.S. security planners replace the five Cold War principles with an alternative set outlined below.

Principle 1: Recognize Multilateral, Multidimensional Threats

The first imperative for U.S. security planners in the post–Cold War era is to grasp the wide array of threats endangering security. In early 1992, referring to the dissolution of the Soviet Union, General Colin Powell, Chair of the Joint Chiefs of Staff, mournfully said, "We no longer have the luxury of having a threat to prepare for."[23] Unfortunately, this statement is not even remotely true, for the United States faces a growing number of significant threats: Both Russia and Ukraine, the two former Soviet republics that continue to possess nuclear weapons, as well as the People's Republic of China, are capable of obliterating the United States in under an hour by using atomic explosions.[24] A dozen "hot spots" around the world such as the Middle East or the India-Pakistan border could explode into regional or global conflicts affecting the United States. The global march of technology means that nuclear, chemical, and biological weapons may soon be—or already are—in the hands of national governments, military factions, or terrorists hostile to American interests. The growth of illegal drug trafficking is causing billions of dollars worth of crime, violence, and addiction in cities across the United States. The worsening trade deficit and the decreasing competitiveness of U.S. goods threaten the jobs and well-being of millions of Americans. In addition, assaults on the global environment such as ozone destruction, climate change, and acid rain may imperil the property, health, and livelihood of every U.S. citizen.

If Americans continue to pretend that one or two villains are at the root of all of the world's problems, the other threats will overwhelm us. *Every* kind of threat to national security—military, political, economic, and environmental—must be carefully weighed. Moreover, threats posed by *every* nation must be examined, whether those threats come in the form of coercion from terrorists trained in Libya, trade barriers in Japan, emigration from Mexico, or unsafe nuclear power plants in Bulgaria. To neglect just one major threat can mean catastrophe for the United States.

Principle 2: Emphasize Conflict Prevention and Resolution

Today, a central objective for security planners must be to avoid war. As advanced weapons technologies spread to more countries, the costs of war are becoming unacceptable. The next time the United States decides whether to fight a war against a "pariah" country like Iraq, Iran, Libya, or Syria, it must consider the possibility that its opponent will be armed with weapons of mass destruction. Nearly all these nations, as well as India, Pakistan, and South Africa, have been acquiring the materials and technology necessary to build nuclear weapons. An even larger number of Third World countries are developing or purchasing ballistic missiles and producing the "poor man's A-bombs"—chemical and biological weapons. The spread of these weapons means that a war, even a small war over a trivial issue, has a greater chance of resulting in horrifying devastation. Would President Bush have been as eager to wage war against Iraq if he had known that Saddam Hussein could explode nuclear weapons in downtown New York or Washington, D.C.?

Even wars involving nations that do not possess weapons of mass destruction endanger U.S. security, because they can escalate and involve countries that do. When the United States decided to fight Iraq over Kuwait, it successfully lobbied Israel, a country having a stockpile of at least one hundred nuclear weapons, to stay out of the conflict. As soon as Desert Storm began, however, Saddam Hussein tried to provoke Israel to enter the war by launching intermediate-range Scud missiles at Tel Aviv and Jerusalem. Had those Scuds released poison gas (which Iraq easily could have equipped them to do), Israel intimated that it would have retaliated against Iraq with atomic bombs. That, in turn, could have turned states like Syria, a coalition partner, and Iran, which was neutral, against Israel. If Syria and Iran had nuclear weapons in their arsenals (Iran probably will in a few years), the Persian Gulf War could have embroiled the entire Middle East in a regional nuclear conflagration. And, to push this terror scenario one unlikely but conceivable step further, had China and the Soviet Union been sufficiently shocked by Israel's nuclear strikes, they could have fired nuclear missiles at Israeli defense installations, which might have induced the United States, an ally of Israel, to attack Beijing or Moscow. The spread of weapons of mass destruction means that a growing number of small wars have the potential to grow into regional or global wars.

Some scholars now argue that the end of the Cold War and the rigid bipolar division of the world between the United States and the Soviet Union mean that small wars are less likely to escalate. Certainly dangerous showdowns like the Cuban missile crisis of 1962 are more improbable now, because Russia no longer maintains the vast commitments to the Third World that the Soviet Union once did. But if the dissolution of the Soviet Union emboldens the United States or its allies to intervene more freely in the Third World, countries fearful of hegemony may rush to acquire nuclear, chemical, and biological weapons, which will increase the risks of small wars escalating.

Besides the dangers of igniting a global war, there are other reasons why U.S. security planners should avoid war. War means the killing and maiming of U.S. soldiers—and many others. It wastes resources that otherwise could be devoted to solving domestic and international problems or to producing greater national wealth. The shooting and bombing of enemy populations can sully the moral reputation of the country. Even so-called realists of international relations recognize (as will be discussed in Chapter 2) that the use of force is becoming an unreliable means to achieve most foreign policy objectives.

At one time, the rest of the world could allow adversaries like Iran and Iraq, Israel and Syria, or India and Pakistan to wage war on each other without suffering any adverse consequences. But the luxury of indifference to other nation's wars is fast disappearing, for a number of reasons:

- □ Wars disrupt global trade and investment activities. The price of a barrel of crude oil, for example, nearly doubled after Iraq took over Kuwait.[25]
- □ Wars sever international transportation and communication links. Saddam Hussein's threat to unleash a wave of terrorism against globetrotting Westerners cut bookings of airlines, hotels, cruise-ship lines, and resorts by nearly 25 percent.[26]
- □ Wars cause environmental impacts that do not respect national boundaries. A nuclear war between India and Pakistan could contaminate U.S. cities, crops, and water supplies with the radioactive debris released by atomic bombs and disabled nuclear-power plants.
- □ Wars send boatloads of refugees to nations thousands of miles away. The UN estimates that current wars and civil strife have displaced 34 million people, with half of them fleeing across one or more international borders.[27]
- □ Wars waste precious time, energy, and resources nations need to solve other problems. An economist from Georgetown University estimates that Iraq's invasion of Kuwait cost the Arab world $438 billion, enough to provide decent shelter for every Arab living in the Middle East.[28]
- □ Wars give neighboring nations an incentive to acquire more armaments, which in turn causes more wars.

For all these reasons, the United States and other nations have an interest in preventing wars, even ones that seem distant and isolated. Obviously, the larger the war and the more U.S. interests implicated, the more urgent it is for U.S. security planners to stop it. As the world becomes increasingly complex, it will be harder and harder to imagine a war that does not threaten some Americans or some important U.S. interests.

U.S. foreign policymakers often profess to have made force a last resort, but from the Korean War to the Persian Gulf War the use of force and the threat to use force—backed up by the world's largest conventional and nuclear arsenal—have been mainstays of U.S. security policy. In 1990, the United States spent twenty times more on military programs and military foreign assistance than on all other nonmilitary international programs put together (see Table 1, p. 257, in the Notes section[29]). A wiser security policy would change these priorities. Beginning with causes, not symptoms, the United States should stress the elimination of the economic and political roots of conflict through persuasion and cooperation. It also should help resolve conflicts that have not yet become violent through stronger, more equitable international rules and institutions. With most conflicts settled long before they produce wars, the demands on the Pentagon would be far more modest.

Principle 3: Make Security Policies Nonprovocative

A key cause of war is *in*security. A nation fearing imminent invasion will be tempted to strike an adversary first. When Egypt, Syria, and Jordan mobilized their forces along the Israeli border in 1967 and closed the Gulf of Aqaba, Israel launched a preemptive attack and achieved a stunning victory in what became known as the Six-Day War. A nation that faces severe shortages of food, water, or energy also may be tempted to wage war against neighbors to obtain fresh supplies. General Hideki Tojo attacked Pearl Harbor in part because the United States had placed an embargo on oil shipments to Imperial Japan.

U.S. national security depends on freeing nations across the globe from all kinds of insecurity—military, political, economic, and environmental. Feelings of insecurity inevitably produce mistrust, arms races, and wars, and the destructive power of nuclear bombs makes these risks unacceptable. Therefore, an important objective of U.S. foreign policymakers also must be to increase the security of adversaries such as China, Iran, Iraq, Libya, and North Korea, and to convince them, by argument and example, that they too should increase the security of other nations.

Provocative foreign policies are counterproductive—they cause adversaries to seethe with enmity, to acquire offensive weapons, and to launch preemptive strikes. Nonprovocative foreign policies, in contrast, increase trust among nations and remove incentives for arms races or wars. For the United States to abandon provocation does not mean becoming isolationist, nor does it mean abandoning the use of force to protect vital national interests. It simply means trying, whenever possible, to engage other nations, whether friends or adversaries, through persuasion and cooperation instead of through coercion and violence.

In 1992, after the Soviet Union dissolved, the Pentagon argued in *Defense Planning Guidance 1994–99* that one reason the United States should retain an armed force of 1.6 million and most of its nuclear weapons was to create a "hedge against the possibility that democracy [in Russia] will fail, with the potential that an authoritarian regime bent on regenerating aggressive military power could emerge in Russia, or that similar regimes in other successor republics could lead to spreading conflict within the former USSR or Eastern Europe."[30] But if the Pentagon is really worried about resurgent militarism in Russia, the United States could pursue policy alternatives that are less expensive and less risky than retaining a huge army and large nuclear weapons stockpile:

☐ The United States could help Russian parliamentarians put stronger democratic checks and balances over their military forces by helping them enact analogues to the U.S. War Powers Act and the Freedom of Information Act, both of which put restraints (however imperfectly) on the U.S. military.

☐ It could help Russians obtain the food, minerals, energy, and technology they need through trade, investment, and loans so that they have no incentive to obtain these by force; indeed, their chief incentive would be *not* to endanger these relationships with force or threats of force.

☐ It could recruit Russia, Ukraine, Kazakhstan, and Belarus to join new collective security arrangements in Europe, perhaps overseen by the UN, that would obviate the need for any of these countries to maintain an enormous army or navy.

Even if all these options failed, the United States could still protect its security against resurgent Russian militarism through a nonprovocative military option. The United States could deploy sufficient defenses, for itself and for its allies, to ensure that any attack by Russia would fail. Unlike NATO's defenses in the 1980s, which Soviet worst-case planners believed were capable of facilitating an offensive NATO sweep across Eastern Europe, these nonprovocative defenses would be unambiguously defensive, capable of deterring Russia without encouraging it to acquire more arms or to attack preemptively.

Principle 4: Favor Multilateral Approaches

The collapse of the Soviet Union has led some commentators to argue that the United States is now the sole superpower left in the world. *Defense Planning Guidance 1994–99* suggests that one of the key U.S. missions will be "convincing potential competitors that they need not aspire to a greater role or pursue a more aggressive posture to protect their legitimate interests."[31] In other words, the United States should strive to convince Japan, Germany, Russia, and other states not to challenge U.S. primacy in international affairs.

But can the world's biggest debtor really pretend to be the world's preeminent superpower? As James Chace of Bard College notes, "Without the $54 billion in aid that the Bush Administration received for the Gulf operation, the U.S., with a budget deficit projected for 1992 of about $400 billion, could not have afforded to mount such a campaign. It is highly unlikely that we will receive support for similar foreign policy adventures, certainly not to police the world as the Pentagon intends us to."[32]

The United States may have the strongest military forces on earth, but economically it is losing ground to other countries. As Chapter 3 details, U.S. industries have been bypassed by European, Japanese, and Korean competitors. The relative decline of the U.S. economy has caused devastating problems at home for Americans. "Of the industrial democracies," notes Robert Borosage, director of the Campaign for New Priorities, "we suffer from the most poverty, the most crime, the worst public health care, and the highest infant-mortality and illiteracy rates."[33]

The economic decline of the United States does not disqualify it from exerting leadership in the world. It does mean, however, that its ability to command instead of cooperate is fast disappearing. The fact is that no one nation has the power, resources, or legitimacy to police the globe. The world's conflicts are too complex and intractable, and the proliferation of nuclear weapons has proceeded too far for any one nation to dominate.

The United States already recognizes the advantages of multilateralism, at least in some of its behavior. For forty years it shared the costs of NATO's defenses, albeit inequitably, with the nations of Western Europe. It sought the endorsement of the UN Security Council and recruited other national military forces before conducting Desert Storm. It pushed hard to establish international rules for trade in the General Agreement on Tariffs and Trade (GATT). It also signed a wide range of international treaties protecting endangered species, stratospheric ozone, and Antarctica. Nonetheless, the United States still does not feel entirely comfortable with multilateralism. It is harder to persuade the world to act than to act oneself. And there is always the danger that others might not go along.

Still, multilateral cooperation is worth pursuing because it carries greater legitimacy and costs less than unilateralism does. Desert Storm was a poor example of multilateral action because the United States dominated decisions concerning if, when, and how the coalition partners would use force. To the limited extent multilateralism was used, however, it boosted the U.S. effort to expel Saddam Hussein from Kuwait. The imprimatur of the UN broadened the alliance, tightened the embargo, and deterred countries from siding with Hussein. Cost-sharing enabled the United States to defray most direct expenses of the operation. It seems implausible that the war could have achieved its small successes had the UN not been so deeply involved.

A stronger UN can offer every nation a way to lower defense expenditures without compromising its security. Impoverished countries might find it cost-effective to hand over the job of protecting their borders to UN troops and to invest the savings in economic development. Even powerful nations such as the United States could lower defense spending if UN forces were able to interdict drug traffic, apprehend terrorists, keep sea lanes open, and protect democracies from interstate aggression.

Multilateralism also may be the only way to successfully tackle threats that are truly global in nature. Control of the proliferation of nuclear weapons, for example, ultimately will require tight international control over fissionable materials, heavy water, and nuclear technologies *everywhere* in the world. Depletion of the ozone layer in the atmosphere can be stopped only if *every* country stops using chlorofluorocarbons and halons. The frenzied competition among nations to lower wages and weaken environmental regulations to attract multinational corporations can be stopped only if global standards are set for these firms to behave responsibly.

Obviously, not every multilateral action is in the United States' interest. The principle of subsidiarity, a fundamental tenet of Jeffersonian democracy, says that every problem should be handled at the appropriate level of government closest to the people. Following this principle, the United States should press the world for the *minimal* set of international norms, laws, and institutions necessary to protect world security.

Principle 5: Promote Democratic Policies

The final principle for a new security policy is to maximize citizen participation. Perhaps the most insidious assumption held by most security planners is that foreign policy should remain their exclusive domain. Security experts occasionally pay lip service to the importance of public involvement, but they bristle at any suggestion that the public could actually help to *make* national security policy. Most security "experts," whether conservative or liberal, generally prefer that the public butt out.

Even though Americans believe they live in the world's best democracy, they have come to accept security policy being set secretly by the president and the National Security Council, a small group of appointed advisers. Congress has been reduced to denying occasional budget authorizations or blocking certain weapons systems. The judicial branch could weigh in, but generally has dismissed security policy lawsuits as raising "political questions" that it is incompetent to answer, no matter how glaring the actual violations of law. In the 1960s and 1970s, for example, the Supreme Court studiously avoided hearing lawsuits that questioned the constitutionality of the undeclared war in Vietnam. The only other source of popular control left is the press, which sometimes provides independent scrutiny but too often uncritically reports official "disinformation" and is reluctant to challenge policies for fear of alienating high-level sources.[34]

Compounding the inaccessibility of national decisionmakers is official secrecy. Much information about U.S. nuclear policy, including the exact characteristics of weapons and strategic doctrines governing their use, is classified. Secrecy prevents informed public debate, and the result is a runaway foreign policy establishment geared toward continuous military mobilization and resistant to public opinions that might point security policy in a new direction.

Polls indicate that most Americans are generally satisfied with presidential conduct in foreign affairs but are profoundly disenchanted with presidential actions on a growing number of specific security issues. For instance, although between 70 and 80 percent of the U.S. public in the early 1980s favored a bilateral nuclear-weapons freeze, the Reagan administration consistently refused to put a freeze proposal on the negotiating table.[35] By leaving security policy to the "experts," Americans have allowed the development of a security policy that emphasizes weapons, threats of force, and military intervention.

The security system we propose here seeks to open U.S. foreign and military policy to meaningful democratic participation by citizens, religious organizations, civic groups, corporations, and local governments. Using their traditional powers to act on environmental and economic issues that once were deemed entirely "domestic" matters, Americans can help to resolve global conflicts. Americans also can wield enormous persuasive and cooperative powers abroad with their constitutionally protected freedoms to speak, associate, travel, and trade. In two areas where common sense suggests that policy ought to remain centralized, namely weapons deployments and wars, a commitment to participation would place new, more rigorous checks and balances on political and military leaders. This would help ensure that leaders everywhere increasingly pursued a security agenda of, for, and by the people, rather than one dictated by security planners.

Organization of the Book

The chapters that follow build on these five post–Cold War principles. In Part 1 we examine three of the principles in more detail—why security planners need to take into account an expanding array of security threats (Chapter 1), why conflict prevention and resolution must be given stronger priority than force (Chapter 2), and why nations should avoid provocative policies that produce arms races (Chapter 3).

Following the logic of the second principle—addressing conflict at its roots—Part 2 suggests ways to resolve conflicts before they become violent. We show how the United States can undertake policies to eliminate the political, environmental, and economic roots of conflict (Chapters 4, 5, and 6), and how it can help resolve conflicts through stronger international rules and institutions (Chapter 7).

In Part 3 we apply the principles to military policy. We suggest the virtues of three new kinds of military policies—nonprovocative defense, collective security, and nuclear disarmament (Chapters 8, 9, and 10).

Part 4 shows how these elements can work together as a system. We identify opportunities for citizen and community participation (Chapter 11) and demonstrate how our recommendations, taken together, constitute a coherent system that can offer Americans more protection at a lower cost (Chapter 12).

One caveat is necessary before we proceed. This assessment has been written more as a road map than as a specific plan. Major landmarks, topographic features, and general directions are shown, but not fine details. Some questions are answered only briefly and others are set aside altogether. We hope this book stimulates experts in many fields—including military strategists, career diplomats, economists, and ecologists—to proceed with much-needed planning.

The key to security without war, we believe, is not some magic weapons system or a clever formula for arms reduction, but rather the development of an entirely new framework of international relations in which offensive force postures and war-making habits are gradually replaced by dependable, widely recognized methods of conflict prevention and resolution. Achieving security without war is a problem not of technology, but of politics. It requires replacing militarism with participatory democracy, resource overconsumption with cost-effective conservation, unilateral coercion with multilateral cooperation, and saber rattling with sound defenses.

The time has surely come for the United States to lead the world beyond the habits of the Cold War. Those who cling to nuclear weapons and the unilateral use of force sell the United States short. At a time when military force is less and less relevant to global politics, a security policy that continues to focus on force will pillage the U.S. economy, weaken its international influence, erode its democratic decisionmaking, and damage its moral standing. The true strengths of the United States are a dynamic economy and a deep dedication to peace and democracy. By building a comprehensive security system on these virtues rather than perpetuating a rickety system of nuclear deterrence that may sooner or later destroy itself, the United States can guarantee its own security, and the world's, for generations to come.

Part One

Redefining Security

1
New Security Threats

Throughout the Cold War the architects of U.S. foreign policy were able to justify ever greater arms budgets by pointing to the Soviet threat. The threat of a Soviet first strike against the mainland United States required the continual buildup and modernization of a strategic nuclear arsenal. The threat of a Soviet invasion of Western Europe had to be met through a massive mobilization of infantry, tanks, planes, and tactical nuclear warheads by NATO. And the threat of Soviet subversion in the Third World demanded aid, covert actions, and wars in support of anti-Communist governments.

Today, however, the dissolution of the Soviet Union and the rise of a friendlier Commonwealth of Independent States in its place has thrown U.S. security policy into turmoil. Opinion leaders across the political spectrum—from Pat Buchanan to Peace Action—are now calling for reduced spending by the Departments of Defense and State.[1]

Some of the most vociferous anti-Soviet hardliners now believe that the United States has overspent on foreign commitments and underspent on domestic problems. Edward N. Luttwak, who argued for more defense spending in a 1982 article entitled "Why We Need More 'Waste, Fraud and Mismanagement' in the Pentagon,"[2] now decries the "Third-Worldization" of the U.S. economy and contends that "the U.S. is wrongly equipped for the new era, with altogether too much of its talent and capital absorbed by the armed forces and military industries."[3]

But trimming sails is not the same thing as mothballing the ship. Withdrawal from international affairs is not a viable option as long as the United States faces an expanding array of threats to its security. By security threats, we mean forces originating from outside the United States that can harm American lives, property, or well-being.[4] These forces include military aggression, political subversion, economic instability, and environmental destruction.[5] Such threats could come from foreign governments, terrorists, drug lords, criminal cartels, or multinational corporations. A brief look at the threats of greatest concern suggests just how vulnerable the United States is today—and how misguided it is either to exhaust national defenses on any one demon or to ignore any of these threats.

Military Threats

One of the traditional objectives of U.S. security planners has been to keep U.S. soil free of foreign troops, bullets, and bombs. Unlike Europeans, Americans have been spared a major armed conflict on their home territory for more than a century, largely because they are surrounded by two oceans and by friendly neighbors. The only serious attack on the United States since the Civil War was carried out by the Japanese at Pearl Harbor in 1941, at a time when Hawaii had not yet achieved statehood.

But whatever military security the United States may have once enjoyed through geographic isolation has been stripped away by advancing weapons technology. The CIS, while posing less of a threat to the United States than the Soviet Union ever did, has a vast arsenal of missiles, bombers, submarines, artillery, and other delivery systems capable of hitting targets anywhere on earth in under an hour. But even when the first and second Strategic Arms Reduction Treaties (START I and II) are fully implemented in 2003, Russia will continue to have about 5,500 warheads.[6] China, whose relations with the United States have been cordial but cool since the Tiananmen Square massacre in 1989, has 350 nuclear warheads as well as intercontinental missiles. Neither Russian nor Chinese leaders seem likely to pick a nuclear fight with the United States in the near future, but both arsenals nevertheless remain aimed at U.S. cities and could be fired by accident, error, or miscalculation. The nations of the CIS that hold nuclear weapons, historically distrustful of one another, have yet to sort out common arrangements concerning their armies, navies, air forces, and nuclear rockets. The student protests for democracy that rocked the streets of Beijing in 1989 may well happen in China again as elderly hardliners die and reformers take their place. If a revolution or a civil war breaks out in Russia, the Ukraine, or China, the nuclear weapons stockpiles could be grabbed by one faction and fired. When at any moment American lives and property are minutes away from nuclear obliteration, which might be caused by something as trivial and commonplace as a faulty computer chip, how secure *is* the United States?

As noted in the Introduction, a half dozen Third World nations are acquiring the materials and technology to build nuclear weapons. According to the Pentagon, as many as twenty-two nations either possess or are acquiring chemical weapons, and ten are pursuing biological weapons.[7] Some of these nations, such as Iran, Iraq, Libya, and North Korea, remain on America's short list of enemies.

The taboo against using chemical and biological weapons, formalized in the 1925 Geneva Protocol, was seriously breached in the 1980s when Iraq began using mustard and nerve gases against Iran and against its own Kurdish population. Iraq was able to develop these weapons with technical assistance from companies in Belgium, Chile, France, Italy, the Netherlands, Spain, Switzerland, West Germany—and the United States.[8] Knowing full well about Iraq's poison-gas transgressions, the United States nevertheless upgraded relations with that country in 1984.[9]

The chemicals and technology necessary for producing poison gas have spread widely: "The genie is out of the bottle," a State Department official recently commented.[10] In the Middle East the proliferation of chemical weapons and medium-range missiles forced millions of Israeli citizens to learn how to wear gas masks during the Persian Gulf War. Thinking about Israel's nuclear arsenal, a Western diplomat said, "If the Syrians tried to use whatever chemical agents they have against Israel, every Syrian would die."[11] And possibly every Israeli as well.

These same Middle Eastern countries and nearly two dozen others have acquired ballistic missiles capable of carrying advanced conventional, nuclear, or chemical weapons against regional adversaries.[12] Israel has tested a missile with a 500-to-900-mile range; India is developing a civilian space rocket with a 2,500-mile range; and Brazil has considered selling 600-mile-range missiles to Libya.[13] Argentina, South Africa, and Taiwan also are building and selling missiles.[14] The military balance in the Middle East may be tipping against Israel as six of its neighbors (Egypt, Iran, Iraq, Libya, Saudi Arabia, and Syria) acquire medium-range missiles.[15] In June 1988 two Egyptian military officers and three Americans were arrested just as they were about to smuggle 430 pounds of advanced carbon-carbon (a heat-resistant material for rocket nose cones) and other equipment for a medium-range missile under joint Egyptian-Argentinian-Iraqi development.[16] Because of cooperation from companies in West Germany, Italy, France, and Britain, as well as from North Korea, the program proceeded anyway.[17] The simultaneous spread of missile and nuclear technology is particularly terrifying, although the chosen means of delivering a nuclear bomb could be a truck, a small plane, or a duffel bag.

Terrorists may eventually add weapons of mass destruction to their arsenals as well. If an anonymous terrorist organization blew up downtown Manhattan with a small nuclear bomb, what good would the U.S. nuclear deterrent be? Against whom would the United States retaliate? How would the United States respond if terrorists released nerve gas at the Super Bowl? Or if they used simple, low-technology means to cut off vital energy supplies, telecommunications systems, and other fragile parts of the infrastructure on which economic life depends? According to Frank Stunnenberg of the University of Amsterdam, "Almost anyone can obtain large quantities of chemicals for [weapons] production and convert them into war gases without any control."[18] For about $240, for example, a number of chemical companies will sell and deliver the ingredients necessary to produce enough mustard gas to threaten the population of a medium-sized city.[19] Even with only guns and explosives, terrorists will continue to pose a threat to Americans throughout the world. Between 1980 and 1985, Americans were the victims of 458 terrorist incidents in Western Europe, 369 in Latin America, and 84 in the Middle East.[20]

Even if weapons of mass destruction are left aside, the conventional arms race poses daunting challenges to U.S. national security. In the name of fighting the Soviet threat, the United States eagerly sold billions of dollars worth of sophisticated arms to any nation willing to declare its opposition to communism. Between 1983 and 1987, the United States shipped $52 billion worth of arms worldwide, half of which went to the Third World.[21] Besides supporting repressive governments like those in El Salvador and Indonesia and guerrillas who violate human rights like those in Angola and Mozambique, the United States sent weapons to General Manuel Noriega in Panama, whose security forces would later fire them against U.S. troops, and to King Hussein of Jordan, who supported Iraq during the Persian Gulf War.

Wars fought with conventional weapons could threaten the United States if combatants choose to escalate to weapons of mass destruction. The likelihood of a conventional conflict involving and possibly hurting the United States is also greater if security planners define "vital American interests" expansively. The Pentagon's *Defense Planning Guidance 1994–99*, leaked to the press in early 1992, does just that, stating that the United States would consider intervening in any of the following scenarios:[22] if Russia and Belarus invaded Lithuania; if a coup against the civilian government in Panama, staged by right-wing military leaders and Colombian drug lords, threatened U.S. access to the Panama Canal; if Saddam Hussein tried once again to seize control of oil fields in Kuwait; if North Korea invaded South Korea as it did in 1950; or if a coup in the Philippines led to some Americans being taken hostage. Each intervention carries the risk that these states, their allies, or political factions within them then will decide to punish the United States.

The Pentagon's threat list includes the possibility of a conventional conflict in Eastern Europe or in the former Soviet Union spilling over into neighboring countries and ultimately involving the military forces of the United States and the CIS. The borders of the new countries of the East are likely to undergo a radical transformation in the next decade or two as more than a hundred ethnic groups struggle for autonomy. The Czechs and Slovaks have already dismembered Czechoslovakia, and the Albanians are attempting to secede from their Serb overlords in the former Yugoslavia. The Hungarians in Romania are seeking to ally with their brethren in Hungary. As political scientist Valerie Bunce notes:

> Because Eastern Europe generally has very poor correspondence between national and state boundaries, this type of problem is likely to be endemic. One can expect, for instance, that tensions will rise among Bulgaria, Yugoslavia, and Greece over the Macedonian question; between Albania and Yugoslavia over the Albanian minority in Yugoslavia; between Bulgaria and Turkey over the issue of the Turkish minority in the former; and between Yugoslavia and Romania over the Serbian minority in Romania.[23]

Any of these conflicts could become as violent as the civil wars now raging in Yugoslavia, which in turn could tempt Germany, Russia, or some other nation to intervene militarily. If East and West found themselves on opposing sides of such conflicts, World War I could be played out once again—only this time both sides would possess nuclear weapons.

For now, the principal military threats facing the United States do not emanate from the former Soviet Union. Indeed, even during the Carter, Reagan, and Bush administrations, the U.S. military faced direct challenges, not from the Soviet Union, but from Iran, Iraq, Libya, Panama, and Syria. Iran traumatized the United States during the final year of Jimmy Carter's presidency when militant "students" held fifty-two U.S. diplomatic personnel captive in Teheran for 444 days. In 1983 Reagan dispatched U.S. forces to Lebanon, where Islamic factions supported by Syria and Iran battled Christian factions backed by Israel and the United States—a mission that ended tragically when a terrorist driving a truck filled with explosives blew up the Marine compound in Beirut. In 1986, after Libyan terrorists were fingered for planting a bomb that killed two people and injured 200 others (many of them U.S. servicemen) at a West Berlin disco, Reagan sent U.S. warplanes to hit targets in Tripoli and Benghazi. When an Iraqi warplane attacked the USS *Stark,* killing thirty-seven sailors, the U.S. Navy reflagged Kuwaiti oil tankers with the Stars and Stripes and began escorting them and other Western ships through the Persian Gulf. All this prompted the *Wall Street Journal* to observe in 1988: "Instead of facing Soviet tanks in Berlin, U.S. forces have been attacked by French-made Iraqi missiles in the Persian Gulf. A lone Iranian-trained terrorist killed more Americans—241—in a single morning in Beirut than Soviet soldiers ever have."[24]

The disappearance of the Soviet threat has removed one major source of military insecurity, at least for now, but has refocused attention on numerous others. As the Cold War ended, the United States found new villains—the Ayatollah Khomeini, Colonel Qaddafi, Manuel Noriega, Saddam Hussein, Slobodan Milosevic, and others. Unfortunately, there is no shortage of rogue characters around the world who are intent on violating human rights, committing international crimes, or invading their neighbors. According to a count by Freedom House, by the end of 1992 only seventy-five nations could be considered "free," and the remaining one hundred eleven were either "partly free" or "not free."[25] Moreover, wars continue to rage in twenty-four countries, including Afghanistan, Angola, Cambodia, Colombia, Guatemala, India, Indonesia, Lebanon, Liberia, Pakistan, Peru, the Philippines, Somalia, South Africa, and Yugoslavia.[26] As more nations and terrorists acquire weapons of mass destruction—a trend that seems inevitable, at least for now—the United States may well find itself more militarily insecure than ever.

Political Threats

To feel secure, Americans must be not only safe from violence but free as a people. Political independence means that no foreign power, whether Russia, the Palestine Liberation Organization, or even the Toshiba Corporation, should be able to dictate how the American people lead their lives.

To some extent, of course, every nation—including the United States—has been losing its sovereignty, and this trend has not been all bad. The growing interpenetration of global problems and the growing power of international institutions means that nations must surrender some freedom of action to protect the common good of the planet. However, it is one thing to agree willingly that certain activities—oceanic shipping, shortwave radio use, or criminal prosecutions of diplomats, for example—should be governed by international norms, rules, or treaties, and quite another to be *forced* to change behavior. It is here that losses of U.S. sovereignty have been particularly worrisome.

Terrorists have already exacted important concessions from the United States. President Reagan decided secretly to sell arms to Iran (in violation of his administration's official policy), in the hope that Iranian officials could convince terrorists in Beirut to liberate American hostages. After terrorists hijacked the Italian cruise ship *Achille Lauro* in October 1985 and mowed down 125 civilians in the Rome and Vienna airports two months later, many Americans decided their summer travel plans in Europe were not worth the risk. Measures taken to thwart terrorism also encroach on political freedom. Mandatory searches have become such an accepted part of airline travel that few remember that such intrusions without a warrant or probable cause were once deemed unreasonable invasions of personal privacy.

Another encroachment upon Americans' freedom has been the growing international commerce in drugs. The flood of crack cocaine into the United States has transformed U.S. cities into war zones.[27] Most of this contraband has been grown by poor farmers in South America and has been processed and distributed by drug lords who command vast armies and wield unprecedented political and economic power. In Bolivia alone, for example, annual receipts from cocaine exports are now $600 million, roughly the value of all other exports combined.[28] Economists estimate that the total price tag on drug abuse in the United States, including the costs of illness, crime, and law enforcement, exceeds $60 billion.[29]

The huge balance-of-trade deficit facing the United States may further compromise the nation's sovereignty. The Reagan and Bush administrations paid for a massive military buildup by more than doubling the national debt to $4 trillion, which transformed the United States from the largest creditor in the world to the largest debtor.[30] About $430 billion of this new debt was borrowed from Japanese life insurance companies, French banks, Dutch pension funds, Saudi princes, and other foreign sources.[31] The political meaning of foreign investors holding so much of our debt is, as investment banker Felix Rohatyn has pointed out, that "*no* meaningful domestic government decision is [now] free of international consequences."[32] Foreign investors who hold U.S. obligations, especially the Japanese, may well demand from the United States what U.S. bankers demanded from Third World debtors throughout the 1980s: Either close your budget deficit, through austerity measures if necessary, or forget about new loans.

As international investment portfolios become saturated with U.S. debt, foreigners increasingly are buying up U.S. companies and real estate. By the end of 1987, foreign claims on U.S. assets had passed the $1.5 trillion mark—three times greater than the level of foreign holdings in 1980.[33] Rohatyn comments, "Foreign control of American business, especially in light of the scale on which it is likely to take place, is a valid issue of national interest. Control of financial institutions involves our international posture. Control of the media (practically all of book publishing is now foreign-owned) can affect public opinion and our political system. Control of manufacturing will affect the know-how and technology around which much of future growth will be created."[34] Although foreigners cannot own defense companies per se, they can, and do, own many high-tech companies that are indispensable for U.S. defense, such as those producing electronics, computers, and special materials.[35]

Foreign ownership of U.S. property poses no problems as long as the foreign owners and their governments remain friendly with the U.S. government. But as the last half century has vividly demonstrated, yesterday's friends can become today's foes, and vice versa. The Soviet Union, a valued ally in World War II, became the "evil empire" for half a century; Japan and Germany, our sworn enemies before 1945, then became close allies. If relations sour with the foreign owners of U.S. capital, we may find the citadels of foreign power in our country becoming modern-day Trojan Horses.

Economic Threats

Even if the United States can prevent foreign attack, coercion, or political disruption, how secure can it be if external forces are undermining its economy? Forty-five years ago, when the U.S.-Soviet arms race began, U.S. economic dominance in the world was undisputed. Now, however, as Yale historian Paul Kennedy pointed out in his influential book, *The Rise and Fall of the Great Powers*, its relative economic influence is waning.[36] In the late 1940s and 1950s the United States produced 40 to 45 percent of the gross world product, but by the late 1960s its share had fallen by half.[37]

As other countries industrialized and improved their economic performance, the relative decline of the United States was perhaps inevitable, but the Reagan-Bush legacy of unprecedented deficits in federal spending and trade, exacerbated by deep cuts in social spending and sharp increases in military spending, seriously eroded the nation's productive base for the future. Foreign imports have already decimated U.S. industries in electronics, steel, machine tools, automobiles, and computers and may soon do the same in aircraft, telecommunications, and fiber optics.[38] While U.S. competitors have seen economic security and national security as inseparable issues and invest heavily in the health, education, and welfare of their people, the Reagan administration slashed nearly $160 billion from social programs that supported, among others, poor families, children, the elderly, and the sick.[39] Between 1980 and 1990, the U.S. government reduced expenditures for vocational and adult education by one-third, for education research and improvement by one-half, and for employment training and placement by nearly two-thirds.[40] With these cuts, it is hardly surprising that nearly one in six Americans cannot read and that more than one in two cannot read well enough to perform "moderately difficult business tasks."[41]

Economist Hazel Henderson notes wryly, "The Cold War is over. Japan won."[42] Americans in greater numbers are buying Japanese cars, cameras, stereos, and computers. As U.S. products lose their competitive edge and as U.S. jobs are exported overseas, the global power of the United States will continue to decline. This will happen in part because other nations no longer need U.S. technology or products and in part because the United States no longer has the productive base to provide military and economic aid to assist friends abroad or to challenge adversaries. In the years following World War II, the United States reconstructed Western Europe by providing nearly $100 billion (in today's dollars) in grants under the Marshall Plan, which ensured the smooth development of democracy and market economies consistent with U.S. values and interests.[43] A similar level of investment in the Third World today would cost $1.5 trillion—clearly a sum well beyond our means.[44] Likewise, the opportunity to help rebuild Eastern Europe and the CIS through grants, loans, loan guarantees, and joint ventures, and to assure that these countries mature into stable democracies with healthy market economies, will now fall to the more solvent allies of the United States in Western Europe and Asia. Commenting on the Reagan years, Senator Bill Bradley of New Jersey says, "Militarily, we're stronger internationally than we were, but economically we're weaker. And the economic side may be more important."[45]

The United States is now part of a globalized economy in which distant events can lead to dramatic repercussions at home. When other countries drop minimum wages, restrict workers' rights, or tolerate greater pollution, companies with operations in the United States will be tempted to move abroad to lower costs of production. With more than $500 billion circulating through the world's foreign exchange markets every day, a significant drop in a nation's interest rates can set off a devastating tsunami of capital flight.[46] As much as some Americans wish to insulate the country from economic oscillations abroad by erecting trade barriers and building a strong "Fortress America," this is no longer possible. As the nations of the East Bloc discovered during the Cold War, isolated economies are doomed to stagnation and a declining standard of living.

Sudden shortages are another kind of economic security threat facing the United States. When OPEC quadrupled oil prices in the 1970s, gas-station lines appeared across the country and the U.S. economy reeled. Oil prices receded in the 1980s, but the doubling of prices immediately after Iraq's invasion of Kuwait was a pointed reminder of how dependent the country still is on foreign oil. Today the United States imports more oil than it did in 1973; over 40 percent of the nation's annual oil consumption is fed by foreign producers.[47] The U.S. economy also relies on a limited number of countries for raw materials like cobalt, platinum-group metals, chromium, and manganese. Sudden cutoffs of any of these could create serious bottlenecks in the manufacture of steel, stainless steel, high-temperature alloys, electronics, and other products vital for the national defense.[48]

The Third World's mounting debt to First World banks—now over $1.2 trillion—poses an additional threat to U.S. security.[49] Facing annual repayment burdens on the order of $20 to $30 billion, developing countries are seeing their standards of living rapidly erode.[50] "If you ever wanted to give left-wing demagogues a tool with which to beat back incipient democracies and market-oriented economies," Senator Bradley has argued, "it's the debt to U.S. banks. Every dollar Mexico pays to American banks is a dollar they don't invest at home, a dollar they don't spend buying U.S. exports."[51] Mexico is the third largest trading partner of the United States, and its struggle to repay its debt in 1983 alone was estimated to have cost 200,000 American jobs.[52] (Declining consumer demand in Latin America overall was responsible for two-thirds of the reduced level of U.S. exports in the 1980s.)[53] As the burdens of debt worsen economic conditions in the region, increasing numbers of Latin Americans are flocking to the United States, adding significant strains to the country's already overstressed public services, infrastructure, and job market.[54] Between 150,000 and 350,000 Mexicans now enter the United States illegally each year—in addition to 150,000 legal Mexican immigrants.[55] Political scientist Jorge Castañeda recently noted that unemployed Mexicans "will have only three options: the United States, the streets, or revolution."[56]

Environmental Threats

Another component of national security, frequently overlooked as such, is the integrity of the global environment that supports American lives with clean air and water, livable temperatures, abundant agriculture, and variegated plant and animal species. How secure is the United States if global warming, ozone depletion, and acid rain weaken the nation's ability to feed itself? How secure can U.S. allies in Western Europe be if they remain vulnerable to foreign nuclear accidents like the meltdown of the Chernobyl reactor, which irradiated much of Europe, caused billions of dollars of property damage, and ultimately could result in thousands of premature cancer cases?[57]

Five billion people now live on the planet, and a billion more will be here by the year 2000, with nine out of ten of them living in poor countries.[58] At current growth rates the Earth's population will double by the year 2100. The availability of cheap capital, plentiful energy, advanced technology, and strong political institutions can minimize the environmental impacts of a growing population, but the fact remains that these resources are limited, especially in the Third World. Most ecologists believe that exploding populations will put unsustainable stresses on regional ecosystems. The United Nations Food and Agriculture Organization predicts that between thirty-six and sixty-four nations will have critical food shortages by the year 2000.[59] The *Global 2000 Report to the President*, published in 1980, predicted that by the turn of the century overpopulation would lead to widespread starvation and to the catastrophic overconsumption of firewood, forests (especially tropical rainforests), grasslands, croplands, ocean fisheries, and fresh water.[60] These predictions are now coming true. Every year salinization and waterlogging are ruining nearly as much land as economic-development efforts are opening up.[61]

Although many incipient ecological disasters are local, even local problems will indirectly affect U.S. security in at least three ways. First, resource exhaustion will perpetuate—indeed, worsen—global poverty, reducing demand for U.S. products and further upsetting the U.S. trade balance.

Second, the terrible costs of this poverty—disease, hunger, homelessness, unemployment, illiteracy—will leave Third World peoples angry and eager for radical, perhaps even revolutionary, change. In 1984 then secretary of state George Shultz said, "Security and peace for Americans are contingent upon stability and peace in the developing world."[62] As long as the United States stands for the principles of freedom, democracy, and self-determination, it must remain concerned about the economic plight of the world's peoples. Deforestation and soil erosion in Haiti during the past decade, for example, made farming all but impossible, crippled the economy, and left the country so politically unstable that one million people fled, many landing on the shores of Florida in small boats.[63]

Third, environmental exhaustion will mean greater interstate competition for scarce resources. Consider what will happen as nations begin to deplete fresh water sources. When Syria completes a series of dams on the Yarmuk River, it will divert 40 percent of the flow of the Jordan River, endangering the livelihood of both Jordanian and

Israeli farmers.[64] Environmental scientist Norman Myers has re-marked: "So critical are assured water supplies to Israel that one reason it went to war in 1967 was that Syria and Jordan were trying to divert the flows of the Jordan River. Israel still occupies the Golan Heights and the West Bank in part because it wishes to safeguard its access to the river's water. While Israel receives about 60 per cent of its water from the Jordan River, only 3 per cent of the river's basin lies within the country's pre-1967 territory."[65] Iraq almost went to war against Syria in 1975 when the latter built the Thawrah Dam on the Euphrates and endangered the economic survival of three million Iraqi farmers living downstream.[66] In 1980, after Ethiopia announced its plans to divert nearly 40 percent of the Blue Nile's water, President Anwar el-Sadat of Egypt warned that if Ethiopia proceeded "there will be no alternative for us but to use force."[67] One hundred fifty-five of the world's most important river systems are shared by two countries, and fifty-nine by three or more countries.[68] Conflicts over these transnational river systems, which support 40 percent of the world's people, could pose major security problems for the world—and, ulti-mately, for the United States.

Today, the most significant environmental threats facing the United States are truly global in nature. Every year, deforestation in the tropics denudes an area the size of Austria and kills off species of plants and animals at a rate one thousand to ten thousand times faster than natural extinction.[69] These species are important sources of food, energy, construction materials, pharmaceuticals, industrial chem-icals, and natural pest controls.[70] About one-quarter of U.S. prescription drugs, for example, contain ingredients derived from rainforest plants.[71] Deforestation also releases carbon dioxide into the air, which contrib-utes to another problem—global warming.

Most scientists believe that sometime in the next fifty years there will be enough man-made carbon dioxide, chlorofluorocarbons, and methane in the air to warm the earth three to eight degrees Fahren-heit.[72] This climatic change could transform the U.S. grain belt and other productive agricultural areas into dust bowls.[73] Hundreds of millions of poor people around the world could starve to death.[74] As temperatures escalate, forests will die off, heat waves will become more extreme, and bodies of water will evaporate (the Great Lakes could fall a foot and make some critical waterways more difficult to navigate).[75] As the oceans warm, their volume will expand and the polar ice caps will melt; sea levels could rise by one to four feet by the middle of the next century.[76] Up and down the U.S. coasts, dikes might have to be built to stave off the inundation of cities like New York, Washington, Miami, and Boston; the cost could easily be hundreds of billions, if not trillions, of dollars.[77]

Equally ominous is the finding of several recent studies, including one by the National Aeronautics and Space Administration (NASA), that atmospheric ozone in both the Northern and Southern hemispheres has declined significantly over the past two decades.[78] Caused by the increased release of chlorofluorocarbons and halons into the atmosphere, the deterioration of the ozone shield is allowing more of the sun's ultraviolet radiation to reach the earth, increasing the incidence of skin cancers and eye problems and damaging animals, plants, and crops. By the middle of the next century, according to one estimate, ultraviolet radiation could increase by as much as 15 percent, causing 1.5 million additional skin cancers in the United States *each year.*[79]

Still other environmental threats to human beings are now posed by new DDT-like chemicals that can permanently impair the human gene pool, the development of ever more resistant varieties of agricultural pests, and the ecological deterioration of the world's oceans.[80] All together, global environmental disasters caused by human mismanagement have created more than ten million refugees—most from declining land productivity—who themselves are producing a variety of military, political, and economic instabilities worldwide.[81]

A Comprehensive Security Policy

For more than forty-five years U.S. security planners focused almost exclusively on Soviet military power. Now with the "red menace" gone, they have turned their attention to villains like Kim Il Sung, Saddam Hussein, and Fidel Castro. If the United States is to be truly secure, it must understand and confront not just the Saddam Husseins of the world, but *all* threats to its well-being originating from outside its boundaries. A security policy that ignores any of the military, political, economic, or environmental threats to U.S. well-being is unworthy of the name, yet historically U.S. security policy has ignored nearly all of them.

Some commentators have complained that defining security in such broad terms muddles thinking and confuses policymaking.

For example, University of Pennsylvania political scientist Daniel Deudney has questioned the value of lumping environmental threats together with military threats—because each poses a different kind of harm, because the perpetrators of the two kinds of threats have different intentions, and because protection from each requires different institutions.[82]

But there are several important threads tying together the military, political, economic, and environmental threats. All these threats endanger things Americans value—life, liberty, and property. All these threats originate, at least in part, from outside the territorial boundaries of the United States and therefore must be met through foreign policies—that is, through policies that influence foreigners to act differently. And all these threats can only be ameliorated through the expenditure of public funds. Money spent protecting Americans from terrorism cannot be spent protecting them from global warming. The challenge for the United States is to design a security policy that effectively meets *all* threats with balance and economy.

2

The Limits to Force

In a speech to Congress in March 1947, President Harry Truman said, "I believe that it must be the policy of the United States to support free people who are resisting attempted subjugation by armed minorities or by outside pressures."[1] To protect democracy, as well as to defend its business and political interests abroad, the United States built up and maintained a vast interventionary apparatus that included some 700 bases spread across forty countries and territories and a navy with nearly 600 ships patrolling the world's oceans.[2]

Since the onset of the Cold War, there has hardly been a moment when the United States has not been intervening militarily in one part of the world or another. U.S. armed forces fought undeclared wars in Korea, Haiti, Vietnam, Cambodia, Lebanon, Grenada, Panama, and Iraq, and U.S. intelligence agents undertook or supported covert actions in more than forty countries.[3] The morality of these interventions, which killed, maimed, napalmed, bombed, and tortured many millions of people, is dubious. But there are pragmatic reasons to question these actions as well. The recent historical record suggests that neither the United States nor other countries that have relied on force as a primary instrument of foreign policy have much to show for it. Moreover, force has become increasingly counterproductive for democracy, trade, and access to resources—the purposes for which it is typically employed.

The Folly of U.S. Intervention

How well did U.S. interventions during the Cold War serve the national interest? How much more secure did the United States become because of its repeated uses of force? To answer these questions, consider three different ways in which force has been employed: covert actions, proxy wars, and direct intervention.

Covert Actions

Faced with a choice between the unpredictability of revolutionary reform and the certainty of conservative dictatorship, U.S. presidents
have often supported the latter. In a few instances they resolved to
replace popularly elected but left-leaning governments with dictators
who were reliably anti-Communist. Realizing that their actions
might evoke public outrage, they decided to act covertly. Here are
some examples:

- After Mohammed Mossadegh, the duly elected president of Iran,
  expropriated properties held by the Anglo-Iranian Oil Company,
  Exxon, and other major U.S oil companies in 1953, these corporations worked hand in hand with the Central Intelligence
  Agency (CIA) to overthrow the government and put the Shah in
  power.
- A year later United Fruit cooperated with the executive branch
  in the United States to replace the democratically elected president of Guatemala, Jacobo Arbenz, with a tyrannical colonel—
  leading to a succession of military dictators who ultimately
  killed 100,000 civilians.[4]
- In 1960 the U.S. State Department and the CIA worked together
  to remove from power Patrice Lumumba, the first popularly
  elected head of the Congo (now Zaire), and put in power Sese
  Seko Mobutu, whose military dictatorship became one of the
  bloodiest and most corrupt in Africa.[5]
- In the early 1970s the CIA assisted right-wing factions in the de-
  stabilization of an elected Marxist president in Chile, bringing to
  power General Augusto Pinochet, who for nearly twenty years
  terrorized the country with storm troopers, torture, and thousands of executions.

How much security did these violent overthrows gain for the
United States? Socialism was temporarily purged from the body pol-
itic in each of these nations and some U.S. business interests thrived,
but all four covert actions also earned the United States the enduring
resentment of the affected peoples. The CIA coup against Mossadegh
in 1953, for example, brought the Shah to power, ushering in more
than two decades of authoritarian rule enforced by his brutal secret
police force, SAVAK. When the Iranians finally overthrew the Shah in
1979, the new leader, the Ayatollah Khomeini, singled out the

United States as "the Great Satan." The United States created its own enemy, which ultimately undid the Carter administration with the takeover of the U.S. embassy in Teheran and then lured the Reagan administration into a humiliating arms-for-hostages deal.

After closely examining covert and overt U.S. intervention in countries as diverse as Zaire, El Salvador, Guatemala, Liberia, Nicaragua, Pakistan, and Vietnam, *Wall Street Journal* reporter Jonathan Kwitny concluded that the United States has managed to create "endless enemies" for itself: "Forceful intervention by a big power in a Third World country, no matter how well intentioned, is almost always dramatically harmful to the people who live in the country being intervened in."[6] It creates suffering for millions who are murdered, injured, orphaned, or tortured. It turns traditional economic and cultural relationships upside down. It destroys civil liberties, grassroots organizations, and other foundations for real democracy. And all these harms, taken together, incubate rampant anti-Americanism. If the United States wants to assure itself that Third World nations will remain reliable trading partners and resource suppliers, Kwitny recommends that it should "make sure that any leader who comes to power . . . has never been shot at by an American gun."[7]

Proxy Wars

Even without intervening directly, the United States has assisted proxy armies with military aid and training, again sowing seeds of foreign resentment. U.S. military and intelligence agencies helped build such nefarious police forces as Iran's SAVAK and Idi Amin's "public safety unit" and helped organize death squads in Guatemala and El Salvador. Graduates of State Department training programs included Nicaragua's former dictator Anastasio Somoza Debayle, Panama's Noriega, and Chile's Pinochet.[8] Throughout the 1970s, twenty-six of the thirty-five countries using systematic torture received U.S. military and economic aid.[9]

Proxy wars have been fought with forward support provided by U.S. bases, which themselves generate bad feelings in the host countries. Because of concerns ranging from prostitution in neighboring towns to qualms about losing national sovereignty, serious disputes over U.S. bases have arisen in Greece, the Philippines, Portugal, Spain, and Turkey.[10] Opposition has even occurred in pro-American Japan. Asia specialists Selig Harrison and Clyde V. Prestowitz, Jr., have written: "Nationalism is growing in Japan and is likely to take an anti-American direction if the United States fails to keep pace with growing sentiment in favor of a reduced superpower military presence."[11] For many people in Latin America, Asia, and Africa, U.S. military bases, aid, and training programs are despised symbols of U.S. imperialism.[12]

Intervention by proxy not only leaves a legacy of enduring hatred for the United States but also destroys the roots of democratic self-governance. Yes, the United States can overthrow an undesirable regime by providing rebels with enough money, credit, arms, and international support. But in doing so it props up new leaders who are often just as repressive and unreliable, and it tears to shreds the fabric of civil society that is necessary for political participation to flourish.

The Reagan administration's not-so-covert efforts to aid the Nicaraguan Contras is a textbook example of the problems with assisting proxy armies. U.S. assistance contributed to more than 30,000 deaths, heightened anti-Americanism throughout South and Central America, facilitated covert drug smuggling into the United States[13]— and nevertheless failed to dislodge the Sandinistas from power for a decade. It was only after the U.S. Congress *cut off* "lethal aid" for the Contras in 1988 that a real peace process could commence. Elections were then held in February 1990 in which the Nicaraguan people, exhausted by a decade of war and U.S.-sponsored economic sanctions, finally voted Sandinista leader Daniel Ortega out of office.

For Contra partisans, this history still suggests the value of proxy warfare: Without the pressure of frequent Contra attacks and the U.S. embargo of Nicaragua, the argument goes, the Sandinistas might not have been willing to hold fair elections and the Nicaraguan people might not have voted against the Sandinistas (as it was, Ortega got 42 percent of the vote). In fact, the Reagan and Bush administrations effectively tortured a weaker country into submission. By making clear to the Nicaraguan people that it would lift the embargo and halt nonmilitary aid to the Contras only if the Sandinistas were ousted, the United States was able to blackmail swing voters into backing Violeta Chamorro, leader of the National Opposition Union (UNO). And just to be sure, the United States channeled nearly $20 million to UNO through the National Endowment for Democracy and the CIA to buy newspaper advertisements and to help pay for 15,000 door-to-door canvassers.[14]

The real goal for U.S. foreign policy in Nicaragua should have been to promote genuine democracy and development, not to crush the

Sandinistas. Because democratic nations are unlikely to wage war against other democracies, a point elaborated in Chapter 4, a democratic Nicaragua would not be a security threat to the United States or to other democracies in the region. Moreover, a Nicaragua able to provide jobs and decent wages for the majority of its people could ensure a stable environment for U.S. investment and a good market for U.S. products.

The Sandinistas actually did democratize and develop Nicaragua after they overthrew Anastasio Somoza Debayle in 1979. They created a nationwide system of neighborhood organizations and began innovative programs for popular health care, adult literacy training, public housing, and sanitation that became models for development programs worldwide. They held elections in late 1984, which most European observers found fair and in which opposition groups garnered more than one-third of the vote.[15] They encouraged private ownership alongside state enterprises and initially received more aid from Western Europe and the United States than from Soviet-bloc countries.[16]

But all these advances were eviscerated by the U.S.-sponsored war and embargo. National resources were diverted from development to military spending. The cutoff of commerce and credit from the United States, once Nicaragua's most important trading partner, strangled the economy. The emerging civil society was torn apart as the Sandinistas issued emergency powers for themselves and reorganized society with military-style regimentation to win the war. The Contras' violence rallied the Nicaraguan public behind the Sandinistas, provided the government with pretexts for closing newspapers and radio stations, and led the country into a closer alliance with the Soviet Union. As historian Arthur Schlesinger, Jr., pointed out: "Mr. Reagan's military remedies promoted, not impeded, the spread of Marxism. Radical ideas thrive in a culture of hatred, violence, bloodshed, and destruction."[17]

Today Nicaragua is still recovering from the Contra war. Poverty is widespread, the social programs of the early 1980s have been virtually dismantled, and the structures of civil society remain weak.[18] U.S. support for the Contras set back democratization and development of Nicaragua by at least a decade.

Other proxy wars also have boomeranged against U.S. interests. In Angola, U.S. enthusiastic support in the 1980s for Jonas Savimbi's rebels, known human rights abusers, legitimated the presence of

Cuban troops and angered most of black Africa. Cuban troops in turn found themselves protecting Chevron Oil's drilling sites from U.S.-supported rebels. U.S. arms shipments to the mujahadin in Afghanistan may have tipped the war against the Soviets, but also wound up strengthening guerrilla forces holding fundamentalist views of Islamic governance akin to those of the Ayatollah Khomeini. Because of these commitments to the mujahadin, the Reagan administration looked the other way as the rebels cultivated more poppy for heroin—as much as doubling production between 1986 and 1987, according to a State Department report.[19]

Direct Interventions

On numerous occasions the United States has committed armed forces to undertake major military interventions. The dispatch of large contingents of U.S. troops to fight wars in Korea between 1950 and 1953 and in the Dominican Republic in 1965 drew little criticism from the American public. The turning point for public tolerance was the Vietnam War.

What started as a small commitment of military advisers in the early 1960s escalated into a full-scale war that ultimately claimed the lives of 1.3 million soldiers (including 58,000 Americans) and 1.2 million civilians.[20] U.S. use of napalm, white phosphorus, and herbicides defoliated between one-quarter and one-half of Vietnam, with much of the damage to cropland, fisheries, and wildlife irreparable, according to a report by the International Union for the Conservation of Nature.[21] Agent Orange continues to generate cancers, Hodgkin's disease, neurological disorders, liver ailments, and sterility in U.S. veterans.[22] By the time the United States left Vietnam in defeat in 1975, the American public had little stomach left for death and destruction caused by direct interventions.

Ronald Reagan ran for the presidency in 1980, promising to kick the "Vietnam syndrome," but he felt constrained to send troops to conflicts where victory could be achieved quickly and cheaply. Reagan's victories, however, were few and far between. By sending the U.S. military to Lebanon in 1983, the United States wound up complicating the conflict, enhancing Syria's diplomatic position, and getting 241 Marines killed by a terrorist truck-bomb. The U.S. invasion of Grenada that same year ousted a government that was unfriendly, but one that posed no threat to Americans, save possibly a handful of medical students, at a cost of virtually unanimous international censure in the UN General Assembly (not even our allies in Western Europe defended us). The U.S. air attack on Libya in 1986 hardly ended terrorism, though it did succeed in drawing sharp criticism from many of our NATO allies.[23] When the U.S. Navy began patrolling the Persian Gulf in 1987 to protect Kuwaiti and Western shipping, it did little to resolve the Iran-Iraq War.

President George Bush was as determined as Reagan to relegitimate the use of force. In his four years in office, Bush sent large numbers of U.S. military forces into Third World settings three times: in Panama, where U.S. troops removed strongman Manuel Noriega from power and brought him to the United States to stand trial on charges of drug smuggling; in Saudi Arabia, where the United States sent half a million troops to evict an Iraqi takeover of Kuwait and to protect oil fields in the region; and in Somalia, where U.S. forces protected convoys of food earmarked for starving civilians.

Some Panamanians undoubtedly were grateful to the 27,000 U.S. troops who overthrew General Noriega and allowed the duly elected government of Guillermo Endara to come to power, but many others were embittered by the brute force of the intervention. According to former State Department official Charles Maechling, Jr., Operation Just Cause "killed more than 300 [Panamanian] men, women, and children and sent another thousand plus into the hospital minus arms, legs, and eyes."[24] The invasion also was strongly condemned by the UN and by the Organization of American States (where the vote was 20 to 1), whose members rightly feared the precedent of one nation marching into another whenever it decides that the wrong leader is in power. Certainly Americans would have been equally alarmed had the Soviet Union invaded Mexico in 1988 to replace the government of President Carlos Salinas de Gortari after his party henchmen stole the presidential election from Cuauhtemoc Cardenas.[25]

U.S. intervention in the Persian Gulf War produced decidedly mixed results. Saddam Hussein's forces ultimately were removed from Kuwait, and a large fraction of his massive military forces, including chemical and nuclear weapons facilities, were either decimated during the conflict or disarmed afterwards. After the war the United States was able to bring to the negotiating table the key warring factions in the Middle East: Israel, its Arab neighbors, and the Palestinians. Today, with Saddam Hussein remaining in power and with the peace talks thus far producing limited results, the long-term consequences of the Persian Gulf War for Middle Eastern security and U.S. interests in the region are uncertain. Two immediate beneficiaries of the intervention were Iran and Syria, both of which possess chemical weapons capabilities, have long sponsored terrorism, and now, with the weakening of Iraq, can focus their attention on the one priority they share—to destroy Israel.

The war also turned Saddam Hussein into a hero for much of the Arab world. Even if Hussein is ultimately overthrown, many in the streets of Amman, Cairo, and Rabat will remember his stand against the West as an exemplar for future North-South confrontations. "When no one else has been able to do so," writes *Time* magazine's Scott MacLeod, "Saddam offers many Arabs dreams of unity, with which they could finally achieve a respected place in the world; of prosperity, which could be brought about by an equitable distribution of Arab oil wealth; of Israel's defeat, which would enable the Palestinians to have justice."[26]

It is too early to evaluate Operation Restore Hope in Somalia. As a short-term relief operation, it could hardly fail. The Somalian warlords, clan leaders, and bandits who had been battling one another since the brutal dictator Siad Barre fled the country in 1991 were no match for 28,000 U.S. troops carrying the flag of the UN Security Council. The intervention, however, was designed with virtually no consultation with Somalis.

One immediate consequence of the U.S. intervention was that delicate peace arrangements that had been worked out in parts of the country were thrown into jeopardy. In the city of Baidoa, where relief efforts had been working reasonably well, the arrival of U.S. troops provoked a local warlord to pillage the town and forced aid distributors to evacuate. Rakiya Omaar and Alex de Waal, the director and associate director of the human rights organization Africa Watch (until they were fired for opposing the U.S. intervention), explain why this happened: "All the agreements so painstakingly worked out no longer hold force. The only question that matters now is, who will gain from the U.S. occupation and who will lose? In this atmosphere, clan negotiators are paralyzed with uncertainty, while the warlords' eyes gleam with the chance of fresh adventures out of the sight of the Marines."[27]

The U.S. armed forces are not well equipped to oversee negotiations among rival clan leaders, to improve indigenous irrigation, sustainable agriculture, and food distribution, or to strengthen the civil society needed for self-rule. Even if U.S. troops could be trained to carry out these delicate tasks, their credibility in Somalia would be undercut by the fact that the United States embraced Siad Barre, starting in 1977, in order to secure a base in the northern port of Berbera, and generously supplied him with weapons for over a decade. As commentator Alexander Cockburn notes, "Somalis do not forget Siad Barre's massacres in the late 1980s of some 150,000 northerners in the former British Somaliland, or his near-total destruction of northern towns like Hargeise with the help of South African bomber pilots and U.S. logistical backup and diplomatic protection."[28]

A Tragic Legacy

The recent history of U.S. intervention hardly inspires confidence that force is a reliable tool of diplomacy. Covert actions wound up toppling democracies and repressing foreign peoples, who now understandably feel contempt for the United States. Efforts to aid proxy armies backfired into stronger public support for the very governments the United States was trying to topple. Direct intervention failed outright in Lebanon and achieved only limited results in Grenada, Libya, Panama, Iraq, and Somalia. In all these cases the use of force never addressed and sometimes exacerbated the fundamental causes of the conflicts.

Weighed against the dubious benefits of force are a number of significant costs and risks. First, there are the often forgotten victims of war. Except in Korea and Vietnam, U.S. armed forces have not suffered large numbers of casualties in interventions since World War II, but their interventions killed thousands in the Dominican Republic and Nicaragua, hundreds of thousands in Iraq and Indonesia, and more than a million in Vietnam. The Persian Gulf War also led Saddam Hussein to wreak revenge on the West through ecotage. He released several oil slicks that imperiled critically important commercial shrimp and fishing industries and set 600 Kuwaiti oil wells on fire, which released thick plumes of toxic smoke that caused respiratory problems as far away as Turkey, Iran, and India.[29]

There are also economic costs. The Vietnam War cost the United States over $595 billion (1990 dollars), decimated the U.S. economy with more than a decade of double-digit inflation, and removed the once mighty dollar as the peg for other nations' currencies. The direct cost of Desert Storm in fiscal year 1991, according to the Bush administration, was $61 billion. To this figure, however, must be added long-term medical and pension benefits to veterans of the war, which Ralph Estes, an American University accounting professor, has estimated will cost more than $100 billion.[30] Against these costs, payments of $52 billion to the war effort by Germany, Japan, Saudi Arabia, Kuwait, and a handful of others seem niggardly.[31]

Large-scale wars also have become risky enterprises because they can escalate into a catastrophic nuclear war. Every time the United States intervenes militarily—whether in Central America, the Persian Gulf, or Africa—it invites a counterintervention by another nation possessing nuclear weapons. Had the Soviet Union still been a major backer of Saddam Hussein in 1990, as it was a few years earlier, U.S. intervention in Kuwait and then Iraq could have precipitated a serious confrontation between the superpowers. If nuclear weapons continue to spread to more countries, the risk grows that sooner or later a nuclear-armed nation will challenge a U.S. intervention. The security of the most powerful nations on Earth once depended on winning wars; now, in the nuclear age, it depends on avoiding them.

Finally, interventions have hurt U.S. security by providing other aggressors or potential aggressors with moral and legal justifications for violating international norms of nonviolence. For example, despite decades of favorable decisions from the World Court (including one against Iran in 1981), the Reagan administration refused further participation in its proceedings after the court roundly condemned the United States for supporting the Nicaraguan Contras, disseminating manuals promoting political assassination, and laying mines in Nicaragua's harbors. Every time the United States casts aside international laws prohibiting military intervention, however, it tacitly encourages other countries to do the same. U.S. mines in the harbors of Nicaragua provided a precedent for the Iranians to lay mines in the Persian Gulf—and someday could provide the excuse for another pariah nation to mine the harbors of New York or Los Angeles. In this respect, the Bush administration's decision to seek UN Security Council approval of its interventions in the Persian Gulf and in Somalia represented a major step forward.

The Persian Gulf War is a poignant reminder that war is hardly obsolete. The United States and other powerful nations still have the technological capacity to fight and win "hyperwars" with smaller, less powerful nations. But the real question is whether such wars are economically and politically worth the costs. In the Persian Gulf War the U.S. high command resisted the temptation to march to Baghdad because the probable cost in U.S. lives seemed too great and the potential gains too limited. As powerful conventional and nuclear weapons proliferate to more countries, the dangers of resolving conflicts through arms races and battlefields will be greater and greater. A hundred years ago a superpower might have been able to impose its will on a distant country, but now nationalism has joined with technology to give Vietnamese, Afghans, Iraqis, and the rest of the world's peoples machine guns, nerve-gas shells, grenades, anti-tank rockets, and anti-aircraft missiles to thwart outsiders. Weapons technology and nationalist ideologies have become great equalizers in international affairs, helping the smallest nations to stand up to the most powerful.

It is no accident that all but three of the twenty-four wars being fought today are internal conflicts, typically with one ethnic or religious group seeking to topple the repressive rule of another.[32] Other nations are also learning that the use of force against neighboring countries rarely pays.

The Recent Record for Other Users of Force

Many countries in recent times have been disappointed with the political results stemming from using force against their neighbors. Iraq's incursion into Iran in 1980 resulted in one of the bloodiest wars since World War II and settled nothing; its attempt to occupy Kuwait a decade later triggered a Western counterattack that pulverized Saddam Hussein's military forces, killed as many as several hundred thousand soldiers and civilians, and caused $200 billion worth of damage to Iraqi factories, schools, bridges, and other vital infrastructure.[33] Vietnam's occupation of Cambodia bled the country's treasury and kept the Vietnamese among the world's poorest people. The Soviet Union's takeover of Afghanistan poisoned its reputation in most of the Third World, killed and maimed tens of thousands of their troops, worsened (as Vietnam did for us) a domestic drug problem, failed to secure a friendly pro-Soviet regime, and hastened its demise as a nation state.

Under Mikhail Gorbachev, the Soviet Union reluctantly concluded that military efforts to co-opt other countries were no longer worth the cost. The Soviets supported Vietnamese troops in Cambodia and Cuban troops in Angola, but ultimately these proxies ran up against the same problems as direct superpower interventions did, which explains why both Vietnam and Cuba ultimately withdrew from these military quagmires. "Far from dominating Southeast Asia, as the falling-domino model predicted," historian Arthur Schlesinger, Jr., has noted, "Vietnam [was] a rather beleaguered state surrounded by hostility—the result [that] the classical 'balance-of-power' model would have predicted."[34] Vietnam's invasion of Cambodia encountered stiff resistance from indigenous forces like the Khmer Rouge and diplomatic pressure to withdraw from Thailand, China, and the United States.[35] In Angola, the Soviets gained access to airfields and naval facilities, but they were not allowed to build permanent military bases.[36] Meanwhile, Angola sought and achieved closer economic and political ties to the West (starting in 1975 the West provided more aid than East Bloc countries did).

After repeatedly disavowing the Brezhnev Doctrine, in which the Soviet Union had claimed the right to intervene militarily in Eastern Europe whenever socialism was threatened, Gorbachev backed up his words with judicious inaction, never once using force to block change in his Warsaw Pact allies.[37] As one Eastern European country after another tossed out its Communist leaders in the autumn of 1989, Gennadi Gerasimov, the principal spokesperson for the Soviet Foreign Ministry, declared the Sinatra Doctrine: "You know the Frank Sinatra song, 'I Did It My Way'? Hungary and Poland are doing it their way."[38] "We have no right, moral or political," said Gerasimov, "to interfere in events happening there."[39] Even in December 1989, when the revolution in Romania briefly appeared to be headed toward a civil war, and when U.S. Secretary of State James Baker made the astonishing remark that the United States would support the Warsaw Pact if it "felt it necessary to intervene on behalf of the opposition," the Soviet Union abided scrupulously by the principle of nonintervention.[40]

In February 1991, as the United States was readying a ground assault against Iraqi troops dug into Kuwait, it was Gorbachev's foreign policy adviser, Yevgeny Primakov, who worked assiduously to produce proposals for the Iraqis to leave Kuwait before a costly ground war got under way. To the United States and its allies, Soviet efforts to allow Iraq to save face were regarded as unwelcome meddling; to much of the rest of the world, however, these peace initiatives demonstrated that the Soviet Union, and not the United States, was more interested in resolving conflicts without violence.

Force as a Last Resort

Surely if the Soviet Union can recognize the limits of force, so can the United States. This does not mean that force is irrelevant, but in an era when so many powerful weapons have fallen into so many hands, nations no longer can use force reliably against their neighbors. Offensive users of force are increasingly likely to encounter overwhelming defenses, deadly retaliation, and international sanctions. The United States and other nations would therefore be wise to regard force as truly a last resort.

Nations may still be tempted to assist one side or another of an internal struggle, but the historical record of U.S. intervention, whether overt or covert, whether by proxy or by direct invasion, suggests that it creates more problems than it solves. Forceful intervention almost always produces new enemies for the intervenor, impoverishes vast numbers of people, and destroys the roots of democracy that ultimately are necessary to resolve civil, ethnic, religious, class, or political conflicts. It is far better to work constructively in troubled lands to promote participatory democracy, sustainable development, and efficient resource use. Even where force is necessary to stop one side from committing genocide on another, as in Bosnia-Herzegovina (where Serbs began systematically exiling and killing Muslims in 1992), it is best deployed by a legitimate regional institution or by the UN than by a self-righteous superpower.

The American people seem ready to support leaders who will abjure the unilateral use of force. Approximately two out of three Americans consistently opposed U.S. military aid to the Nicaraguan Contras, and half opposed the war in the Persian Gulf prior to its commencement. The enormous outpouring of public support for the Persian Gulf War after the shooting began should not obscure the continued skepticism of Americans toward the use of force. Once a war begins, Americans want to get it over with quickly. Any president deciding whether to undertake another intervention of this magnitude will have to remember that forty-seven senators voted against the war. The number of senators who initially refused to support President Lyndon Johnson's intervention in Vietnam, in contrast, was two.

3
The Dangers of Arms Races

From the outset of the Cold War a guiding principle for U.S. security planners has been that the best defense is a good offense. President Ronald Reagan articulated this conventional wisdom when he said: "I don't know of any country that has gotten into war by being too strong."[1] *Commentary* editor Norman Podhoretz, long an advocate of the United States continually expanding and modernizing its weapons arsenal, has written: "Churchill, thinking of the ancient adage *si vis pacem para bellum* ('If you want peace, prepare for war'), later called World War II 'the unnecessary war.' It could, he thought, have been prevented if the democracies had rearmed earlier instead of allowing the military balance to tip in Hitler's favor."[2]

The United States adhered to this logic throughout the Cold War, as did the Soviet Union, setting in motion the most ambitious arms race in human history. This competition is perhaps best called a controlled arms race, since the two superpowers were periodically negotiating arms control agreements that limited the numbers and types of weapons each side could build. However, the controlled arms race, like all other arms races, did not come without cost. It brought the superpowers dangerously close to a mutually suicidal war. In addition, it burdened both sides with enormous political, economic, and environmental insecurities that will remain for decades to come.

The Controlled Arms Race

When two small nuclear bombs killed more than 200,000 people in Hiroshima and Nagasaki, U.S. security planners immediately reasoned that if these weapons could cut short World War II by months and forestall a costly U.S. land invasion of Japan, surely they could serve other U.S. foreign policy interests as well.[3] They could guarantee that never again would our adversaries dare attack the United States as the Japanese did at Pearl Harbor.

In 1947 the United States deployed nuclear weapons against its greatest postwar adversary—the Soviet Union. Proceeding on the argument that the Soviet Union was inherently expansionist and that only a massive show of military strength could stop it, the United States enlisted Western Europe and Canada to form a gigantic anti-Soviet military alliance—NATO. Central to NATO's defense were long-range bombers with nuclear weapons. By the early 1950s, as the Soviet Union began building its own hydrogen bombs, Secretary of State John Foster Dulles announced the doctrine of "massive retaliation," vowing in effect to respond to any Soviet aggression with a devastating counterattack on Soviet cities.

For the next four decades the United States and the Soviet Union engaged each other in a vigorous arms race. Bombers soon were supplemented by intercontinental ballistic missiles (ICBMs) deployed in silos and on submarines. President John F. Kennedy discovered and closed an alleged "missile gap," propelling each side to deploy more than 1,500 missiles by 1970.[4] Strategic missiles were then given multiple warheads and greater accuracy; by 1980, Soviet long-range missiles were carrying 5,500 nuclear warheads and U.S. long-range missiles 7,300.[5] A decade later, after President Reagan sought to slam shut a "window of vulnerability," the Soviets had a strategic arsenal with 12,300 nuclear warheads and a tactical nuclear arsenal with 15,000 weapons deliverable by short-range and medium-range missiles, artillery, and aircraft.[6] The United States had a strategic arsenal with 8,772 warheads and a tactical arsenal with 6,650 warheads.[7]

The superpower arms race during the Cold War was characterized not only by a continuous buildup of weapons but also by periodic arms control treaties. Some measures like the 1972 Strategic Arms Limitation Treaty (SALT) slowed the rate of buildup, though only slightly. Other agreements like the Limited Test Ban Treaty (LTBT), which banned the atmospheric testing of nuclear bombs, actually accelerated the arms race. Hailed for its potential to impede nuclear-weapons development and eventually signed by 116 nations, the LTBT turned out to be primarily an environmental-protection measure that reduced the level of radioactive fallout in the atmosphere.[8] To get the Joint Chiefs of Staff to support the treaty, President Kennedy promised a more vigorous underground testing program—a promise he and his successors kept. In the two decades following the signing of the LTBT, the United States and the Soviet Union *increased* their annual rates of nuclear testing.[9] The best that arms control could accomplish was not a cessation of the arms race, but a controlled arms race, in which the United States and the Soviet Union steadily expanded and modernized nuclear-weapons forces while simultaneously negotiating a few limits.

Today many security analysts contend that the controlled arms race was a great success because it hastened the collapse of the Soviet Union.[10] By forcing the Kremlin to allocate huge sums of money to defense, according to this argument, the controlled arms race weakened the Soviet economy and stoked discontent in the Soviet people. There is no evidence, however, that the Soviets responded to the Reagan arms buildup by jacking up military spending. According to the CIA, Soviet military spending both before and during the Reagan administration's rearmament program grew at a steady 2 percent per year.[11]

Political scientists Daniel Deudney and John Ikenberry argue that the two Western influences that *were* decisive in ending the arms race had nothing to do with arms buildups.[12] One was President Reagan's embrace of nuclear disarmament, demonstrated at the Reykjavík summit in October 1986, when he proposed to scrap all strategic nuclear weapons. This "provided a crucial signal to Gorbachev that bold initiatives would be reciprocated rather than exploited."[13] It was shortly thereafter, in 1987, that Gorbachev accepted Reagan's proposed "zero option," enabling the two sides to conclude the INF Treaty, the first agreement to eliminate an entire class of nuclear weapons.

Gorbachev capitulated not to the West's hardliners, but to its peace activists, who had argued that it was in the mutual interests of the two superpowers to reduce tensions, to end draining conflicts, and to disengage their military forces in Europe and the Third World. Once Gorbachev pulled Soviet troops out of Afghanistan, pruned his conventional forces, and allowed peaceful change in Eastern Europe, it was easy for the two superpowers to reach agreement on the first and second START treaties and the Conventional Forces in Europe (CFE) Agreement.

Another factor hastening the collapse of the Soviet Union was the attraction of capitalism. "For the peoples of the USSR and Eastern Europe," write Deudney and Ikenberry, "it was not so much abstract liberal principles but rather the Western way of life—the material and cultural manifestations of the West's freedoms—that subverted the Soviet vision."[14] East-West trade and citizen exchanges, which expanded steadily after 1983, made more and more Soviet citizens painfully aware that their living standards were falling behind those of the West.

But the West must be modest about the impact of any of its policies on internal Soviet politics. As George F. Kennan, one of the key architects of the Cold War, argues, "The suggestion that any Administration had the power to influence decisively the course of a tremendous domestic political upheaval in another great country on another side of the globe is simply childish."[15] It was the inefficiency of the bureaucratic state-run economy, coupled with the repressiveness and hypocrisy of communism, that brought hundreds of thousands of Muscovites to the streets on August 20, 1991, to support Boris Yeltsin against a hardliner coup. Once Yeltsin came to power and disbanded the Communist Party, more dramatic arms control deals with the United States then became possible.

Despite these developments, the controlled arms race is still not over. Even with recent agreements, the United States and Russia still have many thousands of nuclear weapons and ambitious programs to modernize and improve their arsenals. Should political relations between the two nations sour, another arms race could begin. To prevent this from happening, U.S. security planners must recognize that an arms buildup is not a cost-free venture.

The War Risks of the Controlled Arms Race

According to the *Canadian Army Journal*, of the 1,587 arms races between 600 B.C. and 1960, all but ten culminated in war.[16] "Many Russians," Thomas Powers has noted in the *Atlantic Monthly*, "cite Chekhov's famous principle of dramaturgy: If there is a gun on the wall in the first act, it will fire in the third."[17] World War I, for example, occurred in part because two rapidly arming alliances became convinced that war was inevitable and that whoever struck the first blow would prevail. Each side amassed such a large powder keg that it took only a single match—the assassination of the Archduke Franz Ferdinand by Serbian-recruited terrorists—to envelop the entire continent in a war that claimed the lives of 13 million soldiers and 13 million civilians.

The controlled arms race similarly brought the two superpowers to the brink of a disastrous war. It encouraged the adoption of dangerous strategies and weapons for fighting nuclear wars, opened conduits for accidental nuclear war, spread nuclear weapons to other nations, and accelerated the development of new, destabilizing weapons.

Strategies and Weapons for Fighting Nuclear Wars

Throughout the Cold War, the United States adopted strategies and acquired weapons to fight and win World War III. The traditional U.S. nuclear strategy of massive retaliation actually embodied two doctrines—deterrence and extended deterrence. Deterrence put the Soviet Union on notice that any attack on the U.S. homeland would be met by a deadly nuclear counterstrike. Extended deterrence was a pledge by the United States to use nuclear weapons to meet any Soviet aggression in Western Europe.[18] Although this doctrine was never well understood by the American public, it meant that the United States was prepared to escalate a conventional war into a nuclear war if Europe appeared to be falling into Soviet hands. In other words, the United States stood ready to be the first side to use nuclear weapons.

Had U.S. security planners wished to deploy a nuclear arsenal capable of assuring the destruction of the Soviet Union, they could have been satisfied with perhaps a few hundred nuclear missiles, as Secretary of Defense Robert McNamara had recommended in the early 1960s. However, these strategists argued that the United States also had to be capable of fighting a nuclear war and "prevailing" in a variety of scenarios, including the defense of Western Europe against a Soviet attack, support for U.S. troops protecting oil fields in the Middle East, and beating the Soviet Union to the button if Communist generals were preparing to attack the United States. By defining more contingencies for possible use, U.S. security planners actually increased the chances that nuclear weapons would be used.

On more than a dozen occasions during the Cold War U.S. leaders threatened to use nuclear bombs.[19] Each time, the president put nuclear forces on higher alert and set in motion a chain of potentially uncontrollable events. In peacetime, tactical nuclear bombs are stored in guarded facilities, and detailed arrangements are made to ensure that no single person can fire nuclear bombs from strategic submarines, missile silos, and bombers; *negative* control is emphasized. In times of crisis, however, to compensate for the vulnerability of command-and-control facilities, the operating procedures ensure that the weapons *will* be fired if the order is given; *positive* control becomes paramount. As a crisis deepens and a president authorizes a higher alert, he is inevitably removing controls and increasing the probability of nuclear war by an accidental or unauthorized firing. Each time U.S. security planners threatened to use nuclear bombs, they increased the danger of the Soviets responding likewise.

Were nuclear coercion an effective tool for foreign policymaking, these risks might have been warranted. In an exhaustive survey of nineteen nuclear crises, however, defense analyst Morton Halperin concluded that "nuclear threats have never been central to the outcome of a crisis."[20] Those who believe in the efficacy of nuclear diplomacy often point to the success of President John Kennedy's nuclear threats in convincing the Soviet Union to remove its medium-range missiles from Cuba in 1962. Yet even if Kennedy's threats achieved their objective, there is little consensus among scholars that they were necessary or prudent. Stanford historian Barton Bernstein, for example, has suggested that Kennedy's behavior may have been negligent since most members of the Executive Committee of the National Security Council had agreed that the new missiles did not significantly alter the Soviet-U.S. strategic balance (Soviet submarines were already off the East Coast).[21] U.S. and Soviet leaders then had thirteen days to resolve the crisis—and they nearly failed. Future nuclear crises may need to be resolved in thirteen minutes or less.

The controlled arms race also led to technical developments that increased the risks of nuclear war. For example, the introduction of highly accurate, multiple independent reentry vehicles (MIRVs) in the early 1970s increased temptations for each side to attack first during a crisis. MIRV technology enables a single missile to carry as many as ten warheads, each bound for a different target. With ten MIRVed missiles, the United States could strike a hundred Soviet missiles and consequently prevent up to a thousand Soviet warheads from ever reaching U.S. targets; the Soviets, of course, had similar incentives to strike U.S. MIRVed missiles first. These pressures to be the first to use nuclear weapons intensified in the 1980s when both superpowers deployed medium-range missiles in Europe capable of striking their targets in six to eight minutes. "Use 'em or lose 'em," security planners would say.

Strategic defenses, which encompass a wide range of technologies such as anti-ballistic missiles (ABMs), X-ray lasers, and space-based interceptors, would only exacerbate these risks. In his March 1983 speech introducing the Strategic Defense Initiative (SDI), President Reagan acknowledged that the possession of both offenses and defenses by either the United States or the Soviet Union could be perceived as "fostering an aggressive policy." Yet this is precisely what many security planners working under presidents Reagan and Bush wanted the United States to do: to deploy SDI while simultaneously building up first-strike weapons. The danger was that these technologies would encourage the Soviet Union to strike the United States first during a crisis, lest a U.S. first strike knock out most of the Soviet missiles and SDI neutralize the remainder. Moreover, some of these defensive technologies have clear offensive potential. For example, so-called brilliant pebbles, small space-based rockets that could intercept missiles flying through space, also could assist a U.S. first strike by knocking out enemy satellites for early warning, communications, and intelligence. For now, most strategic defenses remain confined to the weapons laboratories, but if the arms race resumes with Russia or another nuclear-armed power, pressures will mount to develop and deploy these destabilizing weapons.

Accidental Wars

The strategies and the technologies promoted by the controlled arms race also reduced the decisionmaking time Soviet and U.S. leaders had to determine whether the first indications of nuclear attack were real or merely erroneous instrument readings. During the Cold War, false indications of a Soviet attack were triggered by flocks of geese, a war-games tape, and the rising of the moon. Between 1977 and 1984 the North American Air Defense Command (NORAD) had 1,152 false alarms giving early alerts of a missile attack.[22] With so little time for human decisionmaking, more and more of the nuclear command structure was entrusted to electronic sensors and computers. It is not clear whether either side actually adopted a strict launch-on-warning posture, but decisionmaking increasingly relied on electronic data and computers that were inherently vulnerable to hidden programming errors.[23] Was it prudent of U.S. security planners to put Soviet military staff, who even after two hours could not tell whether a Korean commercial airliner was on a spy mission, in a position to decide in a matter of minutes whether to blow up the world?[24]

The controlled arms race carried the additional risks of human error or criminal behavior leading to a nuclear war. Approximately five thousand U.S. personnel guarding nuclear weapons were dismissed each year during the mid-1970s because of alcoholism, drug abuse, delinquency, or derangement.[25] In 1981 Jack Anderson reported that nine out of every ten soldiers guarding and maintaining nuclear weapons had flunked tests of their basic military skills.[26]

Articulating a common response by security planners, analysts in the Harvard Nuclear Study Group concluded that the unauthorized or accidental use of nuclear weapons is unlikely because of three different safeguards:

> First is the "two-man rule," which requires parallel actions by two or more individuals at several stages in the process of communicating and carrying out any order to use nuclear weapons. Second is the system of Permissive Action Links (PALs), including a highly secure coded signal which must be inserted in the weapons before they can be used. Third, devices internal to the weapon are designed to ensure that an attempt to bypass the PALs system will disarm the weapon.[27]

Yet this sanguine assessment of the security of nuclear weapons from human malevolence or sloppiness is questionable on several levels:

- ☐ Conspiracies by "two or more individuals at several stages" are hardly unprecedented and indeed are characteristic of many large-scale robberies and crimes.
- ☐ Individuals can be overcome, coerced, or bribed. As Amory Lovins writes: "During the 1967 Cultural Revolution in China, the military commander of Sinkiang Province reportedly threatened to take over the nuclear base there. French scientists testing a bomb in the Algerian Sahara apparently had to destroy it hurriedly lest it fall into the hands of rebellious French generals led by Maurice Challe."[28]
- ☐ Even if the PALs and other internal security devices work, a bomb could be hauled away and disassembled and the fissionable plutonium or uranium could be extracted for use in a homemade bomb, or the stolen bomb simply could be equipped with a new arming and firing system to bypass the disabled one.
- ☐ A completely foolproof security system cannot be built, and it takes no bold leap to imagine some combination of insiders' knowledge and PALs' failure that could awaken a dormant warhead.

Human error played a large role in the more than sixty-five serious nuclear accidents to which the U.S. government has admitted.[29] While most of these accidents occurred in the early years of the Cold War, at least one noteworthy event occurred more recently: In 1980 a dropped wrench blew up a Titan missile booster in Damascus, Arkansas, catapulting a nine-megaton warhead into a nearby forest.[30] Again, PALs and other internal security devices may help to prevent accidental detonations, but these security measures become less effective as a nuclear arsenal becomes larger. As any system becomes more complex, it has a greater chance of experiencing a catastrophic breakdown.[31] Lloyd Dumas, a professor of political economy at the University of Texas and an expert on nuclear accidents, believes that "as military systems in which these weapons are imbedded have become more . . . geographically dispersed and technologically sophisticated, there is an increased probability that they will eventually fail."[32]

Wars Through Proliferation

The controlled arms race undermined long-standing efforts to curb the proliferation of nuclear weapons among other nations, terrorists, and criminals. To date, 141 nations have signed the 1968 Non-Proliferation Treaty (NPT), in which nonnuclear nations agreed not to acquire nuclear weapons in exchange for a promise by the nuclear nations to negotiate in good faith complete disarmament.[33] As the NPT was completed, China, France, and India all eloquently objected that it would merely ratify the superpowers' military superiority.[34] To counter these arguments, the United States and the Soviet Union argued forcefully—and hypocritically—that militarily weaker nations would be wise to remain weaker. Were nonnuclear nations to acquire nuclear weapons, the superpowers pointed out, they would risk the dangers of their neighbors acquiring nuclear weapons and heighten the chance of disastrous regional nuclear conflicts. Nuclear-armed nations also might find themselves qualifying as new targets for superpower missiles.[35]

A number of nonnuclear parties to the NPT regarded the Soviet-U.S. controlled arms race as a direct violation of the language and spirit of the treaty. At the NPT Review Conferences in 1980, 1985, and 1990, and also at the United Nations Third Special Session on Disarmament in 1988, representatives of nonnuclear nations excoriated the nuclear nations for failing to move toward disarmament;

some even spoke of abandoning the NPT.[36] Resentments will certainly mount if the United States pursues SDI—a program that most nonnuclear nations believe violates the ABM Treaty, the Outer Space Treaty, and the Limited Test Ban Treaty.[37] Unless the United States and Russia begin to move seriously toward disarmament, nonnuclear nations could decide to repudiate the treaty altogether when the NPT comes up for renewal in 1995.

Existing nuclear-bomb programs, as well as closely interlinked commercial nuclear-reactor programs, have provided key bomb-building materials and technology to Argentina, Brazil, India, Iran, Iraq, Israel, Libya, North Korea, Pakistan, and South Africa, among others.[38] The proliferation of nuclear bombs and medium-range missiles suggests that the U.S. "victory" in the controlled arms race came at a cost of sowing radioactive seeds in another ten or twenty nuclear nations. If the United States finds itself in a crisis with these new nuclear nations, its cities once again will be at risk from assured nuclear destruction. The resounding U.S. victory over Iraq in 1991 would have been a disaster had Saddam Hussein been able to attack Western cities with a handful of nuclear weapons. Even if the use of nuclear weapons is confined to a region, the side effects from a "limited nuclear war"—collateral blast damage to nonmilitary targets, poisonous radioactive clouds drifting downwind, disabled electronic circuits from electromagnetic pulses, ravaged ecosystems—would harm many other nations, including the United States. A nuclear war between India and Pakistan could trigger responses from China or Russia, which then could involve the United States.

U.S. victory in the controlled arms race exacerbated proliferation in another way. The disintegration of the Soviet Union forced the United States to confront four new nuclear powers—Russia, Kazakhstan, Ukraine, and Belarus. As these nations bickered over control and disassembly of the old Kremlin stockpile, U.S. security planners fretted over the dangers of ex-Soviet nuclear weapons being lost, stolen, or sold to other nations or terrorists. Many also worried that thousands of scientists involved in the Soviet weapons-building program might sell their skills to the highest international bidder.

These risks are not unique to the Soviet nuclear weapons program. Revolutionary reallocations of political power are conceivable within at least three other nuclear-armed countries—China, South Africa, and Israel—that could expand the number of fingers on nuclear triggers or throw unemployed builders of nuclear bombs onto the world market. Indeed, any country with an active nuclear-weapons program *inevitably* spreads knowledge, technology, and materials for building bombs. It is only a question of how far and how fast.

Future Wars

Perhaps the most terrifying feature of an arms race is the absence of a credible vision of a secure future. The permanent search for strategic superiority leads to the unending invention, accumulation, and modernization of advanced weapons.[39] If U.S. security planners continue to develop weapons without restraint, tomorrow's arsenals will include the following: directed-energy "third generation" nuclear bombs that could destroy a distant missile within seconds by sending out intense pulses of X-rays or gamma rays; a microwave bomb that could damage an enemy's electronics over a wide area; a hypervelocity pellet bomb that could fire a hail of sand-like grains against targets in space at speeds of up to 350,000 miles per hour; and missiles capable of burrowing deep into the earth and pulverizing hardened missile silos. Roger Batzel, director of the Lawrence Livermore Laboratory, told Congress in 1986 that "we have no reason to believe that we have more than scratched the surface with respect to the potential of these technologies."[40]

An arms race could lead participants to turn to chemical weapons. In December 1987 the United States quietly ended its eighteen-year moratorium on chemical weapons production and began producing new binary designs (although some technical problems remain).[41] Three years later the United States and the Soviet Union agreed to stop producing mustard, nerve, and other chemical agents and to begin disposing of all but 5,000 tons of their massive stockpiles by the year 2002 (the Soviet Union had 50,000 tons and the United States 30,000 tons).[42] Research and development is still permissible, however, and as recently as 1989 the Pentagon was designing new chemicals that can overwhelm gas masks and "knockout bombs" that can kill soldiers hiding in buildings.[43]

U.S. production of biological weapons is apparently not planned right now because that would contravene the U.S. obligation under a 1972 treaty not to develop biological agents for offensive purposes. But the Army, contending that the treaty does not bar "defensive research," still hopes to build a new germ-warfare laboratory at the Dugway Proving Ground in Utah, and since 1983 the United States has actually quadrupled its research budget for biological weapons.[44] Among the agents being explored for military potential are plague, anthrax, rabbit fever, meningitis, typhoid fever, dysentery, influenza, smallpox, yellow fever, dengue fever, encephalitis, as well as toxins cloned from cobras, rattlesnakes, scorpions, and shellfish.[45] The Pentagon also is developing microbes for which there are no known antidotes.[46] Biotechnology critic Jeremy Rifkin has warned, "We're talking about the possibility of powerful new genetic weapons that could rival nuclear weapons in the future."[47]

"All of this," former nuclear-bomb designer Theodore Taylor has observed, "means that without serious negotiations, we will see the surge of a whole new arms race that will make the past 30 years look like a walk and the new arms race look like a marathon, without requiring the registration of entrants."[48]

Political Insecurity

Even if the controlled arms race prevented the Soviet Union and other nations from coercing the United States with nuclear weapons, it did little to address three important sources of coercion Americans will face in the years ahead—terrorism, Big Brother repression, and creditor demands.

Whereas nearly all national leaders, however extreme their views, are rational enough to realize that an act of extortion against the United States invites devastating military retaliation, terrorists have no such compunctions. Although terrorism would probably be a serious global problem with or without an arms race, it is exacerbated by unrestricted arms building. The controlled arms race gave leaders unwarranted confidence that military force could solve political problems, thereby discouraging and deferring policies that might address the real roots of terrorism. For example, U.S. leaders came to believe that the best way to stop Palestinian terrorism was to bomb suspected base camps in Libya or elsewhere rather than address the fundamental political question: How can Palestinian claims for a homeland, regarded as just by most of the world, be addressed in a manner consistent with the security of Israel?

The architects of the controlled arms race never appreciated how their embrace of nuclear deterrence provided a perfect model and justification for terrorism. Richard Falk, professor of politics at Princeton University, has argued: "If the most powerful states insist on their discretion to inflict the ultimate barbarism, then any moral or legal objections directed at those with lesser capabilities are much eroded. Indeed the decline of international law during the last several decades is, in part, a reflection of the unbridled nuclearism by the leaders of world society."[49]

In their reliance on nuclear weapons for national security, U.S. security planners not only steadily eroded the moral and legal underpinnings of nonproliferation, they also made the technology and ingredients for building nuclear weapons widely available. Security planners never *intended* for nuclear weapons to fall into the hands of terrorists, but the spread of the data, technology, specialists, and materials necessary for building nuclear bombs has been an inevitable consequence of their ever-expanding nuclear-bomb programs. It is now widely realized that terrorists have at their disposal numerous affordable means for going nuclear, including stealing bombs from military stockpiles; swiping highly enriched uranium or plutonium from military or commercial nuclear facilities and using it for a bomb; and taking spent fuel from military or commercial reactors, chemically reprocessing it, and fabricating the fissionable plutonium into a bomb.[50] As plutonium becomes an item of international commerce, the opportunities for terrorist bomb-building will expand. By the late 1990s, Britain, France, Germany, and Japan could be circulating thousands of bombs' worth of plutonium each year in hundreds of shipments.[51]

The controlled arms race has carried political costs by threatening Americans' freedom to speak, assemble, associate, and travel. As more U.S. resources, industry, and manpower have come under the command of the military, the coercive manifestations of secrecy— classification schemes, censorship, prior restraints, security clearances, gag orders, travel limitations—have pervaded U.S. society.[52] In early 1987, for example, the government began censoring cost and other data about SDI.[53] The requirements of secrecy also sap the vitality of unofficial institutions such as universities. Noting that Pentagon research contracts with universities have doubled in real terms between 1975 and 1985, Professor John Holdren of the University of California, Berkeley, laments the erosion of free academic inquiry: "The pitfalls are obvious, and most have already materialized in specific instances: pressure for principal investigators on campus to obtain security clearances . . . [and] exclusion of students, faculty or visiting researchers who are not U.S. citizens from certain projects

and even whole laboratories."[54] Arms races threaten to saddle the
United States with the very tyranny from which it sought to protect
itself—without a shot ever being fired.

A final political cost of the controlled arms race is that it made the
United States vulnerable to foreign lenders. Rather than raise taxes to
pay for its massive military buildup, the Reagan administration raised
interest rates to attract huge inflows of foreign capital. While the probability is low that foreign creditors will put pressure on the United
States, IMF-style, to cut federal spending and to balance the budget,
they nevertheless may seek to have some say over U.S. domestic policies. It is ironic that the enormous economic burdens the United
States assumed to protect Japan and Germany in the Cold War era have
given these benefactors significant leverage over U.S. well-being in the
1990s.

Economic Insecurity

It is no accident that the Reagan administration's $1.5 trillion
rearmament campaign, the largest in history, coincided with the
dramatic global economic decline of the United States. Nor is it an
accident that the world's best economic performers—the Japanese
and the Germans—spend relatively low percentages of their gross
national products (GNPs) on military defense (1 percent and 3
percent, respectively, compared to about 5 percent for the United
States).[55] An arms race can severely sap a nation's economic strength
by destroying jobs, wasting precious resources, lowering productivity,
stymieing civilian research and development, and weakening commercial competitiveness.

Military spending undoubtedly creates jobs, but it usually offers
few *long-term* employment opportunities. As Wassily Leontief, a
Nobel Prize–winning economist at New York University, has warned:
"In the long run, [a short-run employment] boom usually turns into
a dangerous bust when all of the arms have been built. The military
industry has a terrible time shifting into the private market. Nor-
mally, millions of defense workers must be laid off, and when this
happens, the civilian economy will not have expanded enough to absorb all the jobless people."[56]

A wide variety of studies indicate that military spending is a relatively poor job producer.[57] For example, the Council on Economic
Priorities concluded that a billion dollars spent on MX missiles would

create far fewer jobs than a billion dollars spent on residential construction, public utilities, or the manufacture of railroad or solar energy equipment.[58] A study performed for the Congressional Joint Economic Committee in 1986 found that a reallocation of $35 billion from defense spending to federal programs for construction, transportation, education, health, social services, and space exploration would create 260,000 jobs.[59]

Advocates of greater military spending argue that a billion dollars spent on weapons stimulates the economy roughly as much as a billion dollars spent on nonmilitary production. But even if the so-called economic multiplier effects of both expenditures were equal—and they are not—the primary impacts are radically different. While a billion dollars spent on health care, for example, leaves Americans with a measurable good (namely, better health), it is not at all clear that a billion dollars spent on missiles leaves Americans with more security. University of Texas economist Lloyd Dumas has noted, "Military-oriented production . . . does not add to the supply of consumer goods or to the supply of producer goods, and so contributes to neither the present nor the future material standard of living."[60] Some military spending, such as the $595 billion sunk into the Vietnam War, may even be a net loss.

But military spending is worse than economically neutral. As former secretary of defense Caspar Weinberger once conceded, the productivity of defense industries is lower than that of other industries.[61] Several factors account for the inefficiency of military production: cost-plus contracts that encourage weapons manufacturers to maximize costs and profits at taxpayers' expense; the absence of competitive bidding for most contracts; poor, understaffed Pentagon contract oversight that allows $400 hammers and $1,000 toilets; a long tradition of fraudulent practices that in 1986 found fifty-nine of the nation's top hundred defense contractors under investigation and by 1988 had become a massive national scandal; and a revolving door between the Pentagon and military industries that prevents arm's-length business or regulatory relationships.[62] Pentagon contractors are so rife with inefficiency that Richard Halloran, a military correspondent for the *New York Times*, has estimated that fully one-third of the military budget, about $100 billion per year, could be saved simply through efforts to eliminate waste and fraud.[63]

In studies of fifteen industrial nations, Ron P. Smith of the University of London and Bruce Russett of Yale University found a correlation between increases in military spending and reductions in civilian investment.[64] Analysts at Employment Research Associates came to a similar conclusion when they examined eighteen industries over the period 1953–1980, and discovered that increases in military spending resulted in statistically significant reductions in investment in eight of them; only one industry, electrical machinery, benefited from military spending, and the other nine were unaffected.[65]

Supporters of military spending sometimes argue that research and development (R&D) for weapons results in valuable civilian "spin-offs." For example, Pentagon investments in military aircraft gave McDonnell Douglas, Boeing, and Lockheed the technical know-how and management skill to produce excellent commercial aircraft. The problem with spin-offs, however, is that they are inefficient ways of advancing technology; many defense investments produce nothing valuable for the civilian economy. Surely, if the U.S. auto industry wants to develop a more efficient car, it makes more sense for the U.S. government to invest R&D money directly in General Motors than to expect a usable spin-off from a General Dynamics tank design. A 1975 study by economist Michael Boretsky revealed that only 5 to 20 percent of military R&D produced substantial commercial spin-offs.[66] A recent study by Jay Stowsky of the Berkeley Roundtable on the International Economy has suggested that spin-offs are becoming even more difficult for several reasons: Procurement decisions are rarely made with spin-offs in mind; the specifications for increasingly complex weapon systems are becoming less applicable to commercial products; and the secrecy and export controls surrounding military innovations keep many of them out of civilian markets.[67]

Because of the national priorities set during the controlled arms race, two-thirds of all federally funded R&D now goes to military programs, up from one-half in the late 1970s.[68] This amounts to between 35 and 40 percent of all R&D moneys invested nationwide. Stowsky argues that these investment priorities are harming the ability of the United States to compete internationally:

Take just one technology—lasers—for example. Nearly all of SDI's X-ray laser research aims at extremely high-power application-specific uses; indeed, the typical Star Wars laser must be powered by a nuclear explosion. Meanwhile, the Japanese government is funding private commercial research into lasers with immediate nonmilitary potential—carbon-dioxide and solid-state lasers designed for industrial uses, such as welding, and semiconductor diode lasers that can power compact-disc players and fiber-optics communications equipment.[69]

The controlled arms race has skewed not only R&D priorities but also the entire U.S. industrial strategy. Although international competitors of the United States have been investing heavily in their commercial sectors, the United States itself has been supporting military manufacturers through guaranteed purchases on cost-plus-profit contracts, incentives for technological innovation, and adjustment assistance for displaced military workers.[70] "Japanese firms," writes Rutgers urban planner Ann Markusen, "without the benefit of a huge defense budget and despite a second-rate university research establishment, are much better positioned to take U.S. defense-generated technologies and apply them to basic industrial production."[71] "What good does it do us," economist Lester Thurow asks, "to dominate the world in missile production if we are at the same time being defeated in toasters?"[72]

One implication of the deterioration of nonmilitary sectors of the U.S. economy is that the Defense Department is now buying a substantial quantity of its electronics components from Japanese firms.[73] "In return," Markusen notes, "the Japanese have requested access to the latest defense-funded research results, and the DOD appears willing to accede."[74] One example is General Dynamics' controversial deal with Mitsubishi Heavy Industries to codevelop for Japan the FSX fighter jet, which trade expert Clyde V. Prestowitz, Jr., argues "will shortly give Japan a big boost toward its long-sought goal: leadership in aircraft manufacture, one of the last areas of American high-technology dominance."[75]

In recent years the United States has all but lost its manufacturing leadership in shoes, apparel, toys, consumer electronics, steel, and automobiles.[76] Unless the country dramatically improves its competitiveness, other industries will fall, too, including capital goods and consumer durables. Many new policies are needed to help U.S. productivity, but one that is absolutely necessary, according to Secretary of Labor Robert Reich, is to "take the nation's research and development efforts out from under the Pentagon and its sister agencies, and turn them over to civilian agencies whose explicit goal is to spur the nation's commercial competitiveness."[77] Equally important are higher investments in education, job training, and the nation's transportation and communications infrastructure, which also will require commensurate reductions in military spending.[78]

The damage of the military spending binge of the 1980s on U.S. economic competitiveness may be irreversible, however. Today the United States is spending 5.1 percent of its gross national product on the military and 3.3 percent to pay interest on the national debt, leaving over 8 percent of its GNP unavailable for economic revitalization.[79] Japan, in contrast, spends a little over 1 percent of its GNP on the military, and as an international creditor enjoys debt repayments every year from the United States, which can be used for economic expansion.[80] One result is that economic competitors like Japan can spend two or three times more on highways, bridges, trains, mass transit, airports, schools, telecommunications, and other forms of civilian infrastructure that are essential for economic competitiveness.[81]

The adverse economic impact of military spending has been exacerbated by the simple fact that it was funded by domestic and foreign debt. By 1987 the annual U.S. trade deficit exceeded $100 billion a year, and the dollar plunged to a postwar low against a number of major currencies such as the yen.[82] The declining dollar means that U.S. businesses, developers, and tourists have less purchasing power and influence abroad. The rising interest rates necessary to attract foreign investors also have increased Third World debts and reduced their demand for American products. Between 1982 and 1988, falling consumer demand in the Third World cost the U.S. economy almost 2 million jobs and $60 billion in lost exports.[83]

The sacrifices the U.S. economy had to bear in the 1980s may be just a preview of the future if the United States continues to participate in an arms race. The Pentagon's own estimates for the first phase of implementing SDI range from $69 billion to $115 billion.[84] The Council on Economic Priorities has calculated that the cost of a completed SDI system could be $400 billion to $1 trillion.[85] Former secretary of defense Harold Brown told a Senate committee in 1986 that simply maintaining SDI would cost between $100 billion and $200 billion annually.[86] With current annual defense expenditures at about $300 billion, this new hemorrhage of the Treasury would dramatically decrease the ability of the United States to reduce the deficit, to improve the nation's health, education, and welfare, or to address the wide array of nonmilitary threats to national security.

The deterioration of the U.S. economy has enormous geopolitical consequences. As a borrower rather than a creditor, the United States has less power to influence global economic events through international economic institutions. Germany, Japan, and other economically successful countries will increasingly command the direction of international capital through the World Bank, the IMF, and national banks.[87] The United States no longer will be able to frame development priorities in the Third World as it has in recent years; nor will it be able to veto development loans, as it did against Nicaragua in the 1980s, in pursuit of its own political agenda.

A less competitive U.S. economy also means that the United States has less power to promote sustainable development or democracy in other parts of the world. In November 1987 a number of members of Congress urged the president to launch a "multi-year, multi-national, multi-billion-dollar Marshall Plan" to bolster the government of Corazón Aquino in the Philippines. Because of the massive deficit, the request could not be seriously considered nor could the request by Solidarity in 1989 for $10 billion in emergency loans to assist Poland's transition to democracy (President Bush initially offered a paltry $100 million).[88] The Bush administration promised Russia $24 billion in April 1992 to help move it toward a strong market economy, but in fact it could scrape together only $10 billion, nearly all of it in the form of short-term commercial credits.[89] Increasingly, countries that once turned to us for assistance in cash, technology, and managerial skills will look elsewhere. Right now the largest donor to the Third World is Japan.[90]

Environmental Insecurity

Of all the costs of the controlled arms race, perhaps the most difficult to tally up are the environmental ones. The traditional secrecy cloaking most weapons programs has made the measurement and evaluation of their environmental impacts nearly impossible. But what *is* known is chilling.

The construction of nuclear bombs entails all the public and occupational health risks of the commercial nuclear-power industry. The milling of uranium leaves piles of tailings that emit cancer-causing radon for centuries. Federal reactors that produce plutonium, such as the N-reactor at Hanford, Washington, are designed much like Chernobyl and could experience a comparable core meltdown. Weapons programs have produced nearly all of the nation's transuranic and high-level nuclear waste and about half of its low-level waste, and the technology for disposing of reactor wastes, claimed to be at hand for decades, continues to satisfy none of the constituencies whose jurisdictions have been nominated to become nuclear dumpsites.[91]

Throughout the late 1980s horror stories surfaced about the long history of environmental problems plaguing the government's nuclear-weapons production facilities:[92]

- During the 1940s, Hanford's reprocessing facilities released so much iodine-131 into the atmosphere that the Centers for Disease Control concluded that residents living downwind received more dangerous radiation doses than did Russians living next to the Chernobyl reactor; 30,000 affected children now have a five to fifteen times greater chance of getting thyroid cancer.[93]
- Over a period of twenty years, 4.7 million gallons of chemical wastes and 2.4 million pounds of mercury contaminated the environment surrounding a weapons facility at Oak Ridge, Tennessee—the most serious episode of mercury contamination ever recorded in the United States.[94]
- At the weapons plant run by DuPont in Savannah River, Georgia, strontium-90 was found in a nearby creek and groundwater at levels 42,500 times higher than the EPA's drinking-water standard; nearly two miles away from the plant, pond-slider turtles contained strontium-90 levels one thousand times higher than normal.[95]
- The U.S. government kept secret for decades numerous accidents at the Savannah River reactors, including a meltdown of fuel rods and another melting of a reactor part that ultimately contaminated 900 cleanup workers.[96]

These environmental hazards pose serious threats of premature cancers and other diseases for the more than 600,000 employees who have worked at the nation's nuclear-weapons plants, all of which are outside the jurisdiction of the Occupational Safety and Health Administration and are off-limits to outside labor unions that might push for safer working conditions.[97]

All of these hazards also carry enormous economic costs. For each dollar spent on making the fissionable materials for nuclear weapons, about forty-five cents is already going to waste management.[98] In March 1988, Department of Energy undersecretary Joseph F. Salgado estimated that the federal government would need an additional $100 billion—two-thirds of that year's federal deficit—to clean up the 5,400 toxic chemical and radioactive waste facilities associated with weapons production.[99] The General Accounting Office put the price tag for cleaning up just seventeen major sites at close to $175 billion, and, even then, the sites would remain unusable for any other purposes.[100]

The technologies for SDI could pose additional environmental problems. A report by a special committee of the American Physical Society estimated that SDI might require 100 satellites, each using from 100 to 700 kilowatts of power.[101] The Department of Energy has been trying to put into orbit the SP-100, which would be powered by a 100-kilowatt reactor.[102] An unreleased 1979 Department of Energy study estimated that if a reactor the size of the one aboard the SP-100 fell out of the sky after one year of operation, its vaporized radiation could cause up to 50,000 cancer deaths.[103] Nearly one-fifth of all reactors put into space thus far have failed—some disastrously.[104] The Soviet Cosmos 954, which wobbled out of orbit in 1978 and spread debris across northwest Canada, contained only one three-thousandth as much radioactivity as the SP-100 reactor.[105] It is little exaggeration to observe that SDI gambles our environmental future on the coupled technologies of Chernobyl and the Challenger.

In a renewed arms race, of course, the United States would not stop at SDI. The development of new chemical and biological weapons would open up still more possibilities for environmentally destructive accidents, sabotage, and terrorism. A recent staff report by a Senate subcommittee concluded that Pentagon regulation of chemical and biological research facilities was characterized by "inadequate regulations, lax safety enforcement, and documented safety lapses."[106] In 1988 the Army revealed that for years it had been shipping hazardous germs like anthrax bacterium, dengue-fever virus, and encephalitis-causing viruses through the mail and by overnight courier service.[107]

The Army is currently puzzling over how to destroy its 25,000 tons of outmoded chemical weapons; it estimates that at least $2 billion will be necessary to do the job.[108] While the military proposes burning these chemicals at each of the eight sites where they are now stored, as well as at an incinerator on Johnston Atoll, a Pacific island

730 miles southwest of Hawaii, its history with this technology has hardly inspired confidence among nearby residents.[109] In 1968 the Army accidentally sprayed VX nerve gas into a valley and killed 6,000 sheep.[110] In January 1987 a prototype incinerator in Tooele, Utah, released a liquid nerve agent, GB, at levels thirty times higher than the safety limit (GB causes "nasal congestion, sweating, bronchial spasms, wheezing, muscular twitching, convulsions and ultimately death through paralysis and suffocation").[111]

Not far away from Tooele, citizens living near the Dugway Proving Ground have protested the military's efforts to open the nation's most modern biological warfare laboratory.[112] Among their reasons for skepticism are a series of tests conducted in 1977, when the Army sprayed bacteria on the populations of New York, San Francisco, and Washington, D.C.[113] At the time the Army proclaimed the experiments safe, but later it admitted they were not.

Security Without Arms Races

The United States was not the only country to become more insecure because of the controlled arms race. The Soviet Union suffered all the adverse consequences that the United States did, only more so. The Kremlin found that the more nuclear bombs it built and the more advanced the delivery systems it deployed, the greater were the risks of a nuclear war by design, accident, or proliferation. The systematic repression of citizens in the name of national security was so comprehensive and pernicious that, once given the opportunity in August 1991, the Soviet people dismantled most of the Communist superstate. By one estimate, the Soviets dedicated as much as 25 percent of their GNP to military spending, leaving the country's economy in shambles.[114] Racked with foreign debt, crumbling infrastructure, and uncompetitive commercial products, the Soviet economy was left looking little better than the economies of most Third World countries. The environmental devastation of the controlled arms race in the Soviet countryside also was shocking. In 1967 dust from a radioactive waste dump at the Chelyabinsk-40 nuclear-weapons complex gave 42,000 Soviets a dangerously high dose of strontium-90, and probably hundreds of thousands of others have been radioactively contaminated because of escaping radionuclides.[115]

The legacy of the controlled arms race suggests that security through arms buildups is difficult, if not impossible. The continual building of weapons in the nuclear age is destined to saddle any nation—whether the United States, the Soviet Union, or a new super-power—with political repression, economic exhaustion, and ecological collapse. And that is the best an arms race has to offer. It could well end in a full-scale nuclear disaster.

Part Two

Preventing and Resolving Conflicts

4
The Political Roots of Conflict

Because war has become too costly and risky an instrument for foreign policy, U.S. security planners must seek new ways to prevent it. They should identify and defuse the causes of war long before the missiles start flying.

Why do nations go to war? We believe that the most fundamental roots of war are found in politics. German philosopher Karl von Clausewitz wrote that "war is the continuation of politics by other means." But it is more accurate to say that war represents the failure of politics. Political debate and decisionmaking are the primary means by which conflicts are resolved both within and between nations; when people cannot resolve conflicts through politics, the result is violence.

War begins in the imaginations of the custodians of national armies and weapons arsenals. "The deformed human mind," British historian E. P. Thompson has argued, "is the ultimate doomsday weapon—it is out of the human mind that the missiles and the neutron warheads come."[1] If war between countries is to be prevented, those with the power and inclination to wage war must be controlled. Leaders constrained by democratic checks and balances usually must go through the burdensome and uncertain process of gaining public support before they can launch a war. Dictators, in contrast, can go to war on a whim, with or without public support.

Undemocratic countries are also more susceptible to secessionist movements and civil wars, because they are less able to resolve internal conflicts. Fundamental to a democratic system is the goal of involving citizens in the process of settling some of the most important questions—and conflicts—of political life: What principles should govern national affairs? How should scarce resources be allocated?

Who should make, interpret, and enforce rules and laws? In a strong democracy people have an opportunity to debate these questions, and even those who lose a debate know they can reopen an issue on another day. In a dictatorship, in contrast, a minority can tyrannize the majority, and in a weak democracy the majority can tyrannize minorities. When people in dictatorships or weak democracies do not have access to peaceful means of protecting their interests, they resort to force.

A healthy dose of democracy therefore is a vital antidote to both interstate and intrastate war. It is an antidote U.S. security planners should administer liberally both at home and abroad.

Strong Democracy and Interstate Peace

Several empirical studies of conflicts between nations over the past two centuries reveal that although democracies and nondemocracies have been equally likely to fight wars with nondemocracies, wars *between* liberal democracies have been exceedingly rare.[2] Indeed, since World War II, none of the members of the Organization for Economic Cooperation and Development (OECD) (a grouping of industrialized democracies that includes the United States, Canada, Western Europe, Japan, Australia, and New Zealand) have gone to war against one another, nor have they expected war or prepared for war with one another.[3] This condition of peace has been enjoyed by more than three-quarters of a billion people for nearly fifty years.[4] "By the standards of world history," writes Yale political scientist Bruce Russett, "this is an extraordinary achievement."[5]

Democracy, of course, does not make war impossible. The behavior of colonial powers like France, Great Britain, and the Netherlands, whose brutality set the stage for the wars of liberation fought in the twentieth century, suggests how democracies can cause war. The history of U.S. foreign policy since World War II, as Chapter 2 demonstrated, also is replete with wars—some of which U.S. leaders started. The democratic features of a country can intensify battles and make peaceful settlements more difficult. As Brandeis political scientist Seyom Brown argues:

> [In democratic states] those who wanted to use war as an instrument of national policy would need to whip up widespread popular fear and anger over the issue at hand to assure that a particular conflict with another

country was infused with great significance for the entire nation—its honor, its glory, its way of life, its very survival. Once the country was readied in this way for war, negotiated compromises to resolve the precipitating conflict short of war would be more difficult to achieve. And war, once it did start, would be much more difficult to keep limited in its intensity. The enemy, now defined as venal, would need to be severely punished, if not totally destroyed.[6]

But none of these nuances undercut the central point: *Because democracies almost never fight one another, the spread of democracy can lower the probability of war.*

The exception that proves the rule is covert action. In the early 1970s, for example, the United States helped overthrow an elected Marxist, Salvador Allende, in Chile. Yet this historical instance underscores that wars between democracies are so politically unsustainable that they must be fought secretly. Put another way, the United States sought to sabotage other democracies only by using essentially undemocratic means.

Intuitively, most Americans believe that democracy fosters interstate peace. The collective sigh of relief by Americans over the recently elected democratic governments in Argentina, Brazil, the Philippines, and South Korea reflects their recognition that leaders accountable to a vigilant people are more likely to act responsibly in international affairs. Conservatives and liberals alike enthusiastically supported glasnost in the Soviet Union, prodemocracy protests by Chinese students, and the "velvet revolutions" in Eastern Europe. If there is any core value that can become the basis of a bipartisan U.S. foreign policy, it is global democratization.

Democracy helps constrain interstate conflict for several reasons. Even though a leader of a democracy bent on war must imbue his or her people with images of a brutal enemy worthy of destruction, democratic forces also make exaggerated or dehumanized images of an enemy difficult to create and maintain. If the citizens of a democratic country can meet and speak freely with citizens of an adversary, they often discover that the enemy is not nearly as nefarious as government and private-interest propaganda maintains.

Citizens in a democracy also can form relationships with the supposed enemy more easily, creating pressures on both sides for leaders to maintain peace. Businesspeople want to protect their trade contracts, scientists and academicians want to complete their joint research projects, and artists want to continue cultural collaborations. After President Carter imposed an embargo on grain sales to the Soviet Union in January 1980, for example, many U.S. farmers who had benefited from earlier grain sales to the Soviets became vocal advocates of restoring economic relations. By 1983, according to William Bundy, then editor of *Foreign Affairs,* President Reagan "responded to heavy domestic political pressures from the U.S. farm belt" when he scrapped the embargo and signed a new five-year contract that prohibited interruptions for political reasons.[7]

The web of relationships made possible by democratic pluralism in the United States also has helped to reduce American hostility toward China. Widely regarded in the late 1960s as a "yellow menace" against which the United States considered building a "light" ABM system, China became an ally of the United States because of what Arthur W. Hummel, Jr., the U.S. ambassador there in the early 1980s, called "an amazing web" of relationships. These people-to-people ties, said Hummel, "perhaps the majority of them having nothing to do with the U.S. government [are] a genuine stabilizing force and a force which through the decades will produce much better understanding."[8] Even after Chinese troops killed thousands of prodemocracy protesters in and around Tiananmen Square in June 1989, these relationships allowed Americans to express their anger through dialogue, protest, and divestment rather than through a nuclear-arms race or a war.

Another way democracy promotes peace is by permitting citizens to undertake peacemaking initiatives with "the enemy" that constructively supplement and improve official relations. In formal negotiating, leaders protect national interests and make worst-case assumptions about an adversary's intentions. But informal negotiating, according to Joseph V. Montville, a foreign service officer in the State Department, and William D. Davidson, a psychiatrist specializing in foreign affairs, is "always open-minded, often altruistic, and . . . strategically optimistic, based on the best-case analysis. Its underlying assumption is that actual or potential conflict can be resolved or eased by appealing to common human capabilities to respond to goodwill and reasonableness."[9] Thus, during the late 1950s the democratic nature of the United States enabled *Saturday Review* editor Norman Cousins to launch the annual Dartmouth Conferences—high-level, off-the-record Soviet-U.S. discussions that played an important role in helping the superpowers reach formal agreements for expanding trade, banning above-ground nuclear tests, installing the original "hot line," and allowing direct commercial air service between the United States and the Soviet Union.[10]

A final reason democracies behave more peacefully than nondemocracies is that war is far more costly to the ordinary people who must fight on the bloody battlefields than it is to the leaders who plan the fighting in sterile war-rooms. As the Vietnam War demonstrated, popular support in a modern democracy for military involvement abroad can crumble as young friends and neighbors return maimed or in coffins, as news reports graphically depict atrocities on the front lines, and as international opinion-leaders condemn the supposedly just cause. In a democratic culture, negative news spreads to the people, who can then pressure leaders to avoid or halt a war. Thus, political pressures against the Vietnam War were able to build more rapidly and decisively than did analogous domestic pressures in the Soviet Union against its misadventure in Afghanistan. (Once Gorbachev's policy of glasnost began, however, public outrage over the 10,000 young Soviet men killed and the 20,000 wounded surfaced and spread rapidly in antiwar rallies, essays, poetry, and films.)[11] Democratic political structures allow the public to act on its abhorrence of war. What many have called the Vietnam syndrome is really Americans' (and now the Russians') learned antipathy toward protracted foreign military adventures.

Together, these arguments suggest how public participation can improve the intelligence and morality of security policy. Democracy can render leaders accountable to a more informed set of views about the enemy, and make them more aware of the benefits of peacetime relationships and the human costs of warfare. Public participation acts as a check against abuse, zealotry, and rash exercises of power.

Strong Democracy and Intrastate Peace

Fundamental differences between groups *within* a country also can lead to war. In settings as different as Northern Ireland, the Punjab, the Basque region of Spain, and Quebec, minority groups are battling for autonomy and self-determination, while the majority stubbornly resists change in the name of national unity or cultural hegemony. The great colonial empires of Britain, Spain, Portugal, Belgium, and France imposed national boundaries on nearly every continent that bore little resemblance to the actual distribution of ethnic, religious, or linguistic groups. These groups temporarily teamed up to oust the colonial powers after World War II, but after they achieved independence they aimed their guns at one another. Hindus and Muslims, for example, successfully worked together to kick the British out of India, but then fought a civil war until they agreed (uneasily) to partition the country into two states—India and Pakistan.

The end of the Cold War has lifted the lid from a boiling cauldron of nationalist aspirations worldwide. The worst fighting in Europe since World War II broke out in the former Yugoslavia in 1991, when Croats, Slovenes, and Bosnian Muslims began seeking independence from the repressive rule of Serbia. Once the hardliner coup in the Soviet Union failed in August 1991, the country blew apart into fifteen new nations within a matter of days. Latvia, Estonia, and Lithuania were the first to declare their autonomy. Eleven of the other former Soviet republics loosely affiliated in the CIS, while Georgia decided to go its own way. Even these new states are internally unstable; the former Soviet Union actually contained more than one hundred distinct ethnic groups. Thousands have died in the Nagorno-Karabakh region of Azerbaijan as the Armenians and Azeris living there have struggled for control over the territory.

The process of nations dividing and multiplying is far from complete. The Slovaks divorced the Czechs in December 1992. The Ndebelens, locked out of key government positions in Zimbabwe for over a decade, soon may demand autonomy from the Shonas. The Hausa, Yoruba, and Ibo tribes never have had more than a tentative truce in Nigeria. The East Timorese cannot wait to escape their cruel Indonesian overlords, and massacre-weary Mayan Indians would gladly part company with Guatemala. Quebec continues to indicate its desire to separate from Canada. Even in the United States, Alaska, Washington, Oregon, and northern California have considered secession. Each of these nascent divisions poses a potential source of conflict in the years ahead.

One tempting solution, of course, is to demand that nations capitulate to minority demands and allow secession more freely, but the potentially endless process of subdivision can create more political problems than it resolves. Some of the most persistent conflicts of the Cold War years—North Korea versus South Korea, North Vietnam versus South Vietnam, China versus Taiwan, Israel versus Palestinians, West Germany versus East Germany—were the result of partitions. An estimated 13 million people have died in wars involving states that were divided after 1945.[12] After studying links between partition and war, historian Robert Schaeffer concludes:

> The division of countries into separate states has been a singular failure. Partition uprooted millions from their homelands and compromised the meaning of citizenship where they made their new homes. Partition undercut the meaning of sovereignty for newly independent states and sharpened the competition between divided or sibling states. And partition led to internecine war within and between divided states and drew superpower states into intractable regional wars.[13]

The basic problem with partition is that it perpetuates habits of intolerance.[14] It gives nations an excuse not to develop fair political institutions or legal protections for minorities, and consequently new states created by partition often perpetuate the oppressive habits of the old states. The partition of Palestine created an Israel insensitive to the rights of Palestinians and allowed Arab states to remain intolerant of Jews. The Lithuanians, Latvians, and Estonians, formerly repressed by Russians living in the Baltic states, celebrated their independence by denying voting rights to minorities and by requiring government officials to use indigenous languages or lose their jobs.[15]

Another way to prevent wars of independence, of course, is to repress minority groups. Throughout the Cold War so-called realists in international relations argued that stability (usually a code word for dictatorship) is preferable to democracy if it prevents potentially explosive regional conflicts. "We may . . . wake up one day," wrote University of Chicago political scientist John Mearsheimer about the newly independent states of Eastern Europe, "lamenting the loss of the order that the Cold War gave to the anarchy of international relations."[16] However, the choice is not between stability-loving dictators and bomb-throwing freedom fighters, because sooner or later people being repressed will revolt anyway. The choice is between repression and civil war on the one hand and strong democracy on the other.

Unlike weak democracy, strong democracy requires more than majority rule and periodic voting.[17] Strong democracy is characterized by constitutional protections for minorities, by the principle of subsidiarity, and by a vibrant civil society. Each of these political tools can help inoculate a country against civil unrest and civil war.

In a democracy where the majority can rule without limit, minorities are persecuted and seek protection through autonomy. In a democracy where the rights of minorities are protected, a pluralistic society becomes possible. For example, the Fourteenth Amendment to the Constitution, passed just after the Civil War, protected American minorities with the following injunction: "No state shall make or enforce any law which shall abridge the privileges or immunities of citizens of the United States; nor shall any State deprive any person of life, liberty, or property, without due process of law; nor deny to any person within its jurisdictions the equal protection of the laws." It took nearly a hundred years for the Supreme Court to enforce this constitutional provision and to strike down systematic discrimination based on race, ethnicity, or religion. As a result of these protections, most civil rights movements in the United States (including those for blacks, Asians, Hispanics, Catholics, and Jews) have fought for pluralism and fairness, not secession and separatism.

The principle of subsidiarity states that governance should always proceed from the level closest to the people. Communities should bear the primary responsibility for governing themselves, because citizens can oversee local officials more easily than they can oversee state or national politicians. Only those policies that absolutely require state or national intervention should be taken away from communities. For example, communities might be given primary responsibility for overseeing the disposal of solid wastes, with the national government only intervening to set basic standards concerning pollution resulting from solid waste disposal.

One objective imbedded in the principle of subsidiarity is that a decision should be made by all those affected by it, no more and no fewer. If a decision is made at too low a level—if, for example, upstream communities can dump solid wastes into a river—local decisionmakers will tend not to take into account the "external" effects of their actions. If a decision is made at too high a level—if, for example, the federal government issues thousands of regulations for local trash collection and disposal—public input will be attenuated, those excluded will be resentful, and local creativity will be stifled. The inability of the top-down Communist bureaucracy to administer every detail of daily Soviet life stands as a warning that decisionmaking at too high a level can lead to inefficiency, corruption, and frustration.

The principle of subsidiarity suggests that an alternative to partition is confederation. Whereas partition splits one nation into two, confederation creates two or more relatively autonomous states within the original nation. Canada, Germany, and Switzerland are all examples of countries that are really confederations of very diverse, autonomous states. So is the United States, which keeps a heterogeneous population united by allowing each of the fifty states to have a relatively high degree of self-governance.

Intractable ethnic conflicts might be resolvable if the supervising national governments granted greater freedom to the regions in turmoil. Catholics in a more autonomous Northern Ireland might no longer feel the need to throw Molotov cocktails at British troops. A more autonomous Quebec could achieve its aspirations without seceding from Canada. Creation of additional states in India might prevent further bloodshed among Muslims, Sikhs, and Hindus. In all these instances, however, the national government still should hold the preponderance of force and stand ready to protect the rights of minorities.

Another element that can help resolve ethnic violence is civil society—the web of nongovernmental groups, organizations, and movements that empower citizens to solve their own problems. Imagine how discordant the United States would be if there were no National Association for the Advancement of Colored People fighting racial injustice, no National Organization of Women seeking fair treatment of women, no labor unions demanding better working conditions, no United Way helping the elderly or the homeless. Without these organizations, citizens are forced to turn to the government, and if government is incapable of helping or unwilling to help, which often is the case, citizens inevitably turn *against* the government. Civil society provides a critical mechanism for releasing steam from potentially explosive social problems and for resolving problems through grassroots inventiveness.

Not surprisingly, nongovernmental organizations are the ones breaking new ground for resolving ethnic conflicts in various ongoing combat zones. The Neve Shalom kibbutz, located between Jerusalem and Tel Aviv, has set up the only Jewish-Arab bilingual school system in the country as a means of promoting reconciliation. Northern Ireland's Lagan College, founded in 1981 by Catholic and Protestant parents, teaches secondary students of all denominations how to be tolerant of religious differences and how to live in an integrated society.[18] South African labor unions have been important proponents of equal protection in the workplace for blacks and whites.

Just as strong democracy reins in the excesses of national leaders, it also checks group conflict. If the rules of the game are fair, people are willing to play and occasionally lose. By creating protections for minorities, moving more decisionmaking power to communities, and helping nongovernmental organizations to flourish, strong democracy offers a hope—perhaps the only hope—for resolving internal strife through politics instead of bullets.

Promoting Strong Democracy Abroad

Can the United States export strong democracy to other countries? The answer is yes, with an important qualification—the United States must adhere to the principle of nonprovocation. Many U.S. military interventions, covert actions, and weapons shipments have been rationalized as efforts to promote freedom and democracy. U.S. security planners must seek instead to help individuals abroad to reform their governments according to *their own* values and visions, to help them exercise more fully the very democratic rights Americans seek to exercise themselves. And Americans should stand ready to accept the results of democratic processes even when they seem ideologically disappointing. In the past such tolerance would have led U.S. leaders to approve of the Chilean presidential election of 1970, even though it brought to power Salvador Allende, a parliamentary Marxist, rather than to take the view of then national security adviser Henry Kissinger, who said, "I don't see why we need to stand by and watch a country go communist because of the irresponsibility of its own people."[19]

During the Cold War, U.S. security planners recognized that sowing seeds of democracy in the Soviet Union would reduce its ability to threaten the United States. Aaron Wildavsky, a political scientist at the University of California, Berkeley, argued: "The larger the number of independent centers of power within the USSR, the more the Soviets will be constrained to secure domestic consent for their foreign policy. . . . When the domestic constraints on foreign policy in the two [superpowers] tend to be more equal, so will their incentives for accommodation at lower levels of violence."[20] Unfortunately, most U.S. efforts to promote pluralism in the Soviet Union were provocative and counterproductive. Congress tried to pressure the Kremlin to give Soviet citizens greater freedom when it passed the Jackson-Vanik amendment to the Trade Act of 1974 (signed into law in 1975), withholding most-favored-nation status until the

Soviet Union loosened its emigration policies. The provocation backfired. After the bill became law Soviet leaders reduced emigration to a
trickle, precisely to show that they would not be pushed around.[21]

Another U.S. approach to democratizing the Soviet Union—beam-
ing Radio Liberty from Vilnius to Vladivostok to spread pro-U.S. information and to foment dissent—was problematic as well. Many of
the transmissions were so clearly antagonistic to the Soviet government that they did little more to spawn revolt than continuous
broadcasts of Radio Moscow might have done in the United States.[22]
Surveys suggest that fewer than one in ten Soviets tuned in to Radio
Liberty even once a month, and that most of those who did were
tuning into entertainment programs.[23]

In the 1980s tens of thousands of Americans *did* start to promote
constructive change in the Soviet Union while adhering to the principle of nonprovocation. Some helped convince recalcitrant Soviet
officials of the virtues of democracy; others assisted Soviets who were
already committed to democratizing the system. Whether or not
they realized it, these Americans were walking-talking banned books,
expressing facts and attitudes at odds with the prevailing party line.
Because Soviet citizens were more likely to trust their American
friends than some faceless Radio Liberty announcers, one wonders
if the hundreds of millions of dollars annually spent on these
radio broadcasts might have been better invested in citizen exchange
programs.

Citizen exchanges with the Soviet Union even put restraints on the
foreign policy behavior of Kremlin leaders. In the early 1980s
the goodwill of American visitors often stood in sharp contrast to the
Nazi-like depictions of Americans in *Pravda* and reduced the ability of
Soviet leaders to characterize Americans as barbaric monsters worth
going to war against. As more Soviets entered into relationships with
Americans, whether economic, scientific, cultural, or personal, they
began to put pressure on Communist Party leaders, in their own
small ways, to improve ties with the United States. According to the
Christian Science Monitor, some exchange experts believe "that 30
years of travel to the U.S. by the Soviet political, cultural, and scientific elite ... fueled demand for Gorbachev's reforms."[24] Meetings
between American citizens and Soviet officials in the mid-1980s
played a prominent role in convincing the Soviets to halt nuclear
testing unilaterally for eighteen months, to release prominent dissidents, and to allow on-site inspection of their nuclear test sites by the

Natural Resources Defense Council, a U.S. environmental group.[25] American "citizen diplomats" also may have nudged the Soviet government toward rejecting strategies for fighting a nuclear war. For example, Dr. Bernard Lown, cofounder of the International Physicians for the Prevention of Nuclear War, managed to persuade Soviet officials in 1982 to broadcast (during prime time) a frank, uncut discussion among Soviet and American doctors about the medical consequences of nuclear war and the uselessness of the Soviet government's civil defense program.[26]

In the early 1980s a high-level adviser to President Reagan prepared a memo recommending U.S. initiatives in Eastern Europe and the Soviet Union that would be "aimed at subtly strengthening free market forces, private ownership of land, worker ownership and self-management of industry, decentralized economic (and ultimately political) decision-making . . . and ultimate integration of the [East Bloc economies] into the relatively free market economies of the OECD."[27] The memo urged technical assistance to help East Bloc countries privatize national industries, give workers more control of their factories, develop profit-sharing plans, establish small family-sized farms, set up urban and rural credit unions, and establish genuine cooperatives for farmers, consumers, producers, and renters. The attraction of these policies was that they would have been simultaneously nonthreatening to the recipient governments, consistent with the direction of East Bloc reform, and capable of being undertaken by U.S. churches, civic organizations, and local governments. Unfortunately, the Reagan administration was so consumed with rearmament that it never translated these proposals into policy.

However, many U.S. businesses and citizens recognized that greater trade with the West could open up Soviet society. In 1985 Samuel Pisar, an international lawyer specializing in East-West trade, wrote, "The new Soviet leaders know that the choice before them is fateful: either to face up to the challenges of an advanced economy, with the free movement of ideas, people and goods that this presupposes, or to isolate themselves in an armed fortress condemned to obsolescence."[28] The old guard did try to keep foreign "ideas, people and goods" away from the general Soviet populace, but the hundreds of thousands of foreigners who entered the country for business relations inevitably developed ties with millions of individual Soviet citizens. As the Soviet people came into contact with more Western products, they began to see the virtues of other economic systems and became more supportive of internal reform and greater East-West trade. Franz Schurmann, a professor of sociology and history at the University of California, Berkeley, suggests that Soviet leaders situated the first McDonald's near Red Square to expose Muscovites to the efficiency of American fast food and thereby increase their support for perestroika.[29] Sometimes these business ties exerted influence over Soviet foreign and military policy. After PepsiCo purchased from the Soviets seventeen submarines, a cruiser, a frigate, and a destroyer for scrap metal, Donald Kendall, the company's president, chided Brent Scowcroft, President Bush's national security adviser: "We're disarming the Soviet Union faster than you are."[30]

Another useful leverage point for Americans was computerization. As the *Economist* argued in 1987, information technologies "have shown themselves time and again to be destructive of centralized control, in private companies or dictators' states. A Russia stuffed with Xerox® machines, personal computers, and electronic telephone switches humming with too many conversations to be monitored is more the West's kind of Russia."[31] In the early 1980s a number of Americans helped to interest top Soviet officials in personal computers and international computer networks, and through their efforts the Soviet Union agreed by late 1988 to allow Americans to send computers, diskettes, and videotape recorders to Soviet friends.[32] IDG Communications began a joint venture in April 1988 to print and distribute a Russian edition of *PC World* magazine to 50,000 paid Soviet subscribers.[33] The dispersion of personal computers, laser printers, and desktop publishing equipment resulted in the rapid proliferation of *samizdat* (unofficial press) on controversial issues of foreign policy, economic reform, and human rights.[34] Political publications were assisted by the appearance of public photocopy shops established by Western companies.[35]

As Gorbachev began opening up the Soviet Union, American groups found various ways to assist the development of Soviet civil society:

□ The Madison Avenue advertising firm, Ogilvy & Mather, taught Soviet entrepreneurs the fine points of producing television spots, newspaper ads, and marketing.[36]

□ American Jews concerned about the plight of Soviet Jews established a Jewish Cultural Center and a B'nai B'rith lodge in Moscow.[37]

□ The American Bar Association provided seven-month intern-
ships for seventeen young Soviet lawyers in 1989, allowing them
to gain experience in U.S. law firms, law schools, corporations,
and criminal courts.

□ The Gallup organization and the National Geographic Society
amplified the influence of Soviet citizens by conducting opinion
polls alongside those produced by the Soviet Institute for Sociological Research.[38]

□ U.S. book dealers, churches, and public interest groups distributed to Soviet citizens a wide variety of once-forbidden books,
including the Bible and the Talmud.[39]

Inspired by these grassroots initiatives, the U.S. government began
to pump money into prodemocracy initiatives abroad. Between 1985
and 1988 the U.S. Congress and the National Endowment for Democracy (NED) provided more than $5 million in cash assistance to
Solidarity and other underground groups to bring printing presses,
ink, publications, radio equipment, microfiches and microfiche readers, and videocassettes and videocassette players into Poland.[40] In
Chile, NED gave $1 million to help fund political parties opposing
General Pinochet and to assist voters in getting free photographs for
their registration cards prior to the October 1988 election.[41] As noted
in Chapter 2, NED helped finance Violeta Chamorro's 1990 presidential campaign against Daniel Ortega in Nicaragua. And in countries as
diverse as Chile, Haiti, Pakistan, Panama, and the Philippines,
the U.S. government helped the National Democratic Institute for
International Affairs (an affiliate of the Democratic Party) and the
Center for Democracy monitor elections for instances of fraud or
other irregularities.[42]

Enormous opportunities for U.S. influence are now opening up
throughout the world. In Eastern Europe and the former Soviet
Union, Americans could help inoculate the region against authoritarianism by making loans, providing debt relief, and entering joint
ventures.[43] In Central America, the United States could supply advanced communications technologies to oppressed minorities like
the Miskito Indians in Nicaragua. In South Africa, Americans might
form stronger personal relationships with Afrikaaners and might be
able to sway them toward compromise (even while boycotting
all-white businesses) and simultaneously equip the black majority

with technical, financial, and educational assistance.[44] Now that the Ayatollah Khomeini is gone, relationships with true Iranian moderates might be developed, not for illegal arms transfers, but for joint projects in agriculture, medicine, science, and law. Throughout the Third World, Americans can help developing political cultures adopt constitutions that protect free speech, promote the separation of church and state, check and balance military power, and ensure fair judicial review.[45]

Three cautionary notes about these kinds of activities are worth emphasizing. First, not every act of citizen exchange, trade, or technology transfer will naturally strengthen the position of ordinary people. Americans need to design exchanges carefully so that they benefit citizens and not just officials, especially those in the military or police who are responsible for repression. (Of course, exchanges that reform military and police units, teach them the virtues of abjuring torture and other inhumane practices, and open them up to greater civilian control are all desirable.)

Second, following the principle of nonprovocation, Americans should propose ventures that the people in other countries regard as in their own interest. Soviets adopted American small-scale business and agricultural practices, not because these practices had the potential to transform Soviet society, but because they were economically useful. The key is to help people abroad with constructive areas of reform that they have chosen for themselves.

Finally, at what point does providing people with the tools of democracy become buying an election and subverting democracy?[46] Perhaps the best way to answer this question is to ask what kinds of external assistance Americans would tolerate in the United States. Generally, U.S. law draws a line at electoral politics: Foreigners can contribute money, equipment, or in-kind assistance to any group or individual within the United States, provided that these contributions are not being used to support a political party and specific candidates. Moreover, foreigners are greatly restricted in how they can lobby for specific pieces of legislation. This distinction between nonpartisan and partisan political activities is a reasonable one for the United States to apply as it promotes democracy abroad. NED and other U.S. agencies would be wise to invest in foreign think tanks, education campaigns, and election monitoring, but they should avoid deliberate interference with foreign elections or legislative processes.

Promoting Strong Democracy at Home

If a U.S. policy to promote strong democracy abroad is to survive criticism that it is simply another form of "cultural imperialism," Americans also should be willing to promote a strong democracy at home. Just as democracies have more numerous and effective mechanisms for constraining foreign policy adventures than nondemocracies do, so higher levels of participation within democracies can increase the degree of self-constraint. U.S. security planners should strengthen the democratic checks and balances on leaders within the United States. At least two different strategies might accomplish this: giving Americans greater access to foreign policy information; and strengthening the political restraints on the government's war-making powers.

Increasing Foreign Policy Information

With more and better information, Americans can assess the magnitude of threats to their national security and the relative value of competing policies. Unfortunately, under the rubric of "national security," U.S. leaders have been able to keep much significant information from the American people, causing ordinary citizens to feel left out, disaffected, and powerless. Attempts to restrict public access to information reached a new height in late 1986 when the Reagan administration tried—unsuccessfully—to create a new "sensitive" category of classification, giving every federal department the power to withhold from public scrutiny "those unclassified matters that are related to the national defense or foreign relations of the U.S. government."[47]

Certainly, there are legitimate reasons for some government secrecy. The United States should avoid releasing information that would embarrass its allies, endanger its agents and sources, or provide opportunities for adversaries or terrorists to weaken national security. Yet the need for secrecy must be continually weighed against the costs. In many instances U.S. leaders have used secrecy not to outwit adversaries abroad, but to silence critics at home. A telling example is the U.S. Navy's policy of refusing "to confirm or deny" the presence of nuclear weapons on its ships. Because Soviet intelligence knew a great deal about the status of the U.S. ships it tracked, this policy resulted in the American people knowing less about U.S. security policy than the Soviet military did.[48]

Closure of the U.S. foreign policy apparatus has not served national security interests. In a climate of more open dissemination and evaluation of information, some of the most serious foreign policy blunders in modern U.S. history might have been avoided. If the public had known the strength of the Vietcong, which the Pentagon consistently underreported to present a more sanguine evaluation of the U.S. war effort, the Vietnam War might have been cut short by several years.[49] President Carter's secret agreement to bring the Shah of Iran into the United States for medical treatment triggered the takeover of the U.S. Embassy in Tehran and brought down Carter's presidency. President Reagan's secret executive deals to trade arms for hostages and funnel profits to the Contras in Nicaragua became the turning point of his political fortunes. In all these cases the public was excluded or deceived not out of a principled concern for the interests of Americans, but because successive administrations concluded that their policies could not withstand informed public scrutiny. To view these events simply as misjudgments within each administration is to miss the larger point. Scandals and bad judgments are inevitable without vigorous public scrutiny, and the more they are covered up, the worse they become.

Besides being counterproductive, secrecy also may be increasingly obsolete. We are living in an era of expanding mass communications. Smart, agile reporters are roaming the globe. Broad networks of people are communicating with one another through telephones, radios, and computers.[50] A growing number of "eyes in the sky" satellites are making high-resolution photos available for private purchase.[51] In today's world very little information can long remain under national lock-and-key—even information about relatively closed societies like Albania and China.

The accountability of U.S. leaders could be improved by greater public openness about their strategic doctrines, weapons deployments, and intelligence activities abroad. This might be accomplished by narrowing the national security exceptions to the Freedom of Information Act. Another helpful reform would be to force the Pentagon to identify more of its "black budget" line items for highly classified facilities and activities that are virtually immune to congressional scrutiny. Currently, these hidden line items total more than $35 billion annually.[52]

U.S. national security advisers would be well advised to listen to, as well as inform, the general public. A good model is the National Environmental Policy Act (NEPA), which requires environmental impact statements and public review for every major federal action. Just as NEPA often has led to decisions that are less expensive and environmentally more sound, an analogous process requiring national security impact statements, with public review for major, nonemergency shifts in foreign or military policy, could help prevent costly mistakes.

Restraining Military Adventures Abroad

Another strategy for promoting strong democracy within the United States would be to put more political checks and balances on the president's ability to use military force. The Founding Fathers placed the war powers in the hands of the Congress to prevent precisely the kinds of military adventures and entanglements that presidents have initiated throughout the twentieth century. Alexander Hamilton, a stalwart advocate of a strong executive, said, "The history of human conduct does not warrant . . . [committing] interests of so delicate and momentous a kind, as those which concern [a nation's] intercourse with the rest of the world, to the sole disposal of . . . a president of the United States."[53] Yet Congress has allowed its powers to be bypassed and undermined. According to Eugene V. Rostow, former director of the Arms Control and Disarmament Agency, presidents ordered U.S. armed forces into combat more than 200 times between 1789 and 1973, while Congress made only five declarations of war.[54]

Congress tried to retrieve its checks on presidential adventures in 1973 by passing the War Powers Resolution. Enacted over President Nixon's veto, the act requires the executive to notify Congress within forty-eight hours whenever he or she sends U.S. troops "into hostilities or into situations where imminent involvement in hostility is clearly indicated." Congressional consent also is required for the troops to remain in action more than sixty days, or ninety days if the president certifies an "unavoidable necessity."

Despite repeated presidential uses of force since 1973, Congress has never once used its sixty- or ninety-day clocks to approve or terminate a military action.[55] One problem is that the War Powers Resolution is vague about when hostilities are to be considered "imminent." When President Bush announced to Congress in August 1990 that he was sending 100,000 troops to Saudi Arabia, he carefully stated, "I do not believe involvement in hostilities is imminent."[56] This deliberate circumvention of the law went largely unchallenged by the legislative branch (except for a handful of congressional members who filed a lawsuit in federal court). If congressional controls over the president are to be made effective, the act will need radical revision.

At a minimum, writes J. Brian Atwood, one of the authors of the resolution, "[Congress] must make sure that consultations become politically and legally unavoidable *before* United States forces are introduced into hostilities."[57] On March 16, 1988, President Reagan sent 3,200 troops to Honduras to help repel the Nicaraguan forces that had chased the Contras across the Honduran border. Reagan took this action the day after his secretary of state, his national security adviser, and his chief of staff each had assured Congress that no such policy was being contemplated.[58] Clearly, in this case, as in so many others, if Congress is consulted only after forces are deployed, it is often too late.[59] Atwood has suggested creating a special "leadership committee" made up of the political leadership of both houses of Congress and the ranking members of the Foreign Affairs, Armed Services, and Intelligence committees. Another alternative, suggested by Donald Robinson of Smith College, would be to give some members of Congress seats on the National Security Council.[60] In May 1988 a bipartisan group of senators proposed setting up a "permanent consultative group" to confer with administration officials before, during, and after a military operation.[61]

Possibly the best way to reform the War Powers Resolution would be to follow the first version the Senate passed—an outright prohibition on the president's use of force without congressional approval unless a true national emergency exists. Under this original bill, Senator Alan Cranston of California has noted, "the decision to initiate involvement in a war situation—the modern-day equivalent of a declared war—was restored to Congress, as the Framers of the Constitution clearly provided."[62]

The most serious yet least discussed presidential usurpation of war powers relates to the command structure that controls nuclear bombs. As Princeton political scientist Richard Falk has written, "War plans and decision procedures involving nuclear weapons are completely cut off from democratic notions of agreed-upon guidelines or modes of accountability, much less citizen or even Congressional participation."[63] That the president can, at his sole discretion, use his war powers unilaterally to launch a nuclear first strike, committing the United States to a war that would kill more people than all previous wars combined, underscores the need to develop greater constraints on the use of nuclear weapons. The trend toward "launch-on-warning," and other forms of automated launch, threatens to remove human decisionmakers from the critical question of when and under what circumstances nuclear retaliation should be authorized. Responding to these trends, Jeremy Stone, executive director of the Federation of American Scientists, has suggested that a nuclear planning committee of Congress be established to work closely with the president's national security advisers and to exercise decision-making power over the first use of nuclear weapons.[64]

Short of a major commitment of U.S. troops or nuclear weapons, presidents also have involved the United States in smaller international adventures through covert actions. After World War II covert actions undertaken by the CIA became a convenient way for the executive branch to attempt to assassinate foreign leaders, destabilize elected governments, spread disinformation, and implement other policies that could not win popular support. When these actions were publicized in 1975 by the Senate Special Select Committee on Intelligence Activities, Frank Church, committee chair, argued that they had done little to help the national interest: "I suggest we have lost—or grievously impaired—the good name and reputation of the United States from which we once drew a unique capacity to exercise moral leadership. . . . In the eyes of millions of once-friendly foreign people, the United States is today regarded with grave suspicion and distrust."[65]

The Church committee concluded that covert actions are inherently unreliable means for accomplishing foreign policy objectives. Clandestine operations must be undertaken quickly enough and on a scale small enough to remain secret, requirements that put severe constraints on their usefulness. To preserve secrecy, they must be undertaken by a small number of decisionmakers, yet this increases the probability of serious errors, such as the misguided belief by the Kennedy administration that the Cuban people would support the U.S.-backed Cuban exiles over Fidel Castro during the Bay of Pigs invasion. Moreover, as Harvard political scientist Stanley Hoffmann has argued, "When the operations entail the manipulation of foreign elements with their own agenda (the Cuban exiles mobilized for the

Bay of Pigs landing, or the Nicaraguan contras, or the anti-Allende factions in the Chilean military), American ability to control them is often limited."[66] Indeed, as detailed in Chapter 2, many U.S. covert actions have hurt the nation's interests substantially: Coups undertaken with covert American support in Iran, Guatemala, and Chile all produced extraordinarily repressive dictatorships and infused opposition groups with a deep hatred of the United States.

The Church committee seriously considered banning all covert actions, but settled for establishing a permanent structure of intelligence committees to review all covert actions confidentially. The president was obligated to provide "timely notice" of new operations to Congress. Congress could raise objections, but the ultimate power of deciding whether to embark upon any action resided wholly with the president (except, of course, if Congress passed special legislation prohibiting an operation or stripping away funding). Senator Church's arguments about why some covert actions should still be allowed won the day: "I can conceive of a dire emergency when timely clandestine action on our part might avert a nuclear holocaust and save an entire civilization. I can also conceive of circumstances . . . where our discreet help to democratic political parties might avert a forcible take-over by a communist minority, heavily subsidized by the Soviets."[67]

Today these arguments seem unpersuasive. The kinds of national emergencies Senator Church described are actually part of the president's constitutionally defined power as commander-in-chief. Moreover, if Congress wanted to do so, it could exempt emergencies more clearly and still impose a general ban on covert actions (though even in emergencies the president should be required to consult Congress before undertaking covert actions). It is hard to see how the overt participation of the U.S. government would be more damaging to the political situation in other countries than the political fallout that occurs when covert operations are unmasked. Leaving aside the inevitability of leaks to the press, few covert operations can long remain secret. While serving as director of the American Civil Liberties Union's Center for National Security Studies, Morton Halperin argued, "U.S. arms sales to Iran . . . were discussed so often with so many people over so many insecure channels of communication that interested governments and arms merchants all over the world knew about them."[68] That Congress now routinely and openly debates whether to fund covert programs has caused even former UN ambassador Jeane Kirkpatrick to "tentatively" conclude "that, within any sensible meaning of the term, covert action isn't a viable policy option in the post-Watergate era."[69] As for alternatives to covert action, this book suggests a wide range of options.

Even with congressional oversight, covert actions invite presidential abuse. The Reagan administration simply tossed prescribed procedures aside when it supported the Nicaraguan Contras. After the Iran-Contra scandal revealed a pattern of officials lying to the intelligence committees, the administration tried to assure Congress that it would be more cooperative in the future.[70] But many observers have come to agree with Morton Halperin that prevarication is a problem *endemic* to covert actions: "Covert operations breed a disrespect for the truth. Officials start out lying to the enemy, then to the public, then to Congress, then to other agencies and finally to the person in the next office. They lie about the essentials, and once they discover how easy that is, they start lying about other aspects of the operation. . . . If it is effective to lie about aid to the contras, why not about an imminent invasion of Grenada or about arms for hostages?"[71]

Neither the Congress nor the president is helped by rules that allow some covert actions some of the time. The current procedures make it difficult for members of Congress overseeing covert actions to advocate stopping a program they dislike. Since opposition to a program means acknowledging its existence, the procedures wind up gagging precisely those legislators otherwise most capable of stopping misguided adventures. At the executive level, the current procedures encourage subordinates not to inform the president about covert operations. Admiral John Poindexter explained during the Iran-Contra hearings that his goal was to allow the president to "plausibly deny" any knowledge of the operations. As the Church committee's final report declared, "Any theory which, as a matter of doctrine, places elected officials on the periphery of the decision-making process is an invitation to error, an abdication of responsibility and a perversion of democratic government."[72]

The cause of strong democracy would be well served by a complete abolition of covert actions, except perhaps during well-defined national security emergencies. Another helpful reform would be to take these remaining military operations out of the CIA's hands and put them, instead, under the control of the Department of Defense, where better-established procedures for congressional oversight exist.[73] The CIA could then be returned to its original responsibilities for gathering and analyzing information.

These new restrictions on covert action would not compromise covert intelligence gathering, which accounts for approximately 95 percent of the CIA's budget.[74] Nor would the detailed implementation of specific policies have to be made public. In any case, the American people and their elected representatives should be better able to assess the costs and benefits to the nation of involving itself in a conflict abroad before such involvement begins.

Perpetual Peace

Two hundred years ago the celebrated philosopher Immanuel Kant made the following prediction:

> If the consent of the citizens is required in order to decide that war should be declared (and in [constitutional democracies] it cannot but be the case), nothing is more natural than that they would be very cautious in commencing such a poor game, decreeing for themselves all the calamities of war. Among the latter would be: Having to fight, having to pay the costs of war from their own resources, having painfully to repair the devastation war leaves behind, and, to fill up the measure of evils, load themselves with heavy national debt that would embitter peace itself and that can never be liquidated on account of constant wars in the future.[75]

The striking absence of war between democracies suggests that Kant was right—democracy *is* a cause of peace. It is not the only cause of peace nor is it a perfect cause, but as Yale's Bruce Russett writes, "This is perhaps the strongest non-trivial or non-tautological statement that can be made about international relations."[76]

For the first time in human history nearly a majority of the world's peoples live in democracies. Unfortunately, many of these political systems lack the characteristics of strong democracy. They do not protect minority rights, they eschew the principle of subsidiarity, they have weak civil societies. Moreover, the foreign policy establishment of almost every democracy is characterized by secrecy, hierarchy, and authoritarianism. As nuclear bombs and other weapons of mass destruction proliferate, the "national security state" within every democratic state will be tempted to classify more information, demand more security clearances for decisionmakers, suspend more civil liberties, and further weaken political oversight of national war powers. If U.S. security planners wish to establish a world of peaceful republics, they will need to promote democratic reforms everywhere, including their own backyard.

It is critical, however, to avoid the temptation to promote democracy through force or threats of force. Recent history contains few examples in which one nation has been able to *compel* another to become democratic. Many U.S. covert actions, such as those in Iran, Chile, and Guatemala, resulted in governments that were far less democratic than the previous ones. As long as the United States acts around the globe to dispose of governments not to its liking, other countries will have an excuse to do the same, and every nation's security will be diminished. But if it promotes democracy through persuasion and cooperation, through small-scale businesses and large-scale exchange projects, through the spread of fax machines and personal computers, through the strengthening of war powers and the renunciation of covert actions, and through the encouragement of other nations to do likewise, the United States can bring the world perpetual peace through peaceful means.

5
The Resource Roots of Conflict

For the first time in human history the basic requisites of every nation's security—air, water, land, and life itself—are in danger of being permanently destroyed. The protective ozone layer in the stratosphere is vanishing, the climate is dangerously warming, fresh water supplies are being contaminated by toxic chemicals, and thousands of species are disappearing each year. "In spite of all our propagandists can do," writes Wendell Berry, "the foreign threat inevitably seems diminished when our air is unsafe to breathe, when our drinking water is unsafe to drink, ... when our forests are dying from air pollution and acid rain, and when we ourselves are sick from poisons in the air. Who *are* the enemies of this country?"[1]

The mismanagement of natural resources not only is ruining every nation's life support systems but also is increasing the probability of interstate war. The United States felt compelled to go to war against Saddam Hussein, for example, largely because it failed to achieve energy independence and feared his control of one-fifth of the world's supply of oil. An important way to prevent war, therefore, is to conserve resources and to transform national consumption and production patterns so that they are more sustainable. The United States can increase its security by using energy and strategic minerals more efficiently. And it can increase the security of other nations by encouraging them to do likewise.

The Connections Between Resources and Conflict

There are at least four different ways that natural-resource policies can cause or exacerbate international conflicts. Direct competition for resources like oil or water can pit nation against nation. Environmental degradation resulting from resource mismanagement can create global friction. The vulnerability of a resource infrastructure to sabotage or siege can encourage adversary nations or terrorists to attack. And resource mismanagement can mean lost dollars—and lost opportunities—that otherwise could strengthen national security.

Direct Competition for Resources Abroad

Economies, particularly those of the major global powers, inevitably consume many types of resources. No nation has an unlimited supply of every important resource. The United States is very dependent, for example, on imported oil and imported minerals like chromium and cobalt. When distant suppliers turn off their oil spigots or close their mines, the United States behaves as other nations have done for centuries—it considers using force.

For the past five hundred years, the quest for tea, tobacco, spices, gold, oil, and other resourses has been the driving force behind the expansion of the Spanish, Dutch, and British empires. More recently, nations have battled over phosphates in the Western Sahara (1976 to the present), hoped-for oil in the Paracel Islands (1974), various minerals in Katanga (1960–1964), fish near the shores of Iceland (1972–1973), and oil in the Persian Gulf (1979 to the present). The struggle for resources also has intensified conflicts triggered by other causes. The question of who should control the iron ore in Alsace-Lorraine was a salient issue in both world wars, and conflicts over the control of oil intensified wars in Biafra (1967–1970), Angola (1974 to the present), and the Falklands/Malvinas (1982).[2]

In the twentieth century the Industrial Revolution put the search for sources of energy onto the strategic agendas of most nations. Cheap, plentiful fuels were necessary for industrialization. Oil was essential for vehicles, ships, and aircraft, and became the principal feedstock for the growing petrochemical industry. As this appetite for oil grew, the emerging industrial powers turned to their colonies for new supplies. Britain's long involvement in the Middle East (which set the stage for many of today's political troubles) was driven largely by a need for oil. Germany's need for oil has been cited as one reason for its entry into World War I.[3] Two decades later Nazi Germany justified its military expansion in part by calling for greater Lebensraum—not only "living space" but also access to the natural resources of neighboring nations. The Third Reich was eager to secure agricultural resources in the Ukraine, timber in Poland, and oil in North Africa.[4] Imperial Japan built public support for its military ambitions by sounding the alarm over the paucity of its natural resources.

Like the colonialists and belligerents of earlier epochs, nations today deem their demands for resources to be incontrovertible "national interests" and deploy military force to protect or advance those interests. Although the Iran-Iraq War during the 1980s was primarily a religious and political conflict, the oil deposits in the Persian Gulf, approximately 60 percent of the world's economically recoverable oil reserves, transformed the war into a dangerous arena for superpower rivalry. To gain influence in the region, the United States, the Soviet Union, and many other countries stationed military forces in the Gulf and sold some $50 billion worth of arms to Iran and Iraq between 1981 and 1985, which dramatically increased the bloodshed between the two countries.[5] In 1986, fearful that the Iran-Iraq War could terminate its access to oil in the Persian Gulf, the United States spent about $47 billion to maintain its central command forces in the region.[6] The United States and its allies then paid $61 billion for Desert Shield and Desert Storm to wrest the oil fields of Kuwait from Iraqi control and to return them to the pro-Western al-Sabah dynasty.[7]

Conflicts over oil dominate the headlines, but international fights have been brewing over other resources too. Competition for dwindling water supplies, as noted in Chapter 1, is worsening relations among Egypt, Ethiopia, Iraq, Israel, Jordan, and Syria. Americans and Canadians have had a long-standing conflict over fishing rights, with more than ten violent incidents since 1987.[8] If the world's population continues to grow at exponential rates, demands and confrontations centering on land, water, food, and other resources will almost certainly increase.

Environmental Impacts of Resource Use

Another potential source of conflict is the environmental devastation caused by the extraction, consumption, and disposal of resources. When acid rain crosses national borders, for example, it damages crops, buildings, and people, and strains relations between neighbors. By 1986, more than half of all the trees in West Germany had been damaged by acid rain, and in twelve other

European countries between one-fourth and one-half of the forested areas had been harmed.[9] Acid rain also has killed most of the fish in hundreds of lakes in Canada, Finland, Sweden, and the eastern United States and has left thousands of other lakes dying.[10] Thus far, those nations harmed by acid rain have called for negotiations, not war, but clearly the potential exists for greater conflict.[11]

The Chernobyl nuclear accident provides another compelling example of how resource mismanagement can undermine international security. The long-term health effects across the Ukraine and Europe now are predicted to include between 12,000 and 290,000 thyroid tumors and between 3,500 and 70,000 premature cancer deaths.[12] In the weeks following the accident, fresh vegetables in many parts of Europe had dangerously high radioactivity levels, and the livestock grazing on contaminated grass and lichen produced radioactive milk and meat. In the British highlands some grazing restrictions apparently will continue indefinitely, and for the indigenous peoples of northern Europe the radio-cesium contamination of the lichen-reindeer ecosystem may spell the end of millennia of traditional hunting and culture. The Chernobyl disaster generated a surge of anti-Soviet feeling across Europe among officials and citizens alike. Several Western governments tried to recover billions of dollars in agricultural losses from the Kremlin and threatened to press their claims, if necessary, at the World Court in The Hague.[13]

Maurice Strong, secretary general of the 1992 UN Conference on Environment and Development (UNCED), predicts that "up to 40 potential Chernobyls are waiting to happen in the former Soviet Union and Central Europe."[14] The International Atomic Energy Agency (IAEA), historically an avid promoter of nuclear power, warns that twenty-six reactors in the East have "serious" safety deficiencies and fourteen have "considerable" ones.

Disagreements concerning the safety of other nuclear facilities have created numerous cross-border tensions. Local governments in Germany tried to stop France from building the Cattenom reactor near the Franco-German border because it failed to meet German safety standards.[15] When the Austrian government requested that Germany cancel a proposed reprocessing facility at Wackersdorf that was designed to separate nuclear bomb–grade plutonium from spent reactor fuel, the German foreign minister defiantly replied that his government was going ahead with construction.[16] (The plant, a pet project of the late Bavarian politician Franz Josef Strauss, has since been cancelled on economic grounds.) Irish officials have asked the British government to close the Sellafield reprocessing facility because it is illegally dumping large amounts of radioactive waste into the Irish Sea, but so far, the British have refused.[17] Sweden likewise has ignored Danish pleas to close the Barseback nuclear plant, easily visible across the strait from Copenhagen. Hong Kong is anxious about China: The proposed 1,800-megawatt Daya nuclear plant would be located just fifty kilometers from Hong Kong.[18]

The dramatically increased use of pesticides in agriculture since 1960 has been another international irritant. Although chemical fertilizers and pesticides have boosted grain harvests in the Third World, they also have posed serious threats to human health. Each year between 400,000 and 2 million people in the Third World, most of them poor farm workers, are poisoned by pesticides, and between 10,000 and 40,000 of them die.[19] These deaths inevitably inflame Third World resentment toward the First World corporations and governments marketing such chemicals.

Industrial accidents have created serious transboundary disputes. The blowout of British oil wells in the North Sea resulted in heated protests from the people who live near contaminated beaches in Scandinavia. A Swiss industrial fire in November 1986 dumped some thirty tons of toxic chemicals into the Rhine, killing half a million fish, temporarily spoiling a major water supply for millions of Europeans, and reigniting a long-smoldering European debate about toxic waste disposal. Accidents at substandard production facilities in the Third World—epitomized by the toxic chemical leak in Bhopal, India, that killed some 2,500 people—have deepened the distrust and antipathy felt by many of the world's poor toward those in developed countries.

Beyond the highly visible traumas and the political tension associated with major accidents is the cumulative impact of low-level pollution.[20] Global deaths directly attributable to pesticide poisoning each year are four to sixteen times higher than the number of people killed in Bhopal. The total weight of chemicals released in the accidental contamination of the Rhine by the Swiss is about equal to a single day's normal discharge of chemicals at the river's mouth.[21] (Even the relatively high quantity of mercury released in the accident, 200 kilograms, amounts to less than a week's normal discharge.) Add to these environmental burdens the continuous emission of carbon dioxide into the earth's atmosphere, the daily disposal of hazardous waste into landfills, and the ongoing release of low-level radionuclides, and the gravity of the environmental threats to the security of every nation is apparent.

Slowly, nations are awakening to the dangers of ecological abuse. At a 1989 economics summit, the leaders of Britain, Canada, France, Italy, Japan, the United States, and West Germany issued a joint communiqué that proclaimed, for the first time, that "environmental considerations must be taken into account in economic decision-making."[22] When Soviet president Mikhail Gorbachev gave a speech on new security proposals to the UN General Assembly in December 1988, he referred to the environment more than twenty times.[23] And in June 1992, the largest meeting of heads of states ever recorded—UNCED—was convened in Rio de Janeiro to discuss global environmental problems.

Vulnerability of Resource Production and Delivery Systems

The industrialized nations have built a highly centralized infrastructure for extracting, processing, and delivering energy and other resources. These systems are now extremely vulnerable to accidents, sabotage, or outright attack. The massive power failure of 1965, which blacked out most of the northeastern United States and two Canadian provinces, and the 1989 oil spill by an Exxon tanker in Valdez, Alaska, just begin to hint at the potential magnitude of deliberate destruction. A study for the Pentagon concluded that in a single night, without ever leaving Louisiana, a few saboteurs could cut off three-quarters of the oil and gas of the eastern United States for more than a year.[24] It also found that low-technology sabotage of any one of the nation's more than one hundred nuclear power stations could induce a catastrophic core meltdown, inflicting a Chernobyl-like accident, or worse, on the United States and its neighbors.

The same vulnerability exists at any of the several hundred large nuclear reactors and chemical processing plants worldwide. If a large-scale war ever occurs again in Europe, the fragility of the continent's energy systems might be far more decisive than any other aspect of combat. Serious damage to any one of the operating plutonium reprocessing plants in France and Britain could render most of Europe uninhabitable for centuries.[25] The collateral damage from a conventional bomb exploded in any of the power reactors now operating in northern Germany could send megaton-range fallout drifting downwind. (This fact alone, quite apart from U.S. and NATO nuclear-weapons deterrents, should have made the Soviet Union think twice about waging war in Western Europe.)

The vulnerability of energy-production facilities to military attack is not hypothetical. The Allied bombing of Hitler's synfuel plants greatly accelerated the final phases of World War II, and after the war Nazi leaders said that earlier bombing of their electrical power plants would have shortened the war by at least two years.[26] U.S. military planners evidently learned this lesson, bombing the Yalu River hydroelectric plants during the Korean War and a Cambodian oil refinery during the *Mayaguez* incident in 1975. From the CIA's attack on a Nicaraguan fuel storage depot in Corinto in 1983 to Israel's bombing of Iraq's Osiraq nuclear reactor in 1981, key resource facilities are now among the first military targets. In recent years more than fifty countries have reported significant attacks on their energy systems:[27] Power grids were long the leading targets of Chilean and Salvadoran guerrillas. A blackout by saboteurs in the midst of a nationwide broadcast by President Salvador Allende of Chile contributed to his overthrow. Early in the 1967 Six-Day War, it took Israeli warplanes only thirty minutes to destroy virtually all of Syria's oil installations and two of its major power plants. Rhodesian premier Ian Smith found his national deficit increased by about 18 percent moments after an attack on an oil depot in 1978 (an attack that the African National Congress often has sought to repeat at South Africa's synfuel plants—with some success). And at the end of the Persian Gulf War, Saddam Hussein's retreating army set fire to 600 Kuwaiti oil wells, causing one of the worst environmental disasters in human history.

Opportunity Costs of Resource Mismanagement

The fourth way resource decisions can undermine a nation's economic and political security results from these decisions being made foolishly. In response to the worsening energy crisis of the 1970s, the United States unwisely launched crash projects to develop synthetic fuels and build more nuclear power plants, both among the most expensive energy options available. The Synthetic Fuels Corporation was given $15.6 billion but never produced a single barrel of oil. The nuclear-power program received more than $100 billion in federal subsidies and a like amount in private investment, yet now generates less energy than wood.

These poor investments have imposed significant "opportunity costs" on U.S. national security. Because the federal government failed to invest in efficiency measures and renewable energy resources during the past two decades, the United States imports nearly as much oil today as it did in the mid-1970s. The United States has squandered opportunities to make its economy more energy-efficient, and, in doing so, it has exacerbated its federal and trade deficits and undermined the nation's economic security. Americans today pay more for wasted energy (energy that could be saved using today's best efficiency technologies) than for the *entire* U.S. military budget.[28]

The costs other nations have incurred for mismanaging their resources have been far greater. Poor agricultural planning led to food shortages, price hikes, and riots in the Sudan (1981), Tunisia (1983–1984), and Morocco (1984). Rising food prices in the Sudan sparked strikes and riots again in 1985 and eventually toppled the government. Increases in food prices were also the catalyst for the collapse of the Polish government in 1980 and the establishment of a military government a year later.[29] In 1977 hungry Ethiopian peasants seeking improved conditions migrated to the country's lowlands near the Somalian border, causing Somalia to launch a preemptive invasion of Ethiopia.[30] In all these cases, better agricultural policies might have prevented riots, civil wars, and border clashes.

Alternative Resource Policies

Because of the myriad links between natural resources and security, better management of energy and mineral resources can increase both national and international security. As the largest consumer of resources in the world (and as one of the least efficient), the United States can play a particularly important role in conserving global resources and reducing ecological stresses on the planet. Moreover, by recasting its foreign assistance programs to promote better resource management abroad, the United States can improve the security of other nations—and therefore its own security as well.

Energy Security Policies

Federal investments in cost-effective energy efficiency measures would reduce U.S. reliance on nonrenewable supplies of fossil fuels and on electricity produced by nuclear-power plants and thereby help eliminate the four sources of national insecurity described above. To begin with, extensive energy efficiency could enable the United States to reduce its dependence on foreign oil supplies and lessen concomitant foreign policy risks. Facing unstable political conditions in the Middle East, and a seemingly insatiable domestic appetite for imported oil in the late 1970s and early 1980s, the United States created the Rapid Deployment Force (RDF), a flotilla of ships, planes, weapons, and troops that could be sent on short notice to guarantee Western access to "vital interests" in the Persian Gulf. Whatever the successes of the RDF, the risks entailed were substantial: The deployment of battleships equipped with nuclear weapons in the Middle East, an area adjacent to the Soviet Union, increased the chances that the superpowers would stumble into a nuclear war. Investing *a single year's* RDF budget in improving energy efficiency, in contrast, could have eliminated the U.S. need for Middle East oil, and lessened the risks posed by the RDF itself.[31] Looked at another way, had the United States invested as much as half of the direct cost of its 1990–1991 war against Iraq in energy savings, the country could have unplugged itself from the Persian Gulf permanently. Just increasing the efficiency of American cars by three miles per gallon could have replaced all U.S. oil imports from Iraq and Kuwait.[32]

Indeed, the potential savings are far larger than that. Net imports of oil in 1986 amounted to 5.4 million barrels per day, of which about 1 million barrels per day were coming from the Persian Gulf. Because motor vehicles consumed some 7 million barrels per day, switching from a 20-miles-per-gallon fleet of cars to one averaging 60 miles per gallon would have eliminated virtually all oil imports. Indeed, had the Reagan administration not rolled back light-vehicle efficiency standards in 1986, the United States could have saved as much oil as it imported that year from the Persian Gulf.[33] Weatherization of buildings with wall and roof insulation, double-paned windows, and other energy-saving devices could save a year's worth of oil imports from the Persian Gulf before a nuclear-power plant or a synthetic-fuel plant, ordered now, could deliver any energy whatsoever—and at one-tenth the cost.

Investing in energy efficiency would enable the United States to reduce the grave environmental impacts of running nuclear reactors and burning fossil fuels. An 18-watt compact fluorescent lamp, for example, produces as much light as a 75-watt incandescent lamp for about thirteen times as long, saving over its lifetime about $20 (the cost of buying and installing a dozen incandescent bulbs).[34] By saving electricity that would have been produced in a coal-fired plant, this same superefficient lamp will prevent a ton of carbon dioxide and more than seventeen pounds of sulfur dioxide from being dumped into the atmosphere.

The ecological problems associated with conservation, in contrast to those associated with coal or nuclear plants, are generally small and localized; they can be managed with simple technologies. For example, the problem of radon gas accumulating in well-insulated, airtight houses can be eliminated with air-to-air heat exchangers, which recapture the heat from radon-contaminated air as it is pumped outside. (Heat exchangers are now being mass produced at affordable prices.)

The full use of the best electricity-saving technologies now on the market could save as much as four times the electricity generated by all commercial U.S. nuclear plants combined, for far less money than the cost of *merely operating* those plants.[35] The implementation of these technologies could result in net economic savings exceeding $50 billion a year, allowing the United States gradually to dispense with nuclear-power plants and even most coal plants. Superefficient light bulbs, variable-speed motors, and high-efficiency appliances can eliminate most of the side effects of coal and nuclear plants, including nuclear accidents, weapons proliferation, climatic changes, and acid rain—any one of which could cause a major international upheaval.

Today's best lighting technologies alone could save up to three-quarters of the lighting energy we now use, displacing dozens of large power plants.[36] These technologies would allow the country to avoid spending some $200 billion on power-plant construction and would save about $30 billion a year in operating costs. Similarly, a 1989 analysis of thirty-five types of improvements to electric motors and their components found a potential to save about half of all motor electrical input, which is over half of all electricity used in the world, at a fraction of the cost of fueling a coal or nuclear plant.[37] By 1990, the Electric Power Research Institute, the utilities' think tank, agreed with this conclusion.[38]

Cost-effective efficiency innovations have yet to be fully implemented for several reasons. Many producers and consumers are not aware of the best technologies, which change almost every year. Those buyers who are aware of these technologies often demand that investments in energy efficiency pay for themselves in a year or two, far faster than the twenty-to-thirty-year horizons used by utility planners. Utilities that want to get into the business of marketing energy efficiency are discouraged by obsolete (though changing) state rules that prohibit public monopolies from selling anything but electricity and that give utilities a greater rate of return for selling more electricity rather than for cutting customers' bills. And there are dozens of messy institutional barriers, ranging from "split incentives" between builders and buyers or between landlords and tenants, to perverse fee structures that reward architects and engineers for inefficient designs and penalize them for efficient designs.[39]

Less reliance on nuclear and fossil energy sources would reduce the vulnerability of the U.S. energy infrastructure to sabotage and attack as well as to technical failure or natural disaster. If the supply of imported oil ended tomorrow, the pipeline inventory from wellhead to gas pump could run U.S. automobiles for only a month or so. A fleet of cars averaging sixty miles per gallon, in contrast, could run on this inventory three times as long, giving the United States a bigger cushion against a sudden cutoff by the Organization of Petroleum Exporting Countries (OPEC). Nuclear plants that have been shut down make less tempting targets for terrorists.[40] Small-scale, dispersed energy sources such as houses with passive solar designs, industrial cogeneration facilities, and windmills are inherently more resilient than large-scale coal or nuclear-power plants and can greatly diminish the destructiveness caused by accidents or attacks by terrorists or hostile nations.[41]

Finally, increased energy productivity would reduce U.S. insecurity by directly improving our economic well-being and competitiveness. National payments for energy now constitute about $430 billion per year, two-fifths more than payments for all military activities. Improvements in efficiency since 1973 have already reduced energy payments by about $150 billion per year. If the United States were as efficient as its Western European competitors, it could save another $200 billion annually.[42] Systematic investment in cost-effective efficiency measures conceivably could save *several trillion* of today's dollars over the course of a few decades.[43] The resulting boost to the national economy would shore up the nation's sagging trade position, help pay off the national debt, enhance its economic and political influence abroad, and release resources for other alternative security initiatives.

The ability of the United States to reap the economic benefits of efficiency is not theoretical. Market forces have been driving the economy in this direction for the past decade. Between 1979 and 1986 the United States derived more than seven times as much new energy from improved efficiency as from *all* net expansions of its energy supply.[44] During this same period the United States obtained more new energy from the sun, wind, water, and wood than from oil, gas, coal, and uranium combined.[45] Renewable sources of energy, alleged by many to be impractical, are now supplying at least one-tenth of the nation's total primary energy and are the fastest-growing source except for efficiency.[46] Improved efficiency has already cut the energy required per dollar of U.S. GNP by one-fourth, the oil and gas consumed per dollar of GNP by one-third, and OPEC's market share by one-half.[47] All this happened with little help, and not a little hindrance, from federal policymakers. Yet even these impressive achievements barely scratch the surface of the potential now available.

Mineral Security Policies

Precious minerals also are scarce global resources that U.S. security planners once regarded as "vital." In 1986, when the country debated whether to impose sanctions on South Africa, some officials worried that Pretoria might play its "minerals card." This was one reason President Reagan urged the country to support his policy of "constructive engagement." "Strategically," Reagan said, "this is one of the most vital regions of the world. . . . Southern Africa and South Africa are repository of many of the vital minerals—vanadium, manganese, chromium, platinum—for which the West has no other secure source of supply."[48] That year, South Africa was producing 43 percent of the world's platinum-group metals, which are commonly used for automobile-exhaust catalytic converters, electronics components, and chemical and refining processes.[49] With the Soviet Union producing approximately half the world's platinum-group metals, some analysts warned that the West was in danger of losing control over almost 95 percent of the world's supply. The same argument was raised with respect to manganese and chromium, both of which are used in the manufacture of steel, because together the Soviet Union and South Africa accounted for 58 percent of the world's supply of manganese and 72 percent of the chromium.

Today, a global shift away from scarce minerals to new materials and to more efficient use and recovery of materials has rendered most of these security concerns obsolete. According to a recent article in *Scientific American:* "Substitution of one material for another has slowed the growth of demand for particular materials. So have design changes in products that increase the efficiency of materials use. Perhaps more important, the markets that expanded rapidly during the Era of Materials are by and large saturated. And new markets tend to involve products that have a relatively low materials content."[50]

Consider, for example, U.S. use of steel. U.S. steel consumption per dollar of real GNP has now fallen below its 1860 level, because Americans have lighter cars made out of other materials and because they spend proportionally more of their incomes on services. New steel production also has fallen sharply because of increased recycling. Even military equipment now requires less steel. The Army's latest designs for tanks and troop carriers use new plastics, ceramics, and fiberglass compounds for armor.[51]

What has happened to steel is happening with many other once-scarce natural resources. Advanced materials, substitutions, reuse, re-manufacturing, recycling, and more efficient designs have gradually lowered U.S. dependence on many minerals—and much more is possible. A recent report by the Office of Technology Assessment concluded that if the United States fully employed all available techniques, the "prospects for substantial reduction in current levels of U.S. dependence by the year 2000" are "fair" for chromium and manganese and "good" for cobalt and platinum-group metals.[52]

Another reason not to worry about catastrophic mineral shortages is the growing volume and complexity of international trade. As John P. Holdren, a professor in the Energy and Resources Group at the University of California, Berkeley, has concluded: "The international flows of energy, nonfuel minerals, food, manufactured goods, technology, money and information have grown so large, so multifaceted, so ubiquitous, and so mutually indispensable that the idea of any country or group of countries waging systematic economic warfare against others by restricting a subset of these flows is becoming less plausible all the time."[53]

To the extent that U.S. military missions remain driven by the desire to secure access to scarce minerals (the Pentagon's *Defense Planning Guidance 1994–99*, written in 1992, contains these kinds of arguments),[54] they could be obviated or substantially scaled back if the United States took full advantage of existing technological trends.[55] The Reagan and Bush administrations, however, wed to the belief that the government should not interfere with the marketplace, adamantly opposed any national efforts to invest in new technologies except those with military potential. Were the United States to begin investing in research and development of new materials and new production techniques, it could free itself of foreign resources and renounce all coercive means of acquiring them. To the extent that the United States still might need foreign resources, Jonathan Kwitny argues in *Endless Enemies* that "the best way the United States can insure access to vital resources is to make itself a trading partner that any country seeking peaceful commerce would naturally want to deal with."[56]

Policies for Resource Security Abroad

U.S. security depends not only on managing its own resources more wisely but also on its helping other nations to do so. If its NATO allies are drawn into another conflict in the Middle East because of their dependence on oil, the United States will be in danger of being drawn in too. Pollution of the Baltic Sea could create new tensions between Scandinavia and Russia. The concentration of oil refineries and pipelines in Saudi Arabia, tempting targets for Iraq, also imperils U.S. economic security. Because of these interconnections, the United States should help other nations address the resource roots of conflict.

Improvements in energy efficiency in other nations offer the same kinds of security-enhancing benefits as they do for the United States. If Western European countries were less dependent on Middle Eastern oil, the burdens on NATO would be fewer. If Americans worked with the new nations of Eastern Europe and the CIS to increase their energy efficiency—as groups such as the Natural Resources Defense Council, the Rocky Mountain Institute, and Princeton's Center for Energy and Environmental Studies are doing—global carbon dioxide emissions could be significantly reduced. If Americans promoted energy efficiency and renewable energy systems in Third World nations, they could improve the economic well-being of those countries and eliminate pretexts for Third World leaders to acquire proliferation-prone nuclear reactors. In Haiti, where the average person spends as much as a quarter of his or her household income on electricity, mainly for lighting, simply giving away quadrupled-efficiency light bulbs would dramatically lower Haitians' electricity bills and increase their disposable income by as much as 20 percent. This would enable the hard-pressed Haitian government to divert scarce funds from power plants to reforestation and agricultural reform.

U.S. security also could increase through the promotion of better agricultural practices abroad. Simply phasing out subsidies for pesticides in the Third World—currently between 19 and 89 percent of the real retail costs of these items[57]—would make sustainable methods of pest control more economically attractive. U.S. aid programs geared to improving water efficiency, especially in irrigation, would simultaneously reduce the need for foreign capital, prevent the environmental devastation caused by large-scale dams, increase food production, and improve the ability of many countries to provide clean drinking water (probably the most important single factor for improving public health). The United States could support natural pest-control programs like those of the Nigerian-based International Institute of Tropical Agriculture, which has successfully used wasps to eradicate a mealybug that was endangering crops throughout Africa (scientists working for the U.S. Agency for International Development had pronounced the program unworkable).[58] At home and abroad the United States could spread solar-drying technologies, integrated agriculture-aquaculture systems, and solar-driven pumps.[59] Improving the nutrition and health of people in the Third World without increasing their dependence on First World technology or money would eliminate precisely the kinds of desperate needs, environmental hazards, and vulnerabilities that foster conflicts.

Security Through Sustainability

In 1987 the World Commission on Environment and Development, chaired by Gro Harlem Brundtland, recommended the universal pursuit of the goal of sustainable development. Sustainability occurs, according to the report, when nations meet "the needs of the present without compromising the ability of future generations to meet their own needs."[60] Defined in this way, sustainability also is a means to prevent war.

Nations that operate their economies sustainably would minimize consumption of nonrenewable resources and be immune to sudden cutoffs. By using solar, wind, and geothermal energy sources instead of oil, coal, and uranium, these nations would no longer threaten other nations with climate change, acid rain, or nuclear meltdowns. With a dispersed energy-supply system, they would not be as vulnerable to sabotage or attack. A world of nations that were self-sufficient in energy, water, food, and other essential resources would trigger fewer wars than today's world of conflict-producing dependencies, externalities, vulnerabilities, and inefficiencies.

Greater military security, of course, is not the only reason for the United States to become more sustainable and to help other nations do likewise. There is an emerging consensus that if nations continue living unsustainably—if carbon dioxide continues to build up and warm the global climate, if chlorofluorocarbons and other synthetic chemicals continue to eat away the ozone layer, if toxic chemicals continue to enter the food chain, if deforestation continues to upset the biological balance of the planet—the survival of humanity will be imperiled. None of these ecological trends will create sudden disasters. Their costs will appear more gradually in the form of more cancer deaths, lower agricultural yields, more intense storms, and reduced GNP. But no country can be secure for long if these planetary wounds are allowed to fester.

Protecting the earth's environment must now become a centerpiece for national security planning. High on every nation's action list should be the following: phase out the burning of fossil fuels, perhaps by imposing a carbon tax; replace automobiles, particularly gas-guzzlers, with high-efficiency cars and mass-transit systems; design manufacturing processes to use less energy and fewer nonrenewable resources; minimize pollution through stricter regulation and higher taxes on smokestack emissions; recover and recycle nonrenewable resources; protect existing ecosystems and restore ravaged ones; and employ new measures of economic well-being that can show whether a nation is depleting or conserving its natural resources.

Two things can be said about this ambitious agenda. First, realizing the goal of sustainability will not be cheap. Maurice Strong, the secretary general of UNCED, estimates that developing countries, together, will need $125 billion per year to make the transition, or about $70 billion per year more than they currently receive from the First World in foreign aid.[61] This means that it is essential to reduce military expenditures and invest the savings in global environmental protection. Second, the global nature of ecological problems requires global solutions. Unprecedented cooperation will be necessary to transfer technology, to provide necessary capital to poor countries, to ban certain chemicals, and to negotiate new international regulations.

The United States will help determine whether this agenda for ecological security succeeds or fails. The Bush administration consistently belittled concerns about global warming, resisted financial commitments to developing countries, and fought environmental treaties that might burden business in the short term. Were the United States to adopt a more constructive attitude toward global environmental protection, were it to support greater energy efficiency and sustainable agriculture, were it to provide $10 billion per year for global cleanup and development and press its allies to do likewise, its good example and power of persuasion could set the world on a fundamentally different course.

6
The Economic Roots of Conflict

U.S. security planners understood at the beginning of the Cold War that sound economic policies can prevent war. They remembered Versailles, where a $33 billion reparations bill was imposed on Germany after World War I and brought to power a popular demagogue who promised to repudiate these humiliating debts—Adolf Hitler. John Maynard Keynes resigned in protest from the British negotiating team at Versailles, accurately predicting that "by aiming at the destruction of the economic life of Germany, [the Treaty] threatens the health and prosperity of the Allies themselves."[1] U.S. security planners were determined not to make the same mistake after World War II. Through the stewardship of General Douglas MacArthur and the generosity of the Marshall Plan, the United States helped rebuild the economies of Japan and Western Europe and, in doing so, created a prosperous economic order.

That order, however, was built upon the global primacy of the U.S. economy. Today, Pax Americana is breaking down, and the absence of a new economic order to replace the old one is causing resentment, conflict, and disorder. Outraged by Tokyo's restrictions on imports of U.S. auto parts, computers, and rice, Americans have demanded retaliatory trade barriers and demolished Japanese cars with sledgehammers. The crushing burden of foreign debt is destabilizing young democratic governments in Latin America. The lure of quick profit is drawing thousands of companies into the arms trade and sowing the seeds for new conflicts. U.S. security planners must now examine all these connections between economics and war, and they must devise new policies at home and abroad that increase the chances for peace. Today's economic order must be strengthened with a package of debt relief for the Third World, a corporate code of conduct, a regime of fair trade, and a new approach to development assistance. And economic conversion of arms factories and military institutions must move forward on a planetary scale.

The Bretton Woods Economic Order

In 1944 representatives of the emerging victors of World War II met at a conference in Bretton Woods, New Hampshire, and agreed to create the International Bank for Reconstruction and Development (now called the World Bank) and the International Monetary Fund (IMF). The World Bank was created to provide long-term loans for postwar rebuilding and development, and the IMF was intended to provide short-term credit and to help stabilize exchange rates between currencies. The United States designed these institutions to create a thriving global economy that was both resistant to war and congenial to U.S. interests.

With the World Bank, the United States sought to boost the economic recovery of Europe and to jump-start the Third World, at all times ensuring that economic development was consistent with democracy and market capitalism. In the late 1960s Robert McNamara led the World Bank to shift its investments away from big development projects (such as dams, irrigation projects, and power plants) and toward rural development, population control, job training, and literacy education.

With the creation of the IMF, the United States sought to make the dollar the pivotal currency of international trade. Because the United States had by far the world's most powerful economy after World War II, the nations represented at Bretton Woods agreed to fix their currency exchange rates in relation to the U.S. dollar. The U.S. government, in turn, promised to redeem paper dollars for gold at a rate of $35 per ounce.

Integral to these institutions was a belief that the U.S. economy would remain the world's strongest. What U.S. security planners did not foresee was how their policies of deterrence, containment, and intervention would steadily erode the nation's economic base. Today, after several decades of subsidizing the defense of Western Europe and Japan, the United States finds itself falling behind its allies economically.

One indicator of declining U.S. economic power is the reduced influence of the dollar. Bretton Woods made the dollar as good as gold and assumed that the United States could continue to operate as the world's central bank. But the Vietnam War shattered this assumption. Financed through deficit spending, the war racked the United States with serious inflation and trade deficits for more than a decade, which caused foreigners to lose confidence in the dollar and exchange dollars for gold. By 1971, the U.S. gold supply had became so depleted that it could no longer cover outstanding international claims.[2] President Nixon responded by suspending gold convertibility. Two years and two devaluations later, Nixon formally severed the link between the dollar and gold. What has emerged since is a system of floating exchange rates that was designed to eliminate deficits and surpluses more readily. Although the dollar remains the preeminent global currency for some transactions (most oil, for example, is still bought with and sold for dollars), it is fast becoming an equal among other international currencies. In 1975 about 85 percent of all government reserves worldwide consisted of dollars; today the figure is 56 percent.[3]

Another key component of the Bretton Woods order was created in 1948, when most of the world's countries—with the notable exceptions of the East Bloc and some developing countries—signed the General Agreement on Tariffs and Trade, an institution designed to promote "freer and fairer trade" by encouraging signatory nations to lower their tariffs and nontariff trade barriers. Between 1950 and 1975 successive rounds of GATT negotiations helped merchandise trade for industrial nations grow at an average rate of 8 percent per year, double the average growth rate for their GNPs.[4]

The World Bank, IMF, and GATT served the interests of world peace. They prevented destabilizing trade wars and currency fluctuations. They raised rates of literacy and life expectancy for millions of people in poor nations. By increasing global flows of goods and finance, they enriched many participating countries and provided them with strong incentives not to upset beneficial economic relations through the use of force. But the Bretton Woods economic order also *created* significant new sources of conflict and war.

The Insecurities of Cold War Liberalism

Economic relations are conducive to peace only if they are secure, balanced, and safe. If one nation can cripple another by severing economic relations suddenly, or if one nation derives more benefits from trade than its partner, or if some people outside a trade transaction are seriously harmed, then these economic relationships can lead to resentments and war. Regrettably, the Bretton Woods economic order has facilitated all of these dysfunctional types of economic relations.

Risky Dependencies

As we saw in the previous chapter, developed nations like the United States have become dangerously dependent on oil from unstable Third World countries, particularly those in the Persian Gulf. Despite assurances from neoclassical economists and the architects of Bretton Woods that two countries always can realize economic "gains from trade," the *political* reality is that Arab sheikdoms can shut down the world's foremost industrial economies by turning off the spigots. As long as the nations of the West remain so vulnerable, they will continue to arm their favorite potentates and stand ready to launch military operations such as Desert Storm whenever their oil supplies are threatened.

Political scientists draw a distinction between interdependence and vulnerability.[5] Interdependence occurs when two trading partners specialize in certain forms of production but cannot hurt each other by cutting off the relationship. Guatemala, for example, sells vegetables to the United States, and the United States sells computers to Guatemala. If the relationship were to end, both countries could easily find other sources of supply. If, however, the United States was the sole supplier of computers in the world, and if the Guatemalan economy was dependent on U.S. computers, Guatemala would be vulnerable to a sudden cutoff.

As more countries in the world produce a wider variety of goods, the ability of any one country—even a powerful one like the United States—to hurt another by cutting off trade is diminishing. Moreover, there are probably only a few types of goods that are so important that a nation would be willing to go to war to secure them. The prospect of the United States launching missiles against countries that refused to sell high-definition color television sets, for example, seems farfetched. One could more easily imagine the inability to secure supplies of food, water, fossil fuels, and medicine causing a nation to resort to violence.

The Bretton Woods institutions pay almost no attention to the issue of vulnerability. The World Bank and the IMF rarely give loans or balance-of-payments assistance that would help recipient countries become self-sufficient in necessities. Indeed, efforts by the World Bank (as well as by the U.S. Agency for International Development) to support heavy industry, roadways, large dams, and export-oriented agriculture have saddled Third World nations with long-term dependencies on First World technology, spare parts, and loans.

Conflict-Ridden Imbalances

Almost every nation complains about the fairness of the current international economic order. Europeans and Japanese express anger over U.S. pressure to accept "voluntary export restrictions," while Americans carp about European Economic Community (EEC) agricultural subsidies and Japan's restrictions on rice imports. Despite public posturing about the virtues of free trade, the Reagan and Bush administrations actually raised barriers to foreign imports. After the stock market crash of October 1987, various U.S. industries criticized the EEC's trading practices (regarding agricultural goods and steel), as well as Japan's (regarding semiconductors), and China's (regarding textiles).[6] By the end of 1987, Washington had erected nontariff trade barriers to protect 35 percent (by value) of the goods produced in the United States, up from 20 percent in 1980.[7]

Many economists fear that the world is breaking up into three regional trade blocs overseen by the EEC, Japan, and the United States.[8] Even though the United States pushed its allies to strengthen GATT in the Uruguay Round, it also hedged its bets by putting negotiations for a North American Free Trade Agreement (NAFTA) on a "fast track." If GATT breaks down, the three blocs could find themselves in trade wars with one another. The American public already considers Tokyo's economic power one of the most significant threats to U.S. national security and fears, as suggested by the title of a 1991 book by George Friedman and Meredith LeBard, *The Coming War with Japan.*

Even if the Uruguay Round collapses, however, developed nations are unlikely to scrap GATT altogether and resort to full-scale protectionism. Trade is too valuable to too many interest groups to imagine democracies withdrawing from the world economy. Despite rhetorical "bashing" on both sides, Japan and the United States remain each other's biggest overseas trading partners, with $140 billion in goods flowing between them in 1991.[9] The high value placed on trade motivated the seven biggest trading partners in the world (Britain, Canada, France, Germany, Italy, Japan, and the United States) to begin meeting in the mid-1980s as the Group of Seven, or G-7.

Far more serious threats to world peace are posed by the imbalances that the Bretton Woods institutions have created between North and South. A growing choir of critics now blames these institutions for perpetuating, even worsening, Third World poverty. The IMF conditioned many of its loans to developing nations on draconian changes in their domestic macroeconomic policies. By the 1980s it was placing conditions on three-quarters of its Third World loans (which totaled a cumulative $464 billion in 1985), typically requiring borrowing governments to slash their welfare spending, wages, credit, and public-sector employment.[10] Although the purpose of these cuts was to lower consumer demand for imports and thereby improve the recipient nations' balance of payments, the consequences for the lives of people were often catastrophic. According to Oxford economist Francis Stewart, countries receiving IMF loans in the 1980s tended to experience declining income, increasing unemployment, stagnating investment, and poorer social services, yet saw no improvement (and sometimes a serious deterioration) in their balance of payments.[11] After a number of African governments cut their food subsidies, there was a rise in malnutrition among children.[12] In Latin American and Caribbean nations, where most debt to First World institutions is held (Latin America's total debt was roughly $420 billion in 1990), the purchasing power of the minimum wage fell by 25 percent in 1983, 8 percent in 1984, 1 percent in 1985, and 11 percent in 1986.[13]

While the IMF insisted that Third World clients dismantle their welfare systems, it seemed less concerned that its loans were often squandered by corrupt officials who purchased needless military hardware, indulged in frivolous shopping sprees, or simply lined their own pockets. Moreover, many of the loaned dollars did not stay in the debtor countries. According to J. P. Morgan & Company, by 1982 some of the richest citizens of Mexico, Brazil, and Argentina had converted their assets into dollars and had deposited some $87 billion of borrowed funds into foreign bank accounts to earn interest.[14]

IMF policies hurt Third World countries in other ways, too. By encouraging countries to cut expenditures, the IMF fostered deflation and reduced demand for Third World products. By encouraging too many countries to specialize in the same exports (typically, primary commodities like coffee and cocoa), IMF and World Bank programs glutted the market with these exports and lowered their global prices, which cut earnings for the exporting countries.[15]

The World Bank worked with the IMF in encouraging austerity measures in the Third World. Its 1988 *World Development Report* fingered deficit spending in developing countries as a principal cause of economic problems and encouraged Third World governments to charge more for public services like health and education.[16] Only recently has the World Bank begun to suggest that these deficits might be reduced by cutting military spending.[17]

In 1984 it was estimated that an increase of 1 percent in U.S. interest rates would add about $3 billion per year to the Third World's debt.[18] When the Reagan administration funded its military buildup and its tax cuts by raising interest rates to attract foreign capital, it placed tremendous new burdens on the Third World. As Sherle Schwenninger and Jerry Sanders of the World Policy Institute noted in early 1987:

> The Third World's resentment of U.S. policy is understandable. The United States first pushed the world economy into deep recession through tight money and high interest rates, then drove up the Third World's debt-servicing burdens and further drove down their commodity prices . . . all of which created an economic dynamic that made Third World growth dependent on U.S. consumption. Now, on top of all of this, America is threatening to close its markets to many developing countries, all the while applying pressure on them to open theirs in order to help reduce the U.S. trade deficit.[19]

Other U.S. macroeconomic policies have had equally deleterious consequences. For Latin American nations dependent on American consumers (in 1984 these countries sold nearly 85 percent of their exports to the United States), the recent surge in U.S. protectionism has meant severe setbacks in economic growth, further cuts in government services, and even political instability.[20] Some Third World analysts estimate that trade barriers imposed by the First World in 1987 cost their countries over $80 billion—twice the level of non-military aid the First World donated that year.[21]

The net result of rising debt payments and falling sales is that the total capital flow *from* the developing countries for the repayment of loans to the industrialized countries has become greater than the capital flow *to* the developing countries. According to the World Bank, the Third World transferred $24 billion more to the First World than it received in new loans in 1986 (the amount rose to $34 billion in 1987, $38 billion in 1988, and $43 billion in 1989).[22] The United Nations Children's Fund (UNICEF) has put these numbers in human terms: Setbacks in Third World development attributable to this capital outflow in 1988 alone caused the otherwise preventable deaths of half a million children under the age of five.[23]

Increasing resentment toward First World banks threatens U.S. corporate interests abroad with nationalization, radicalizes students and political factions, and contributes to Third World political instability. Time and again, cuts in food subsidies have sparked riots—in Egypt in 1977, in Liberia in 1979 (culminating in the ouster of the Tolbert regime), and in Tunisia in 1984.[24] Violent street demonstrations followed Brazil's announcement in 1986 of new austerity measures and an end to price controls. Following Venezuela's decision in February 1989 to double gasoline prices to meet the IMF's austerity program requirements, bloody clashes between police and rioters left 300 dead.[25] Peru's debt burdens resulted in economic and social chaos, which in turn strengthened the hand of drug lords and the Shining Path guerrillas and gave President Alberto Fujimori an excuse in early 1992 to dissolve the legislature, suspend the constitution, and stage a de facto coup d'état. For fragile democracies such as Brazil, Argentina, Paraguay, Peru, and Uruguay, instabilities caused by IMF and World Bank policies may make the difference between democracy and military coups, between peace and civil war—or, from the perspective of the United States, between coexistence and military interventions.

Harmful Effects on Workers, Consumers,
and the Environment

Another problem with the Bretton Woods institutions is that they encouraged economic transactions that hurt outsiders and caused what economists blithely call "externalities." These institutions gave corporations from the First World permission—and, in some cases, subsidies, loans, and promotional support—to do business anywhere in the world, without assuming responsibility for harm they cause to people along the way. The rules of GATT allow companies (but not workers) to move freely across boundaries, prescribe no minimum standards for labor rights or environmental protection, and remove from community governments important freedoms to regulate, invest, or enter contracts as they see fit.[26] More or less unaccountable to any national government, multinational corporations are now moving from country to country in search of the best deals for buying natural resources and labor, and the best markets for selling their wares. To make themselves competitive, governments everywhere are easing environmental standards, removing product safety laws, and lowering wages and benefits. A frenzied competition is at work, "harmonizing" and driving downward standards to protect the environment, consumers, and workers.

This "harmonization" will not be complete for a number of years. So for the time being, First World corporations are locating plants in the Third World to evade First World safety standards. A grim example of the consequences of this trend is provided by the disastrous toxic chemical leak at a Union Carbide plant in Bhopal, India. In retrospect, the Bhopal "accident" was a predictable result of a long history of poor safety procedures. According to the *Multinational Monitor,* between 1978 and 1984 six serious accidents occurred at the Bhopal plant, resulting in dozens of injuries and at least one death.[27] The plant was chronically plagued with faulty equipment, its workers inadequately trained, and its management lax. One of Bhopal's chemical engineers called it "grossly underdesigned" from the beginning.

The Bretton Woods institutions also have made the Third World a waste dump for toxic pollutants from the First World. One indicator of U.S.-Mexican free trade is that hundreds of thousands of gallons of hazardous waste from southern California, for example, have found their way to a field in Tecate, Mexico.[28] Lawrence Summers, while serving as chief economist for the World Bank in 1992, wrote in a confidential memo to his staff, "Just between you and me, shouldn't the World Bank be encouraging more migration of dirty industries to the [less developed countries]?"[29] Noting that "underpopulated countries in Africa are vastly underpolluted," Summers argued, "I think the economic logic behind dumping a load of toxic waste in the lowest wage country is impeccable and we should face up to it." The reaction in the Third World to attitudes like these is understandably one of outrage. According to the Federation of American Scientists, "Press reports in Central and South America about rumored exports have fueled negative images of 'big brother' to the north dumping garbage on them. One official of the United Nations Environment

Program in New York even went so far as to say that 'governments could fall because of this.'"[30]

Rather than attempt to raise living standards of people in Third World countries, the Bretton Woods institutions encourage First World corporations to take full advantage of low wages. In countries like Malaysia, Thailand, the Philippines, Sri Lanka, and India, multinational corporations pay workers who produce clothing, footwear, and electronics an average wage of less than $25 per month.[31] In Somoza's Nicaragua, long supported by the U.S. government, electronic-assembly workers were paid twenty-five cents an hour.[32] Can we really be surprised when Nicaraguan or Filipino peasants turn to radical ideologies or to armed struggle to rid themselves of this kind of oppression?

Even efforts by the Bretton Woods institutions to promote development in the Third World have hurt many of the supposed beneficiaries. Consider the Green Revolution, in which the United States and other First World nations introduced new high-yield crops to the Third World, which required heavy applications of fertilizer, carefully controlled irrigation, and increased mechanization. These techniques, adapted primarily from agricultural successes in the First World, had unexpected harmful effects on social and economic structures in developing countries. The Pakistan Planning Commission estimated that mechanization of farms reduced the need for labor by 50 percent, putting many poor farmers out of work.[33] To make the Green Revolution work, farmers had to evict their tenants, buy out their neighbors, and increase their own land holdings. Those farmers and laborers who were displaced then migrated to cities in search of jobs, finding instead only more impoverished people like themselves living in large shantytowns.[34] To be sure, the Green Revolution produced more food, but it did not reduce hunger. It merely encouraged fewer people to grow more food for export and thrust more people into urban poverty, thus widening the gap between rich and poor.

The technologies of the Green Revolution also created new problems for Third World agriculture. The new single-strain crops had less natural resistance to drought, insects, and disease than the native plants they replaced, and large amounts of pesticides and fertilizers were needed to compensate for these deficiencies. Fertilizer consumption increased so rapidly that it became a major expense for many developing nations, which suggests why First World petrochemical companies manufacturing the fertilizer were such Green

Revolution enthusiasts. Between 1960 and 1967 the proportion of India's total export earnings required just to finance fertilizer imports rose from 2.5 to 20 percent.[35] The Green Revolution relied also on the heavy exploitation of groundwater, causing droughts in some parts of India.[36] A study by the Center for Science and Environment concluded that the number of Indians harmed by drought increased from 18 million in 1960 to 191 million in 1984.[37]

The damage from the Bretton Woods economic order and U.S. policies has caused deep resentment in the Third World and fueled calls for revolutionary change. By not devising economic policies that genuinely improve the well-being of the majority of the world's people who are poor peasants or workers, the United States and other First World countries have set the stage for civil and interstate wars.

Failure to reduce poverty in the Third World, as noted in Chapter 1, is diminishing U.S. national security in other ways as well. Millions of Mexicans, Haitians, and Salvadorans are entering the United States illegally and overwhelming the financially stretched communities in which they settle. Impoverished farmers in Bolivia, Colombia, and Peru are attempting to eke out a better living by growing coca and opium, which winds up killing or addicting thousands of Americans each year. Deforestation in the Amazon, funded in part by the World Bank to open more land for Latin American farmers, is worsening the global greenhouse effect and reducing the number of animal and plant species available for agriculture and medicine.[38]

Security Through Development

The United States should join with other First World nations to promote sustainable development in the Third World. As the Marshall Plan demonstrated, development assistance is more than just charity—it can result in stable democratic economies that can better resist and deter foreign domination and that have fewer reasons to threaten their neighbors. U.S. assistance for Third World development is an investment to prevent dangerous arms races, revolutions, civil wars, and military adventures in the decades ahead. It is also a way to slow South-to-North immigration, to cut narcotics supplies, and to protect the global environment.

If the United States is serious about promoting sustainable development in the Third World, it will have to revamp the international economic system in four ways: forgive Third World debt, create a binding code of conduct for multinational corporations, rethink the rules of global trade, and reorient development assistance.

Debt Relief

A top priority for the United States should be to reduce the debts of developing countries. After riots against Venezuela's IMF-imposed austerity measures left 300 dead in early 1989, Treasury Secretary Nicholas Brady reversed the U.S. long-standing refusal to consider debt reduction and proposed that commercial banks reduce Third World obligations in exchange for shares of Third World businesses and new "exit bonds," essentially smaller loans with fixed interest rates.[39] Backed by promises from the World Bank and the IMF to provide $25 billion over three years to guarantee interest payments, the Brady plan was a small step in the right direction. However, with the Third World's debt still towering at over $1.2 trillion, ambiguous exhortations that commercial banks should voluntarily reduce these loans and take financial losses are not nearly enough.[40]

Sooner or later the U.S. government will need to think seriously about forcing banks to reduce the debts, paying off the debts with funds from the national treasury, or both. In July 1989 the United States set an important precedent when it agreed to cancel $1 billion of official U.S. loans to sub-Saharan Africa.[41] It should now require U.S. banks to lower substantially the debt burden on Third World countries. In 1989 Third World countries owed U.S. banks, at least on paper, about $280 billion.[42] The secondary market value of this debt, though, was only about $97 billion. According to Harvard economist Jeffrey Sachs:

> The stock market values of those commercial banks holding the developing countries' debts are also deeply discounted, in line with the secondary market prices of the debt. For example, the stock market seems to value Citicorp as if each $1 of its claims on Mexico were actually worth about $0.40, i.e., the price of the debt in the secondary market. This fact is very significant. It suggests that if Citicorp were to sell $1 of Mexican debt at the price of $0.40, the stock market value of the bank would remain unchanged, even though the bank would report a $0.60 book loss on the transaction. Thus, the banks can now afford to accept large losses on their portfolios without further reducing the banks' market value.[43]

The U.S. government should require U.S. banks to apply sound accounting practices and "write down" their loans to $97 billion, and it should encourage other lender nations to do likewise. Spread over five to ten years, this action would reduce the Third World debt burden by two-thirds while saddling U.S. banks with a manageable penalty (but also one that is well deserved, given how carelessly they made the loans in the first place).

Debt relief is particularly urgent for fragile democracies like Argentina, Brazil, and Mexico. The leaders of the Latin American Group of Eight argue that their political systems have little chance of surviving and gaining popular legitimacy if their economies continue to plummet under the pressure of steep interest payments.[44] No U.S. security goals are served if these nations revert to military dictatorships and their populations blame U.S. banks, the IMF, and the World Bank for new eras of repression.

Corporate Code of Conduct

One way the United States could help remold the global economy and reduce Third World hostility is to promote stronger international norms and laws to regulate the behavior of multinational corporations. It could begin by tightening domestic laws governing U.S. corporations operating abroad. These firms should be held to the same standards of behavior whether they are doing business inside or outside the United States. The export of materials banned for domestic use, such as DDT, should be prohibited. Excusing ourselves from regulating corporations on the grounds that other countries will gain a competitive advantage is not only morally indefensible but also bound to stoke future Third World anger—and future conflicts.

Ultimately, of course, the effectiveness of domestic laws will depend on whether the United States can convince other major countries to adopt more stringent laws as well, preferably through stronger international treaties. The UN has drafted a model code of conduct for multinational corporations that could serve as the basis for international regulation and perhaps even be made a part of GATT.[45] The code would protect both the environment and consumers, obligate corporations to respect basic standards concerning human rights and worker rights, outlaw corporate bribery, require firms to disclose information about their operations, and ensure that corporations receive fair compensation for nationalization. As Esther Peterson of the International Organization of Consumers Unions argues, "The Code will benefit the public in every country by setting up standards of decency, fair competition, fair market prices and greater honesty in the operation of businesses worldwide."[46]

Fair Trade

The U.S. pursuit of free trade through GATT and NAFTA must give way to a more nuanced approach that emphasizes fairness and self-reliance. Without these adjustments, free trade will result in exploitation, resentment, and conflict.

Most industrialized nations have learned (the hard way) that markets only work if economic freedom is exercised according to reasonable ground rules. Every business in the United States must pay a decent wage, observe labor laws, produce goods that conform to basic safety standards, and adhere to environmental regulations. The nations of the EEC recognized that they could eliminate barriers to trade within their region only by simultaneously enacting a Charter of Fundamental Social Rights.[47] The economic global system overseen by GATT, in contrast, has no ground rules regarding the treatment of workers, consumers, or ecosystems. Until a social charter is inserted into GATT, further deregulation of global trade will be an invitation to abuse.

A GATT social charter could work within the existing legal structure. Any country found paying substandard wages, tolerating child labor abuses, or allowing environmental destruction would be guilty of an "unfair trade practice," which other countries then could penalize by raising tariffs against the offender's exports.

GATT should define floors for national, state, and local regulations, not ceilings. If a global minimum wage is set at $1 per hour, the United States should still be permitted to enact a minimum wage, if it wishes, of $6 per hour, and California should be permitted to make its minimum wage $8 per hour. Some of the proposals on the table during the Uruguay Round, however, would have GATT standards quash national laws concerning public health and safety.[48] U.S. trade representatives have suggested that local health and environmental laws relating to food and agricultural goods be replaced by uniform international regulations. With the aim of harmonizing these laws across the world, the Bush administration proposed delegating the power to promulgate health and environmental standards to an agency in Rome called Codex Alimentarius, or Codex. This agency, largely dominated by executives from chemical and food companies, would have been given the authority to declare what levels of various chemicals in food were safe. Any standards that were more stringent, whether they came from Congress, the states, or cities, would be preempted.

Consider DDT. The U.S. Congress wisely banned food imports containing anything more than very low "background" levels of the pesticide. But if the Bush proposals are accepted, the Codex standard, which allows much higher levels of DDT, would suddenly become U.S. law. According to Anne Lindsay, director of pesticides registration at the U.S. Environmental Protection Agency, about one out of every six pesticide standards set by Codex is weaker than those set by U.S. law.

Advocates of free trade have it completely backward. An unfair trade practice occurs not when a country or city protects its environment, but when a jurisdiction can exploit the environment to manufacture cheap goods and undercut more responsible producers. Goods produced at the expense of workers' safety, public health, or environmental protection are the ones that should be branded as unfair trade practices. Once these kinds of rules of trade are set, corporations no longer will be able to play countries and communities against each other.

The commerce clause in the U.S. Constitution provides a reasonable model for how to balance the benefits of free trade with the democratic virtues of allowing countries and localities to pass their own health, safety, and environmental regulations. Basically, if a U.S. court concludes that a regulatory measure is protecting a local industry, it will strike down the law. However, if the regulation is reasonably serving the public's welfare and equally burdening locally and nationally produced goods, the court will uphold the law. An analogous system could operate within the framework of GATT and empower national courts to scrutinize national, state, and local regulations and to apply these kinds of standards. Regulations that draw no distinction between locally produced and foreign goods would be presumed legitimate.

Sustainable Development

Ultimately, the advancement of the Third World economies depends on long-term investment. Grants and loans from the First World can be helpful, but only if they adhere to the following five guidelines.

Address Poverty. First and foremost, if development assistance programs are meant to eradicate poverty and its attendant conflicts, they should be aimed at helping the world's poor. Current U.S. foreign aid programs, which consist largely of lump-sum transfers of weapons, foodstuffs, or cash, are based not on people's economic needs but on the strategic importance of their government. Among the largest current recipients of U.S. aid are Israel, Egypt, Turkey, Greece, Pakistan, and El Salvador. Until U.S. programs are *designed* to assist the poor, no one should be surprised when they fail to contribute much to development.

Support Basic Needs. Finance, technology, and training should be aimed at helping developing nations become self-sufficient in basics such as food, water, shelter, clothing, and health care. In 1983, six of the top ten recipients of U.S. emergency food aid were net *exporters* of food, and most of the food they were exporting consisted of nonnutritious items like coffee and cocoa, the cash crops they were encouraged to develop under IMF and U.S. Agency for International Development policies.[49] A better alternative would be to help rural farmers grow food and clothing fibers for themselves and their fellow citizens. The United States should be wary of expecting or encouraging the poorest nations to compete on a global commodities market before they can meet their own basic needs.

Promote Self-Reliance. Unlike the Green Revolution, future development assistance programs should not foster increased dependence. Technologies that require exotic training, spare parts, or materials available only in the First World should be avoided. Far better opportunities for investment are available.[50] The United States might support farming methods that depend on locally produced fertilizers, tractors, water pumps, and tools. It might help establish small- and medium-scale industries that produce clothing, bicycles, refrigerators, and other basic consumer goods for domestic consumption. For countries that are already meeting their basic needs and are ready to begin exporting, the United States might provide loans for indigenous factories that can process farm products like coffee and thereby ensure that their exports generated more income for the domestic economy.

Encourage Redistribution of Land, Resources, and Income. Third World nations can begin to pull themselves out of misery only if their consumers have real purchasing power. Increased domestic production depends upon increased domestic demand. After observing the enormous income gap between the wealthy elite and a vast impoverished underclass in most Third World nations, economists Robin Broad and John Cavanagh have suggested that the First World should condition

future loans on "spreading income more evenly," which would require "extensive land reform, progressive taxation policies, and guarantees of worker rights."[51]

Minimize Environmental Impacts. To avoid sowing further resentment in the Third World and to promote environmental security, development assistance should emphasize technologies that do not
damage the environment. The First World must learn the lessons of
recent development projects that have resulted in ecological catastro-
phes. For example, Brazil's Tucurui hydroelectric dam on the Amazon
(which cost over $8 billion and could have been rendered unneces-
sary by much cheaper energy efficiency measures) flooded half a million acres of forest, forced the resettlement of 30,000 people, and,
when Agent Orange was used for defoliation, resulted in the deaths
of forty people.[52] According to Susan George of the Transnational
Institute in Amsterdam, the Grande Carajas iron-ore project in Brazil,
one of the world's largest development schemes, will "cost an estimated $62 billion and entail partial or total deforestation of an
area larger than France and Britain put together."[53] As even the
World Bank is beginning to concede, projects like these that sacrifice
long-term environmental integrity for short-term economic gain are
flimsy bases for development.[54]

Initiatives that meet these criteria will tend to be much smaller,
simpler, and more ordinary than the IMF's and the World Bank's
flashy megaprojects. The United States might support, for example,
cooperatives such as the Women's Working Forum in India, which
has provided job training, loans, and family planning to 82,000 poor
women in southeastern India.[55] Like the Grameen Bank of Ban-
gladesh, the Women's Working Forum typically gives loans under
$100 and has achieved a repayment rate of over 96 percent. U.S. de-
velopment programs might forego building large dams and fertilizer
factories and instead focus on giving peasants small biogas digesters
to transform dung and garbage into methane energy and natural fertilizer.[56] Now used by more than 30 million Chinese, these digesters
require no exotic foreign materials and encourage peasants to stop
dumping untreated sewage and stripping forests for firewood.

The United States also might spread awareness of decentralized
political structures that can better promote economic self-reliance.
For example, it might help towns and villages to consider reorga-
nizing themselves along the same lines as Villa El Salvador, a 300,000-
person self-help community in Peru.[57] The city runs on a highly

decentralized, bottom-up system of management and decision-making, in which more than one hundred 2,500-person residential groups each plan their own small businesses, prepare communal meals for poorer families, and participate in drawing up the community's Popular Integral Development Plan.

Whether the World Bank and IMF ever will be capable of supporting these kinds of development initiatives remains an open question. The historical tendency of these institutions to promote export-driven development instead of self-reliance, to give communities and nongovernmental organizations secondary status, and to ignore distribution issues and environmental impacts is not encouraging. The United States should demand reform of these institutions, and, if change proves to be impossible, it should consider withdrawing support from them and creating new institutions to replace them.

The World Bank and the IMF were created with a vision of development based on the values of the free market.[58] What is now needed is a Green Bank, built on the values of sustainability and equity. This bank might make only small grants and loans to projects that protected the environment and helped the poor. Nations receiving Green Bank assistance would have to live by a different set of conditions; they would have to lower military spending, strengthen democratic institutions, restore ecosystems, redistribute land, and improve the social safety net. The existence of such a fund would strengthen the hand of Third World leaders who were committed to eliminating the underlying causes of war, including poverty, ecological havoc, authoritarianism, and arms buildups.

Conversion Planning

Requiring Third World recipients of grants and loans to demilitarize is just a small part of a larger economic challenge facing the world—namely, how to convert military establishments, armed forces, weapons laboratories, and munitions factories to peacetime uses. Economic revitalization worldwide requires every country, from the lagging superpowers to the debt-ridden countries of the Third World, to reduce levels of military spending and to reinvest the savings in productive nonmilitary enterprises.

With worldwide military expenditures running at nearly a trillion dollars per year, there are powerful vested interests committed to continuing, or to increasing, global military spending. The armed forces of the world provide jobs to approximately 26 million people (with another 40 million serving in reserve units), and millions of others are employed in research, development, testing, deployment, and marketing of weapons systems.[59] Munitions manufacturers are so influential that even dedicated peace crusaders like Sweden's Olof Palme and Czechoslovakia's Václav Havel found themselves becoming reluctant salesmen and apologists for their country's arms exports. As long as so many people find military spending essential to their livelihood, movement toward planetary demilitarization will be difficult, if not impossible.

Thus far, U.S. security planners have given little attention to how to retool weapons industries and how to retrain defense workers at home and abroad. But conversion planning is an essential part of preventing war. Conversion not only minimizes costly economic dislocations but also nullifies pork-barrel arguments to continue military spending. If every soldier, every bomb builder, and every arms merchant knew that he or she would not become unemployed because of military cuts, much of the political opposition to demilitarization would dissipate.

The United States should set up a national fund to facilitate economic conversion and encourage other developed nations to do likewise. In addition, a special international fund might be set up—perhaps as a division of the Green Bank—to help financially strapped Third World countries demobilize their armed forces, restructure their arms industries, and decommission weapons.

Ultimately, controls on arms industries worldwide should be made part of the global code of conduct governing all multinational corporations. It may be utopian to envision an international regime banning sales of conventional weapons, but certainly one *regulating* the arms trade is feasible. Every international weapons transaction should be reported to a UN agency and taxed, perhaps with the collected revenues used to support sustainable development and conversion in Third World countries. A violation of the code, as noted earlier, would be deemed an unfair trade practice, and countries not enforcing the code would have retaliatory tariffs slapped onto their exports. As the world's biggest arms supplier, the United States could play a major role in drafting and securing global support for such a code.[60]

Simultaneous promotion of sustainable development, equity, and demilitarization could be a tremendous boon to U.S. national security and economic well-being. Countries that were able to meet the needs of all their people equitably, without ruining the environment and without becoming arms merchants, would make reliable trading partners interested in preserving world peace. As more nations strove to make their economic activities environmentally sustainable, the dangers facing Americans (and others) from global warming would diminish. Better-paid workers in Latin America, Africa, and Asia would be able to purchase U.S. exports—and employ millions of Americans. Increasingly, U.S. security depends on improving economic security for every person living on the planet, so that those desiring the tangible manifestations of "life, liberty, and the pursuit of happiness" do not seek these blessings through military means.

7
Conflict Resolution

No matter how successfully the sources of conflict are uprooted, some nations inevitably will have needs, desires, or whims that reach beyond their borders and are difficult to reconcile in a peaceful manner. A goal for U.S. security planners must be to resolve these disagreements before nations resort to violence. Conflict resolution, however, has never been a strong point for U.S. foreign policy.

Throughout its relatively short history, the United States has responded to conflicts by retreating to isolationism or by acting unilaterally. According to public opinion analyst William Schneider of the American Enterprise Institute: "Prior to 1948, the noninternationalist public tended to hold sway over foreign policy. . . . Isolationism had a long history in American politics and was associated with both the Left (Progressivism) and the Right (conservatism)."[1] It took two world wars to shake Americans out of their global complacency and into a role of world leadership. But lacking experience in international relations, U.S. leaders became too willing to use military force unilaterally in support of the nation's values. This predilection for "going it alone" waned somewhat after the debacle in Vietnam, but surged again during the Reagan administration. Without consulting other nations, even U.S. allies, President Reagan unilaterally deployed military forces in Lebanon for peacekeeping, in the Persian Gulf to protect Kuwaiti and American oil tankers, in Honduras to intimidate the Sandinistas in Nicaragua, and in Libya to retaliate against Colonel Qaddafi's support of terrorism. As we have described, this unilateralism did not serve U.S. interests very well and fostered anti-Americanism around the globe.

Even though unilateralism cannot work, the proper response to conflict in the world is not a return to isolation. Modern economics, technologies, and politics have made isolation all but impossible. Any nation's decision to build a nuclear-power plant threatens neighboring countries with potential Chernobyl-like disasters and the proliferation of nuclear weapons. Any nation's decision to burn more coal exacerbates global warming and increases the likelihood of massive droughts, widespread starvation, and coastal flooding world-wide. Any nation's decision to adjust its rates of interest, currency exchange, government spending, and tariffs will reverberate through-out the global economy. Any nation's decision to deny human rights to its people sets off large-scale migrations, such as the exodus of the boat people from Vietnam. As more and more domestic decisions carry international consequences, leaders have no choice but to talk, negotiate, and compromise.

Isolationism can do little to protect national security. The United States cannot hope to secure itself militarily or politically unless the conventional and nuclear-weapons arsenals of all other nations are restrained. Its military security now depends on a dozen or so de-cisionmakers in Russia or China and on the leadership of a dozen other nations with nuclear weapons or near-nuclear capabilities. The United States cannot secure itself economically unless it convinces other nations to sell their resources at affordable prices and to open their markets to U.S. products. Nor can it secure itself environmen-tally unless it can persuade other nations to eliminate acid rain, con-serve atmospheric ozone, and slow (and, if possible, arrest) global warming.

Greater global interconnectedness is a mixed blessing, of course. For every nation, it simultaneously opens new opportunities for cooperation and new avenues for coercion and conflict. Worrying about the military dangers posed by a fundamentalist Islamic govern-ment to its south, the Soviet Union decided to "involve itself" in the affairs of Afghanistan—by invading and brutalizing the Afghani people for a decade. Israel "took an interest" in Iraq's becoming a nuclear-weapons power by bombing the Osirak research reactor in 1981. Fearful of being swamped with cheap Japanese semiconduc-tors, automobiles, and stereos, the United States "persuaded" Tokyo to establish "voluntary" export limitations. Distinctions can be drawn between manipulation through protracted warfare on the part of the Soviets, an isolated use of force by the Israelis, and economic arm-twisting by the United States. Yet in each of these cases the tar-gets of coercion—the Afghanis, the Iraqis, the Japanese—resented it and fought back. The imposition of "solutions" by stronger nations inevitably breeds further conflicts.

As weaker nations acquire more powerful weaponry, develop stronger nationalist identities, and establish more resilient economies, they will become less susceptible to *any* coercion. The United States and other powerful nations will have to discard noncooperative modes of diplomacy, not out of altruism or idealism, but in the sober recognition that coercion rarely succeeds and that even in the few instances in which it might work, the resulting resentments create enduring enemies and new conflicts.

The only realistic alternative to coercion is cooperation; nations must harmonize their interests in ways that are mutually beneficial. In this chapter we examine four different ways the United States can cooperate with other nations: closer bilateral ties, stronger norms of international behavior, regional and international regimes, and global institutions like the UN and the World Court. None of these means of cooperation is a panacea. But each has a proven track record in resolving conflicts peacefully. And the national security of the United States would be bolstered if the practitioners of U.S. foreign policy tried each means before employing force—the most unreliable, unpredictable, and immoral means of resolving conflict available.

Bilateral Cooperation

The most obvious and familiar way two nations can resolve a disagreement is through compromise and cooperation. It is so obvious and familiar that sometimes Americans forget what an important role it has played throughout U.S. history. Since the Rush-Bagot Agreement of 1817, for example, the United States has been able to keep its northern border demilitarized and to settle disputes with Canada without violence. Despite some deep disagreements, Americans developed habits of negotiation with Canadians over issues of water use, navigation, fishing, pollution, extradition, electric power, and commerce that made threats, arms races, and wars obsolete.

Sean Lynn-Jones, managing editor of the journal *International Security,* and Stephen Rock, a political scientist at Vassar College, have identified five specific ways "cooperation breeds cooperation" and can strengthen national security:

> First, cooperative ventures—such as contacts, trade, and functional interaction—may provide both sides with more and better information about one another's capabilities and intentions. Such information may enable

them to forego worst-case analyses and to engage in further cooperative efforts that would otherwise have seemed too risky. Second, cooperation may help each side appreciate the legitimacy of the other's interests. This "realistic" empathy may enhance both sides' willingness to compromise. Third, cooperation may cause the states to redefine their own interests. This might occur because of the internalization of a norm of cooperation, which would increase the benefits of one's own cooperation and the costs of defection. Alternatively the experience of cooperation might modify perceptions of the other side. One will be more willing to risk a cooperative strategy if the other seems likely to reciprocate. Fourth, because cooperation reduces tensions, it facilitates the settling of disputes. . . . Finally, cooperation promotes a trusting, friendly atmosphere in which sensitivity to similarities and common interests is increased, while the salience of differences is minimized.[2]

Certainly, Soviet-U.S. cooperation in the 1980s demonstrated all these mechanisms. After the Soviets invaded Afghanistan in late 1979, relations between the superpowers all but collapsed. President Carter embargoed grain sales to the Soviet Union, cutting total U.S. exports there by half. Fewer than one-third as many Americans visited the Soviet Union in 1980 as did in 1979. The Reagan administration was elected in large part because of its anti-Soviet platform and, once in office, it refused to renew the Soviet-American cultural exchange agreement, denied visas to many Soviet visitors, and increased restrictions on the movements and activities of the Soviets it did allow in. But, one by one, cooperative initiatives began to repair these frayed relations. The grain embargo was rescinded and trade slowly increased. Tourism, exchanges, and joint scientific ventures built on one another, and by 1989 they reached an all-time high. Americans' images of the "evil empire" gradually gave way to a more nuanced appreciation of the strengths and weaknesses of Soviet society, and similar changes occurred in Soviet attitudes toward Americans. Better information and more durable personal relationships helped both sides find more areas for cooperation, including space travel to Mars, energy and resource efficiency, environmental restoration, and disease control in the Third World.[3]

All these cooperative ventures brought together high-level Americans and Soviets, who then began to tackle tougher security questions. In January 1988 the U.S. Navy sent two helicopters to help a Soviet naval vessel disarm a mine in the Persian Gulf.[4] An informal working group of Soviets and Americans meeting in Moscow in early

1989 came up with a number of proposals for combatting terrorism, including exchanges of antiterrorism technologies and joint anti-terrorism exercises and simulations.[5] A cooperative study by the USA-Canada Institute of the Soviet Academy of Sciences and the American Committee on U.S.-Soviet Relations formulated working principles for a nonintervention agreement.[6] Even the KGB suggested that its top directors meet with those of the CIA to "(1) promote détente by allowing officers from the two agencies to get to know each other and (2) authorize joint reviews of past clandestine operations in order to avoid misinterpretations of motives in the future."[7]

One specific way U.S. security planners can facilitate bilateral coop-eration with other nations is to totally familiarize themselves with recent writings on improved negotiation methods that encourage diplomats to define national interests broadly and to search crea-tively for accommodation.[8] They also might try to teach these skills to diplomats from adversary countries. In 1989 the Harvard Negotia-tion Project did just that when it held classes for mid-career Soviet negotiators on the finer points of consensus-building.[9]

New teachings about negotiation can point First and Third World nations in a new direction as they consider looming conflicts over global warming. No matter how persuasive First World scientists are in showing the need for Third World nations to reduce their burning of oil, gas, and coal and to protect their rainforests (which absorb car-bon dioxide), Third World leaders will inevitably resist First World in-junctions to limit industrialization and development. Why shouldn't rich nations reduce their own level of economic development, in-stead? The old school of negotiation would have led each side to defend its own behavior and to criticize the behavior of others, with each side's gain being viewed as the other side's loss. The new school of negotiation shows the way that both sides can recognize a *mutual* interest in preventing global warming and encourages them to think creatively about cooperative solutions. Following this method, nego-tiators might decide to embark upon an international program of energy efficiency that would enable both North and South to win at neither's net expense. Indeed, as we saw in Chapter 5, energy effi-ciency simultaneously saves money, prevents conflicts over scarce resources, and ameliorates a wide range of environmental problems.[10]

When bilateral negotiations become intractable, third-party media-tion can help. Just as a marriage counselor can help a couple to sur-mount seemingly irreconcilable differences, third-party mediation can help nations to see areas of common interest and reach agreement. President Carter's Camp David mediation between Prime Minister Menachem Begin of Israel and President Anwar el-Sadat of Egypt was critical in securing a peace accord between these two historical adversaries. In the mid-1980s the leaders of Argentina, Greece, India, Mexico, Sweden, and Tanzania, through the organizing efforts of Parliamentarians for Global Action, tried to bring together Americans and Soviets to resume negotiations on a comprehensive nuclear-test ban. Though a test-ban treaty has not yet been achieved, the six-nation initiative helped convince enough signatories of the Limited Test Ban Treaty to trigger its formal provision for holding a new conference on transforming the limited ban into a comprehensive one.

Bilateral agreements are the simplest, and most appropriate, means to resolve conflicts between two nations. However, a growing number of security issues affect the interests of many, most, or all nations, and these must be dealt with in regional or global agreements. If the United States and Russia were to make deep cuts in their nuclear arsenals, their military security could nevertheless be threatened if nations such as India, Israel, and South Africa continued to acquire nuclear bombs. An agreement by the United States and Western Europe to tighten safeguards on their civilian nuclear-power facilities would not prevent nuclear terrorism if the same safeguards were not in place in reactors in Third World countries. The removal of Manuel Noriega from Panama did little to rid U.S. ghettos of narcotics because drug traffickers in Colombia, Peru, and Bolivia remained in business. An agreement between the United States and Canada to reduce the burning of coal could help eliminate acid rain but would do little to prevent climate change unless Western and Eastern Europe, Russia, China, and other countries also agreed to cut air pollution. Approaching security problems exclusively through bilateral agreements will ultimately prove cumbersome and inadequate.

International Norms

For a growing number of global security problems, nations need to develop universally respected rules of conduct. Just as no complex society can long endure within its own borders without some rules to guide the behavior of all its members, the security of international society requires rules to guide international behavior. Harvard political scientist Stanley Hoffmann has noted, "It is ... in everybody's interest to arrive at a network of global rules—and deep disagreements on the rules do not prevent a very wide recognition of this interest."[11]

To be respected, international rules require general global agreement on certain norms, on what is right and wrong. Without norms, rules tend to be disrespected. U.S. laws based on weak norms, such as alcohol prohibition in the 1920s and the 55-mile-per-hour speed limit in the 1980s, were regularly violated, which brought the laws into contempt. When rules accurately reflect public norms, they tend to be obeyed even in the absence of formal enforcement mechanisms. The development of global norms, therefore, would allow international rules to evolve that are more or less self-enforcing, minimizing the risks of tyranny that would result if every rule had to be enforced by a powerful global police force.

Most of today's international law is really a set of widely observed norms governing the behavior of nations. For example, there are norms concerning how ships on the high seas identify themselves, send distress signals, and deal with pirates. These norms have risen to the status of international law—that is, what nations believe all nations *ought* to do—because nearly all nations have found their observance beneficial.

Norms can be found as readily in what nations say as in what they do. Two hundred years ago, much of the world considered aggressive warfare, slavery, and torture perfectly acceptable. Although instances of these barbaric practices can still be found today, they are becoming less common and no one brags about them. Nearly all leaders now insist that their military adventures are defensive and they disavow slavery and torture. However cynical, these pronouncements matter: They lead citizens to expect their leaders to behave according to their rhetoric, and when leaders transgress these norms, citizens clamor for a change either in national behavior or in national leadership.

One important norm, implicit in the five security principles laid out in the Introduction, is the Golden Rule—do unto other nations as you would have them do unto your nation. The United States should favor comprehensive, preventive, nonprovocative, multilateral, and participatory security policies because it wants to enjoy the benefits of similar policies being adopted by other nations. Whether one regards this as applied Christianity or pragmatic politics, the United States should claim no more territorial sea than it would have others claim, it should abjure all trade barriers it would not want raised against American goods abroad, and it should forswear interventions it would not want practiced on itself. One way of evaluating U.S. policy toward Nicaragua in the early 1980s is to imagine the reaction in the United States had Nicaraguan agents blown up a U.S. oil depot or mined U.S. harbors, as the CIA did in Nicaragua.

The norms for international conduct growing out of the Golden Rule ultimately should stimulate myriad international agreements. There are, of course, numerous other norms that could be especially helpful in facilitating worldwide acceptance of our security proposals. Three examples suggest the range of possibilities.

First, the United States should promote norms that reduce the basic causes of conflict. For example, to address the resource roots of conflict, the United States might promote the norm of conserving exhaustible resources like tropical rainforests and stratospheric ozone. Or it might promote the international norm of cleaning up all major environmental messes, including ocean pollution and orbiting junk in space. It might adhere to the International Astronomical Union's dictum that "no group has the right to change the Earth's environment in any significant way without full international study and agreement."[12]

A second type of valuable norm would view international dialogue as unconditional. Conflicts cannot be resolved unless the concerned parties are willing to discuss them. If nations wish to prevent or to resolve conflicts instead of applying force, they must always be ready to talk. If the United States were to follow this norm, it would begin talks with Vietnam, North Korea, and Cuba to reopen mutually beneficial economic and political relations. Exemplary behavior by the United States might persuade other nations to adhere to this norm, and critical impasses might then be broken in the Middle East or in the Koreas, where neighbors have been reluctant to negotiate for decades.

Third, the United States should promote a norm against unilateral military intervention. When a nation is under siege and its defenses are failing, the first resort should be UN collective security, not the Marines or Kremlin-style "fraternal assistance." This norm would strengthen the universally recognized UN Charter, which outlaws military intervention "against the territorial integrity or political independence of any state." The charter carves out exceptions for "the inherent right of individual or collective self-defense." Unfortunately, defense or collective self-defense has been offered as the basis for almost every military adventure since 1945. Self-defense was the justification for the U.S. attack on Libya in 1986, when it bombed that country in retaliation for Qaddafi's support of terrorists.[13] Collective self-defense was the rationale for the U.S. military involvements in Korea, Vietnam, and Grenada and for the Soviet military interventions in Hungary, Czechoslovakia, and Afghanistan. As long as a nation is its own judge and jury on what constitutes defense or collective self-defense beyond its borders, the norm of military non-intervention will be nearly meaningless. Far simpler and stronger would be a ban on *any* unilateral military operations on another nation's territory. Nations eager to strengthen the security of others could still do so through economic assistance, political cooperation, and defensive-weapons exports. Plus, there would always be the option of UN peacekeeping, which is discussed in Chapter 9.

To promote these norms, U.S. leaders must explicitly endorse them and regularly refer to them in speeches, policy statements, and legal documents. They must ensure that U.S. security policies scrupulously adhere to them, and they must insist that other nations do likewise. Every time the president or the Congress acts with explicit reference to these norms, more people in the United States and other countries will begin thinking about them, debating them, refining them, and ultimately conforming to them.

International Regimes

International norms can set the stage for a fundamental system of international rules, but, ultimately, the rules need to be articulated, refined, codified, interpreted, and enforced. Short of an all-powerful world government, global norms become more like rules through what political scientists call "regimes."[14] According to Stanford political scientist Stephen Krasner, "Regimes can be defined as sets of implicit or explicit principles, norms, rules, and decision-making procedures around which actors' expectations converge in a given area of international relations."[15] Regimes are essentially contracts in which nations bind themselves to behave over a narrow range of issues in mutually beneficial ways. Traditional regimes have ranged from alliances like NATO to treaties like GATT. They have included organizations like the International Monetary Fund and the World Bank. Even tacit understandings, such as informal East-West agreements in areas such as crisis control and nuclear nonproliferation, can be considered regimes.[16]

The key to regimes is that their adherents feel some sense of obligation—but they cannot be forced to obey. Any nation that wishes to quit a regime can do so, although quitting usually means losing the benefits of membership. To withdraw from the IMF or the World Bank would mean losing influence over or access to the flow of capital in the world. To repudiate GATT would mean risking massive tariff increases against one's exports.

Nations are beginning to recognize that today's most significant threats must be met through more and better regimes. Problems like nuclear-weapons proliferation, conventional arms trafficking, terrorism, drug smuggling, AIDS, economic instability, environmental destruction, and population growth must be addressed through well-planned, multilateral action.[17]

Regimes help nations become more secure in four important ways.[18] First, regimes allow nations to share the costs of otherwise unaffordable international enterprises. While few nations, if any, can afford to build on their own the huge proton-storage rings and colliders now necessary to study particle physics, a global science regime could raise the funds. The NATO security regime allowed the United States and the nations of Western Europe to deploy a massive defense system against the possibility of a Soviet invasion, which none of the allies could have deployed alone.

Second, regimes bolster security by facilitating the flow of information between nations, which in turn helps them identify more common ground for cooperation. By helping nations monitor the petroleum stocks of other nations to plan for shortages, the International Energy Agency has reduced panic buying by governments and oil companies that could boost prices.[19] Regimes also encourage information-sharing as negotiators develop more trusting, personal relationships with one another; the real negotiations, it is often said, begin in the bars (or, in the case of the U.S.-Soviet INF accord, in the woods).

Regimes help nations avoid the inadvertent generation of new conflicts by exposing them to the interests of a much larger number of nations. Before GATT, for example, nations often made bilateral trade agreements that created difficulties and resentments with their other trading partners. By approaching trade barriers as a global problem, GATT has enabled participating nations to remove tariffs and other trade barriers from expanding portions of their economies without fear of bilateral reprisals.

Finally, regimes induce nations to begin bending their own behaviors to adhere to international norms. Even as U.S. administrations have changed, the NPT helped motivate Democratic and Republican administrations alike to keep nonproliferation high on the foreign policy agenda.

Regrettably, the Reagan administration's insistence on unilateralism allowed several opportunities for multilateral problem-solving to slip through its fingers. Had the administration signed the Law of the Sea Treaty, instead of rejecting it to shield a small number of mining companies from losses that might result from the treaty's regulations on the extraction of seabed mineral nodules, it could have helped implement a clear and fair set of rules to govern the use of the high seas—rules that included limits on other nations' claims on coastal territory, which the United States had sought since the 1970s.[20] By cutting U.S. financial support for the UN Fund for Population Activities because of its birth control and abortion programs, Reagan weakened efforts to stem global population growth and exacerbated an underlying cause of illegal migration into the United States.[21]

In these cases the immediate costs of U.S. unilateralism were manageable. In the future, however, as more nations acquire nuclear and chemical weapons, develop more competitive economies, and operate more environmentally dangerous technologies, continued U.S. unilateralism could be catastrophic. As Columbia University international law scholar Richard Gardner has argued, "The case for multilateralism will be particularly compelling as we face a new era in which our relative power has declined and we will need to share economic burdens and political responsibility, not just with Europe and Japan, but with emerging power centers in the developing world."[22]

U.S. security now depends on working closely with other nations to strengthen existing regimes and to create new and better ones. Four rules of thumb would be especially useful. First, the United States should open international regimes to more participation. "With increased power over their natural resources and over vast chunks of the neighboring seas," Stanley Hoffmann has argued, "more actors will have to be taken seriously and become involved in the quest for international regimes."[23] Although it is true that insisting on the full participation of nations with little at stake in a given issue—for example, Togo's interest in international space travel—can impede the progress of a regime, most nations have defined security problems too narrowly and have underestimated the global impact of many security threats. An agreement to restrict the emission of chlorofluorocarbons into the atmosphere might best be negotiated by the biggest polluters in the First World, but if a hundred Third World nations were excluded from the negotiations, they might be tempted to ignore the agreement and use chlorofluorocarbons freely for their own economic development. As monumental as the Camp David Accords were in settling antagonisms between Israel and Egypt, the exclusion of the Palestinians caused resentment throughout the Arab world and provoked violence against both parties. The growing interconnectedness of the world means that more and more global problems must be tackled by regimes that are universal or nearly universal.

Second, to become more stable and to be more effective, international regimes will need a higher level of public awareness and participation. Today the people of the world have practically no role in international regimes. The World Bank, IMF, and GATT all fail to provide meaningful entry points for nongovernmental organizations, political parties, or citizen participation. The consequences, predictably, are low public awareness of, interest in, and commitment to these regimes—all of which subvert the effectiveness of regimes.

An example of the need for public participation is provided by the International Convention on the Physical Protection of Nuclear Materials, which was designed to prevent terrorists or other unauthorized groups from obtaining the ingredients for nuclear bombs. Although nearly everyone would agree that nuclear terrorism is undesirable, the terms of the convention extended much further and outlawed nonviolent antinuclear protest. The hermetic process by which the treaty was negotiated enabled those interested only in stifling dissent against nuclear energy to frame the treaty's language so sweepingly that it is now an international crime—on a par with genocide, slavery, or piracy—to plan a peaceful demonstration or any other action that might, however briefly and improbably, delay a shipment of nuclear fuel.[24]

One way to increase public participation in regimes, suggested by the European Parliament, is to create directly elected bodies. The United States might propose, for example, the creation of an elected Democratic Assembly in the UN to parallel the General Assembly, with representatives for every five million people. A less radical approach might be for nations to provide more observer-status seats for local governments and nongovernmental organizations, a reform that is beginning to occur in the International Whaling Commission and some specialized UN agencies. *Los Angeles Times* columnist Ernest Conine once suggested that, to reduce the discontinuities in U.S. policies toward Russia, summits ought to involve both the president and a representative from the party currently out of office.[25]

A third reform the United States should promote is to give regimes enough flexibility to manage day-to-day problems. The entire area of arms control could profit from this kind of reform. Since its inception, arms control has meant protracted negotiations, sometimes lasting five to ten years, followed by long, uncertain ratification periods. By the time these treaties are ratified, they are often out of step with current technology and politics. An alternative to this sluggish process, suggested by Oxford international relations scholar Mitchell Reiss, would be to create an international arms control agency with its own tenured staff, empowered to rein in specific areas of arms competition.[26] Such an institution might be designed so that, once a treaty creating it was approved by the U.S. Senate, separate ratification of certain well-defined areas of regulation would no longer be necessary. This agency could develop an arms control civil service that would add continuity to long-term policy, respond to new weapons systems and geopolitical developments on an ongoing basis, and facilitate more politically palatable step-by-step deals.

Fourth, the United States should increase its financial commitment to regimes and encourage other nations to do likewise. Stanley Hoffmann has observed that nations "should be willing to commit, in advance, certain kinds of resources—money for aid or for stabilizing export earnings, stocks of food products, reserves of important raw materials, and also soldiers and weapons for peace-keeping forces."[27] Today the level of U.S. support for various international organizations outside of NATO is trivial. The average annual contribution of each American to the UN is less than $3 —compared to $1,200 for the Pentagon.[28]

Global Institutions

The recommendations we have made for strengthening international regimes would create dozens of overlapping institutions to manage the world's various security problems. No matter what these treaties and organizations accomplish, however, their multiplicity and complexity would engender confusion, contradictions, and noncompliance unless some centralized institutions emerge to harmonize and enforce their rules. The best institutions the world thus far has created for these tasks are the UN and the World Court, which have always held the promise of becoming, respectively, the principal legislator and the principal adjudicator of international law.

The frequent criticisms hurled at the UN by neoconservatives inside and outside government have obscured some of the important successes of its affiliated organizations. UNICEF has saved the lives of between 750,000 and 1 million children each year through programs promoting oral rehydration, and another 1.5 million children each year through its immunization programs.[29] After a ten-year, $300 million campaign, the World Health Organization (WHO) has virtually eliminated cases of smallpox.[30] By extending tiny loans (often $50 or less), the International Fund for Agricultural Development has helped as many as 180 million rural poor people reach "food security."[31] The United Nations Development Fund for Women (UNIFEM) has supported more than four hundred projects, giving impoverished women labor-saving machinery, providing job training, and setting up women's farming cooperatives.[32] Even the often-ridiculed General Assembly has become an important articulator of global norms; between 1970 and 1986, the General Assembly faced twenty-five key resolutions on war and peace issues, and *every* time it upheld the UN Charter's prohibition on the use of force.[33]

Despite these successes, everyone realizes that the UN has failed to resolve the most pressing threats to international security, including most interstate disputes, civil wars, and resource shortages. Similarly, the World Court's influence, always precarious, has been declining precipitously. Since World War II, international courts and formal arbitrations have been presented with only half as many disputes per year as between the two world wars, and cases now trickle in at a rate of about one a year.[34]

Most political scientists dismiss the UN and the World Court as overly ambitious pipe dreams. While teaching at Harvard, Robert

Keohane and Joseph Nye, Jr., for example, criticized the UN General Assembly as an example of the periodic, unrealistic, grand designs of the United States, which are "more valuable as sounding boards than as decision-making bodies," and which "only rarely are . . . likely to provide the world with instruments for collective action."[35] These criticisms overlook the most fundamental reason the UN and the World Court have failed—not that they are too ambitious, but that they lack enough power to fulfill their ambitions. Because the UN General Assembly was given virtually no power except to pass nonbinding resolutions, it *inevitably* became a debating society. In the areas where the General Assembly has been empowered to act—providing money for cooperative programs like UNICEF, WHO, and the Food and Agriculture Organization (FAO)—it has done rather well. But most of the UN's real enforcement power, whether to declare trade embargoes or to dispatch peacekeeping forces, resides in the Security Council, which has rarely acted because of the veto power held by each of the five permanent members. The declining role of the World Court also reflects its lack of any real enforcement powers.

Even though more than two-thirds of the American public favored giving the UN more power in the 1980s, the Reagan administration systematically attempted to weaken the body, often with the quiescent support of Congress.[36] The administration abandoned the UN Educational, Scientific and Cultural Organization (UNESCO). It threatened to walk out of the FAO and the UN Conference on Trade and Development (UNCTAD). It cast more than one-third of all the U.S. vetoes since 1946. It diluted the UN norm of nonintervention by defending in the Security Council its invasion of Grenada and Israel's invasion of Lebanon, in both instances defying its allies.[37] One of its representatives even said that he would cheerfully wave good-bye from the docks of New York if the organization "sailed off into the sunset."[38]

The Bush administration's treatment of the UN was more ambiguous. While running for president in 1988, George Bush declared: "A President can't subordinate his decision-making to a multilateral body. He can't sacrifice one ounce of our sovereignty to any organization."[39] Yet in 1990 Bush responded to Iraq's invasion of Kuwait by organizing sanctions and a military response through the Security Council. Two years later he also turned to the Security Council for a resolution before sending troops into Somalia. Still, Bush (along with a complacent Congress) allowed the United States to fall behind in its dues by over \$400 million[40] and, in the words of the *New York Times,* to assume "the dishonorable role once played by the Soviet Union: number one U.N. deadbeat."[41] "The withholding of legally owing [sic] payment," Richard Gardner argued, "undermines U.S. leadership, compromises international programs that serve our national interests, and sabotages budgetary and organizational reforms that were set in motion on the promise that we would meet our financial obligations."[42]

The Reagan administration also reversed decades of unwavering U.S. support for the World Court. After the United States received very favorable verdicts concerning the Iranian hostage crisis and a Canadian-U.S. fishing-rights dispute,[43] the administration changed course and withdrew from the Court when Nicaragua successfully challenged the U.S. effort to overthrow the Sandinista government, a change that was deplored by, among others, the 4,500-member American Society of International Law. In April 1988 the United States shunned the World Court again when that body deliberated over the legality of a U.S. statute ordering the Palestine Liberation Organization to close its UN mission in New York.[44]

High on a new U.S. security agenda should be a concerted effort to strengthen the UN and the World Court, an effort that no U.S. administration has seriously undertaken since the inception of these institutions. There are a host of constructive reforms currently being debated at the UN that the United States might promote. By integrating more due process into UN deliberations, the United States could help protect countries like Israel that are often condemned without an adequate hearing. By enlarging the UN's financial base and expanding the power of certain agencies, the United States could help the UN hire more qualified staff and improve the organization's programs to promote human rights, fight terrorism, interdict black-market flows of drugs and plutonium, check the spread of AIDS, restore damaged ecosystems, and promote energy efficiency and sustainable agriculture.

But these reforms represent relatively minor tinkerings. The most significant power to act lies with the secretary general and the Security Council, not the General Assembly. With U.S. support, the secretary general could better employ his (or her) good offices to mediate conflicts. Recent successes, achieved largely without U.S. support, show what a key role the secretary general can play. When the United States considered a negotiated withdrawal of the Soviet Union from

Afghanistan farfetched, Secretary General Javier Pérez de Cuéllar spent seven years shuttling proposals back and forth between Afghan rebels and the Soviets (the two sides never met face to face).[45] His efforts finally succeeded in mid-1988 when the Soviets announced their departure from Afghanistan. The secretary general and his assistant, Jan Eliasson, also served as mediators between Iran and Iraq and helped engineer an end to their bloody, eight-year-long conflict.[46] According to Brian Urquhart, former UN undersecretary general, the Iranian government found it politically easier to avoid admitting defeat and instead to point to UN resolutions and the secretary general's mediation proposals as a way to "explain to its people it was bowing to overwhelming international will."[47] Pérez de Cuéllar's crowning achievement was to complete a peaceful settlement of the decade-long civil war in El Salvador on the day of his retirement in December 1991.

As for the Security Council, the United States and Russia might support a long-standing French proposal to establish an international satellite verification system and create a reliable source of public information about global military deployments. Robert Johansen, director of the Institute for International Peace Studies at the University of Notre Dame, has written:

> A UN monitoring agency could provide objective information to warn of, and hence possibly deter, surprise attacks such as Iraq launched against Iran, to accumulate evidence to confirm or deny alleged border violations between Nicaragua and Honduras, to monitor and implement cease-fires such as the Israeli withdrawal from Sinai in 1982, to assist UN peacekeeping missions and observer patrols, to discourage clandestine tests of missiles or warheads, to hamper covert operations aimed at manipulating political events in small countries, and to reinforce confidence-building measures.[48]

Better information about national deployments of arms and troops would also more clearly identify and deter cheating on arms control agreements and undercut the ability of nations to fabricate "windows of vulnerability" that often are used to justify arms races. UN reconnaissance missions might be permitted to fly through the airspace of all nations at low altitudes, below the clouds, where they could produce higher-resolution pictures than those taken by superpower satellites in outer space.[49] By publicizing this information, the UN could help strip away the secrecy employed by military establishments, which prevents effective oversight by civilian leadership. If the UN agency performed impartially and accurately, its powers gradually could be expanded. Perhaps it could serve as an international intelligence agency, capable of monitoring the spread of ballistic missiles, chemical and biological weapons, and nuclear materials and technology. As Zachary Citron has argued: "The world's top intelligence agencies, such as the CIA, the KGB, and the Mossad, would, whenever they felt like it, plug in information they've gathered. This voluntary sharing of information would turn out to be surprisingly comprehensive; in just about every case, it would be in *some* nation's interest to share relevant information."[50]

The United States also could strengthen its commitment to the World Court and encourage other nations to follow. It could set a good example by reinstating its acceptance of the Court's compulsory jurisdiction, as forty-six other nations have done, thereby agreeing to appear if named as a defendant in a proper lawsuit and to abide by the Court's ultimate verdict.[51] (Most of these nations, however, have some restrictions on their acceptance of compulsory jurisdiction.) Under the old Connally Reservation, the United States accepted the Court's jurisdiction except over matters "essentially within the domestic jurisdiction of the United States of America as determined by the United States of America." In other words, the United States reserved the right to be its own judge and jury. If the United States believes that international law should be taken seriously, it should rescind the Connally Reservation and be willing to go before the Court to defend its actions. At a minimum, it should be prepared to bind itself to the Court's compulsory jurisdiction over the small number of criminal areas on which most nations agree, such as piracy, genocide, terrorism, torture, and drug trafficking. In each of these areas the World Court might set up a system of trial courts and prisons, and it might encourage subscribing nations to extradite their pirates, terrorists, and drug traffickers back to the World Court. Once a workable, reliable system of international criminal justice was established with regard to a small number of issues, the expansion of its jurisdiction to other, tougher areas could proceed.

Reform of the UN and the World Court will not be easy, but in recent years reform has been stalled because of U.S. intransigence. If the United States used its considerable clout to strengthen the secretary general's good offices and to set up a worldwide verification and intelligence apparatus, these reforms could be enacted—and every nation's security would be enhanced.

The End of History?

In his essay on the "end of history," Francis Fukuyama worried that the end of the Cold War would mean the end of the world's most challenging conflicts:[52] "The end of history will be a very sad time. The struggle for recognition, the willingness to risk one's life for a purely abstract goal, the worldwide ideological struggle that called forth daring, courage, imagination and idealism, will be replaced by economic calculation, the endless solving of technical problems, environmental concerns and the satisfaction of sophisticated consumer demands."[53] Yet the mundane, technical nitty-gritty of global problem-solving has always been at the heart of international relations. Americans should be delighted that the ideological fog of the Cold War that kept their leaders from addressing so many conflicts is finally lifting. U.S. security planners finally can set aside the obsolete games of war, coercion, and arms buildups, and commence the more fruitful process of identifying, discussing, and settling key differences.

The United States clearly has many tools for resolving conflict without violence. It can work with other nations bilaterally or multilaterally. Or it can strengthen norms, regimes, and institutions. Far from being a dull enterprise, the peaceful resolution of conflicts will call on Americans' fullest faculties of "daring, courage, imagination and idealism." Security planners can rest assured that as they begin to settle the world's pressing conflicts through persuasion, cooperation, and compromise, history will be just beginning.

Part Three

Military Defense
Against Aggression

8

Nonprovocative Defense

National security planners should emphasize the prevention and resolution of conflicts, but they also must prepare contingency plans for occasions when adversaries resort to force. No country can afford to ignore the possibility of military aggression. Some roots of conflict will remain undetected or be too deep to weed out. Some ongoing conflicts will be beyond the reach of bilateral cooperation, international norms, and global regimes. Some national leaders will be driven by xenophobic dreams of conquest and domination. And some countries will undertake military aggression out of irrationality or by mistake. The alternatives discussed so far can substantially reduce the probability and severity of an attack, but as long as military threats exist, prudent national security planners must prepare to deflect and repulse potential aggressors.

In keeping with our five security principles, however, military planners should change their current habits in two ways. First, military force should be employed truly as a last resort, consistent with the principle of emphasizing conflict prevention and resolution. Second, force should be structured and used *exclusively* in defensive ways, following the principle of nonprovocation. The term we use to describe a strategy of pure defense is *nonprovocative defense* (NPD).

In this chapter we discuss the historical roots of NPD, its advantages, its components, and its critics. We ultimately recommend that NPD become the organizing principle for the military forces of every nation and every alliance.

The European Offensive Arms Race

Most of the work on NPD was done in the 1980s by Europeans who were terrified of the prospect of a Soviet-U.S. nuclear war.[1] When the Reagan administration first came into office, its weapons buildup and nuclear-war-fighting strategy spurred many of Europe's most creative minds to rethink the concept of security. Europeans, East and West, were particularly alarmed that the superpowers were deploying weapons and designing strategies that were intended for aggression— exactly what happened seventy years earlier when an offensive build-up culminated in a disastrous trench war.

The fear felt by Europeans was certainly understandable. In 1987, Jonathan Dean, former head of the U.S. delegation to the NATO– Warsaw Pact force reduction negotiations, called the East-West arms race in Europe "the largest peacetime military concentration in human history." He described it in the following terms:

> [There are] over 10 million men in active-duty military forces, over 200 ground force divisions, 40,000 heavy tanks, 10,000 combat aircraft, and over 2,600 naval vessels in the seas bordering Europe. In addition, about 15,000 nuclear warheads for tactical and intermediate-range delivery system are deployed in Europe, including the western Soviet Union, not to mention the strategic warheads targeted at this same area by both superpowers. This huge force concentration consumes at least two-thirds of the total yearly expenditure for armed forces of all the countries of the globe, now running about $1 trillion annually. It accounts for well over half the military budget of the United States and at least 60 percent of the Soviet military budget.[2]

The offensive arms race in Europe began at the end of World War II, when the Soviet Union occupied much of Eastern Europe, established Communist puppet regimes, and set up and maintained huge conventional forces seemingly poised to expand into Western Europe. The response of the United States was to organize NATO and to implement a policy of extended deterrence, by which the NATO allies declared their intention to use any means to defend against a conventional attack in Europe, including, if necessary, the first use of nuclear weapons. The Soviet Union countered with its own nuclear buildup, setting in motion a regional nuclear-arms race that culminated in the early 1980s with the deployment of Soviet medium-range SS-20s and, in response, U.S. Pershing II and cruise missiles.

It was only when the INF Treaty in 1988 eliminated a whole category of Soviet and U.S. nuclear weapons that the European offensive arms race began to slow down. But even after this important step, much of the regional arms race remained uncontrolled. The British and French nuclear forces were left untouched by the INF Treaty, as were other categories of offensive nuclear weapons, including air-launched and sea-launched cruise missiles, upgraded short-range nuclear weapons (such as multiple-launch rocket systems), new nuclear artillery shells, and strategic nuclear weapons retargeted for Europe.[3]

The INF Treaty also did not address conventional weapons capable of supporting offensive incursions. After World War II, the Soviet Union positioned over a million troops and tens of thousands of tanks along its western frontier, which NATO interpreted as evidence that the Kremlin was planning a quick sweep across West Germany and France. NATO responded by building a conventional force for forward defense, defined by Sam Nunn, the chair of the Senate Armed Services Committee, as "defense as near to the inter-German border as possible, with the aim of conceding minimum West German territory."[4] Forward defense was good politics, since it promised to keep war away from most civilians in the West, but it also carried military liabilities. It meant that NATO soldiers on the front lines would bear the full brunt of any attack and be unable to use Western European territory to their own advantage, which might induce NATO to resort to nuclear weapons more quickly.

To remedy this problem, NATO's military planners in the early 1980s devised a deep-strike strategy called Follow on Forces Attack (FOFA). The idea behind FOFA was that, if the East attacked the West, NATO would strike deep into Warsaw Pact territory and disrupt second-echelon forces. Once these follow-on forces were routed, the Warsaw Pact would be unable to sustain its attack on the front lines. The necessary weapons for FOFA were long-range cruise and ballistic missiles armed with conventional explosives, manned attack aircraft, and target acquisition and kill-assessment sensors.[5] Since FOFA could only succeed if it stopped second-echelon Warsaw Pact forces before they reinforced the front lines, probably a few days after a war began, it had to work quickly. FOFA, therefore, relied on weapons and delivery systems ready to strike with lightning speed. Strategist Edward Luttwak argued, "Technically, the proposed 'deep-attack' systems would exploit Western, and especially American, technological advantages by combining accurate sensors, computer-assisted battle management centers, aircraft attack pods and carrier missiles to finally launch precision-guided sub-missiles at the individual targets."[6] These weapons would be launched at the earliest stages of the battle, which also made them prone to being fired by computer error or accident.

The most dangerous characteristic of FOFA was that a prudent Warsaw Pact commander had to interpret it as an offensive strategy. The same long-range weapons that were supposed to attack second-echelon forces also could be used to initiate an attack against the Soviet Union. Western assurances that NATO's weapons would be used only to repulse Soviet aggression were no more believable in the East than Soviet assurances to NATO that Warsaw Pact tanks and troops were strictly for defensive purposes. From a military perspective, verbal promises do not matter very much—only capabilities do. Because FOFA, like the Soviet war strategy, *could* have been used for aggression, it contributed to the European arms race and military instability.

Warsaw Pact and NATO military planners spent so many years fretting over their vulnerability to surprise attack and planning countervailing strategies that they had little awareness of how their respective strategies caused the other side to increase offensive nuclear and conventional forces. Offensive buildups by one side begot offensive buildups by the other and decreased the security of both. This result should not have been surprising, because historically most efforts to achieve security through threats and counterthreats have failed. Offensive arms races almost always leave both sides more insecure and impoverished—and they often culminate in war.

Political changes in Europe since the fall of the Berlin Wall have led to the dissolution of the Warsaw Pact and deep cuts in NATO's forces. The threat for which NPD was originally designed has dissipated. Nevertheless, NPD proposals remain relevant for Europe and elsewhere. As long as nations and alliances maintain military forces, it will be wise to structure them defensively.

Advantages of NPD

The essential value of NPD is that it can create for two competing countries or coalitions a stable condition of *mutual defensive superiority*. "What a nation or alliance needs for security at the nonnuclear level," according to Cambridge economist Robert Neild and University of Copenhagen science theorist Anders Boserup, "is that the defensive capability of its nonnuclear forces be superior to its potential opponents' nonnuclear offensive capability. Mutual security requires that this condition be satisfied for both sides."[7]

NPD implicitly recognizes the principle in the UN Charter that every nation has the right to protect itself from foreign attack.

Nations adhering to NPD could deploy as many troops and weapons as they felt were necessary to dissuade potential adversaries from attacking. The only restriction is that the overall force structure, strategy, and military training would need to be defensive. NPD seeks to transform a nation's forces so that it has "the capacity to inflict heavy losses on any invading force, but at most only a limited capacity to mount offensive operations in the enemy's territory."[8]

The rationale for NPD is simple. Unless a nation restricts its military forces to unambiguously defensive purposes, it will motivate its adversary to counter them in ways that inevitably weaken the security of both sides. Offensive deployments, or deployments that are equally useful for defense and offense, instill in an adversary the fear that an attack is being contemplated. The adversary then responds by deploying its own fear-inspiring weapons, setting in motion a dangerous arms race.

It is useful to think back to the 1980s and ask how NPD could have defused the offensive arms race in Europe if the revolutionary political changes in the East had never occurred. An understanding of how NPD could have increased the security of Europe when hostilities were high suggests the role NPD can play in defusing volatile conflicts elsewhere in the world.

Suppose, to consider just a simple example, the Warsaw Pact had replaced tanks with precision-guided anti-tank weapons in fixed, heavily fortified positions. Because these anti-tank weapons are incapable of long-range mobile assaults and are useful almost exclusively for defending against attack, their deployment would have reduced Western Europe's fear of a Soviet invasion without motivating NATO to acquire new, counterbalancing offensive weapons. The security of both alliances would have been improved. A Warsaw Pact buildup of tanks, on the other hand, would have provoked a counterdeployment by NATO of more tanks (or cries for more theater nuclear weapons), and the result would have been an intensified offensive arms race.

A more comprehensive transition to NPD would have generated even more relief. Had NATO believed that all Warsaw Pact forces were useful only for defending Eastern Europe from attack and useless for attacking Western Europe, NATO military planners might have begun phasing out their plans for fighting nuclear wars. Likewise, had NATO made all its forces unambiguously defensive, the Soviet Union would have no longer needed to plan preemptive attacks against Western Europe and could have justified withdrawing many of its troops and tanks from Eastern Europe. NPD reduces mutual fears of attack and creates an environment conducive to trust, cooperation, and conflict resolution.

Because the security of Europe would have been best served if both NATO and the Warsaw Pact scrapped their offensive forces and fully deployed NPD *simultaneously*, many NPD promoters, such as the West German Social Democratic Party, wanted to implement it through bilateral negotiations. It is worth noting, however, that NPD can be beneficial even if only one side implements it. Unless NATO harbored a hidden agenda to overrun Eastern Europe and the Soviet Union, it would have lost nothing by shedding its offensive capabilities years ago. Had NATO still feared aggression from the East, it could have compensated by building more defensive capabilities. NATO might have unilaterally replaced its tank and deep-strike aircraft forces with more anti-tank weapons, more short-range aircraft, and more troops (stationed far away from the front lines). This not only would have neutralized NATO's half of the European powder keg but also would have eliminated the excuses for the Warsaw Pact to maintain and expand its half.

Unlike its offensive counterpart, a defensive arms buildup tends to decelerate over time. If the Soviets had dug more tank traps between East and West Germany to impede either side from mounting an attack, NATO would have hardly felt more insecure. Nor would NATO have felt greater insecurity if the Soviets acquired more fixed anti-tank weapons or more fixed anti-aircraft weapons, which could only be used to repulse a NATO attack on Warsaw Pact territory. As economist and defense analyst Dietrich Fischer has observed:

> If we build defensive arms, their main effect is to add to our security, and they reduce the security of an opponent only slightly. He will want to acquire some additional [defenses] to compensate for that loss of security, but he will add a smaller quantity than we did. The chain of mutual reactions will very soon come to a halt when both sides feel sufficiently protected. The surprising result, therefore, is that if the two countries use sufficiently defensive arms to protect themselves, the arms race will eventually stop, even in the absence of any mutual agreement, provided that each side seeks only to maintain its own security.[9]

NPD encourages nations to shape defenses to meet particular threats and eschews mirror-imaging of the other side's weapons deployments, a practice that continually accelerated the arms race in

Europe throughout the Cold War. For example, instead of matching a Soviet fighter squadron with its own fighter squadron, NATO might have increased Western Europe's supply of precision-guided anti-aircraft weapons.

NPD, therefore, provided an opportunity for either NATO or the Warsaw Pact *on its own initiative* to reduce regional tensions and wind down the conventional arms race in Europe long before political changes in the East. Indeed, reduced military tensions in Europe might have brought about these political changes much sooner—and saved hundreds of billions of dollars of military expenditures. The question that loomed over the entire NPD discourse in the 1980s was one of realism. How could both sides really make their forces effective yet manifestly defensive?

Components of NPD

NPD requires more than an announcement of defensive intentions. Clear, unambiguous *actions* are necessary. Forces must be structured so that an *adversary* deems them primarily defensive. Had NATO adopted NPD in the 1980s, it still would have needed to convince the Warsaw Pact that it possessed neither the intention nor the capabilities for aggression.

The historical wisdom about offense and defense is well summarized by Albrecht von Müller, director of the Max Planck Institute's program on security and defense policy, and Andrzej Karkoszka, senior fellow of the Polish Institute for International Affairs: "The attacking force has the advantages of preemption, surprise, and local superiority. To exploit them, it must have a capability for preemptive deep strikes and a high degree of strategic mobility. . . . The defender has the advantage of fighting on well-known and possibly prepared territory."[10] The key to creating a credible NPD, therefore, is to have weapons and a force structure that are incapable of preemptive deep strikes or strategic mobility and that, at the same time, are capable of maximizing the defenders' advantages of fighting on home territory.

Nonprovocative Weapons

The line between defensive and offensive weapons is sometimes blurry, but some classes of weapons are easy to categorize. Anti-tank weapons are more defensive than tanks; short-range fighters are more defensive than long-range bombers; naval destroyers are more defensive than aircraft carriers. Defensive weapons can be distinguished qualitatively from their offensive counterparts by looking at four factors: range, vulnerability to preemption, concentration of value, and dependence on local support.

- ☐ *Short Range.* Unlike offensive weapons, which must travel long distances to attack an adversary's homeland, defensive weapons only need to repel nearby forces. For example, to demonstrate its defensive intentions, Sweden has deliberately not acquired long-range bombers and has kept the fuel tanks of its other military aircraft small to limit their range.[11]
- ☐ *Low Vulnerability.* Any weapon that is vulnerable to sudden attack invites preemption or escalation in a crisis. Invulnerable weapons, in contrast, can be fired at will; there's no need—or temptation—to fire them preemptively or early in a battle. Following this principle, Switzerland hides its fighter planes in bunkers carved out of mountains, so they do not have to take off until a battle actually begins.[12]
- ☐ *Low Concentration of Value.* Weapons of extremely high value, such as large battleships or weapons-support facilities like airfields, invite preemptive attack. The Argentinians discovered this when the British began the fighting in the Falklands/Malvinas War by sinking the large Argentinian battleship *General Belgrano*. Defensive weapons have a relatively low value and can be dispersed over a wide area.
- ☐ *Dependence on Local Support.* Since weapons that require long, vulnerable supply lines are good targets for preemption, defensive weapons should depend on local support. As Dietrich Fischer writes: "If tanks depend on fuel depots in fixed positions, they are limited in their mobility and serve essentially defensive functions. If they are accompanied by fuel trucks or pipelines for long-range advances, they can serve offensive functions."[13]

By these criteria many, if not most, of the weapons in the NATO and Warsaw Pact arsenals in the 1980s were offensive.[14] The bulk of the Warsaw Pact forces were designed for a blitzkrieg-style attack on NATO, a war-fighting strategy in which masses of tanks, backed up by infantry and supported by air forces, suddenly and quickly could pierce NATO's defenses, establish territorial control, and roll onward.[15] To defend against a possible blitzkrieg, NATO amassed forces similar to those of the Warsaw Pact—tanks, mechanized infantry units, attack helicopters, long-range air power, extensive support forces, and a sophisticated command-and-control structure. These highly mobile weapons violated the first and fourth characteristics of nonprovocative weapons because of their long range and mobile supply lines.

Both sides also had highly vulnerable forces that invited attack. NATO's thousands of battlefield nuclear bombs in West Germany were often described as "use 'em or lose 'em," weapons because if they were not fired early in a battle they would be destroyed or overrun. Moreover, both sides had unfortified airfields, supply depots, troop camps, and command centers that provided tempting targets for an early strike.

Finally, rather than dispersing their valued military assets, NATO and the Warsaw Pact concentrated more and more value in fewer and fewer weapons. For example, at the end of World War II the U.S. Navy had close to 7,000 ships; after Reagan's huge defense buildup there were fewer than 600, each representing an enormous concentration of value. A typical aircraft carrier costs over $1 billion to build and another $1 billion or so to equip (with the full panoply of escort ships, the cost per carrier task group is closer to $15 billion). Today's tanks cost more than seven times as much as their World War II predecessors.[16] A B-2 Stealth bomber, the Air Force's newest air weapon, costs over $520 million *per plane*.[17] These valuable weapons, and their foreign analogues, invite preemptive attack.

If NATO had adopted a policy of NPD in the 1980s, it would have gradually eliminated these offensive weapons and armed itself instead with short-range anti-tank and anti-aircraft weapons deployed in dispersed, invulnerable positions. It also would have dispersed its supply depots and command-and-control facilities and increased its reliance on local support. Rather than being concentrated at the Warsaw Pact border, forces would have been spread throughout NATO territory. This brings up the second essential factor in NPD planning—a nonprovocative force configuration.

Nonprovocative Deployment

To be credibly nonprovocative, NPD weapons must be deployed in unambiguously defensive ways. One option for NATO might have been to withdraw some of its forces from the Warsaw Pact border, as Norway did. The Norwegians defended their 200-kilometer border with the Soviet Union by using mountainous terrain to their advantage and emplacing fixed defenses some 150 kilometers away from the border. The deployment pattern complemented Norway's declared policy of minimizing tension in the region.[18] As a result, the Soviet Union had neither reason nor pretext to build up offensive forces on its border with Norway. (An additional benefit was that the Soviet Union also did not have any pretexts for building up offensive forces along the nearby Finnish border.)

To make its navy invulnerable, Sweden decided to conceal many of its ships in granite coastal caverns.[19] Its navy in the early 1980s consisted of twelve submarines, two destroyers, thirty-five fast attack craft, and various minelayers and minesweepers, all dedicated to coastal defense.[20] To emphasize neutrality, the radio frequencies of the Swedish forces were kept incompatible with those of both NATO and Warsaw Pact forces.[21] And the Swedish army, following a philosophy of "defense in depth," was deployed throughout Swedish territory rather than just along its borders.[22]

After Tito broke with Stalin in 1948, Yugoslavia also successfully used defensive deployments to deter a Soviet invasion.[23] Like the Swedes, the Yugoslavians had a small navy capable only of coastal defense, and they stressed defense in depth. Local jurisdictions had their own militias, trained in guerrilla tactics, which supplemented the national army.

Learning from the examples of Norway, Sweden, Switzerland, and Yugoslavia, European security planners envisioned nations or alliances adopting NPD with some of the following features:[24]

Defensive Barriers. To make aggression by enemy ground forces more difficult, a defender should place ditches, walls, mines, boulders, tank obstacles, and even dense forests along vulnerable borders. Some analysts suggested laying a pipeline along a tense border that in times of crisis would be filled with an explosive slurry and blown up, leaving behind a deep trench to trap tanks. Jochen Löser recommended establishing a defense zone with barriers that would channel attacking tank forces toward well-prepared, concentrated anti-tank forces.[25] Norbert Hannig and Albrecht von Müller wanted to create a four-to-five-kilometer corridor along the border, a no-man's-land in which advancing Warsaw Pact forces would face intense firepower.[26]

Techno-Commando Units. Horst Afheldt suggested that NATO deploy

10,000 fighting units, each consisting of twenty to thirty men and armed with short-range artillery, anti-tank weapons, and Stinger-like anti-aircraft missiles.[27] Each unit would be responsible for defending ten to fifteen square kilometers. By becoming intimately familiar with its sector, a unit could use the terrain effectively to achieve a defensive advantage. A decentralized communications network would link the commando units so they could help each other when necessary. Afheldt envisioned units close to the border with East Germany as active duty forces, while those in the rear would consist of reservists who would be called only during a crisis. (The armies of Sweden and Switzerland actually consist of reservists, who make up about 10 percent of their total populations and can be fielded quickly in defensive formations.)

Civilian-Based Defense. The deliberate training of civilians to resist any foreign invasion, a policy called civilian-based defense (CBD), has been practiced for centuries by the Swiss and more recently by the Swedes.[28] Under this strategy, citizens are trained to make their country nonfunctional and ungovernable in the face of an attack. A country with a well-rehearsed CBD would become a clear burden rather than an asset to any occupier. Citizens can be taught, for example, how to resist military occupation (or, for that matter, domestic tyranny) through strikes, boycotts, noncooperation, and obstruction.[29] In Switzerland, CBD consists of well-defined plans to deny any attacker the fruits of warfare by destroying valuable economic assets and key transportation points if the country is invaded. During World War II these plans, backed by the Swiss threat to blow up railway tunnels linking Germany with Italy, apparently helped to dissuade the Nazis from attempting to conquer the country.[30]

Any credible NPD force structure would probably employ all these ideas in multiple layers of defense. Frontal barriers would stop or slow advancing forces. Forces breaking through would next face techno-commando units. Then enemy occupiers would have to cope with civilian-based defense units. At all times, an attacker would face continued resistance from short-range aircraft and artillery, as well as from reinforcements deployed by neighboring countries.

Criticisms of NPD

Few nations have adopted NPD, in part because its theory and practice really only became widely discussed in the 1980s. Some defense analysts have raised important and troubling questions concerning NPD. Perhaps the most frequently voiced concern is that NPD condemns a defending nation to the certainty that the destruction of war will occur on its own territory. Commenting on the applicability of NPD during the Cold War along the border between East and West Germany, Edward Luttwak observed:

> To imagine such a defense in depth for the NATO central front in Germany is ... to indulge in sheer fantasy—and malevolent fantasy at that. For that zone of deep combat happens to correspond to the territory where tens of millions of Germans live. Quite rightly, what the Germans demand is not merely an eventual ability to defeat an aggression at some ultimate point in time and in space, but rather an actual provision of security for themselves, their families, their homes, and their towns.[31]

Luttwak's concern for the German people, however sincere, was disingenuous, for in the 1980s it was hard to conceive of *any* major battle for Europe that would not result in their slaughter. Compared to NATO's declared strategy of raining thousands of tactical nuclear warheads onto advancing Warsaw Pact troops, NPD offered the prospect of dramatically less damage if war ever erupted. This explains why some of NPD's most stalwart proponents were Germans, who were indeed concerned about "security for themselves, their families, their homes, and their towns." Dietrich Fischer also has noted that this kind of argument "misses the whole point. As history has shown, the true choice is rather between a concentration on defense, which helps avoid war, and an offensive posture, which is likely to draw a country into war."[32]

Other critics of NPD have simply *assumed* that defenses would be inadequate against a determined aggressor. Stephen Flanagan, while serving as a senior fellow at the Strategic Concepts Development Center at the National Defense University in Washington, D.C., wrote: "A state that relies on the pure form of deterrence by denial, inherent in the nonprovocative defense concepts, runs the risk of tempting a potential aggressor to wear down its defenses."[33] But why would an attacker's forces necessarily be more robust and durable than the defender's? Could not the defender just as easily wear down an attacker's forces? Once a defender adopts NPD, its goal is to build defenses until it has a very high level of confidence that it can outsmart and outlast any foreseeable offensive. Moreover, NPD does not rely exclusively on "deterrence by denial"; once an attack is under way, defending forces might counterattack on the aggressor's territory. As von Müller and Karkoszka have argued: "To compensate for the attacker's advantages of surprise and local superiority the defender needs some mobility, too—but not on a strategic scale."[34] Even though a defender could not traverse the entire continent of Europe, it still could maneuver over a range of several hundred miles.

Flanagan also criticized NPD concepts as "largely reactive measures to be undertaken after an attack has begun, [which makes] them highly vulnerable to surprise attack."[35] Again, he assumed that a nation that adopts NPD would make inadequate preparations against a surprise attack. In fact, NPD's emphasis on decentralized forces, defense-in-depth, and dispersed command, communication, and control would have been better suited to blunt a surprise attack than NATO's force structure in the 1980s, which concentrated troops and weapons in a small number of border positions.

Flanagan questioned whether "nonprovocative defense concepts [would] deter a state with clearly hostile political objectives[.] For example, would a nonprovocative defense posture [by Iraq] have deterred Iranian attacks [during the Iran-Iraq War]?"[36] Flanagan assumed the answer was no. If Iraq had adopted NPD in the 1970s, though, it certainly would have prevented its attack on Iran in September 1980, the first blow in the decade-long conflict. Once the Iran-Iraq War began, it is hard to evaluate whether an NPD posture *then* could have dissuaded Iran from further aggression against Iraq. Flanagan suggests that the long-brewing antagonisms between the two countries and the religious fanaticism of the Ayatollah Khomeini meant that nothing would have deterred an Iranian counteroffensive. Ultimately, however, even Khomeini had to face military reality. Certainly if Iraq had possessed better defenses, Khomeini would have been *more* eager to pursue nonviolent diplomacy. Of course, if Iraq had limited itself to defenses, its aggression against Kuwait in 1990 and the Persian Gulf War that followed would have been impossible.

The most legitimate criticism of NPD is that much of it remains theoretical. The lessons from countries that have implemented NPD are instructive but of limited use; Switzerland, for example, is protected on all sides by mountains and possesses no critical resources like oil that might attract an aggressor. It is true that most of the NPD proposals for Europe came either from analysts outside the military or from military planners who were no longer on active duty, but this is a problem of engineering details, not of theory. The fundamental principle that defense will reduce the twin dangers of an adversary's building offensive arms and launching a preemptive attack is based upon political, psychological, and historical judgments, not just military ones.

NPD Today

Europe has changed so radically since the political revolutions of 1989 that the NPD proposals may seem like good ideas whose time has passed. Yet the initial euphoria over the downfall of the repressive governments of Eastern Europe has given way to a sobering, even chilling, recognition of the daunting task of political and economic reconstruction that lies ahead. Ideas about how to defend Europe are now adrift. The Warsaw Pact has been formally disbanded and there is an emerging recognition that NATO is obsolete, yet no one is quite sure what institutions should replace them. Much talk has focused on reviving the moribund Western European Union, creating a military arm of the EEC, or giving more substantive powers to the 35-nation Conference on Security and Cooperation in Europe (CSCE). Dozens of proposals for new regional security structures have been floated, each involving different configurations of members and substantive powers.[37] Which of these institutions, if any, will carry the principal responsibilities for defending the continent will depend on each European nation's perception of the military threats it faces. If more conservative Russian leaders come to power, bent on reestablishing military hegemony over Eastern Europe, NATO not only will find a new lease on life but also might adopt the Czech Republic, Slovakia, Hungary, Poland, and other nations as new members. European security planners, however, are more likely to be concerned about the numerous conflicts within and between the new nations of Eastern Europe and the CIS.

Whatever the new strategic architecture of Europe, NPD will be relevant. Every nation of Europe and every alliance within Europe would be wise to phase out offensive forces. The more nations and coalitions that emphasize defense in their military structures, the fewer the pressures for costly arms races or disastrous wars.

As suggested by the Iran-Iraq example, NPD also has relevance outside Europe. Any country facing hostile adversaries can use NPD to increase its security without reducing the security of its adversaries. Under the Camp David Accords, the demilitarization of the Suez, monitored by a multinational peacekeeping force, interposed defensive barriers between Egypt and Israel. Similar defensive zones, coupled with NPD, could put an end to what have been decades of threats and attacks along Israel's borders with Lebanon, Syria, and Jordan.[38] To create a lasting settlement for the Persian Gulf, NPD should become a central objective for the reconstituted defense establishments of Kuwait, Saudi Arabia, and Iraq. In Northeast Asia, where the U.S. military has its second largest commitment of forces, NPD might help reduce forty years of tension between North and South Korea. Wherever the dangers of transborder aggression can be found—between Vietnam and Cambodia, India and Pakistan, Mozambique and South Africa—NPD offers an important framework for preventing future wars.

U.S. security planners should try to convince friends and adversaries alike to adopt NPD, and there is no better way to start than by setting a good example. Besides entering into more agreements with the Russians and the Europeans to scrap remaining offensive weapons and strategies, the United States should export only defensive arms, and even these should only go to countries that explicitly embrace NPD. The United States could lead the world in setting up norms and regimes that would forbid nations from exporting or importing offensive arms. Countries addicted to selling, buying, or building offensive arms should be isolated and stigmatized. Finally, the United States should help to establish a defensive collective security system run by the UN (as described in the next chapter) that would guarantee the defeat of any aggressor in the world.

Fortunately, NPD has gradually moved from the think tanks of Europe into official policy. The completion of the CFE Agreement formalized the elimination of many offensive forces by both NATO and the Soviet Union. Arms control agreements reached by Bush and Gorbachev in late 1991 removed short-range nuclear weapons from Central Europe and weakened each side's ability to launch a preemptive first strike with strategic weapons.

But many more agreements will be necessary for the countries of Europe and the CIS to complete their transition to NPD. Cuts agreed to so far have not covered naval forces or a substantial fraction of air forces. As Randall Forsberg, Rob Leavitt, and Steve Lilly-Weber have observed, "After this first CFE Treaty is implemented, Europe will still be the most heavily armed region of the world, with many more weapons than were deployed at the end of World War II."[39] Future rounds will have to include discussions on regulating uncovered weapons, limiting troop deployments, establishing a system of aerial inspections, and putting further restrictions on military exercises. Ultimately, *all* unambiguously offensive weapons, deployment patterns, and doctrines in the regions will have to be eliminated.

Perhaps the most significant aspect of NPD that has yet to be discussed in Europe is the need for a radical restructuring of all U.S. and Russian forces. Because an NPD plan in Europe must eliminate forces capable of aggression against any European country, long-range forces ultimately must be pruned away. As long as the United States maintains long-range air forces and ocean-going naval forces at bases all over the world, the Russians will be concerned that U.S. carrier-based aircraft in the Mediterranean and North Atlantic and NATO land-based attack aircraft will be able to strike the CIS.[40] The same U.S. F-111s based in England that attacked Libya in 1986 could also attack key military positions near the Russian city of St. Petersburg. Similar insecurities are posed for NATO and the new nations of Eastern Europe by Russian long-range air and naval forces. An integral part of NPD, therefore, must be the gradual elimination of long-range U.S. and CIS offensive forces, including foreign bases and rapid-deployment forces. In addition, all the navies stationed in Europe will have to be restructured so that they have the capability to protect sea lanes but not to intimidate other countries.[41]

Because the same forces capable of mounting offensive actions in Afghanistan or Iraq also can be used for offensive actions against countries in Europe, a stronger global norm against First World intervention in the Third World may be necessary to perfect NPD in Europe. Only as the interests of the First World in Third World intervention shrink might they be willing to renounce offensive aircraft and naval forces. Thus far, Russia has abjured such intervention—but the United States has not. U.S. security planners should follow suit and advance U.S. interests in the Third World through resource efficiency, sustainable development, democratization, and better regional and international institutions. To the extent that the nations in the Third World still want military protection from the First World, they should do so through an improved collective security system at the UN.

9
Collective Security

Nonprovocative defense should be a country's first line of military protection, but relatively weak countries will resist NPD because they lack the financial and technological resources to defend against powerful aggressors. If the combined might of the United States, Britain, France, and two dozen other countries was necessary to dislodge Saddam Hussein from Kuwait, it is hard to imagine how Kuwait could have built an NPD structure capable of withstanding the million-man Iraqi army. To be sure, stronger Kuwaiti defenses might have deterred Iraq from invading in the first place. Nevertheless, small and vulnerable countries will only feel secure if they have an additional layer of defense for protection. The best military option available for such countries is collective security.

Some small countries choose to compensate for their vulnerability by acquiring offensive capabilities. Israel has gone this route. When serious military threats emerge, the Israeli Defense Forces wipe them out through preemptive attack. In 1967, for example, when several Arab states were mobilizing troops near the Israeli border, Israeli jets obliterated the air forces of Egypt, Syria, and Jordan before they got off the ground, and Israeli tanks swept across the Sinai Desert in six days. Israeli divisions invaded Lebanon in 1978, and again in 1982, ostensibly to destroy guerrilla bases of the Palestine Liberation Organization. The Israeli air force bombed the Iraqi Osirak reactor in 1981 to destroy Saddam Hussein's nascent nuclear weapons program. Even before that, the Jewish state had become a semi-superpower by building up an arsenal of an estimated 150 nuclear weapons and an impressive array of missiles capable of reaching the cities of any Arab adversary.

Israel's offensive posture has enabled it to survive in a hostile environment, but it also has increased the insecurity of its neighbors. Indeed, Israel's provocative behavior has accelerated offensive arms races throughout the region and inspired its adversaries to stockpile chemical weapons and to develop nuclear weapons. If every country in the Middle East—including Egypt, Iraq, Iran, Jordan, Kuwait, Libya, Syria, and a half-dozen others—were to follow Israel's example by going nuclear and intermittently attacking one another's arms-production facilities, a cataclysmic nuclear war in the Middle East would be all but inevitable.

Long-term security in the Middle East, as in Europe, depends on finding a way to help vulnerable countries achieve a condition of mutual defensive superiority with their neighbors. Local arms control arrangements can help, but unless every nation in the region agrees to abide by these treaties—a great improbability—small countries will still feel vulnerable and will be tempted to acquire offensive arms, whatever the risks. Vulnerable nations in the Middle East and elsewhere will only lay down offensive arms if another layer of defense is available.

Establishing a protective alliance with more powerful countries is another possibility, but a problematic one. A small country must worry about whether its allies would come to the rescue at the critical moment. Moreover, junior partners in an alliance are often pressured to accept bases, to cope with infringements on national sovereignty, or to support unwise foreign policies of senior partners. Sometimes senior partners may use calls for assistance as an excuse for hegemony. Thus, even though governments of South Vietnam and Afghanistan asked the United States and the Soviet Union, respectively, to intervene for "defensive" purposes, in both cases the superpowers manipulated their junior partners for their own geostrategic designs.

Another problem with traditional alliances is that they encourage senior partners to maintain interventionary forces. If the United States were to enter a formal alliance with Israel, for example, it would need to project force in the Middle East through battleships, long-range aircraft, and intercontinental missiles. These forces, despite any proclaimed defensive intent, would carry offensive capabilities. Whenever the boundaries of one partner are not contiguous with another, an alliance can motivate the partners to maintain highly mobile forces that can be used for offense.

A better means for weaker nations to protect themselves, one that is more consistent with the principle of nonprovocation, would be to set up an international collective security system. This system would be built on one simple principle: A UN military force will stand ready to stop and reverse any interstate aggression.

UN Collective Security

From its inception, the UN Charter envisioned setting up a global military force that could come to the rescue of one nation under siege from another.[1] The countries that emerged victorious from World War II were convinced that long-term world peace required the creation of a powerful army, navy, and air force under UN supervision that could mobilize against future Hitlers. If a nation knew that attacking another nation would trigger UN-sponsored economic sanctions and a UN-commanded military response, it might think twice about its extraterritorial designs. Under the provisions of the UN Charter, all members were obligated to contribute money, weapons, and troops to set up this force.

Unfortunately, collective security became the first victim of the Cold War. The five permanent members of the Security Council could not reach agreement on how to assemble, let alone deploy, contingents of troops from member states.[2] The superpowers, particularly the Soviet Union, were nervous about a global military force that was more powerful than their own armies and that someday might be wielded against their own interests. With the United States and the Soviet Union on opposite sides of most military security questions, Security Council resolutions to activate UN forces were vetoed.

Stalin's fears of U.S. hegemony in the UN were not wholly unfounded, for the first military action taken by the Security Council in 1950 was against a Soviet ally, North Korea, which had just invaded South Korea. When the Soviet Union briefly boycotted the Security Council for not seating mainland China, the United States seized the opportunity and convinced the council to take collective action against North Korea. Realizing that the Soviet Union would soon return to the Security Council and attempt to scuttle the intervention, the United States then convinced the General Assembly to pass the Uniting for Peace Resolution, which transferred authority for peacekeeping to the General Assembly. Just like Desert Storm four decades later, Uniting for Peace was essentially a U.S. operation with a token deployment of troops from other countries.

Uniting for Peace and Desert Storm were both ad hoc arrangements. Despite periodic meetings of the Military Staff Committee of the Security Council, a standing UN military force was never established. (Only today is the secretary general pushing seriously for this.)[3]

Starting in the mid-1950s, however, Secretary General Dag Hammarskjöld attempted to circumvent the superpowers by organizing contingents of national troops under the UN flag to *monitor* hostilities and to stand between combatants. Since then, the Security Council has dispatched UN troops more than a dozen times to oversee cease-fires. These peacekeeping arrangements differed from the original conception of collective security in several ways. Whereas collective security was designed to mobilize UN forces against an aggressor, peacekeeping troops never took sides and only fired weapons in self-defense. Moreover, UN peacekeepers entered a battlefield only after hostilities had abated and both sides had invited the troops to police the cease-fire. Despite these limitations, nearly a thousand UN peacekeeping troops have died in the line of duty.

The record of UN peacekeeping, in Columbia professor Richard Gardner's view, has been stellar:

Without UN peacekeeping, the disengagement agreements in 1973 between Israel and Syria and Israel and Egypt (and therefore the Camp David agreements) would not have been possible, the former Belgian Congo would have been dismembered, and Greece and Turkey might have gone to total war. [Three of the] main UN peacekeeping operations still in existence—in southern Lebanon, on the Golan Heights, in Cyprus—remain the most politically useful means anyone can think of to contain violence in those areas.[4]

Unlike unilateral military deployments, UN peacekeeping operations have consistently provided face-saving ways out for belligerents and have prevented hostile forces from taking advantage of cease-fires or interim settlements.[5] In Cyprus, 50,000 fully armed British soldiers in the early 1960s were unable to keep violence from breaking out between Greeks controlling the southern half of the island and Turks controlling the northern half, but since then several thousand lightly armed UN troops have kept the peace.[6]

If the United States had actively supported UN peacekeeping missions in the 1980s, most of its ill-fated unilateral adventures would have been unnecessary. In Beirut, a UN peacekeeping force would have been far more effective at containing violence than the dispatch of U.S. troops was (the U.S. force, according to a Pentagon report, failed to adhere to its intended neutrality and lost 241 Marines and sailors to a terrorist truck-bomb).[7] In Central America, a UN peacekeeping force along the Honduran-Nicaraguan border, which was formally proposed by Honduras and then squelched by Contra supporters in the United States, could have helped deter attacks from both sides. The Pentagon estimated that a force of 1,300 observers with an annual budget of $40 million would have done the job.[8] (Ultimately, UN forces did play a major role in disarming the Contras and ensuring their safe reentry into Nicaraguan society.) Instead of the U.S. Navy protecting Western and Kuwaiti ships in the Persian Gulf during the late 1980s, a policy that tilted toward Iraq and may have intensified the Iran-Iraq War, a UN escort fleet could have protected the free and safe passage of *all* international shipping.[9] Such a policy could have been the precursor for a permanent UN collective security force in the region that might have obviated the need for U.S. troops in Desert Storm.

Unlike many efforts at collective self-defense in which the "helping" nation starts taking sides and may even occupy the nation being helped (as the Soviet Union did in Afghanistan), UN peacekeeping forces have a history of impartiality and fairness. It is for this reason that nations wishing to stop fighting are increasingly turning to the 44,000 active-duty UN peacekeeping troops for help—so much so that the organization received the 1988 Nobel Peace Prize.[10] In that year, blue-helmeted UN troops began monitoring the departure of Soviet military forces from Afghanistan, the cease-fire between Iran and Iraq, the pullout of 50,000 Cubans from Angola, and the transition of Namibia to independence.[11] All these operations proceeded smoothly, except in Namibia, where the UN force was initially too small to keep South West Africa People's Organization guerrillas separated from South African police units.[12]

More recently, the UN has designed and implemented peacekeeping operations for other conflict-torn regions, such as the former Yugoslavia, Western Sahara, El Salvador, Guatemala, Haiti, Cambodia, Afghanistan, Kashmir, and Mozambique.[13] These operations have provided packages of services that include bringing together opposing sides for mediation, monitoring elections, disarming hostile forces, and policing armistice agreements. For these operations to succeed, the UN estimates that its annual peacekeeping budget needs to be enlarged substantially. But the United States has been reluctant to pay its share, even though it constitutes less than one-half of one percent of the Pentagon's budget.[14]

The United States could boost world peace by meeting its financial obligations and promoting the establishment of a *permanent* UN peacekeeping force. Currently, most peacekeeping troops are recruits from national military forces, whose loyalties are more to their own national governments than to the UN and who can be withdrawn by national leaders on a moment's notice. In 1967, Egypt's announcement that it was removing its troops from UN forces along the Egyptian-Israeli border led to the dissipation of the force and, ultimately, to the Six-Day War.[15] A better model is provided by the UN troops from Denmark, Finland, Norway, and Sweden, who are trained and deployed as an integrated, multinational Scandinavian force.[16] If all UN peacekeeping troops were similarly integrated, no nation could withdraw its personnel on short notice and the peacekeepers would be more loyal to the UN and to international law.

The secretary general might be empowered to send UN peacekeeping forces to any border at any time, not only in reaction to a crisis but also to prevent a crisis, to halt the escalation of hostilities, or to deter intervention by other nations.[17] If the secretary general had deployed several thousand peacekeeping troops along Kuwait's border with Iraq in July 1990 as soon as Iraq's military mobilization became clear, the Persian Gulf War might have been averted. To give the secretary general this kind of flexibility, the five permanent members of the Security Council might forgo, perhaps on an experimental basis, their veto power and instead require only a two-thirds majority vote on proposed peacekeeping actions. Robert Johansen has pointed to numerous conflicts that a UN peacekeeping force, unencumbered by the veto, might have "prevented, shortened, or at least reduced in scale": "Border violations across the Kampuchean-Vietnamese-Chinese borders encouraged full-scale Vietnamese occupation of Kampuchea. The ease with which Iraq was able to prepare a cross-border attack on Iran led to a war. . . . Syrian and Israeli attacks on the PLO in part grew out of the failure of Lebanon to maintain the integrity of its own borders. UN peacekeepers might have also averted the violent Falklands-Malvinas dispute."[18]

Although past UN peacekeeping teams have acted primarily as observers, the UN might try to reorganize them for more assertive military missions against an aggressor, but these should remain purely defensive. For example, if a nation were under siege, it could request assistance from UN peacekeepers, who would be under strict orders to repulse the invaders and to return the borders to the status quo ante. Nations might even be given the option to become UN-protected, gradually replacing their own military apparatus with

UN peacekeeping forces and banking the savings from lower military expenditures. Any nation that sought to attack a UN-protected country would face the prospect of immediate international condemnation and retaliation—a prospect that could provide a compelling deterrent to aggression.

Defensive Collective Security

Following Iraq's attempted takeover of Kuwait in August 1990, global thinking about collective security has assumed a new urgency. The Security Council, no longer hamstrung by the Cold War, responded by passing twelve resolutions against Iraq, the last of which authorized the U.S.-led coalition to evict Iraq by force. However, what was an unprecedented opportunity to activate the UN military apparatus was reduced to a permission slip for unilateral U.S. military action. Despite the presence of small contingents of troops, ships, and planes from other countries, the United States provided nearly all of the troops and weapons and oversaw the command and control of the forces. President Bush declared that Desert Storm marked the beginning of the new world order, but it really showed how a powerful superpower could finesse UN approval for its own military designs— just as the United States had done in 1950 when General Douglas MacArthur led forces flying the UN flag into Korea. Since routing Iraq from Kuwait, the United States has taken no serious steps to create a permanent UN security force.

Nevertheless, the Persian Gulf War was a reminder of the *promise* of collective security. There was nothing about Desert Storm that the UN could not have done with greater legitimacy. The allied forces' smart weapons, bombers, battleships, and troops all could have been put under a UN command. If Saddam Hussein had known that his invasion of Kuwait would face the full wrath of an international military force, he might have been deterred from attacking. The prestige Hussein gained in the Arab world by challenging the U.S.-led "infidels" would have been seriously undercut had he faced blue-helmeted UN troops. For the United States, a UN force supported by equitable dues from 186 nations would have been cheaper than running the whole operation itself and then passing the hat for monetary contributions.

One long-term goal of a UN collective security system is for nations to begin surrendering parts of their military establishments to the

UN. Rather than investing billions of dollars in nuclear and chemical weapons to prevent a future Iraqi attack, Kuwait might invite UN troops to stand along its borders. Once the blue-helmeted troops established a good reputation for protecting borders, larger countries also might subscribe. Just as it is not cost-effective for every household to have its own fire engine as long as the community has a reliable fire department, countries might prefer a cheap, reliable international force over an expensive national defense apparatus. Most countries probably would not disassemble their military forces entirely, nor would they have to. Simply putting some national military functions under international control could save money and augment security. Defense of sea lanes, a perennial goal of most national military establishments, for example, could be assumed by a UN navy.

A UN collective security system would probably work best if it adhered to the principles of NPD as rigorously as nation-states and alliances should. No one wants to risk the possibility of a UN force becoming the world's newest and most powerful aggressor. Shorn of offensive capabilities, a UN collective security force would be limited to protecting subscriber nations from *external* aggression. This force would deploy primarily defensive weapons, configured in defensive positions. It would have some mobility, but not enough to be capable of offensive military actions. And it would renounce weapons with nuclear, chemical, or biological warheads altogether.

Generally, UN forces should resist getting involved in civil wars or purely internal conflicts. The UN cannot retain its impartiality if it is in the business of choosing winners and losers from among competing political parties, military factions, or ethnic or religious groups. To side with existing governments would support many dictators and their human-rights abuses, but to side with rebels would promote insurrections and instability throughout the world. Probably the most UN forces should attempt to do in such circumstances is Hammarskjöld-style peacekeeping, in which they monitor hostilities, stand between combatants, and enforce a cease-fire. Recent operations in El Salvador, Bosnia, and Somalia suggest that UN peacekeeping forces also can help guard shipments of food and aid, deter human-rights violations, mediate between warring parties, and enforce disarmament and demobilization agreements. In the cases of El Salvador and Somalia, UN forces were invited by both sides, and in the case of Bosnia they were invited by one side. A formal request for assistance by at least one side of a civil war, and preferably by two, should be a prerequisite for any UN intervention.

However sensible it might be to create a UN force ready to help any nation facing attack by another, the UN might be wise to make the force available only to nations that "go defensive." This kind of restriction could convince many nations to continue adhering to the NPT, to give up production of chemical and biological weapons, to sign conventional arms control agreements, and to refuse involvement in the offensive weapons business. One could imagine a special department of the UN Security Council producing guidelines about what weapons, force configurations, training exercises, and R&D activities were permissible, and issuing regular reports on which countries were violating the rules. A further part of the arrangement might be to require subscribing nations to open factories, warehouses, laboratories, and ports to UN inspectors, who would ensure that offensive weapons were not being secretly designed, produced, imported, or exported. If offensive weapons were found or inspections resisted, UN protection would be withdrawn, and if the violations were major, the UN might fortify the defenses of neighboring countries.

A collective security system oriented strictly to defense would have approached Saddam Hussein's invasion of Kuwait very differently than Operation Desert Storm did. First, the principal mission of a defensive UN force would have been to prevent aggression, not to reverse it. Using its own satellite monitoring and other intelligence information, as suggested in Chapter 7, the UN would monitor the globe for telltale signs of aggression. Rarely can an attack proceed without some advance signals being observed. Troops and tanks must be moved to the front lines, aircraft must be fueled and loaded, ships must leave ports, provisions must be assembled for resupply, reinforcements must be mobilized. Prior to Iraq's invasion of Kuwait, U.S. intelligence followed Hussein's troop movements southward but explained them away as a bluff. A defensive collective security system would take no such chances. At the first sign of aggression against a subscriber nation, the UN would send troops and additional defensive weapons. Here, Desert Shield, which preceded Desert Storm, provides a better model. Just as the United States quickly positioned troops along Kuwait's southern border and deterred Iraqi aggression against Saudi Arabia, the UN would dispatch its forces whenever an attack against a protected country seemed imminent. As a potential aggressor came to grips with the entire United Nations standing ready to repel the invasion, it would probably be dissuaded from mounting the offensive.

If aggression nevertheless occurred before its troops could prevent it, the next response of the UN would be nonviolent sanctions. Again, Desert Shield is instructive. Before authorizing the use of force, the UN sought to pressure Iraq to leave Kuwait through the imposition of an economic embargo. Many believe that if the United States (as well as the other nations in the UN Security Council) had shown greater patience with the embargo, the whole war would have been unnecessary. After comparing 115 uses of embargoes since World War I and noting Iraq's high dependence on trade (half its economy ran on earnings from oil exports), political scientists Gary Hufbauer and Kim Elliott concluded that the embargo on Iraq had between an 85 and 100 percent chance of working, though it probably would have required another year or two.[19] There are many other kinds of sanctions short of war. Physical assets and bank accounts worldwide can be frozen. Air traffic to and from the aggressor nation can be cut off. Membership in the UN and in other international bodies can be stripped. All nonviolent options should be exhausted before UN forces attempt to dislodge aggressors.

Finally, the military mission of a defensive collective security system would not be to decimate the aggressor, but to restore national boundaries to the status quo ante. Unlike U.S. efforts in Desert Storm to destroy Saddam Hussein's military establishment and to trigger a civil war in the country, a purely defensive operation would have focused on the narrow task of pushing Iraq out of Kuwait. Obviously, whenever UN forces find themselves in the position of trying to recover lost territory, military tactics may demand some offensive maneuvers (hence the need to give forces some mobility). But the tactics that the United States employed against Iraq, including 100,000 bombing sorties to eliminate Iraq's nuclear- and chemical-weapons facilities and to decapitate Saddam Hussein's command-and-control system, went far beyond anything the UN should ever contemplate.

This system could work only if the UN Security Council were reformed in the ways suggested in Chapter 7. As long as five nations possess the power to veto any collective security action, a small nation will not have confidence that the UN will come to its defense at a crucial moment. A better approach would be to insist that proposed collective security actions receive a two-thirds or three-quarters vote in the Security Council. If only half the Security Council members believe that an act of aggression has taken place, it seems prudent to not commit UN forces. A higher standard is called for, but one that is not so high that a single nation could veto the operation for partisan reasons.

Democratizing the UN also is an important requisite for collective security to succeed. The U.S. effort to buy Security Council votes prior to Desert Storm does not inspire confidence that the UN always will make objective, principled decisions concerning the use of force. Strengthening the standards of due process in UN procedures and opening up its deliberations to oversight from citizen groups, churches, and nongovernmental movements would make members more accountable and help fracture and reduce the power of hegemonic nations.

A UN collective security system would create a powerful new deterrent to interstate aggression, one that was entirely consistent with NPD. The question remains, however, how a defensive world can remain secure if a half dozen nations (and soon many more) possess nuclear weapons. How can any country defend itself against a nuclear neighbor? How can a UN collective security force, shorn of offensive weapons, deter a nuclear aggressor? The answer to these questions lies in the elusive goal of disarmament.

10
Control of Nuclear Weapons

Nonprovocative defense and collective security can deter and repel most forms of aggression, but as long as some nations retain weapons of mass destruction these strategies cannot completely succeed. One more puzzle piece is necessary to achieve security without war: Nuclear weapons must be put under strict international control.

Even though nuclear weapons can deter attacks, they are poor candidates for defense because they always can be used offensively. Indeed, they are designed not to defend a nation's homeland but to devastate an adversary's. Even the smallest nuclear bomb can destroy a wide area. Hiroshima was annihilated by a relatively small nuclear blast that released a force equivalent to 14,000 tons of TNT.[1] This single explosion killed more than 100,000 people and permanently traumatized survivors and their offspring both physically and emotionally.[2] The largest chemical-explosive bombs in World War II, by comparison, had yields one-thousandth as large.

Nuclear weapons pose special problems for NPD because a defender can do little to protect its population against atomic or hydrogen bombs. By the time President Ronald Reagan left office, he was forced to concede that his dream of creating an "Astrodome defense" over the United States was technically and financially infeasible. He ultimately heeded the advice given both by the Defense Science Board and the Joint Chiefs of Staff to emphasize a more modest mission for SDI—defending U.S. missile silos and military installations.[3] By 1990, SDI salesmen were reduced to calling for a minimal shield made up of thousands of small rockets orbiting in space. The technology for space-based interceptors has been ridiculed by, among others, former Joint Chiefs of Staff chair David Jones and former Defense Department secretaries Harold Brown and James Schlesinger.[4] Even if the technology were effective, adversaries could turn to unconventional means of delivery such as trucks, boats, or luggage. The inherent limitations of strategic defenses mean that a nation with a strong NPD will nonetheless remain vulnerable to an adversary possessing nuclear bombs.

Nuclear weapons also are incompatible with UN collective security. Collective security can work only if UN forces can overpower an aggressor's forces, but meeting this condition may be impossible if an aggressor is armed with nuclear weapons. A Hitler-like leader possessing nuclear weapons could obliterate UN command structures and metropolitan areas throughout the world.

These arguments do not mean that NPD and collective security are not worth implementing. Both strategies will deter or halt most forms of aggression, most of the time, especially if our other proposals for conflict prevention and resolution are fully used. However, NPD and collective security cannot defend against a determined aggressor with nuclear bombs—no strategy can do that. The terrible truth of the nuclear age is that any nation, faction, general, criminal syndicate, terrorist group, or madman in possession of nuclear bombs has the power to pulverize large areas anywhere on earth. As the materials and technology for making these weapons fall into more hands, every nation's vulnerability to nuclear attack is bound to increase. The only way out of this conundrum is to put *all* nuclear materials and technology under international supervision.

There are three steps the United States should take to reach this goal: deep arms control, denuclearization, and disarmament. With the Cold War over and the Soviet Union gone, the United States already has entered into several significant agreements with Russia to reduce the size of the world's largest nuclear-bomb stockpiles. But it can and should go further. It should shrink remaining nuclear arsenals to the lowest levels possible consistent with minimal deterrence. It should then try to phase out all nuclear activities, both peaceful and military. Finally, it should try to wean every country, including itself, away from nuclear deterrence once and for all.

Deep Arms Control

In Chapter 3 we suggested that the continual buildup and modernization of nuclear arms carries several serious costs. By engaging in a vigorous arms race for more than four decades, the United States and the Soviet Union constructed repressive national security structures,

wasted trillions of dollars on unproductive weapons, and created legacies of deadly nuclear wastes that will linger for hundreds of generations. Moreover, the nuclear-arms race brought the superpowers
perilously close to fighting a nuclear war through terror, error, or
insanity.

The dangers of building nuclear arms are so serious that arms control must remain a central element of U.S. security policy. Whatever
the failures and limitations of arms control agreements in the past,
the United States must try to head off future arms races through
more ambitious measures. The United States should reformulate its
weapons deployments, policies, and negotiations in accordance with
six guidelines: abandon first-strike capabilities, promise never to use
nuclear weapons first, phase out extended deterrence, replace the
strategy of "rough parity" with one of minimal deterrence, halt all
verifiable modernization, and search for substitutes for nuclear deterrence. Each step not only will increase U.S. security but also will make
it easier to reach two essential long-term goals—global denuclearization and disarmament.

Abandon First-Strike Capabilities

U.S. security planners must abandon the technical and strategic illusion that the United States can fight and win limited nuclear
exchanges. In the 1980s nuclear strategists who favored giving U.S.
nuclear forces the capability to knock out some or all Soviet nuclear
forces in a first strike assumed that a nuclear war could be controlled
like a water faucet, turned up or down at will. The entire theory of
"escalation dominance" for fighting a nuclear war rested on the belief that, whatever level of force the Soviets might choose to use, U.S.
commanders could choose a response that was just a little higher—
high enough to persuade the Soviets to halt the conflict, but not so
high as to provoke further Soviet escalation. Once the warheads start
flying, however, it is hard to imagine the conflagration remaining
controlled for very long.

If a U.S. president learned that Soviet missiles had destroyed "only"
several U.S. military bases, or "only" London and Paris, the political
and psychological pressure to retaliate and destroy equivalent Soviet
targets would be enormous. This retaliation could then set in motion
an uncontrollable, rapidly escalating nuclear war. Scientists Spurgeon
Keeny, Jr., and Wolfgang K. H. Panofsky have argued:

The destructive power of nuclear weapons, individually and most certainly in the large numbers discussed for even specialized application, is so great [that] the collateral effects on persons and property would be hard to distinguish from the onset of general nuclear war. But more fundamentally, it does not seem possible, even in the most specialized utilization of nuclear weapons, to envisage any situation where escalation to general nuclear war would probably not occur given the dynamics of the situation and the limits of the control mechanisms that could be made available to manage a limited nuclear war.[5]

Even if the political leadership at the top resolved to keep the war limited, escalation could occur if officers on the battlefield lost communication with their superiors and felt compelled to fire their nuclear weapons. This possibility is particularly worrisome since the electromagnetic pulses emitted by the first bombs would probably cripple, early in a conflict, the command-and-control systems linking leaders with field commanders. Moreover, because each side's primary objective would be to destroy the other's leadership and command-and-control centers, John Steinbruner of the Brookings Institution has concluded that "a nuclear war would be uncontrollable shortly after the first tens of weapons are launched, regardless of what calculations political leaders might make at the time."[6]

As former defense secretary Robert McNamara has concluded: "I do not believe we can avoid serious and unacceptable risks of nuclear war until we recognize—and until we base all of our military plans, defense budgets, weapon deployments, and arms negotiations on the recognition—that *nuclear weapons serve no military purpose whatsoever. They are totally useless—except only to deter one's opponent from using them.*"[7] In other words, nuclear weapons should only be used in a retaliatory second strike; all first-strike capabilities must be eliminated. And to be effective, this principle must be applied in every context, including, as will be discussed, NATO's defense of Western Europe.

To refashion the U.S. nuclear arsenal so that it is *only* capable of a retaliatory second strike, the weapons that compose it would have four basic characteristics:

☐ *Survivability.* A retaliatory arsenal must be capable of surviving a first strike by any nuclear aggressor. This means deploying mobile launchers such as submarines instead of immovable launchers such as land-based silos, which are sitting ducks for a preemptive attack. Small submarines could be particularly effective because they can move freely along the U.S. coasts and perhaps even in U.S. lakes, areas that would not be vulnerable to any foreseeable advances in an adversary's antisubmarine warfare technologies.[8]

□ *Limited Accuracy.* A nuclear bomb is so powerful that a missile carrying it can destroy an entire city, even if it misses its precise target by hundreds of yards or even many miles. The only reason to build highly accurate nuclear-weapons systems is to be able to destroy small, hardened targets such as missile silos, and the only reason to hit missile silos is to be able to launch a first strike (because if an adversary strikes first, its silos will be empty). In other words, high accuracy is useful only for a first strike, not for retaliation.

□ *Single Warhead.* As already discussed, multiple-warhead missiles provide incentives to strike preemptively: Better to launch ten U.S. MIRVed missiles first to knock out a hundred Russian MIRVed missiles than to let the Russians use those hundred MIRVed missiles to knock out a thousand U.S. missiles. Replacement of multiple-warhead missiles with single-warhead designs would eliminate these perverse incentives to start a nuclear war.

□ *Slow Delivery Time.* The faster a missile can hit a target, the more military commanders worry about a surprise attack. An important feature of a second-strike weapon, therefore, is that its delivery time should be relatively long. The difference between "slower" delivery times of twenty to thirty minutes and "faster" delivery times of six to eight minutes may seem trivial, but to military commanders those extra minutes may be critical for avoiding catastrophic mistakes. Soviet security planners, for example, were greatly relieved when the INF Treaty eliminated Pershing II missiles, which were capable of traveling from launchers in Western Europe to Soviet silos in less time than it takes to smoke a cigarette.

As long as the United States has an adequate second-strike capability, it sacrifices no security by eliminating first-strike weapons. Second-strike weapons deter; first-strike weapons provoke. Nevertheless, because the world would be safer if the two countries with the largest nuclear-weapons stockpiles got rid of their first-strike capabilities simultaneously, U.S. security planners should engage Russia (and, if necessary, the Ukraine) in vigorous proposals—far beyond the

START agreements—to eliminate bilaterally the 90 percent or more of both arsenals that are unnecessary for simple deterrence. Alternatively, the United States might make unilateral gestures and promise to go farther, pending Russian reciprocity. The flurry of proposals from George Bush and Mikhail Gorbachev in the autumn of 1991 demonstrated how gestures and countergestures can set in motion a security-strengthening arms race in reverse.[9]

Adopt a Policy of No First Use

The most significant step toward abandoning a first-strike posture would be for the United States to declare its refusal to use nuclear bombs first in any circumstance and to back up this declaration with weapons and deployment patterns that could only facilitate a second strike. During the Cold War, the United States threatened to respond with nuclear bombs to a Soviet assault on Western Europe, even if that meant it would be the first side to use them. This policy was challenged in the early 1980s by four of the most prominent arms controllers in the United States—McGeorge Bundy, George F. Kennan, Robert S. McNamara, and Gerard Smith. In an influential article in the journal *Foreign Affairs,* the so-called Gang of Four expressed "the gravest doubt about the wisdom of a policy which asserts the effectiveness of any first use of nuclear weapons by either side."[10] They suggested that the United States should continue to protect Europe through NATO, but exclusively with conventional weapons, unless the Soviet Union used nuclear bombs first.

Questions about the wisdom of the first-use posture, as well as the political revolutions in Eastern Europe, finally led NATO in early 1990 to repackage the doctrine and to make nuclear weapons a "last resort." But as Senator Joe Biden of Delaware noted, this was "a rhetorical shift, not a policy shift."[11]

The first-use doctrine never made much sense, even when the huge concentrations of Warsaw Pact forces were deployed along the border between East and West Germany. It was based on the farfetched notion that the United States could fight and win a "limited nuclear war" in Europe, and thereby courted the very disaster it was designed to deter. Daniel Charles of the Federation of American Scientists argued that during a crisis NATO's preparations to use nuclear weapons—an integral part of its first-use policy—could "inevitably stimulate measures on the part of the Warsaw Pact, and vice versa.

Through action and reaction, an operational momentum leading toward nuclear use could be created . . . [and] NATO's leaders may be unable, in the short time available to them, to create political and even military alternatives to nuclear use."[12]

Today the dangers of any country or combination of countries in Eastern Europe or the former Soviet Union mounting an attack on Western Europe have become practically nonexistent. Far more likely is a war *between* two or more nations in the East, which continuation of the NATO first-use policy, even as a last resort, can do nothing to deter. A better approach would be for the United States and NATO to reassure the countries of the East that a conventional conflict in Europe would *not* escalate to nuclear war.

Phase Out Extended Deterrence

Even if the United States abandons first use in Europe, the question remains whether it should consider supporting its NATO allies with nuclear bombs if Europe is struck by nuclear weapons first. In the late 1980s several arms controllers argued that the United States could remove tactical nuclear bombs from Europe and still maintain a posture of extended deterrence, because U.S. strategic missiles stationed in submarines or in silos in South Dakota could do the job.[13]

Like the doctrine of first use, however, extended deterrence was built on a hard-to-believe assumption. Would U.S. leaders really risk destroying their own country to save Europe? Even a "limited nuclear war" in Europe seemed destined to escalate into a full-scale nuclear war between the superpowers, and almost everyone knew that SDI would not protect the U.S. homeland against retaliation. The fact remains that whether the United States "promised" to defend Europe by using nuclear weapons first or second, the promise was, and is, delusionary.

It is also obsolete. Europe no longer faces a potential aggressor armed with nuclear bombs. The era of the Russian bear threatening the security of Germany, France, and Britain is over. One can still concoct, as the Pentagon regularly does, farfetched scenarios of the Russian military staging a coup, renouncing arms control commitments, rebuilding conventional forces, and trying to regain a foothold in Europe. Or a new Caesar could assume the helm in Romania or the Ukraine, acquire nuclear bombs, and conduct a campaign of conquest across Europe. Surely these developments would not occur overnight—the United States (as well as the UN Security Council) would have ample time to devise an appropriate response. So would nuclear-armed British and French forces.

Instead of maintaining a posture of extended deterrence, the United States should help its European allies develop nonprovocative conventional defenses. It also should strengthen the capabilities of UN collective security forces.

Replace Rough Parity with Minimal Deterrence

The traditional view of U.S. strategic planners is that the United States should maintain "rough parity" with its most formidable adversary. During the Cold War this meant matching Soviet deployments both numerically and qualitatively—bomb for bomb, missile for missile. Because each side, as a matter of prudence, underrated its own weapons and overrated its adversary's, the logic of rough parity continuously spurred the competitors to find and fill gaps, thereby perpetually fueling an arms race.

An alternative to rough parity is "minimal deterrence," in which the United States would retain the fewest number of weapons necessary to deliver a devastating second strike against any adversary. While advocates of rough parity argue that the United States should match 3,000 Russian missiles with 3,000 missiles of its own, advocates of minimal deterrence might argue that a hundred missiles would be plenty, provided they were invulnerable to a Russian first strike.

No one can say with certainty what size arsenal would constitute an adequate minimal deterrent for the United States, but clearly it would be much smaller than today's stockpile. Today the United States faces only three potential adversaries with large nuclear stockpiles—Russia, the Ukraine, and China—and none of them poses the kind of threat the Soviet Union did in the 1980s. Prior to the dissolution of the Soviet Union, the United States had 20,000 warheads, the Soviet Union had 29,000, and China had 600.[14] Under START I, START II, and other recent initiatives, the Ukraine will hand over all its nuclear weapons to Russia, and the U.S. and Russian arsenals will be reduced to about 5,500 warheads each.[15] Strategic planners on both sides believe they can go farther. Former president Jimmy Carter has suggested that the United States and Russia restrict themselves to small arsenals in well-hidden submarines and well-fortified missile silos.[16] Robert McNamara now believes that the two adversaries could maintain sufficient deterrents with 500 warheads each.[17]

Minimal deterrence is not without risks. All of the potential problems, however, merely underscore the importance of implementing minimal deterrence with other well-crafted arms control measures:

☐ Critics contend that because large stockpiles of nuclear weapons can thwart an opponent's first-strike plans, deep cuts on one or both sides, unaccompanied by the elimination of first-strike weapons, may increase the temptation of either superpower to launch a knockout first blow. This concern can be addressed with concomitant commitments to eliminate offensive nuclear weapons. If nations agree to phase out missiles that have great vulnerability, high accuracy, multiple warheads, and short delivery times, they can cut deeply their strategic arsenals without incurring any increased risk of a devastating surprise attack.

☐ Michael D. Intriligator, director of the Center for International and Strategic Affairs at the University of California at Los Angeles, has argued that large arsenals "provide a type of insurance against technological breakthroughs that could make a first strike [against the United States] possible."[18] This danger can be eliminated, however, by following another principle for better arms control, as described below—that modernization should be proscribed by treaty if reliable verification is possible. By agreeing to bans on the testing of warheads and missiles, the United States and Russia can substantially slow their technical development programs. Getting other nations to adhere to these bans, of course, can further strengthen the dam against breakout.

☐ Some analysts contend that strategic defenses become more realistic if only hundreds of missiles need to be intercepted (instead of thousands). If the side deploying Star Wars weapons decides to attack and then protect itself against retaliation, minimal deterrence can help it successfully execute a first strike. This problem can be eliminated, though, by strengthening the ABM Treaty's prohibition against antimissile defenses and banning *all* weaponry in space, both conventional and nuclear.

☐ Another concern is that deep cuts might make security guarantees to other nations less credible and might encourage them to build up their nuclear, chemical, and biological weapons. Here, it is worth recalling that many leading politicians and thinkers in countries allied with the United States believe that the gradual elimination of superpower nuclear bombs from their soil, particularly those earmarked for first use, would *increase* their national security. In countries such as Britain, Canada, the Netherlands, New Zealand, and Germany, many millions of people believe they would be more secure without the U.S. nuclear guarantee. Nevertheless, if deep cuts in the U.S. arsenal leave the allies feeling less secure, the United States can shore up their security through a variety of nonprovocative, nonnuclear measures.

□ Even if minimal deterrence does not *cause* other nations to build up their arms, it nevertheless may weaken the United States vis-à-vis nations, such as Libya, that choose to go nuclear. But if an adversary like Muammar Qaddafi acquires nuclear weapons, minimal deterrence allows the United States to deploy additional nuclear weapons to ensure its ability to retaliate against the new threat. Minimal deterrence cannot eliminate the vulnerability of the United States to nuclear attack—*no strategy can do that*. However, it can guarantee that a nuclear attacker would be destroyed, which is all rough parity can guarantee anyway, and at the same time it can help free the United States from a costly, dangerous arms race.

□ A final concern about minimal deterrence is the danger of cheating. How can U.S. security planners really be sure that Russia had eliminated, say, 90 percent of its stockpiles? Besides the usual "national technical means," which include ultra-sensitive satellite photography capable of discerning a football from 500 miles in space,[19] other arms control measures can help. A cutoff of plutonium production, which would be relatively easy to verify because heat-detecting satellites can monitor large-scale plutonium-production reactors, would put a ceiling on each nuclear nation's arsenal of fission bombs. Another verifiable step would be a cutoff in the production of tritium, which would allow the decay of fusion and fusion-boosted fission bombs at a rate of about 6 percent per year—or a reduction of 50 percent within a decade.[20] Like plutonium, tritium is produced in nuclear reactors that typically produce enough heat to be detected by satellite. Verification of these measures, of course, can be improved through on-site inspection.

The United States should begin pressing all nuclear-armed nations to embrace minimal deterrence, verified by teams of international inspectors. If it simultaneously seeks other arms control measures, it can have all the benefits of smaller arsenals while limiting the risks. If minimal deterrence were in place, nuclear-armed states would continue to be deterred from attacking one another, only they would have fewer bombs and less provocative arsenals. The risks of accidental nuclear war or of nuclear weapons being stolen or sabotaged would be greatly diminished. Meanwhile, nuclear nations would be better able to tolerate asymmetries between their arsenals. No longer compelled to match each other's weapons development, they would stop practicing the kind of mirror-imaging that has been one of the principal stimulants of the arms race.

Halt All Verifiable Modernization

Another goal for arms control is to undertake any halt to weapons modernization that can be reliably verified. The history of the Soviet-U.S. arms race is replete with new developments that promised greater security, yet were matched by the other side and opened new areas for dangerous and costly competition. Every generation of arms controllers bemoans the opportunities it missed because of its misguided drive to modernize. Negotiators of the LTBT of 1963 regret that they failed to achieve a comprehensive ban on nuclear testing. Negotiators of the SALT agreements lament that they failed to eliminate multiple-warhead missiles. Must today's negotiators regret, a decade from now, that they missed ripe opportunities for controlling modernization?

Among the most promising opportunities currently available for halting modernization are:

- a comprehensive ban on warhead testing, which would reduce confidence that a new weapon design would work as planned;[21]
- a comprehensive ban on missile launch testing, which would reduce confidence that a new missile design would accurately and reliably hit its target;[22] and
- a ban on all weapons and weapons components in space (including anti-satellite weapons), which would prevent nuclear-armed nations from starting a new, costly arms race.[23]

All these measures, which should be signed by all countries, could be easily verified through seismic monitoring, satellite and jet photography, and a modest level of on-site inspection.[24] Russia has already shown interest in each of these measures. Moreover, as demonstrated with the INF Treaty and the CFE Agreement, Russia is willing to allow an unprecedented level of on-site inspection. What is still lacking in the effort to halt modernization is sufficient political will on the part of the United States.

Search for Substitutes for Nuclear Deterrence

Arms control, wisely practiced, can prevent destructive arms races, but it still has a fundamental problem—it is based on perfecting nuclear deterrence. In the early 1980s, after being convinced of the deadliness of nuclear war, many Americans bristled at security experts' admonishments that they learn to "live with" nuclear deterrence by entrusting humanity's fate to imperfect leaders and computers.[25] Some began supporting measures for serious disarmament. Others latched on to the one vision of a nonnuclear future that was being officially promoted—SDI. Arms controllers appear to believe that better education can sell the public on a modest level of nuclear deterrence, not realizing that the problem lies in the genocidal threats embodied in nuclear deterrence itself.

People resist nuclear deterrence because it is morally abhorrent. Under classical just-war theory, wars must be fought with means of violence proportional to the ends sought, and belligerents must scrupulously avoid acts of violence against noncombatants. Yet, in the case of nuclear bombs, observation of these rules is impossible. What ends could possibly be worth the end of civilization? How can noncombatants be protected when even a limited use of nuclear bombs could destroy an entire society? As political philosopher Michael Walzer has written, "Nuclear weapons explode the theory of just war. . . . Nuclear war is and will remain morally unacceptable, and there is no case for its rehabilitation. Because it is unacceptable, we must seek out ways to prevent it, and because deterrence is a bad way, we must seek out others."[26]

In 1983 the Catholic bishops of the United States formally adopted this position in a pastoral letter to their constituents, urging the world's people to make a "moral about-face": "The whole world must summon the moral courage and technical means to say no to nuclear conflict; no to weapons of mass destruction; no to an arms race which robs the poor and the vulnerable; and no to the moral danger of the nuclear age which places before humankind indefensible choices of constant terror or surrender. Peacemaking is not an optional commitment."[27]

There is also a practical reason the public cannot put its trust in deterrence—no one expects it to last forever. True, if arms control achieves unprecedented success, it might eliminate many of today's most dangerous instabilities. But then what? University of Colorado economist Kenneth Boulding has argued: "At the moment nuclear war looks rather like a hundred-year flood; that is, its annual probability is probably not more than 1 percent. However, the probability of a hundred-year flood happening sometime within any given hundred years is about 63 percent, and its occurrence sometime within a thousand years is 99.995 percent: it becomes a virtual certainty."[28]

Nuclear genocide cannot be rehabilitated—morally, politically, or strategically. Instead of trying to find additional clever intellectual justifications for living with nuclear weapons, U.S. security planners should lead the American people in a creative dialogue on how we can live without them.

Denuclearization

One reason deterrence cannot stave off nuclear war indefinitely is that as long as some nations have nuclear weapons, incentives will be high for others to acquire them. Nuclear bombs pose a classic "tragedy of the commons," where the rational behavior of each actor undermines the social good for everyone. Because nuclear weapons can deter aggression, every rational nation will find some value in having them; but once every nation goes nuclear, the rising risks of nuclear war will imperil the security of the world. In the 1968 Non-Proliferation Treaty both nuclear and nonnuclear nations acknowledged that global security would be boosted by ridding the world of nuclear weapons. Nonnuclear nations agreed to forswear nuclear weapons, in exchange for a promise by nuclear nations, expressed in Article VI, "to pursue negotiations in good faith on effective measures relating to cessation of the nuclear arms race at an early date and to nuclear disarmament, and on a treaty on general and complete disarmament under strict and effective international control."

As the nuclear-arms race between the superpowers winds down, renewed attention has been brought to the problem of nuclear proliferation. Unfortunately, the materials and technology needed to build atomic bombs have become so accessible that the only way to prevent the dam of nonproliferation from bursting is to create an international system of control over both civilian and military uses of nuclear energy.

The Ease of Building Nuclear Bombs

The NPT restrained most nations from overtly going nuclear, but it also legitimated proliferation by promoting the development of "peaceful" nuclear-power plants and creating the unrealistic expectation that voluntary "safeguards" could prevent nuclear materials and technology from being diverted into bomb programs. Existing or contemplated safeguards or treaty arrangements, however, including those provided by the International Atomic Energy Agency (IAEA), do not appear capable of preventing the misuse of fissionable material.[29] Technology and materials spread by the NPT's promotion of "peaceful" nuclear-power plants have given virtually every recipient nation the option of going nuclear—in some cases, within days.[30]

Nations have at least three low-cost ways to produce fissionable materials for nuclear weapons. First, a nuclear-bomb builder can make bomb-grade plutonium by obtaining a large supply of uranium, putting the uranium into a crude reactor, and extracting plutonium from the reactor's spent fuel. None of these tasks is particularly difficult. Most nations can obtain uranium through international commerce with few questions asked.[31] Hundreds of tons are sold each year for quite innocent activities like ceramics production.[32] Moreover, uranium is widely distributed in the earth's crust; almost every nation that has looked for it has found enough uranium to support a modest weapons program.[33] Building a small reactor is not particularly difficult either. John R. Lamarsh, a renowned nuclear engineer, estimates that a graphite-moderated reactor using natural unenriched uranium could be put together in a few years at a cost under $30 million.[34] Even spent-fuel reprocessing is relatively straightforward. In 1977, former weapons designer Theodore Taylor testified to the California Energy Resources Development and Conservation Commission: "Contrary to rather widespread belief, separation of plutonium irradiated nuclear fuel, and its subsequent incorporation into nuclear weapons suitable for military purposes, is not potentially beyond the capability of most countries."[35] Oak Ridge National Laboratory confirmed Taylor's assertion by designing a small reprocessing plant that most nations could build in under two years with only a marginal chance of detection.[36] Some of these steps could even be skipped, as energy policy analysts Amory and Hunter Lovins suggest:

> There are . . . disquieting indications that without using any conventional facilities such as [light water reactors] or reprocessing plants, and without serious risk of detection, one unirradiated [light water reactor] fuel bundle could be made into one bomb's worth of separated plutonium in one year by one technician with about one or two million dollars' worth of other materials which, in at least one European country, are available over the counter and apparently subject to no controls.[37]

A second route open to bomb builders is to obtain natural uranium and to enrich it to weapons grade.[38] Enrichment was once thought to be an exotic technology, largely because the U.S. nuclear-weapons program initially used gaseous diffusion plants that were esoteric, expensive, and energy-intensive.[39] However, more than sixteen countries now have built enrichment technologies, many using simple technologies with low costs and low energy intensities.[40] Proliferation experts also have been distressed to discover that once design constraints such as safety, efficiency, and commercial cost-effectiveness are relaxed, virtually any nation can enrich uranium cheaply. In 1972 the U.S. Atomic Energy Commission revealed that twenty-three low-technology methods for enrichment were available.[41] Several years later Edwin Zebroski of the Electric Power Research Institute (EPRI) reported: "We at EPRI mounted two relatively small projects, both of them under half a million dollars. Both of them produced working table models of devices that looked like they would be economic and relatively small scale. . . . I don't think either of the teams that did this were especially smart. They were newcomers to the field and I think that the same smarts exist in 50 other countries."[42] Zebroski also speculated that a large room filled with mass spectrographs, which are widely available in laboratories throughout the world, could create enough enriched uranium in a year for as many as 100 bombs.[43] A centrifuge design capable of uranium enrichment has been in the public literature since the 1960s, and a good machinist could assemble an even better version in a few weeks.[44] Even innocent centrifuges used in universities and hospitals have enrichment potential. Although many of these devices are inefficient and it might take hundreds of machines running for many months even to get one bomb's worth of fissionable uranium, the fact remains that virtually any nation with several tens of millions of dollars could use readily available technology to go nuclear.[45]

However, nonnuclear nations do not need to risk the embarrassment of having clandestine activities uncovered, because there is a third route to obtain fissionable materials—a peaceful nuclear-power program. Under the guise of generating electricity, a nation can amass thousands of pounds of plutonium in spent fuel, build a reprocessing facility, secretly assemble the mechanical innards for nuclear weapons, and then at the appropriate moment kick out the international inspectors, reprocess the spent fuel, and become a major nuclear-weapons state. As the Lovinses argue:

> The power reactor has an innocent civilian "cover" rather than being obviously military like a special production reactor. It is available to developing nations at zero or negative real cost with many supporting services. . . . It bears no *extra* cost in money or time if one were going to build a power reactor anyhow. And unlike a research reactor, or a production reactor of convenient design and cost, it produces *extremely large amounts* of plutonium: so large that theft of a few bombs' worth per year is within the statistical "noise" and can be made undetectable in principle, while nearly a hundred bombs' worth per reactor per year—more than from any other option—is available if overtly diverted.[46]

Once a nation produces fissionable uranium or plutonium, the remaining task of building nuclear bombs is relatively simple. Just after the Soviet Union dissolved, the United States became so concerned about the prospect of 2,000 to 3,000 Soviet bomb-builders auctioning themselves to the Saddam Husseins of the world that Secretary of State James Baker proposed an employment clearinghouse to find them nonmilitary jobs.[47] The Bush administration later pledged $25 million to establish an International Science and Technology Center in Moscow, and a National Academy of Sciences panel recommended increasing its budget by $150 million.[48] But these initiatives will do little to prevent proliferation of nuclear weapons. There are probably *tens of thousands* of people in the world with enough technical knowledge to produce atomic bombs, and their numbers are certain to increase.

Iraq is in some ways a typical nation. As measured by per capita GNP, half the countries in the world are richer than Iraq, half are poorer. Like most countries, Iraq signed the NPT and allowed IAEA inspections of its facilities for nuclear research. Yet despite limited financial resources, despite treaty obligations and international safeguards, despite the Israeli destruction of the Osirak research reactor in 1981, this average country was able to develop a formidable nuclear-weapons program by using the first two routes discussed here. UN inspections after the Persian Gulf War uncovered a small spent-fuel reprocessing facility, small amounts of plutonium and enriched uranium, thirty calutrons capable of low-technology uranium enrichment, and a nearly operational factory to mass-produce centrifuges for enrichment.[49] The Iraqis also were constructing the innards for a nuclear bomb. At the Al Atheer test facility, UN inspectors found vacuum furnaces for casting uranium metal into bomb parts, an isostatic press for compressing high-explosive charges to trigger a nuclear chain reaction, and a mainframe computer with programs to predict nuclear-blast shock waves.[50] Evidence also was found of an Iraqi project to develop a surface-to-surface missile capable of carrying a nuclear warhead.[51] If Iraq had not invaded Kuwait, it would now be well on its way to becoming the second nuclear-armed nation in the Middle East.

Controlling Nuclear Activities

In 1953 President Eisenhower proposed "Atoms for Peace," believing that peaceful nuclear technology could be spread without revealing military nuclear secrets. Today Eisenhower's dream is in shambles. The spread of the peaceful atom has given knowledge, technology, and materials for building nuclear weapons to almost every country on the planet. Undoing this knowledge is impossible, but if national governments are prepared to act quickly and resolutely, they can put nuclear technology and materials under careful global supervision. This would require the simultaneous pursuit of three reinforcing objectives:

□ Place all nuclear materials and related technologies under strict international control.
□ Close down all programs producing nuclear materials, whether military or peaceful in character.
□ Decommission all nuclear warheads and place the constituent nuclear materials under global lock-and-key.

As even the proponents of Atoms for Peace realized, monitoring and enforcement of a nonproliferation regime requires international rules—that is the reason they created the IAEA. But the agency has been a colossal failure. The IAEA only inspects facilities that the host country admits are dedicated to nuclear research or nuclear-energy production. It has few inspectors, uses unreliable inspection techniques, and spends the lion's share of its meager budget promoting nuclear energy. Diversions of nuclear-bomb materials have been detected by IAEA inspectors, yet the incidents were consistently hushed up and little, if any, action was taken.[52] Nonproliferation can only succeed if a stronger inspection regime is created.

Even if the world's nuclear industries were shut down tomorrow, the tasks facing international inspectors would be formidable. They would have to close uranium mines and mills, decommission all reactors, and mothball all enrichment and reprocessing plants. They would have to locate, store, and oversee the more than 215 metric tonnes of plutonium and 1,000 metric tonnes of enriched uranium that already have been produced.[53] They would have to monitor all other materials or technologies with bomb-building potential, such as heavy water, tritium, nuclear-grade graphite and zirconium, nuclear instrumentation, and advanced centrifuges. There is no way of knowing whether this regime could prevent proliferation, but one fact is clear: The chances of success diminish the longer nuclear activities are allowed to continue.

Ongoing production of nuclear materials, either for civilian or for weapons purposes, will necessarily complicate any control regime. Instead of guarding known stockpiles of fissionable materials, inspectors would have to keep track of thousands of bombs' worth of materials traveling annually between countries on trucks, trains, ships, and planes. Instead of being able to eliminate global demand for nuclear engineers, technology, and materials, the international community would have the hopeless task of distinguishing peaceful from military intentions. As the Lovinses argue, closure of *all* nuclear production, both peaceful and military, would make bomb-making technology and materials "harder to obtain; efforts to obtain them would be far more conspicuous; and such efforts, if detected, would carry a high political cost for both supplier and recipient because for the first time they would be *unambiguously military* in intent."[54]

If the United States wishes to persuade other nations to forgo nuclear energy, it must provide them with viable alternatives for energy production, including the devices and techniques for saving energy discussed in Chapter 5. The more double-paned windows, low-flow shower heads, photovoltaic cells, and windmills that Americans can put in the hands of other countries, the lower will be their need to retain nuclear-power industries. Of course, the United States will only be a credible advocate of these energy alternatives if it uses them for its own domestic energy needs. Fortunately, it is now many times cheaper to install many efficiency measures or to produce renewable energy than to run nuclear-power plants. Put another way, it is now cost-effective to shut down the U.S. commercial nuclear-power industry altogether.

The arguments for phasing out commercial nuclear facilities apply also to military facilities, only with greater force. The United States will have difficulty persuading other countries to shut down, or abstain from building, weapons-production facilities if it insists on retaining nuclear bombs for its own security. That is why it is essential that the United States move toward disarmament. As we noted in Chapter 3, the NPT expires in 1995. If the United States wants the treaty to continue, it must be prepared to deliver its end of the bargain.

Making Disarmament Possible

Even if the United States and other nuclear-armed nations adopt NPD, slim down their nuclear arsenals into minimal deterrents, and stop all additional production of nuclear materials, a number of insecurities will remain. Minimal nuclear arsenals could still be launched by human mistake, computer error, malevolence, or insanity. As long as some nations possess nuclear weapons (or other weapons of mass destruction such as those capable of releasing nerve gas and deadly germs), they may be able to coerce adversaries into concessions of territory, resources, money, or policy. Moreover, as long as nations continue to conduct research and development into new weapons, they may conceivably stumble upon innovations that could overwhelm other nations' defenses.

All these dangers suggest why nuclear nations must give renewed consideration to putting all nuclear weapons under effective international control. Over the next few years many nonnuclear nations will be making critical decisions over the acquisition of nuclear bombs. They will follow with great interest decisions made by the United States, Russia, China, Britain, France, India, and Israel.

As Princeton political scientist Richard Falk asks:

> If we're prepared to use nuclear weapons ..., why shouldn't the same option be permitted to all those other nations that have other goals in the world? And why shouldn't those who are weaker follow the example of those who are stronger and more successful in the ways that count—according to what we've taught them? In other words, underlying the whole policy of the nuclear age is the fantastic notion that you can both promote a peaceful world and at the same time retain the domineering capacities that come from having nuclear weapons and the announced willingness to employ them.[55]

By providing a quantum increase in military strength at relatively low cost, nuclear bombs are attractive to militarily weak nations. They can enable even the smallest international actor—Albania, for example—to become a formidable threat to the world's most powerful nations. To emphasize this *technical* reality of nuclear arms, Theodore Taylor once mused that a "fizzle-yield, low efficiency, basically lousy fission bomb" detonated outside the U.S. Capitol building during the president's State of the Union message "would destroy the heads of all branches of the United States Government—all Supreme Court justices, the entire Cabinet, all legislators, and for what it's worth, the Joint Chiefs of Staff."[56] Evolving weapons technologies that allow any nation to inflict intolerable harm on any other will ultimately create a world of thousands of balanced "mutual hostage" relationships that could force nations into more equal positions of power.

Today's hierarchy of nations is breaking down. As Harvard political scientist Stanley Hoffmann contends, "What the United States is facing in today's world is mainly a demand for 'state equality.'"[57] The value of equality is so widely held that no nation will settle for less. Even such "realists" as Michael Mandelbaum of Johns Hopkins concede that "[a] spirit of egalitarianism pervades contemporary international politics" and "is likely to gather force."[58] If nations are unable to achieve equality politically, they will do so militarily—if necessary, through nuclear bombs.

The realities of proliferation and international egalitarianism—realities that *no* foreign policy can entirely eliminate—are making only two kinds of world possible: a world of nuclear anarchy, in which all nations strive to become equal through military strength; or a world of disarmed order, in which all nations equally renounce nuclear weapons and embrace a common system of control. This dichotomy is not meant to suggest that disarmament is a problemless utopia, for badly executed disarmament may very well disintegrate into nuclear anarchy. Nor is it meant to suggest that proliferation will occur quickly. The point is that the only long-term alternative to nuclear anarchy is well-executed nuclear disarmament.

We may be lucky enough to live with nuclear weapons for ten, twenty, or even two hundred more years, but the odds are not very good. In a world of many nuclear nations, small nuclear wars would become a common part of the geopolitical landscape until one or more larger nuclear wars scarred the world beyond recognition. A world of nuclear anarchy would force humanity to teeter continuously on the brink of extinction. As long as nations refuse to put nuclear bombs under permanent international control, the world will remain at the precipice.

A world of disarmed order *is* possible. The year 1995, when the NPT comes up for renewal, could be a turning point. If the United States and Russia halt production of fissionable materials, establish minimal deterrents, cut their nuclear arsenals deeply, and open up all weapons facilities to international inspection, other nations will be persuaded to follow suit. Most nonnuclear nations will gladly sign a new NPT that ends the nuclear apartheid of the original treaty. If nuclear nations finally live up to their end of the bargain, most nonnuclear nations will be willing to live up to theirs by continuing to forswear these barbaric weapons.

Nuclear nations probably need not completely disarm by 1995; the NPT only obligates them to make substantial progress. One good-faith step toward disarmament, as Arjun Makhijani and Katherine Yih have suggested, is for nations to put their bombs in heavily fortified halfway houses protected by international guards.[59] UN inspectors could oversee the removal of nuclear weapons from missile nose-cones, ships, submarines, planes, and depots and could verify the emplacement of the warheads in repositories on each nuclear nation's home territory. Detaching warheads from their delivery systems would greatly reduce the risks of launch by computer error, accident, or a mad general.

Even though UN forces would guard the repositories, nuclear nations would retain the right to boot them out and reactivate their weapons at any time. Because it would take many days, even weeks, before a nuclear nation could reassemble its arsenal, a surprise first strike would be impossible. Makhijani and Yih argue that this would give other nations ample time to respond:

> While it would be physically possible to rearm, it would become politically more and more difficult to do so. A rearming could only occur if there were such a total breakdown in agreement between the nuclear weapons states that they would again consider going on hair-trigger alert. By making it necessary to wait and negotiate for a considerable period before taking this drastic step, the sequestering of nuclear warheads would be a central part of a political process for weaning nuclear weapons states from the doctrine of deterrence.[60]

Disarmament proposals in the past have rarely been taken seriously by policymakers because they presupposed the instantaneous emergence of gigantic international bureaucracies empowered to scrap weapons, verify compliance, and take police actions against cheaters. To many, these presumptions seem improbable and dangerous. For example, despite his deep sympathy for disarmament, economist Kenneth Boulding warned that the international police forces overseeing disarmament would "inevitably either degenerate into a tyranny of one party or group over the others or break up into world civil strife."[61] The halfway houses proposed here, however, would give the UN an opportunity to improve inspection and verification techniques and to develop democratic checks and balances in the system. As trust in the UN system grew, *then* nuclear nations could be convinced to scrap their nuclear warheads and to put the fissionable materials under permanent control. A reliable, rigorous UN inspection system is also the only way to ensure that nations do not develop, deploy, or use chemical or biological weapons.

But the first order of business is to transform the political context in which the disarmament of weapons of mass destruction takes place. By gradually reducing the political, resource, and economic roots of conflict and encouraging nations to become accustomed to the nonviolent resolution of conflict through international institutions, the proposals we are presenting throughout this book would eliminate many of the incentives for nations to cheat and to acquire offensive nuclear weapons in a disarmed world. The defensive transition envisioned here slowly and carefully could build UN institutions for inspection, without compromising the ability of nations to build legitimate defenses. The international procedures for verification and enforcement could grow in reassuring evolutionary steps, not frightening revolutionary leaps. Once global politics renders nuclear bombs obsolete, disarmament will become essentially a question of nuclear-waste disposal.

Now that the Cold War is over, the United States has a unique opportunity to set in motion a global transition to nuclear disarmament. If U.S. security planners move quickly and decisively to phase out nuclear power, cut off nuclear-weapons production, deactivate nuclear warheads, and put all nuclear materials and technology under international inspection, they have a chance to halt proliferation. The genie of knowledge about how to make a nuclear bomb cannot be stuffed back into the bottle, but the construction and operation of national facilities to employ that knowledge can be. The alternative is a drift toward a world of nuclear anarchy, in which other nations mimic our addiction to nuclear bombs and in which nuclear wars become an inevitable part of global life.

Part Four

Implementation

11
Grassroots Participation

Citizens need not rely on enlightened leaders to carry out many of our proposals. It is true that national foreign policymakers have the exclusive power to deploy nonprovocative defenses, to create a UN collective security apparatus, and to dismantle nuclear bombs. But if security policies are seen to include matters of democracy, environment, and economics, a wide range of opportunities for direct participation opens up. Whether citizens choose to act as individuals or through nongovernmental organizations (NGOs), universities, or local governments, they have the power not only to influence security policy but also to *make* security policy.

What Citizens Can Do for Peace

Most books that advocate peace end with a laundry list of suggestions about how to convince leaders to implement desirable foreign policies and to discontinue undesirable ones: Write letters to your members of Congress, cast your vote and register your friends, prepare op-eds for your local paper, educate your neighbors, take a stand. There is nothing wrong with these recommendations, but they reflect a narrow and simplistic view of democracy.

Strong democracy, as we discussed in Chapter 4, means much more than voting for representatives every two, four, or six years. It means being actively engaged in civic life on a day-to-day basis. It means having a sense of social responsibility, taking initiative at the community level, solving problems without politicians. Where politicians must be involved, strong democracy means forging an ongoing partnership with them in the formulation, execution, and evaluation of policy. If Americans are willing to practice strong democracy at home—and millions already are—they can reduce the probability of U.S. leaders taking the nation to war. All the strategies discussed thus far have important entry points for grassroots participation.

Americans can eliminate the political roots of war by promoting democracy at home and abroad. Indeed, as Chapter 4 detailed, that is exactly what thousands of citizen diplomats did with respect to the Soviet Union. They helped open up that Communist society by entering into working relationships with Soviets in the fields of art, business, children's welfare, energy, filmmaking, high technology, law, medicine, negotiation, psychology, religion, science, television, and women's rights. They helped Soviet partners publicize human rights abuses, distribute photocopiers and fax machines, organize small businesses, start underground newspapers, monitor elections, and revitalize the legal system. Americans should now enter these same kinds of relationships with the Chinese, Cubans, Iranians, Iraqis, Libyans, North Koreans, and every other nationality that might be regarded as an "enemy." At the same time Americans can reduce their own bellicose impulses by strengthening U.S. civil society and dismantling the national security state.

Americans can directly eliminate the resource roots of war. Every act of saving energy at home reduces the need for oil from abroad. Despite federal neglect, people across the United States saved seven times as much energy between 1979 and 1986 as all net expansions of the energy supply over the same period. "In the absence of strong federal leadership and a comprehensive federal energy policy," says Tom Curtis of the National Governors' Association, "a lot of states are stepping out on their own." Here are some recent examples:

- □ For nearly twenty years the California Energy Commission has been promoting tougher energy-efficiency standards for appliances, new buildings, and industrial plants.
- □ Washington state recently passed a housing code that requires new houses to be more than twice as energy efficient as those built under the 1977 code.
- □ Connecticut has upgraded standards for its state-owned vehicles, demanding that they achieve 45 miles per gallon by the year 2000.
- □ Iowa now requires its gas and electric utilities to spend between 1.5 and 2 percent of their operating revenues on energy efficiency measures.

□ Massachusetts and the states of the Pacific Northwest insist that utilities consider efficiency before any new power plants are built.

Municipal and county governments also have played a role. Starting in the 1970s, comprehensive energy conservation plans were implemented by such locales as Gevena County and Carbondale in Illinois; Humboldt County, California; Franklin County, Massachusetts; Fulton, Missouri; Salem, Oregon; Philadelphia, Pennsylvania; and Madison, Wisconsin. These programs included block-by-block campaigns to weatherstrip, caulk, insulate, install double-pane windows, and otherwise tighten the thermal efficiency of homes and offices.

Some U.S. organizations have boosted global security by improving the efficiency of energy use in the CIS. In 1987 the Rocky Mountain Institute began working with the Soviet Academy of Sciences to try to spread state-of-the-art lightbulbs, windows, cars, refrigerators, and hundreds of other devices throughout the Soviet Union. The California office of the Natural Resources Defense Council entered into an agreement with the Soviet Academy of Science to draw up a least-cost energy plan for Belarus and the Crimean region of the Ukraine. Russian independence from foreign oil reduces temptations for it to invade petroleum-rich neighbors; less reliance on nuclear power helps to prevent future Chernobyls; less coal burning staves off acid rain and global warming.

In Chapter 6 we noted that small-scale development projects are particularly promising ways of ending poverty in the Third World. Small-scale projects demand more contact between the providers and the recipients of aid, thus facilitating long-term relationships that can help participants better conceive, implement, and evaluate a project. Environmental problems, social dislocations, and political issues are more readily recognized and ameliorated when the providers of assistance personally know the victims. And small-scale projects rely on the Third World's most plentiful resource—people.

Today, tens of thousands of Americans are actively involved in promoting small-scale development in the Third World through such relationships as sister schools, linked day-care centers, ecotourism, alternative trade, and work camps.[1] Over the past twenty-five years the International Executive Service Corps of Stamford, Connecticut, has sent retired businessmen and skilled volunteers to work on 12,000 projects worldwide.[2] The San Francisco–based International Development Exchange (IDEX) matches carefully selected Third World development projects costing under $5,000 with churches, schools, Elks and Rotary Clubs, and other willing donors. The Ashoka Project raises money from American foundations and individuals to cover the salaries of sixty innovative Third World environmentalists, family-planning advocates, cooperative organizers, and other leaders who are dedicated to improving the lives of the poorest 20 percent of the populations of Brazil, India, Indonesia, Mexico, and Nigeria.[3]

Some of the most interesting grassroots initiatives that promote development and environmental protection are debt-for-nature swaps. The World Wildlife Fund and the Nature Conservancy bought $10 million of Ecuador's debt in exchange for government support of Fundación Natura, a local conservation group.[4] Other groups took over an estimated $50 million of Costa Rica's debt in the form of "conservation bonds" that will be used to fund expansion and reforestation of the country's national parks.[5] These swaps have had only a tiny impact on the Third World's total debt, and sometimes they have been undertaken with inadequate participation of grassroots groups in the affected countries. (A deal in which Conservation International assumed $650,000 of Bolivia's $4 billion debt in exchange for the country's agreement to set aside 3.7 million acres of forest for endangered species of cats and monkeys, for example, came under criticism for failing to consult with the indigenous peoples who lived there.[6]) But if debt-for-nature swaps are framed with the full participation of NGOs, and if they respect the principles of self-reliance, equity, and ecology outlined in Chapter 6, they can be valuable tools for promoting sustainable development.

Some Americans invest directly in Third World environmental projects. The Massachusetts Audubon Society decided that the best way to protect birds nesting in New England during the summer was to raise $7 million and purchase 110,000 acres of forest in Belize so that these songbirds would be protected during the winter.[7] Frank Lockyear, a former nurseryman from Wilsonville, Oregon, spent his retirement years planting trees in Costa Rica, the Dominican Republic, Greece, Haiti, Jamaica, South Korea, and Taiwan; in Thailand he mobilized ten thousand college students to help him.[8] Several American research teams produced studies for Brazil that show that harvesting forests for edible fruits, rubber, oils, and cocoa generates nearly two times the economic return of deforesting the same area for timber and cattle grazing.[9]

In Western Europe more than a thousand cities provide schools, medicine, tools, technology, and training directly to towns and villages in Asia, Africa, and South America.[10] Two hundred cities in Belgium have city councilors whose responsibilities include Third World development. In the Netherlands 380 out of the nation's 670 municipalities have their own Third World development policies. One hundred Dutch cities spend an average of 50 cents per capita on town-based development initiatives in the Third World. The German city-state of Bremen, with a population equivalent to that of Washington, D.C., devotes more than $1 million per year for programs in China, India, Mali, and Rwanda. Following the principles of the 1985 Cologne Appeal, these city-to-city relationships stress raising the consciousness of people in the North as well as assisting people in the South. There is no reason why the 719 U.S. sister-city ties with the Third World cannot go beyond cultural exchanges and begin hundreds of analogous small-scale, environmentally sound development programs (some already do).

As demonstrated by the role of citizen diplomacy in improving Soviet-U.S. relations, cooperation between national leaders also can be facilitated by ordinary people. High-profile private citizens such as Anglican envoy Terry Waite can serve as useful intermediaries between national leaders. The broader sweep of unofficial contacts by business partners, churches, human rights organizations, cultural groups, and interested citizens, as detailed in Chapter 7, can erode the enmity that often prevents official cooperation, while putting domestic pressures on leaders to improve cooperative initiatives abroad.

Because the legitimacy of international norms comes ultimately from the people, NGOs already play an important role in developing them. Amnesty International helped in the development of norms against political imprisonment, torture, and capital punishment. INFACT, with its worldwide boycott of Nestlé infant formula, created new norms of ethical behavior for multinational corporations. Greenpeace, in its campaigns to save whales and baby seals, established norms to protect marine life and endangered species.

Stronger international regimes and institutions will require enlightened governmental policies, but many global initiatives may also come from outside national governments. For 125 years the

International Red Cross, now composed of 146 national NGOs and supported by millions of volunteers, has provided food, clothing, shelter, medical treatment, and moral support to the victims of war and natural disasters.[11] Cooperative projects to prevent the spread of AIDS and to promote Third World development have brought together vast international networks of churches, universities, businesses, and foundations. Transnational networks of environmentalists, such as the International Union for Conservation of Nature and Natural Resources, have launched projects to promote species protection, sustainable development, rainforest conservation, and pollution control, and they are intensively lobbying country after country to make their views national policy.[12] The International Organization of Consumers Unions has member groups in seventy countries actively advocating safer products and tighter restrictions on the marketing of pesticides, medicines, and baby formula.[13] All these efforts provide expanding opportunities for citizens to modify the behavior of other nations.

Even some elements of military security can be strengthened through popular action. As more reconnaissance photos are sold publicly and more private communication networks are formed, more military information-gathering functions might come into the hands of citizens. Sweden and India, for example, might launch a satellite verification system financially supported by cities. Citizens also can undertake some types of peacekeeping. In the 1980s the church-based organization Witness for Peace played a major observer role in Central America, analogous to the role of UN peacekeepers, by sending several thousand trained Americans to detail hostilities and human rights abuses along the Nicaragua-Honduras border.[14] It is conceivable that hundreds of cities throughout the world could assemble contingents of peacekeepers, train them in nonviolent resistance, and dispatch them to trouble spots. As long as such efforts were unarmed and nonviolent, they would be consistent with current U.S. laws of neutrality, as well as with our five security principles.

Increasingly, the question facing citizens interested in strengthening global security will be not *what* they can do—the number of options are overwhelming—but *how* they can do it.

Municipal Foreign Policies

In recent years Americans entering the rough-and-tumble of international affairs have discovered that their powers as individuals or as members of NGOs have limits. Unlike national governments, which have vast treasuries derived from taxes, most individuals and NGOs operate on financial shoestrings. Individuals and NGOs also lack the "color of authority" of national diplomats and therefore are much less likely than national officials to get meetings with, let alone influence, powerful officials abroad.

Faced with these realities, millions of Americans seeking world peace have acted at the community level. Many have recruited their local elected officials, who, unlike inaccessible national officials, are rarely farther than a telephone call or public meeting away. And they have discovered that, unlike most NGOs acting alone, communities can carry out grassroots foreign policy activism with legitimacy and money. Although citizens who practice diplomacy abroad do not always have much political clout, mayors do. In 1986 Dianne Feinstein, who was then the mayor of San Francisco, and several other mayors convinced the Soviet Union to allow thirty-six people to emigrate after many analogous private initiatives failed. With regard to resources, few nongovernmental entities can match the coffers of a city. Although most U.S. cities are financially pinched, if they allocated a mere 1 percent of their budgets to promoting international security, as the cities of Hiroshima and Nagasaki do, they could expand the size of the U.S. peace movement more than tenfold.

Today, more than 1,000 local governments in the United States officially involve themselves in foreign affairs.[15] These "municipal foreign policies," once dismissed as trivial, aberrant, or unconstitutional, are exerting an increasingly important influence on U.S. foreign policy. More than 900 local governments passed a nuclear-freeze resolution and helped pressure President Reagan to launch the START talks in Geneva and the INF negotiations in Vienna. By refusing to cooperate with the Federal Emergency Management Agency's "crisis relocation planning" in the early 1980s, more than 120 cities helped derail the government's civil defense program, which was part of its scheme for fighting nuclear war. By divesting their portfolios of more than $20 billion worth of securities from firms doing business in South Africa, seventy cities, thirteen counties, and nineteen states helped to persuade the Congress to replace "constructive engagement" with limited economic sanctions in 1986.

In the years ahead cities will play an increasingly important role in international affairs through a wide variety of means. The following is a sampling of what is already happening:[16]

Education. Both San Francisco and Boulder County, Colorado, produced and disseminated pamphlets arguing for a nuclear freeze. High schools in New York City and Milwaukee now teach courses in peace studies. In the United Kingdom, peace-related educational programs undertaken by cities include special newspapers, leaflets, videos, booklets, speaking tours, conferences, workplace seminars, exhibitions, road signs, plaques, advertisements, postcards, banners, badges, peace parks, town shows, adult-education courses, special libraries, and "peace shops."

Research. Undaunted by the absence of nationally funded peace-research programs, states such as California and Iowa established their own peace programs. Los Angeles, Pittsburgh, and Baltimore passed ordinances requiring their staffs to prepare and publish annual reports on the local economic impacts of military spending.

Lobbying. To convince federal lawmakers of the urgency of eliminating nuclear-bomb testing, more than 800 U.S. local elected officials signed petitions for a comprehensive test ban (CTB), nearly 200 cities passed CTB resolutions, and the U.S. Conference of Mayors approved a special CTB resolution. The U.S. Conference of Mayors has a part-time lobbyist in Washington, D.C., to argue for reversing the flow of moneys from Main Street to the Pentagon, and some cities may soon join this effort.

Policing. Nearly thirty U.S. cities have passed "sanctuary resolutions" ordering their police not to cooperate with the U.S. Immigration and Naturalization Service in its efforts to deport Salvadoran and Guatemalan refugees back to the war zones from which they had fled. After the Soviet Union shot down KAL flight 007, thirteen states used their police powers to pull Stolichnaya vodka from liquor-store shelves.

Zoning. More than 180 U.S. cities are "nuclear-free zones." Half of these simply passed nonbinding exhortations calling for disarmament, but the other half actually prohibit the manufacturing of nuclear bombs within their jurisdiction. A number of jurisdictions such as Chicago and Cambridge, Massachusetts, also help military contractors plan for nonmilitary production.

Contracting and Investing. By spending $500 billion annually and overseeing $300 billion in investments, U.S. local and state governments have become aware of their power in selective contracting and investment. Jersey City, New Jersey, and Marin County, California, are among nearly a dozen jurisdictions that have prohibited municipal contracts with or investments in firms that produce nuclear bombs.

Sister Cities. In 1991 Sister Cities International reported that 898 U.S. cities had active relationships with 1,607 sister cities worldwide, including forty-four in the People's Republic of China and seventy-three in the Soviet Union. Besides enriching the daily cultural life of participating cities, these relationships help citizens to replace the ignorance, fear, and hatred that drive arms races and war with understanding, empathy, and trust.

Trade Agreements. Some 200 U.S. cities are actively establishing economic city-to-city ties abroad by promoting their products or attracting foreign investment. In 1984, for example, Mayor Feinstein of San Francisco signed a trade pact with the Chinese province of Shanghai that within a few years resulted in tens of millions of dollars of additional business for the Bay Area.

Political Agreements. To undertake a joint political endeavor—namely, to challenge U.S. military involvement in Central America in the 1980s—eighty-seven U.S. cities and 200 European cities set up links with communities in Nicaragua. Along with citizen groups, these sister cities provided more humanitarian assistance than the total level of private U.S. aid going to the Contras. Burlington, Vermont, arranged for a ship to carry 560 tons of supplies to its sister city in Puerto Cabezas, including 30 tons of medical supplies collected from local hospitals.

International Organizations. In 1985, to promote policies on behalf of peace with greater effectiveness, a half-dozen U.S. mayors met with 100 mayors from twenty-three countries in Hiroshima for the First World Conference of Mayors for Peace Through Inter-City Solidarity. Other global organizations that help cities coordinate their municipal foreign policies regarding cultural exchange, peace, Third World development, and environmental protection include the United Towns Organisation (Paris), the International Nuclear Free Zone Registry (Manchester), the International Union of Local Authorities (The Hague), and the International Council for Local Environmental Initiatives (Toronto and Freiburg).

Municipal State Departments. In an effort to consolidate their international affairs activities under one roof, some cities created special offices equipped with staff, overhead, and funding. Cambridge, Massachusetts, and Washington, D.C., established official peace commissions. Seattle allocates $225,000 per year for an Office of International Affairs to coordinate foreign trade and relationships with thirteen sister cities.

Over the next decade or two, there may well be enough cities participating in foreign affairs to establish one or more global unions of local officials—permanent, ongoing organizations in which local representatives could devise common global agendas and lobby national leaders through pooled resources. Predicting the exact complexion of these city-based organizations would be premature, but three of their probable features are worth noting. First, many groups that are minorities at the national level are majorities at the local level; city-sized units of representation would therefore give many minorities an effective voice in international affairs. Second, the sheer diversity of participants would increase the chances that embarrassing issues that often get buried at the UN—like torture—would get a real airing. Third, a global union of municipalities might foster new alliances on such bases as size, industry, bioregion, religion, and language—natural alliances that nation-state politics now obscure. While a Camp David–like summit among the national leaders of Israel, Egypt, Syria, Jordan, and Lebanon now seems implausible, it would be less difficult for one or two of the most forward-looking mayors from each country to come together. This actually happened in 1991, when a group of European mayors attempted to mediate between mayors representing the Serbs, Croats, Muslims, Albanians, and other major ethnic groups in former Yugoslavia.

Municipal foreign policies, if continued and expanded, hold the promise of reorienting U.S. security policy in four helpful ways. First, they allow the voices of more Americans to be heard on foreign policy. It is one thing when Americans "speak with one voice" as they did when war was declared against Japan and Nazi Germany. But it is quite another thing when only one voice is heard because the majority of Americans have been silenced, as happened when President Reagan continued to support the Nicaraguan Contras despite opposition by two-thirds of the public. Municipal foreign policies provide opportunities for all Americans to have a voice in international affairs.

Second, municipal foreign policies improve the efficiency of U.S. foreign policy. A staggering number of transactions now take place between the United States and other nations in such areas as communication, tourism, trade, investment, and cultural exchange. For example, the Clearing House Interbank Payments System (CHIPS), which is operated by 140 U.S. banks specializing in international finance, conducts several billion transactions daily. Attempts by the national government to control these transactions too tightly inevitably will scare off international trade and finance and stifle domestic economic growth. Municipal foreign policies, in contrast, allow tens of thousands of people, each expert in his or her own area, to take primary responsibility for these policies. National officials already have begun to recognize that they should set broad guidelines for the ways in which ideas, people, capital, and goods cross borders and leave the details to individuals, corporations, and local governments. To promote international trade, for example, the Department of State has actually briefed activist governors, assisted state and local representatives through its embassies and consulates, and loaned Foreign Service officers to states.

Third, municipal foreign policies encourage nonmilitary, nonprovocative approaches to international relations—precisely the approaches suggested by our five security principles. Because local and state governments cannot meet threats abroad by dispatching troops, shipping weapons, and running covert operations, they are forced to develop more nuanced and nonviolent policies. They can address the political roots of conflict by promoting citizen exchange programs with adversary nations, and they can relieve the economic sources of conflict through Third World development programs. They also can play an important role in developing stronger international norms and institutions for the peaceful resolution of conflicts.

Finally—and most important—municipal foreign policies enhance accountability in U.S. foreign policy. They provide people at the grassroots with more diverse sources of information that they can use to evaluate, criticize, and improve national foreign policies—and they provide more opportunities to participate directly in international affairs. Municipal foreign policies allow more foreign policy decisions to be made at a level of government where public scrutiny is high. Unlike national officials, local leaders cannot classify their deliberations or create secret teams in the basement of City Hall. Indeed, most local governments are dogged by scandal-hungry local newspapers and governed by statutes that demand public meetings for important local decisions.

As municipal foreign policies expand, the federal government may be tempted to reassert its primacy in international affairs. Already some commentators are suggesting that the federal government should set up a special desk within the State Department to track, discourage, and legally stop local meddling in foreign policy.[17] However, given the potential benefits of greater municipal involvement, the federal government would do well to follow far more modest guidelines.

As a first step, the U.S. government should support all local efforts to educate, research, and lobby on foreign policy. In the spirit of the First Amendment to the U.S. Constitution, which protects free speech on foreign policy, and the Fifth Amendment, which the Supreme Court has held grants a broad privilege to Americans to travel abroad,[18] U.S. leaders should be willing to tolerate the freest possible exchange of ideas, people, books, and audio-visual materials. The government has far more to lose if its limits on basic freedoms cause outraged Americans to take to the streets. Congress might begin by narrowing presidential discretion in banning travel abroad and scrapping the 1799 Logan Act, which has unsuccessfully (and probably unconstitutionally) attempted to discourage Americans from meeting with leaders abroad to discuss controversial issues.[19] Specific travel restrictions, such as those that ban Americans from traveling to Cuba, North Korea, or Vietnam (which determined citizens have evaded by using exceptions for visiting family members, journalists, or researchers) should be lifted. Also, the government might help fund local consciousness-raising activities by enlarging the coffers of the National Institute for Peace and channeling these moneys, with minimal strings attached, to municipal programs.

The federal government should accept municipal initiatives unless they pose more than a hypothetical danger to U.S. foreign policy. Cities are making their own foreign policies not to meddle in the federal government's affairs, but to meet legitimate local concerns. Municipalities that create nuclear-free zones, for example, are attempting to address the economic impact of military spending and the health hazards of nuclear-weapons manufacturing. Federal attempts to quash these initiatives will simply anger the people affected and prompt new, equally irksome municipal policies to accomplish the same goals. Where local initiatives arise that pose more than a symbolic danger to national foreign policy, the federal government should try to work in cooperation with the offending municipality. In the same way that federal officials work closely with municipal and state officials to harmonize their trade policies, they should try to involve mayors and other local representatives in the formulation of U.S. policies concerning arms control, resource management, Third World development, and international institutions. Tapping local wisdom not only can mollify unwanted local protest but also can help prevent the kind of foreign policy disasters that have occurred because of a lack of proper checks and balances on leaders.

A final recommendation is to tighten the laws governing those very few nonfederal initiatives that already have caused serious international mischief. The most obvious activities that come to mind, thus far undertaken by citizens and not by cities, are exports of weapons, ammunition, and other combat equipment to countries or rebels with whom the United States is at peace. One possible remedy would be to strengthen the Neutrality Act by enforcing it through an independent prosecutor rather than relying on the political whims of the Justice Department. States themselves might pass their own versions of the Neutrality Act and make it a state crime to ship arms or train belligerents without the approval of the federal government.[20]

Taken together, the proposals in this chapter suggest a fundamentally new direction for U.S. foreign policy. Local officials and citizens are no less prone to error or irrationality than the president. Even so, new forms of public participation in foreign policy offer a broader base of political accountability, unprecedented opportunities for the promotion of peace, and badly needed checks on ill-conceived foreign policy adventures. Whether 250 million Americans can mold policy better than a dozen members of the National Security Council is a matter of political judgment, but it is precisely that judgment which underlies our long-standing faith in democracy. As Thomas Jefferson once said, "The good sense of the people will always be found to be the best army."[21]

12

A Genuine
New World Order

Skeptics will be quick to point out the limitations of our proposals. Democratization will never restrain all future leaders from waging war, nor will more energy efficiency prevent all global competition for resources. International cooperation, norms, regimes, and institutions may help patch up some disagreements, but nations must be militarily prepared for the times when conflict resolution fails. And our defense proposals may look good on paper, but can we really entrust the security of Europe, the Middle East, and other hot spots to defensive weapons and new collective security arrangements?

However valid these criticisms, perfection is the wrong criterion for evaluation. No single security plan can *guarantee* an end to war. What must be asked, instead, is whether these proposals considered *as a system* can work better than today's security system. We believe that our proposals produce a peace sturdier than the mere absence of war, a peace in which conflicts can be eliminated and resolved long before war becomes a possibility. As long-time peace activist W. H. Ferry has written: "Peace is not just a condition but a continuing effort to discern and meet needs, to relieve strains, and to foresee, avert or diminish crises."[1] In the system we propose, military victory would be a symbol of defeat because it would mean that the most critical nonprovocative policies—the tools of economics, democracy, diplomacy, and law—had failed.

A Practical Vision

A security system based on the principles of comprehensiveness, nonprovocation, prevention, multilateralism, and participation is at once visionary and pragmatic. It rejects the technological utopianism of those who seek an impenetrable shield against nuclear bombs that will consume hundreds of billions of dollars and still probably not work. Yet it also rejects the strategic utopianism of arms controllers who believe that the world can coexist forever with thousands of nuclear weapons under the doctrine of mutual assured destruction. What it offers, instead, is a comprehensive framework for preventing and resolving conflicts that renders nuclear bombs and other weapons of mass destruction less and less relevant to national and global security.

Our proposals can diminish the probability of war, yet do so without compromising the other values Americans treasure, such as free trade, environmental protection, political participation, human rights, and international law. Too often mainstream analysts are willing to subordinate these values to national security. For example, in its 1985 book *Hawks, Doves, and Owls,* the Harvard Project on Avoiding Nuclear War criticized U.S. policies aimed at political reform in Eastern Europe and the Soviet Union because they ran "the risk of planting seeds of discord between the East and West."[2] Our policies would have the United States promote democracy through non-provocative means, creating the possibility of political reform *and* stability.

Little of what we propose is revolutionary or untested. Several centuries of experience have shown that democratically self-controlled and economically self-reliant nations rarely go to war with one another. International institutions such as the UN are now experiencing a renaissance as numerous war-weary nations turn to them for mediation, peacekeeping, and collective security. Even nonprovocative defense, a relatively new concept, has withstood the test of time in Sweden and Switzerland.

Unlike arms control, which can work only with step-by-step agreements between nations, many of our proposals can be adopted independently. The United States can substantially increase its own security and that of other nations by conserving energy, promoting sustainable Third World development, enhancing political participation at home and abroad, announcing and abiding by international norms of negotiation and nonintervention, subjecting itself to compulsory jurisdiction in the World Court, shifting to nonprovocative defenses in Europe and Asia, scrapping first-strike nuclear weapons, and closing all nuclear facilities. None of these policies endanger U.S. national security or require the reciprocity of other nations. In some instances, such as nonprovocative defense, bilateral and multilateral agreements can be helpful, but even here, a strong case can be made for taking at least a few steps independently. Just as every decision to deploy weapons systems in the past was made independently, so too can decisions be made independently to trade offensive weapons for defensive ones or to renounce nuclear bombs and other inhumane weapons of mass destruction.

The nonprovocative nature of our proposals encourages reciprocation. As the United States makes it progressively clearer to other nations that it will not and cannot launch an aggressive attack on anyone, its adversaries and former adversaries will have less need to build offensive arms. Even if more conservative leaders rise to power in Russia, the West will be better served by not giving them an excuse to renew an offensive arms race or to reestablish hegemony over Eastern Europe. A concerted effort by the United States to exorcise provocation from East-West relations will enable it to avoid simultaneous insecurity and insolvency.

Our proposals are feasible for another reason. As long as security is defined in terms of more or fewer weapons, it can be pursued only at the highest levels of political governance because virtually all countries, including Western democracies, make their weapons decisions with minimal popular consultation or guidance. By enlarging the agenda for security beyond military policy, our policies invite—indeed, demand—people's informed participation. Acting either individually or through nongovernmental organizations, Americans and other peoples can help promote resource efficiency, Third World development, cultural exchanges, scientific and trade agreements, treaty verification, and perhaps even unarmed peacekeeping. For most of these activities, government cooperation is helpful but not essential.

A Resilient Security System

One of the most attractive features of our proposed security system is its resistance to catastrophic failure.[3] Today's security system pays little attention to the roots of conflict and the value of international norms and institutions in resolving conflicts, and relies instead on *managing* "inevitable conflicts" through the threat of war. As noted in the Introduction, the United States spends roughly twenty times more on military programs than on all nonmilitary foreign programs put together. Tilted so heavily toward provocative accumulations of arms and threats to use force, the current system is extremely fragile. Any number of crises can escalate into a global war. In a world dominated by arms races and force, a crisis typically leads one side to ratchet the conflict upward to show its resolve, causing its adversary to ratchet another notch further, and so on. Conflicts get caught in a cycle that only extraordinary efforts can stop—efforts that must be made at a time when communications are difficult, tensions are high, and offensive forces are on hair-trigger alert.

Imagine yourself as president of the United States in July of 1990. Saddam Hussein has just begun amassing his million-man army and huge numbers of tanks, personnel carriers, and artillery along the Kuwaiti border, poised to invade at any moment. How do you respond? Sitting around a table are your advisers—the secretaries of state and defense, the national security adviser, the chairman of the Joint Chiefs of Staff, and a handful of other policy experts. Your colleagues warn that Saddam Hussein's takeover of Kuwait will be disastrous for U.S. national security, because if he is allowed to succeed he can dictate world oil prices, threaten Israel, and destabilize Arab allies such as Saudi Arabia and Egypt. What are the chances that you would seriously entertain nonprovocative policies? It is already too late to deal with the political or economic roots of the conflict. As for conflict resolution, the secretary of state might mention negotiation, mediation, or international institutions, but these options would probably be dismissed as "soft." "What's needed now," your national security adviser urges, "is not talk but resolve." Because the United States has ignored alternatives for conflict resolution for so long, they *do* seem naive. Moreover, because top U.S. leaders have spent years attacking rather than improving the UN and the World Court, these institutions seem ineffectual.

What remains are the military options, with which the cabinet members have had vast experience. Having nearly all the government's security budget at his or her disposal, the secretary of defense can produce reams of details about different force options. Even though recent uses of force rarely met their objectives, force is appealing because it is tangible and tough. Unless you were an extraordinary leader, you would probably believe that you had little choice but to risk war.

In a world where nonprovocative policies were already in place, you would not be faced with such a Hobson's choice. The conflict would have encountered negative feedback at all stages. To begin with, by focusing on all security threats, not just the military threats posed by the Soviet Union, Nicaragua, Iran, or Panama, you would have taken serious measures to cut the flow of offensive arms (especially materials, parts, and technology useful for chemical and nuclear weapons) to *every* country, especially countries with patently expansionist intentions, such as Iraq. Unlike the Bush administration, which in the months before Iraq's invasion of Kuwait fought congressional efforts to ban militarily usable exports to Iraq, you might have completed a worldwide treaty restricting all transfers and sales of offensive weapons.

You also would have had policies in place removing the roots of aggression. Your program to raise energy efficiency standards for automobiles, homes, appliances, and offices, combined with a tax on foreign petroleum imports, would have virtually eliminated U.S. dependence on Persian Gulf oil. Your efforts to promote efficiency abroad would have greatly diminished the global strategic significance of oil. This would have enabled you to treat Saddam Hussein's threat to occupy Kuwait as a question of territorial ownership, rather than as a threat to the West's "way of life."

Your policies to promote sustainable development in the Third World, especially in poor Arab nations, might have further constrained Iraq's ambitions. One reason Saddam Hussein invaded Kuwait was his irritation over Kuwait's insistence that Iraq repay a debt incurred when it fought Iran in the 1980s. Kuwaiti leaders had provided Iraq with a generous loan, because they feared a fundamentalist victory as much as Hussein did. If the West had given economic assistance to Arab countries—perhaps small-scale loans that could not be diverted to military purposes—it could have rendered ineffectual Hussein's rhetoric about the world's richer countries exploiting impoverished Arab states. A robust economic assistance program supplying Iraq with grain, small-scale development loans, and nonmilitary technology might have made Hussein more reluctant to imperil these economic ties through military aggression.

Of course, well-targeted economic assistance would have gone hand-in-hand with programs to promote democracy. A network of citizen exchanges and sister cities might have been engaged in discovering, reporting, and discouraging embarrassing human rights abuses in Iraq. Properly tailored trade relations might have benefited free-thinking Iraqi farmers, merchants, and intellectuals. A proliferation of U.S.-donated fax machines, personal computers, microfiches, and other communications technologies might have eroded the Baath Party's monopoly on information. Together, these policies might have opened up enough political space for more democratically inclined Iraqis to challenge the militaristic policies of Saddam Hussein.

Real conflict resolution also would have been possible, because the relevant international institutions would have been mature and reliable. With more staff, resources, and credibility, the secretary general of the UN would have been available to mediate Iraq's ostensible disputes with Kuwait, including its demands that Kuwait relax repayment terms on Iraq's loans, cease its slant drilling into Iraqi oil fields, and surrender territories that historically belonged to Iraq. Some of these disputes could have been referred to the World Court, now a stronger and more legitimate body, and others to specially appointed international arbitrators.

With all of these security policies in place, the conflict probably would not have escalated beyond a mere shouting match. But even if Iraq had still contemplated aggression, Saddam Hussein would have faced the prospect of almost certain military defeat. Thanks to a global campaign to promote nonprovocative defense, a growing number of countries, including Kuwait and Saudi Arabia, would have been equipped with strong defenses. The Kuwaiti and Saudi borders with Iraq might have been fortified with multiple layers of minefields, ditches, anti-tank barriers, and precision-guided weapons. Even if these defenses could not withstand the full brunt of the Iraqi army, another tool would have been available—a defensive UN collective security force with a formidable air force, navy, and army. A UN satellite system could have alerted the Security Council to the dangers Iraq was posing to Kuwait and Saudi Arabia. Your proposal that the UN deploy forces to deter an Iraqi attack would have passed handily despite the opposition of a handful of nations sympathetic to Saddam Hussein, because the restructured Security Council would have prevented a minority of nations from vetoing urgently needed action.

This hypothetical scenario suggests how the security system we propose can be far more capable of preventing, resolving, and deterring threats than the current one. Compared to today's uneasy world of arms races and wars, our system provides leaders with numerous safety valves with which to stop a political crisis from flaring into a war.

First, our security system provides *early detection and remedy of crises*. William Ury of the Harvard Nuclear Negotiation Project has argued that one factor that often transforms a conflict into a crisis is the pressure of time. Simply having enough time to think through complex diplomatic developments carefully may make the difference between peace and war. Many years after the Cuban missile crisis, George Ball, one of President Kennedy's senior advisers in 1962, reflected: "Much to our own surprise, we reached the unanimous conclusion that, had we determined our course of action within the first 48 hours after the missiles were discovered, we would almost certainly have made the wrong decision, responding to the missiles in such a way as to require a forceful Soviet response and thus setting in train a series of reactions and counter-reactions with horrendous consequences."[4] The system we propose not only gives decisionmakers more time and options to resolve conflicts, it also reduces the premium on time for decisions. Nonprovocative defenses by their very nature produce stalemates early in a conflict and thereby reduce the urgency leaders might otherwise feel to resort to offensive forces. Adhering to minimal deterrence eliminates the need for launch-on-warning or other trip-wire strategies. Putting atomic and hydrogen bombs under international supervision deters nations from resorting to the nuclear option. By lowering the incentives for preemption, our policies provide more time for negotiation and compromise.

Another advantage of our proposed security system is *redundancy*, the presence of multiple independent policies that work in concert to ensure that the security system can successfully respond to unforeseeable dangers. Strategic planners today boast about redundancy in the strategic triad—bombers, ground-launched missiles, and submarine-launched missiles—because each leg is independently capable of inflicting assured destruction on an aggressor. The nonprovocative military structures we propose work redundantly to stymie an attacker. Supplementing national military forces would be a UN force. If front-line defenses fail, defense-in-depth with numerous techno-commando units still can prevent aggression from penetrating too far. If territorial defenses fail, civilian-based defenses can make foreign occupation as disagreeable as the Afghans did for the Soviets— and then some. Unlike the current system, our policies apply the principle of redundancy to avoiding and deflecting conflicts. A conflict can be avoided by thorough democratization *and* resource policies *and* international institutions *and* nonprovocative defense systems. Because these avenues are very different from one another and because they are not linked by a single command-and-control system, they are unlikely to fail at the same time or in the same way, and the failure of one is unlikely to cause the failure of the others.

A third advantage of our system is the *diversity of national participants*. National security planning by a small cabal of experts deliberating in secret has repeatedly shown itself prone to error, abuse, and militarism. The current system demands that the world's five-plus billion people forever entrust their fate to the discouraging record of this elite. Our policies make peace everyone's business. National leaders, of course, will continue to play a major role in overseeing weapons, negotiating treaties, and laying the ground rules for citizen participation in foreign affairs. However, the nuts and bolts of international affairs—in trade, investment, cultural exchange, global communications, environmental protection, development assistance, and conflict resolution—will fall increasingly into the hands of the people of the world. Our proposed security system rests on millions of transnational threads, which, like the Lilliputians restraining Gulliver, can hold back bellicose leaders and become a part of an alternative, nonviolent fabric of international relations.

Finally, our policies are *synergistic*—each strengthens the others. Because today's security system deals with adversaries primarily through provocations, each of its constituent policies tends to make the others more difficult to achieve. During the Cold War the Soviet and U.S. buildup of provocative first-strike weapons, for example, made all other kinds of U.S.-Soviet relations more strained and dangerous. Each of our policies, in contrast, is mutually reinforcing.

☐ *Exporting Democracy.* Democratization not only puts controls on leaders but also helps to eliminate the economic roots of conflict. Hunger in most countries can be eliminated through land reform, which in turn can only be accomplished by giving the landless poor greater political power. Once participatory forces are unleashed, millions of people will be able to involve themselves in world trade, international norm-building, and even such high-politics areas as arms control verification and international peacekeeping. Participation is contagious. Where participation thrives, citizens may increasingly press their leaders to avoid provocative adventures and arms buildups, and to resolve conflicts through cooperative ventures, negotiation, and the UN.

☐ *Better Economic Policies.* More resource efficiency, sounder macro-economic policies, and more constructive Third World development initiatives will provide the world's people with more wealth, more equitably distributed. The benefits for political participation are obvious. For many of the world's poor, meaningful participation is unthinkable if they do not have adequate food, water, shelter, clothing, medical care, and education. Moreover, Third World governments will never enjoy legitimacy unless their people believe there is economic justice. In the Philippines, Corazón Aquino's government was politically unstable—and its guerrilla opposition much stronger—because she never delivered on her promises of real land reform. Equitable economic development also can produce a larger middle class, which often acts as a force for political moderation. Expansionist demagogues such as Hitler, Mussolini, and Tojo came to power during periods of economic depression, when the middle class was relatively weak. To the extent that better economic policies increase the self-sufficiency of nations, especially in vital necessities such as food and energy, there also will be less reason for nations to intervene or to use force to obtain them.

☐ *Peaceful Conflict Resolution.* Efforts to improve the effectiveness of bilateral cooperation, of international norms and regimes, and of the UN and the World Court will help nations to address the economic and political roots of conflict. A better-constituted IMF or World Bank can begin to remove (not just reschedule) the onerous debt burdens on the Third World. New development programs that emphasize self-reliance, environmental protection, and grassroots participation will improve the Third World's long-term economic health. Better international organizations can reduce the economic roots of conflict by strengthening global norms against polluting the air and waterways, endangering species, and wasting natural resources. A stronger World Court will expose human rights abuses that impede political participation and will promote better global norms against torture, racism, sexism, and militarism. Even when nations face armed threats, the development of more powerful and dependable regional or international collective security forces can provide viable options short of war. If the United States seriously had tried to resolve the conflict between the Contras and the Sandinistas in Nicaragua through the Contadora Group, the Arias Plan, or UN peacekeeping, it might have prevented a war that caused

30,000 deaths and left 18,000 wounded.[5] In the long term, a central task for international regimes and institutions can be to assist nations in implementing nonprovocative defenses.

☐ *Nonprovocative Defenses.* While offensive military structures often are at odds with democracy because they require forced conscription, secrecy, repression of dissent, and a concentration of warmaking powers, NPD promotes a flowering of democracy. It was no accident that the renaissance of cultural, economic, and political freedom in Eastern Europe coincided with the rapid disassembly of the offensive security structures of the Warsaw Pact. NPD increases the domestic and foreign costs of aggression and makes nonviolent means of conflict resolution more attractive. By fully adopting NPD, the nations of Europe can reverse the East-West arms race, permanently bury Cold War distrust, and open up millions of new channels for cooperation, dialogue, and negotiation. In other regions such as the Middle East, Southeast Asia, Central America, and Africa, NPD can help wind down current arms races and prevent future conflicts.

National and International Savings

Besides having a much greater chance of preventing war than the current system, our proposals offer the prospect of recouping much of the more than $1 trillion the world now expends on military forces each year. Although much more detailed study is needed on this question, there are several reasons to expect substantial savings.

One of the largest costs of U.S. security policy today is the maintenance of provocative nuclear and nonnuclear forces in Western Europe. Throughout the 1980s two-thirds of the world's annual military spending was consumed in the East-West arms race in Europe. By eliminating NATO's and Russia's nuclear weapons, demobilizing troops, and creating demilitarized buffer zones, NPD can become the most important strategy for global economic revitalization ever conceived. The macroeconomic decisions over which the political parties of most Western nations feud so furiously—interest rates, government spending levels, money suppliers, exchange rates, trade barriers, and so forth—pale in comparison to the possible savings that would result from permanently replacing the Cold War in Europe with a nonprovocative security system. For the United States alone, savings resulting from a demilitarization of Europe could be as high as $150 billion annually—a sizeable fraction of the federal deficit.[6]

Even if NATO or Russia were to implement NPD unilaterally, each would benefit economically because the cost of defensive weapons is often lower than the cost of offensive weapons. A $4,000 precision-guided munition can destroy a $1 million tank, and a $50,000 anti-aircraft missile can bring down a plane that costs $10 million.[7] Offense requires some combination of tanks, mobile armored vehicles, bombers, long-range attack aircraft, and aircraft carriers, all of which are inherently vulnerable to increasingly cheap, accurate, and reliable precision-guided munitions. As the British Royal Navy learned in the Falklands/Malvinas War (when one Exocet missile sank the HMS *Sheffield*) and as the U.S. Navy learned in its first foray into the Persian Gulf (when one Iraqi missile crippled the USS *Stark*), technology is making defense cost-effective.[8]

But some weapons are cheaper to use offensively than to defend against, and these warrant special international oversight. Nuclear bombs fit into this category. Strategic defenses against nuclear weapons can always be overwhelmed by cheaper missiles, decoys, and space mines. This is why we propose that the United States and Russia, at least initially, adopt a policy of minimal deterrence based on a second-strike capability, which would deter a nuclear attack and still eliminate over 90 percent of their nuclear arsenals. If the United States subscribes to minimal deterrence, for example, it can cut the Trident D-5 missiles, the B-2 Stealth bombers, and SDI, with resulting savings of tens of billions of dollars a year. Additional cuts in nuclear testing and warhead manufacture will save billions more. As President Eisenhower said in 1953: "Every gun that is made, every warship launched, every rocket fired signifies, in the final sense, a theft from those who hunger and are not fed, those who are cold and not clothed. This world in arms is not spending money alone. It is spending the sweat of its laborers, the genius of its scientists, the hopes of its children. . . . This is not a way of life at all, in any true sense."[9]

The creation of a defensive UN collective security force also can prevent the further hemorrhage of national treasuries into wasteful military expenditures. Saddam Hussein's grab for Kuwait will certainly not be the last act of international aggression in our lifetimes. How often can the United States—or any other nation acting alone—afford to spend tens of billions of dollars to halt the latest

Napoleon on the global scene? Our proposals lift this burden from the shoulders of the United States and put it more equitably on all nations. If the United States cedes to the UN some of its foreign bases, battleships, bombers, and other long-range forces, all of which are very costly items, the U.S. defense budget can be cut significantly. U.S. annual dues to UN peacekeeping forces might be substantially increased, but even under current cost-sharing arrangements (which should be made more equitable), the United States pays only 30 percent of the total peacekeeping costs (which is preferable to paying 100 percent of operations undertaken unilaterally). Moreover, creative U.S. diplomacy can persuade Japan, Germany, and other rising economic powers to assume greater financial burdens—and thereby lower the burden to U.S. taxpayers even further.

Additional savings to the United States can result from the nonmilitary policies we recommend. Energy efficiency not only eliminates many roots of conflict but also prevents costly expenditures on expanding the U.S. energy supply, which yields net savings often equal to a substantial percentage of GNP. Promotion of democracy and sustainable development in the CIS, Eastern Europe, and Latin America will prevent expensive arms races and wars, create lucrative markets for U.S. goods, and provide profitable places for U.S. investment. As Václav Havel, then the president of Czechoslovakia, told the U.S. Congress, millions of dollars spent today to stabilize fragile democracies, especially those in the former Soviet Union, will be billions of dollars saved tomorrow. Fairer rules of trade will prime the global economic pump without ruining the environment or stripping U.S. workers of decent jobs. And stronger international norms and laws protecting global commons like the oceans, the air, and imperiled species will prevent trillions of dollars of potential damage to human health and property from air pollution, climate change, ozone depletion, food poisoning, crop failure, and migration.

Throughout the world, peoples and nations are crying out for ways to increase security without dissipating their resources. The 1980 Brandt Commission pointed out that the money saved from every tank not built could be used to produce 4,000 tons of rice, enough to feed 22,000 children for a year.[10] The $20 million not paid for a jet fighter could support 40,000 village pharmacies. One-half of one percent of the world's military expenditures, if redirected, could buy enough agricultural equipment to enable every Third World country to be self-sufficient in food within a decade. Our policies provide a realistic way for nations to protect themselves more effectively and still reallocate parts of their military budgets into these vitally needed investments.[11]

Other Security Threats

Not only can our proposals better prevent war and result in massive economic savings, they also can help address many other pressing national security issues. While the current security system under-values or exacerbates the threats Americans now say they are most concerned with—weapons proliferation, civil wars, terrorism, drug trafficking, economic decline, and environmental disasters—the security system we propose helps address each of them.

Weapons Proliferation

The current system values provocative weapons. As long as the United States, Russia, the Ukraine, France, Britain, China, and Israel are unwilling to disarm their nuclear weapons (as well as their chem-ical and biological ones), how can we be surprised when less powerful countries insist on having them as well? The only credible way to halt weapons proliferation is through global arms control agreements in which *all* nations forswear these weapons. Our proposals to shut down the military and civilian nuclear industries, to promote alter-native energy sources, to end the production of fissionable uranium and plutonium, and to put nuclear materials and nuclear bombs in halfway houses overseen by international inspectors move the world toward denuclearization.

Nations like the United States and Russia will be willing to let go of their nuclear bombs only when they can feel secure without these offensive weapons—a top priority for our proposed system. In a global environment that emphasizes defensive weapons and strat-egies, it will be easier to spot, stigmatize, and counter nations still committed to offense. The UN might produce an annual report eval-uating the relative defensiveness and offensiveness of every nation's arsenal. NGOs might document and embarrass nations unwilling to move toward NPD. Whenever pariah nations cross a certain thresh-old of offensiveness, the rest of the world can act in unison to stop selling them military hardware (today's arms embargoes, in contrast, are usually only against nations that have already begun fighting).

Nations endangered by aggressors might receive special assistance from defensive UN collective security forces.

All of the critical components of nonproliferation—negotiating global security agreements, inspecting existing stockpiles and factories, and punishing cheaters—depend on stronger international institutions. While U.S. security planners currently make institutions like the UN a low priority, repeating self-fulfilling prophesies that they are weak and ineffectual, our proposals move the United States to strengthen, democratize, and regularly use these institutions.

Even if our proposals lead only to serious bilateral arms reductions, they will help the cause of nonproliferation. If the United States and Russia finally fulfill their promise to pursue disarmament in good faith and achieve a comprehensive ban on nuclear testing, there is a much better chance that the nonnuclear signatories to the NPT will renew the agreement when it expires in 1995. Likewise, serious superpower initiatives to outlaw chemical and biological weapons completely (including so-called defensive research) will give them the credibility needed to induce other nations to renounce these cruel weapons.

Civil Wars

The year 1992 was when Americans realized that most conflicts in the post–Cold War world would be civil wars, usually with one ethnic, tribal, or religious faction taking up arms against another. They watched television images of atrocities being committed on nearly every continent: Serbs practicing "ethnic cleansing" of Muslims in Bosnia-Herzegovina, mass graves being unearthed in Guatemala and El Salvador, Somalian warlords laying waste to farms and leaving hundreds of thousands to starve, Indonesian troops firing on unarmed protesters in East Timor. During the Cold War, the United States believed it could respond to regional conflicts in two ways—either by ignoring them entirely or by assisting one side with arms shipments, covert action, or military intervention. However, neither isolationism nor unilateralism did these countries, or the United States, very much good.

Our proposals suggest new ways civil wars can be prevented. Spreading ideas about human rights, strong democracy, civil society, and federalism can help unstable countries reorganize themselves without violence. Helping nations to become more efficient users of resources and to establish more self-reliant and sustainable economies can reduce the frequency and intensity of internal conflicts. A more active UN Secretariat can mediate local fights before they explode into larger civil wars.

When Serbia went to war against Croatia and Slovenia in 1991, everyone predicted that Bosnia-Herzegovina would be its next target. A UN peacekeeping force could have been dispatched to Bosnia in advance, and teams of conflict resolvers could have mobilized civic leaders to preach reconciliation, tolerance, and nonviolence. This might have prevented the hundreds of thousands of casualties that occurred when Serbia helped the Bosnian Serbs rape, pillage, and slaughter their Croatian and Muslim neighbors in 1992 and 1993. Today, the same case can be made for the UN to deploy a large peacekeeping force to Macedonia, and to be prepared to enter Kosovo should Serbian overlords begin to prosecute ethnic cleansing against the Albanian majority.

The biggest threat that civil wars pose to world peace is the possibility of escalation into regional or global conflicts. Our proposals reduce the chances of this happening by creating global systems of inspection and control over offensive conventional weapons and over the materials and technology for nuclear, chemical, and biological weapons. By trimming the overall level of weaponry in nations, our proposals also make future UN peacekeeping operations more manageable. UN forces will be useless if they are constantly ducking bullets, mortars, and shrapnel.

Terrorism

The global cooperation promoted by our proposals is the best defense against terrorism—in three different ways. First, what little progress the world has made against terrorism in recent years is due to greater cooperation among national police forces in tracking, chasing, arresting, and prosecuting terrorists. The best possible deterrent against terrorism is to let offenders know that there is no safe harbor in which to hide. Stronger international laws against terrorism are still needed to ensure uniformly stiff punishments. The development of international norms and laws offers the long-term chance that terrorists caught anywhere on the planet can be brought before an international tribunal.

Second, better global cooperation is the only way to keep high-tech weapons and weapons materials such as enriched uranium and pluto-nium away from terrorists. Currently, the world tries to prevent crim-inal diversions of nuclear-bomb materials through one relatively weak organization, the IAEA. A stronger nonproliferation regime will require not only a substantial overhaul of the IAEA but also the use of other international organizations to monitor flows of industrial chemicals and biotechnology and prevent their diversion to chemical and biological weapons. Our proposals would have U.S. security plan-ners emphasize this kind of multilateral cooperation.

Terrorism is ultimately a political problem, not a technical one. In an open society any public gathering or meeting of leaders is always vulnerable to homemade bombs, nerve gas, over-the-counter poison, and widely available firearms, grenades, and Molotov cocktails. The United States must begin to replace the current anarchy of interna-tional relations, in which might makes right, with a more predictable and respected body of norms and laws in which major political griev-ances have a greater chance of being settled without violence. Once the international community can help groups like the Palestinians or the Irish Catholics attain some of the political rights they seek, these groups may be willing to renounce violence. By emphasizing the pre-vention and resolution of conflict, our proposals are better equipped than the current system to defuse terrorism at its roots.

Drug Trafficking

The international flow of narcotics thrives in part because of the ab-sence of any serious international drug enforcement. Right now, drug traffickers have created elaborate global networks for growing, pro-cessing, and distributing their goods, while nations rely on primitive law enforcement networks to eradicate poppy and coca crops, to pre-vent large-scale laundering of drug profits, and to prosecute drug lords. Criminals can move freely to countries with the weakest anti-drug policies because there are no enforceable international laws. By stressing the development of international organizations and laws that can deal effectively with drug trafficking, our proposals can help nations put globetrotting drug lords behind bars.

Our proposals also would focus U.S. foreign policy on one of the key reasons why Third World farmers turn to growing drug crops—poverty. So long as the average coca farmer can earn an income six times higher than other farmers for a crop that is resistant to most pests and enjoys a relatively stable price, the incentives for illicit agriculture will remain irresistible. Freed of the expense of the arms race and unilateral interventions, the United States can invest in genuine debt relief, sustainable development, and family planning. Today it spends only about $300 million each year on assistance to population, energy, and environmental programs abroad—about one one-thousandth of its total military expenditures, or two-thirds of the cost of a *single* B-2 bomber.[12] Given the magnitude of the economic problems in the Third World, this is a pittance.

Every American city should consider adopting a town or village in Peru, Bolivia, or Colombia, so that U.S. citizens may work side by side with Latin American citizens to promote economic alternatives to growing coca. Like the Europeans who now have nearly one thousand Third World links dedicated to sustainable development, Americans should send sister communities farming equipment, provide small-scale loans, and help build roads, bridges, water systems, and schools. For $25 billion, a fraction of the total cost of the Persian Gulf War, the United States could pay every rural family in Latin America $1,000 not to grow coca (an amount equal to the typical annual income for a coca farmer).[13] That would be half the cost American cities are now paying in terms of crime, sickness, and other damages from the drug war at home.

National Economic Decline

As we have seen, the bloated defense budget and ongoing military adventures have undermined the economic strength of the United States. Contrary to what the economy might have looked like if the United States had invested in nonmilitary programs (or simply if it had not created the huge federal deficit), the Reagan rearmament program, perpetuated by President Bush, spawned a corrupt and inefficient welfare system for defense contractors, debased the education and training of the nation's future labor force, let public infrastructure decay, hired the best and brightest young people to produce better bombs instead of better civilian technologies, and bled hundreds of billions of critically needed dollars away from programs for public health and housing.

The rearmament programs of the 1980s have already left U.S. cities looking like war zones; many soldiers who fought in the Persian Gulf War were statistically safer spending six months on combat duty than they were in their own neighborhoods. During the 1980s the U.S. defense budget increased by $579 billion, while total federal funds to states and cities were cut by $78 billion.[14] Despite escalating problems of crime, crack, and homelessness, for example, New York City in 1990 tried to close a deficit of nearly $1 billion by laying off more than 10,000 municipal workers.[15] According to a 1990 survey by the National League of Cities of 576 communities with populations greater than 100,000, more than half encountered more difficulties in paying their bills than they had a year earlier.[16] Red ink is also plaguing more than half the states.[17] Henry Aaron of the Brookings Institution says, "I think you would have to go back to the Great Depression to find similar anguish, in terms of the number of states that are facing unprecedented cutbacks in service."[18] Unless the United States fundamentally changes its national security policies and stops pouring money into Patriot missiles, Star Wars research, and a permanent troop presence in the Middle East, its urban centers will collapse.

Cutting the U.S. defense budget, of course, is not the only policy that can restore the nation's economic strength. But as long as Americans are unwilling to raise taxes, it is a logical necessity. Trimming a few billion here and there through occasional weapons cancellations, procurement reform, or accounting gimmickry is not enough. Real savings will be possible only if the United States restructures its military commitments to Europe and Asia, creates a UN collective security apparatus, closes its overseas bases, and demobilizes these troops once they return home. By providing clear principles for accomplishing these tasks without compromising the security of U.S. allies, our proposals can help put the U.S. economic house in order.

One by one, the economic competitors of the United States have come to see that their future rests on a strong economy, not on an inefficient military establishment. Japan is nurturing its best industries with generous public investment. Western Europe is increasing its economic competitiveness by solidifying its common market. According to the CIA, between 1978 and 1986 China slashed its military forces by 3 million troops, cut weapons purchases by 10 percent, and reduced overall military spending by 20 percent to improve its domestic economy.[19] And after the collapse of the Soviet Union, the constituent republics decommissioned thousands of nuclear weapons and cut military procurement by 50 to 80 percent.[20] When will the United States wake up to this world of new priorities?

Environmental Threats

Finally, there is the long list of environmental threats—global warming, ozone depletion, acid rain, ocean dumping, toxic wastes—that today's national security planners all but ignore. By any objective standard, these threats are as significant as those that were posed by Soviet expansionism, Libyan terrorism, Manuel Noriega's drug running, or Saddam Hussein's appetite for oil. While computer models continue to crank out ominous estimates of casualties from absurd conventional war scenarios in Europe, millions of people worldwide are dying from cancers caused by ecological abuses. When will the United States begin to pay more attention to the wars that are already raging?

The security system we propose takes these environmental threats seriously and provides the resources for ameliorating them. It helps nations to become familiar with the kinds of international cooperation necessary to address these problems. There is no way that the United States, or any other nation acting alone, can stop destruction of tropical rainforests or prevent destructive releases of carbon dioxide, chlorofluorocarbons, or methane into the atmosphere. These problems are truly global in scope; they require the kinds of international norms and laws that we have suggested the United States begin to foster. Moreover, to undo the damage that has already been done, the new global institutions we propose will be needed to foster multinational efforts at reforestation, environmental restoration, and energy efficiency.

Choices for the Future

The American people can continue to cling to security concepts adopted nearly fifty years ago and observe the moral stature and the economy of the United States decline, or they can redefine these security policies to address a wide variety of military, political, economic, and environmental threats. They can continue to worry about resurgent Russian expansionism while less paranoid allies of the United States invest in loans, joint ventures, and trade deals with the CIS. They can continue to rely on the provocative strategies of nuclear deterrence and extended deterrence—and risk a nuclear war by accident or miscalculation—or they can seriously promote democracy, resource efficiency, international institutions, and nonprovocative defense. They can continue to pray that their leaders will not overreact when a crisis arises, or they can actively search out solutions and do something about conflicts and problems long before shots are ever fired. They can continue to keep the American people out of foreign policy, a hopeless effort that cannot succeed without endangering the most basic civil liberties, or they can help to harness the intelligence, creativity, and enthusiasm of millions of their fellow citizens through grassroots action and municipal foreign policy.

In recent years the National Security Council has consisted primarily of the secretaries of state and defense, military analysts, and Sovietologists. To their ranks should be added leading experts on democracy, international economics, global environmental problems, and the Third World.[21] This newly constituted NSC should produce an annual compendium of security threats and recommend an array of policies to defuse each of them, including actions that can be taken by American citizens, religious organizations, corporations, and local governments. People should gather at open meetings across the country to discuss this report and to prepare ideas for the following year's report. U.S. security policies should be formulated and implemented not to manipulate public opinion, but instead to embody the wishes and values of the American people.

As long as the United States sees its security in terms of arms building or uses of force, nuclear war may be inevitable. As Kenneth Boulding's example of the hundred-year flood suggests, even if there is only a 1 percent chance of nuclear war in any given year, sooner or later it is bound to occur. The security system we have proposed suggests that a very different kind of world order is possible. It will not eliminate all conflict from the planet—no security system can assure that. It will, however, begin to make war as unlikely as is humanly possible. The panoply of proposals we have presented cannot be implemented overnight, universally, or simultaneously. Some are more controversial than others, and some will entail greater risk. But the risks, whatever they may be, pale in comparison to the known dangers of the current system.

If we had no alternatives, we could despair of the hopelessness of the human condition. But the alternatives beckon and provide an urgent challenge to American idealism and ingenuity. The notion that security is possible through economic justice, political freedom, respected laws, and a common defense is what inspired our forefathers in the summer of 1787 to produce one of the most influential political documents of modern times. Today, over two hundred years later, we, the people of the United States—and we, the people of the world—have the opportunity "to form a more perfect union, to establish justice, insure domestic tranquility, provide for the common defence, promote the general welfare, and secure the blessings of liberty to ourselves and our posterity." All we need is to lift up our vision, summon our courage, and commit ourselves to begin.

Notes

Introduction

1. Ronald Reagan, "I'm Convinced that Gorbachev Wants a Free-Market Democracy," *New York Times*, 12 June 1990, p. A21.

2. Francis Fukuyama, "The End of History?" *National Interest*, no. 16 (Summer 1989):18.

3. Christopher Flavin, "The Cold War Ends, The Oil War Begins," *Christian Science Monitor*, 10 August 1990, p. 19.

4. "The Stakes in the Gulf," *Wall Street Journal*, 15 August 1990, p. A8.

5. Quoted in Robert L. Borosage, "How Bush Kept the Guns from Turning into Butter," *Rolling Stone*, 21 February 1991, p. 20.

6. William M. Arkin, Greenpeace, personal communication, 5 January 1993; and John G. Heidenrich, "The Gulf War: How Many Iraqis Died?" *Foreign Policy*, no. 90 (Spring 1993):108–125. See also William M. Arkin, "The Gulf 'Hyperwar'—An Interim Tally," *New York Times*, 22 June 1991, p. 15.

7. Harvard Study Team Report, "Public Health in Iraq After the Gulf War," May 1991 (monograph). Available from the Public Affairs Office at the Harvard School of Public Health.

8. "Notes and Comment," *New Yorker*, 1 October 1990, p. 29.

9. Americans Talk Security, "A Series of Surveys of American Voters: Attitudes Concerning National Security Issues," in *National Survey No. 12* (Winchester, MA: Americans Talk Security, January 1989), p. 15.

10. See George F. Will, "Reagan's Disarmament," *Newsweek*, 21 December 1987, p. 78.

11. Amy Kaslow, "U.S. Government, Firms Courted Iraq in Late '80s," *Christian Science Monitor*, 19 November 1990, p. 7; Glenn Frankel, "How Saddam Built His War Machine," *Washington Post*, 17 September 1990, p. 1; Jim Hoagland, "Soft on Saddam," *Washington Post*, National Weekly Edition, 16–22 April 1990, p. 29.

12. Alan Friedman, "BNL Hell," *New Republic*, 9 November 1992, pp. 18–20.

13. Stephen Kinzer, "Gulf War Sets Off Crisis for Germans," *New York Times*, 17 February 1991, p. 15.

14. See warnings from, among others, Jacob Goldberg, "The Illogic of Saudi Arms Sales," *New York Times,* 19 September 1990, p. A29.

15. Michael T. Klare, "Fueling the Fire: How We Armed the Middle East," *Bulletin of the Atomic Scientists* 47, no. 1 (January-February 1991):19–26.

16. Robert Kuttner, "Thanks for Sharing," *New Republic,* 31 December 1990, pp. 17–18.

17. *World Almanac and Book of Facts—1988* (New York: Pharos Books, 1987), pp. 338–339.

18. Barton Gellman, "Fading Memories, Evanescent Victory," *Washington Post,* National Weekly Edition, 20–26 January 1992, p. 11.

19. "A Nation's Global Role," *Newsweek,* 11 March 1991, p. 72.

20. Henry Kissinger, "False Dreams of a New World Order," *Washington Post,* 26 February 1991, p. A21.

21. Don Oberdorfer, "Eased East-West Tension Offers Chances, Dangers," *Washington Post,* 7 May 1989, pp. A1, A32.

22. Ibid., A32.

23. Quoted in Robert L. Borosage, "Defensive About Defense Cuts," *Nation,* 9 March 1992, cover page.

24. At the time of the dissolution of the Soviet Union, its nuclear weapons were spread among four republics: Russia, Ukraine, Belarus, and Kazakhstan. Under the START agreements all nuclear weapons are supposed to be transferred to Russia. As of this writing, Kazakhstan has done so and Belarus has announced its intention to comply; the Ukraine, however, continues to debate whether it will ratify START and denuclearize.

25. Matthew L. Wald, "Price of Oil Jumps Past $40 a Barrel," *New York Times,* 10 October 1991, p. A1.

26. Asra Q. Nomani, Jeffrey Taylor, and Scott Kilman, "It May Be Irrational, but Terrorism Anxiety Spurs Plunge in Travel," *Wall Street Journal,* 13 February 1991, p. 1.

27. Doris Meissner, "Managing Migrations," *Foreign Policy,* no. 86 (Spring 1992):68.

28. Barton Gellman, "Fading Memories, Evanescent Victory," *Washington Post,* National Weekly Edition, 20–26 January 1987, p. 11. Two years after the war, a report by the Arab Monetary Fund and two other Arab economic institutions estimated that the total cost of the war to the region (excluding environmental damage and lost economic growth) was $676 billion. Youssef M. Ibrahim, "War Is Said to Cost the Persian Gulf $676 Billion in 1990 and 1991," *New York Times,* 25 April 1993, p. 14.

29. See Table 1 for comparisons of military and nonmilitary expenditures in 1990.

Many of the "nonmilitary expenditures" actually have substantial military purposes. Foreign aid is often used for military education and training. PL-480 Food Aid has sometimes been resold by recipient countries for

Table 1   Fiscal Year 1990 Expenditures

Expenditure	$ Billion
Military Expenditures	
Department of Defense total	289.8
Department of Energy expenditures on nuclear weapons	9.0
Defense-related expenditures	0.6
Foreign military financing	4.8
Military training and other	0.1
Total	$304.3
Nonmilitary Expenditures	
International development and humanitarian assistance	
Economic Support Fund	$4.0
AID for Eastern Europe	2.6
Multilateral development banks	1.5
Food aid	1.0
Refugee programs	0.5
Voluntary contributions to international organizations	0.3
State Department narcotics assistance	0.1
Peace Corps	0.2
Other	0.1
Conduct of foreign affairs	
State Department salaries and expenses	1.8
Foreign buildings	0.3
United Nations program	0.7
Other	0.1
Foreign information and exchange	
U.S. Information Agency	0.9
Board for International Broadcasting	0.4
International financial programs	
Export-Import Bank	0.6
International Monetary Fund	0
Other	0.1
Total	15.2

SOURCE: *The Budget for Fiscal Year 1992* (Washington, DC: U.S. Government Printing Office, 1992), pp. 183, 194.

military aid. The Department of State's administrative funding is frequently harnessed for military diplomacy.

30. "Excerpts from Pentagon's Plan: 'Prevent the Re-Emergence of a New Rival,'" *New York Times,* 8 March 1992, p. 14.

31. Patrick E. Tyler, "U.S. Strategy Plan Calls for Insuring No Rivals Develop," *New York Times,* 8 March 1992, p. 1.

32. James Chace, "The Pentagon's Superpower Fantasy," *New York Times,* 16 April 1992, p. A17.

33. Robert L. Borosage, "Imagine Peacetime," *Mother Jones,* January-February 1992, p. 20.

34. One prominent example of official disinformation is the White

House's efforts to destabilize the Libyan government by planting a story in the *Wall Street Journal* about an imminent U.S. attack on Libya. See Bob Woodward, *Veil* (New York: Pocket Books, 1987), pp. 548–552. For extensive discussions of the timidity of the American press, see Noam Chomsky, "The Bounds of Thinkable Thought," *Progressive,* October 1985, pp. 28–31; Noam Chomsky, "All the News that Fits," *Utne Reader,* February–March 1986, pp. 56–62; and various issues of the magazines *Deadline* (available from the Center for War, Peace, and the News Media, New York University, 10 Washington Place, New York, NY 10003) and *Extra!* (available from Fairness & Accuracy in Reporting, 130 West 25 St., New York, NY 10001).

35. Daniel Yankelovich and John Doble, "The Public Mood: Nuclear Weapons and the U.S.S.R.," *Foreign Affairs* 63, no. 1 (Fall 1984):46.

Chapter 1

1. See, for example, Patrick J. Buchanan, "Now that Red Is Dead, Come Home, America," *Washington Post,* 8 September 1991, Outlook section, p. C4; and SANE/Freeze referendum passed by the city of Chicago in April 1991, cited in "National Budget Priorities," *Global Communities,* August 1991, p. 7. (SANE/Freeze is now called Peace Action.)

2. Edward N. Luttwak, *The Meaning of Victory: Essays on Strategy* (New York: Simon and Schuster, 1986), pp. 85–115.

3. Edward N. Luttwak, "America's Setting Sun," *New York Times,* 23 September 1991, p. A17.

4. Our definition of security threats explicitly does not include problems originating primarily from *within* the United States. To broaden the definition that far would open the book to a discussion of all policies on all issues.

5. An interesting early effort to redefine national security is made by Richard H. Ullman in "Redefining National Security," *International Security* 8, no. 1 (Summer 1983):129–153.

6. "Nuclear Notebook: Proposed U.S. and C.I.S. Strategic Forces," *Bulletin of the Atomic Scientists* 48, no. 4 (May 1992):48–49; and William M. Arkin, personal communication, 5 January 1993. By 2003, the United States will have roughly the same number of warheads—5,500.

7. John H. Cushman, Jr., "The Race to a More Elaborate Arms Race," *New York Times,* 3 July 1988, p. 3; and E. A. Wayne, "U.S. View of Chemical Arms Meeting," *Christian Science Monitor,* 6 January 1989, p. 7.

8. "Selling Ways to Wage Chemical War: A Booming Business," *Christian Science Monitor,* 13 December 1988, p. B4 (chart).

9. Robert S. Greenberger, "Iraq Opened Dangerous Pandora's Box by Using Chemicals in War with Iran," *Wall Street Journal,* 1 August 1988, p. 12.

10. Ibid.

11. George D. Moffett III, "Israel, Determined not to Be a Chemical Target," *Christian Science Monitor,* 13 December 1988, pp. B15–16.

12. Ibid., B16.

13. Ernest Conine, "Missile and Nuclear Arms Heighten Third World Risk," *Los Angeles Times,* 15 January 1988, p. II-15; and Jack Anderson, "New Weapons from Brazil," *San Francisco Chronicle,* 28 March 1988, p. A25.

14. Jonathan Power, "Private Arms Cartel Often Flaunts Law," *San Francisco Chronicle,* 10 February 1988, Briefing section, p. 5.

15. George D. Moffett III, "Modern Missiles Add Twist to Mideast Arms Spiral," *Christian Science Monitor,* 15 July 1988, p. 1.

16. Philip Shenon, "U.S. Accuses 2 Egyptian Colonels in Plot to Smuggle Missile Material," *New York Times,* 25 June 1988, p. 1; and Mel Elfin, "Behind the Condor Carbon-Carbon Smuggling Scam," *U.S. News and World Report,* 25 July 1988, p. 38.

17. John Wolfsthal, senior research analyst, Arms Control Association, personal communication, 5 January 1993.

18. Gary Yerkey, "Experts Study Threat of Chemical Weapons in Terrorists' Hands," *Christian Science Monitor,* 29 August 1986, p. 9.

19. Ibid.

20. David Ignatius, "Terrorism? So What Else Is New?" *Washington Post,* National Weekly Edition, 28 April 1986, p. 24.

21. Michael T. Klare, "Deadly Convergence: The Perils of the Arms Trade," *World Policy Journal* 6, no. 1 (Winter 1988–1989):147. Figures are in 1985 dollars.

22. Patrick E. Tyler, "7 Hypothetical Conflicts Foreseen by the Pentagon," *New York Times,* 17 February 1992, p. A8.

23. Valerie Bunce, "The Struggle for Liberal Democracy in Eastern Europe," *World Policy Journal* 7, no. 3 (Summer 1990):423–424.

24. Walter S. Mossberg and John Walcott, "U.S. Defines Policy on Security to Place Less Stress on Soviets," *Wall Street Journal,* 11 August 1988, pp. 1, 16.

25. Freedom House, "Democracies Increase Again This Year," 17 December 1992 (press release).

26. "World at War—1992," *Defense Monitor* 21, no. 6 (1992):1–16.

27. David Gergen, "Rebalancing Justice's Scales," *U.S. News and World Report,* 27 March 1989, p. 96.

28. Peter Andreas and Coletta Youngers, "'Busting' the Andean Cocaine Industry," *World Policy Journal* 6, no. 3 (Summer 1989):541.

29. Stephen Labaton, "The Cost of Drug Abuse: $60 Billion a Year," *New York Times,* 5 December 1989, p. D1.

30. Gerald Epstein, "Mortgaging America," *World Policy Journal* 8, no. 1 (Winter 1990–1991):27.

31. Richard J. Barnet, et al., "American Priorities in a New World Era,"

World Policy Journal 6, no. 2 (Spring 1989):205. See also Anne B. Fisher, "Who's Hurt by Salomon's Greed?" *Fortune*, 23 September 1991, p. 71.

32. Felix Rohatyn, "America's Economic Dependence," *Foreign Affairs* 68, no. 1 (America and the World issue 1988–1989):55.

33. Ibid., 60.

34. Ibid., 63.

35. Ibid., 62–63.

36. Paul Kennedy, *The Rise and Fall of the Great Powers: Economic Change and Military Conflict from 1500 to 2000* (New York: Random House, 1988).

37. Samuel P. Huntington, "The U.S.—Decline or Renewal," *Foreign Affairs* 67, no. 2 (Winter 1988–1989):81.

38. Barnet, et al., "American Priorities in a New World Era," 205.

39. American Federation of State, County and Municipal Employees, "The Republican Record: A 7-Year Analysis of State Losses of Federal Funding (FY 1982–FY 1988)," August 1988, p. 1. (Available from the American Federation of State, County and Municipal Employees, AFL-CIO, 1625 L St., NW, Washington, DC 20036.)

40. "Levels of Federal Assistance to State and Local Governments," *Global Communities*, Autumn 1991, p. 3.

41. Barnet, et al., "American Priorities in a New World Era," 208.

42. "An Interview with Hazel Henderson," *Whole Earth Review*, Winter 1988, p. 5.

43. Charles William Maynes, "Coping with the '90s," *Foreign Policy*, no. 74 (Spring 1989):43.

44. Roughly 270 million Europeans (including Turks) received $100 billion in 1989 dollars from the Marshall Plan—or about $370 per person. There are now 4 billion people living in the South.

45. Mossberg and Walcott, "U.S. Defines Policy," 16.

46. Richard J. Barnet and John Cavanagh, "National Interest and Global Realities," *IPS Briefing Paper #2* (Washington, DC: IPS, January 1992), p. 4.

47. Matthew L. Wald, "Gulf Victory: An Energy Defeat?" *New York Times*, 18 June 1991, p. D1.

48. Office of Technology Assessment, "Strategic Materials: Technologies to Reduce U.S. Import Vulnerability," OTA-ITE-248, May 1985, p. 3.

49. Rohatyn, "America's Economic Dependence," 57.

50. Ibid.

51. Mossberg and Walcott, "U.S. Defines Policy," 16.

52. Norman Myers, "Environment and Security," *Foreign Policy*, no. 74 (Spring 1989):35.

53. Francis Stewart, "Back to Keynesianism: Reforming the IMF," *World Policy Journal* 4, no. 3 (Summer 1987):472.

54. Barnet, et al., "American Priorities in a New World Era," 205.

55. Myers, "Environment and Security," 36.

56. Quoted in ibid., 36.

57. "The Accident at Chernobyl—Economic Damage and Its Compensation in Western Europe," *Nuclear Law Bulletin* 39 (June 1987):58–65.

58. Jessica Tuchman Matthews, "Redefining Security," *Foreign Affairs* 68, no. 2 (Spring 1989):162–163.

59. Carl Haub, "The World Population Crisis Was Forgotten, but Not Gone," *Washington Post,* National Weekly Edition, 5–11 September 1988, p. 23.

60. *The Global 2000 Report to the President on Entering the Twenty-first Century* (Washington, DC: U.S. Government Printing Office, 1980).

61. Matthews, "Redefining Security," 165–166.

62. Quoted in Myers, "Environment and Security," 24–25.

63. Jodi L. Jacobson, "Abandoning Homelands," in *State of the World 1989,* ed. Lester R. Brown (New York: W. W. Norton, 1989), p. 64.

64. Myers, "Environment and Security," 28–29.

65. Ibid., 28.

66. Ibid., 29.

67. Ibid., 32.

68. Ibid., 29.

69. Matthews, "Redefining Security," 165.

70. Ibid.

71. "Ecologists Make Friends with Economists," *Economist,* 15 October 1988, p. 25.

72. Matthews, "Redefining Security," 169.

73. Ibid.

74. John P. Holdren, "Cross-Cutting Issues in Integrated Environmental Assessment of Energy Alternatives: Distribution of Costs and Benefits," Energy Resources Group—Working Paper 80-10, October 1979 (monograph), p. R-1, note 2.

75. David A. Wirth, "Climate Chaos," *Foreign Policy,* no. 74 (Spring 1989):9.

76. Matthews, "Redefining Security," 170.

77. Wirth, 12; Stephen H. Schneider and Robert S. Chen, "Carbon Dioxide Warming and Coastline Flooding: Physical Factors and Climatic Impact," in *Annual Review of Energy* 5 (Palo Alto, CA: Annual Reviews Inc., 1980), pp. 116–117.

78. Philip Shabecoff, "Most Authoritative Study Yet Shows Declining Ozone Layer," *New York Times,* Western Edition, 16 March 1988, p. 1.

79. Dick Russell and Russell King, "Politics of Ozone: Delay in the Face of Disaster," *In These Times,* 17–30 August 1988, p. 6.

80. "Don't Go Near the Water," *Newsweek,* 1 August 1988, p. 42; Paul R. Ehrlich, Anne H. Ehrlich, and John P. Holdren, *Ecoscience: Population, Resources, Environment* (San Francisco: W. H. Freeman, 1970), pp. 565, 631; J. Parry, "Nations Unite to Fight Pollution," *Sea Front* 29 (May-June 1983): 143–150; Jodi L Jacobson, "Swept Away," *Worldwatch* 2, no. 1 (January-

February 1989):20–26; Philip Shabecoff, "Acid Rain Called Peril to Sea Life on Atlantic Coast," *New York Times*, 25 April 1988, p. 1.

81. Jacobson, "Abandoning Homelands," 59–60.

82. Daniel Deudney, "Environment and Security: Muddled Thinking," *Bulletin of the Atomic Scientists* 47, no. 3 (April 1991):22–28.

Chapter 2

1. Quoted in John Lewis Gaddis, *The United States and the Origins of the Cold War* (New York: Columbia University Press, 1972), p. 351.

2. Robert Greenberger and Tim Carrington, "Network of U.S. Bases Overseas Is Unraveling as Need for It Grows," *Wall Street Journal*, 29 December 1987, p. 6.

3. William Blum, *The CIA: A Forgotten History* (London: Zed Books, 1986).

4. Ruth Leger Sivard, *World Military and Social Expenditures—1991*, 14th ed. (Washington, DC: World Priorities, 1991), p. 22.

5. Jonathan Kwitny, *Endless Enemies: The Making of an Unfriendly World* (New York: Penguin Books, 1984), pp. 1–103.

6. Ibid., 108.

7. Ibid., 109.

8. Frances Moore Lappé, Rachel Shurman, and Kevin Danaher, *Betraying the National Interest* (New York: Grove Press, 1987), pp. 45–49.

9. Ibid., 47.

10. Greenberger and Carrington, "Network," 1. See also Seth Mydans, "Talks on Bases in Philippines Spur Defiance Toward U.S.," *New York Times*, 25 June 1988, p. 1.

11. Selig S. Harrison and Clyde V. Prestowitz, Jr., "Pacific Agenda: Defense or Economics?" *Foreign Policy*, no. 79 (Summer 1990):62.

12. Joseph Gerson and Bruce Birchard, *Confronting the Network of Foreign U.S. Military Bases* (Boston: South End Press, 1991).

13. Between 1981 and 1983 the Reagan administration refused to investigate reports by U.S. agents that the Honduran military was dealing in drugs, because of that nation's support for the Nicaraguan Contras. Elaine Sciolino and Stephen Engelberg, "Narcotics Effort Foiled by U.S. Security Goals," *New York Times*, Western Edition, 10 April 1988, pp. 1, 10.

14. Dennis Marker, "A Catalogue of Constant U.S. Interference," *Christian Science Monitor*, 14 February 1990, p. 25.

15. Saul Landau, *The Dangerous Doctrine: National Security and U.S. Foreign Policy* (Boulder: Westview, 1988), pp. 142–143.

16. Ibid.

17. Arthur Schlesinger, Jr., "Reagan Is Crying Wolf on Nicaragua," *Wall Street Journal*, 25 March 1988, p. 18.

18. Lee Hockstader, "Nicaragua's Economy Stumbles as Wary Investors Stay Aloof," *Washington Post*, 7 February 1992, p. A20.

19. Elaine Sciolino and Stephen Engelberg, "Narcotics Effort Foiled by U.S. Security Goals," *New York Times,* Western Edition, 10 April 1988, pp. 1, 10.

20. Ruth Leger Sivard, "Wars and War-Related Deaths Since 1945," *World Military and Social Expenditures—1983,* 9th ed. (Washington, DC: World Priorities, 1983), p. 21.

21. Robert A. Rice and Joshua N. Karliner, "Militarization: The Environmental Impact," *Environmental Project on Central America (EPOCA) Paper #3,* 1986, pp. 3–4. (Available from EPOCA, c/o Earth Island Institute, 300 Broadway, Suite 28, San Francisco, CA 94133.)

22. Bill McAllister, "Viet Defoliant Linked to More Diseases," *Washington Post,* 1 May 1990, p. A8.

23. Terrorism experts Robert H. Kupperman and Jeff Kamen wrote: "Reagan Administration efforts notwithstanding, terrorist incidents have not substantially decreased following our raid in Libya in 1986." "A New Outbreak of Terror Is Likely," *New York Times,* Western Edition, 19 April 1988, p. A19. Opinions on the raid ran 2-1 against in Britain and 3-1 against in West Germany. See Jonathan Dean, *Watershed in Europe: Dismantling the East-West Military Confrontation* (Lexington, MA: Lexington Books, 1987), p. 16.

24. Charles Maechling, Jr., "Washington's Illegal Invasion," *Foreign Policy,* no. 79 (Summer 1990):121.

25. Andrew Reding, "Mexico Under Salinas: A Facade of Reform," *World Policy Journal* 6, no. 4 (Fall 1989):685–729.

26. Scott MacLeod, "In the Wake of 'Desert Storm,'" *New York Review of Books* 38, no. 5 (7 March 1991):6.

27. Rakiya Omaar and Alex de Waal, "Somalia's Uninvited Saviors," *Washington Post,* 13 December 1992, Outlook Section, p. C4.

28. Alexander Cockburn, "Beat the Devil," *Nation,* 21 December 1992, p. 762.

29. Eric Schmitt, "Fouled Region Is Casualty of War," *New York Times,* 3 March 1991, p. 19.

30. Since no one is planning to cover these bills by raising taxes, another cost will be the interest paid to Japanese people and others who buy U.S. Treasury Bonds. Estes calculated that interest charges will be several hundred billion dollars, paid out over the next three decades. Estes's revised estimates are summarized in Richard J. Barnet and John Cavanagh, "Unequally Sharing the Costs and Dividends of War," *Christian Science Monitor,* 14 March 1991, p. 19. His original estimates, made before the end of the war, appeared in Ralph Estes, John Cavanagh, and Felicia Kornbluh, "And Who Will Pay the Piper?" *Los Angeles Times,* 10 February 1991, p. M5.

31. David E. Rosenbaum, "U.S. Has Received $50 Billion in Pledges for War," *New York Times,* 11 February 1991, p. A13.

32. Center for Defense Information, "World at War—1992," *Defense Monitor* 21, no. 6 (1992):1.

33. For estimates of Iraqi deaths during the Persian Gulf War, see Introduction, infra. For an estimate of Iraqi property damage from the war, see Sivard, *World Military and Social Expenditures—1991,* p. 21.

34. Arthur Schlesinger, Jr., "Reagan Is Crying Wolf on Nicaragua," *Wall Street Journal,* 25 March 1988, p. 18.

35. Elizabeth Becker, "Up from Hell," *New Republic,* 17 February 1992, pp. 32–37.

36. Center for Defense Information, "Soviet Geopolitical Momentum: Myth or Menace?" *Defense Monitor* 15, no. 5 (1986):12–13.

37. See, e.g., Bill Keller, "In Moscow, Tone Is a Studied Calm," *New York Times,* 18 August 1989; and Henry Kamm, "Gorbachev Said to Reject Soviet Right to Intervene," *New York Times,* 2 April 1989, p. 15.

38. Bill Keller, "Gorbachev, in Finland, Disavows Any Right of Regional Intervention," *New York Times,* 26 October 1989, p. A1.

39. Ibid., A12.

40. Thomas L. Friedman, "Baker Gives U.S. Approval If Soviets Act on Rumania," *New York Times,* 25 December 1989, p. 13.

Chapter 3

1. Quoted in Jeanne Larson and Madge Micheels-Cyrus, *Seeds of Hope* (Philadelphia: New Society Publishers, 1986), p. 35.

2. Norman Podhoretz, *The Present Danger* (New York: Simon and Schuster, 1980), pp. 83–84.

3. For a compelling argument that the Japanese were ready to surrender anyway and that the use of nuclear weapons on Japanese cities was unnecessary, see the updated version of Gar Alperovitz, *Atomic Diplomacy* (New York: Penguin, 1985).

4. Robert S. McNamara, *Blundering into Disaster: Surviving the First Century of the Nuclear Age* (New York: Pantheon, 1987), pp. 154–155.

5. Ibid.

6. "Estimated Soviet Nuclear Stockpile," *Bulletin of the Atomic Scientists* 47, no. 6 (July–August 1991):48.

7. "U.S. Strategic Nuclear Forces," *Bulletin of the Atomic Scientists* 48, no. 1 (January-February 1992):49; "U.S. Nuclear Weapons Stockpile," *Bulletin of the Atomic Scientists* 47, no. 5 (June 1991):49.

8. Admittedly, putting testing underground did stop some weapons development. For example, first-strike enthusiasts have not been able to test fully the effects of electromagnetic pulses on various weapons and command-and-control systems. But this is a far cry from stopping all weapons modernization. John P. Holdren, personal communication, July 1987.

9. Ruth Leger Sivard, *World Military and Social Expenditures—1983,* 9th ed. (Washington, DC: World Priorities, 1983), p. 29 (Chart 19).

10. The argument is reviewed and rebutted in Daniel Deudney and G.

John Ikenberry, "Who Won the Cold War?" *Foreign Policy,* no. 87 (Summer 1992):123–138.

11. William W. Kaufmann, *Glasnost, Perestroika, and U.S. Defense Spending* (Washington, DC: Brookings, 1990), Table 2.

12. Deudney and Ikenberry, "Who Won the Cold War?" 123–138.

13. Ibid., 127.

14. Ibid., 134.

15. George F. Kennan, "The G.O.P. Won the Cold War? Ridiculous," *New York Times,* 28 October 1992, p. A21.

16. Quoted in Sidney Lens, "Deterrence Hardly Deters," *New York Times,* 25 December 1983, section 4, p. 13.

17. Thomas Powers, "What Is It About?" *Atlantic Monthly,* January 1984, p. 48.

18. The Soviet military threat to Western Europe was seriously and greatly exaggerated. Newly declassified intelligence estimates from the 1940s and 1950s show that U.S. officials knew that the Soviet army, much of which still relied on horse-drawn carriages for transportation, was in no condition to launch an offensive against Western Europe. Matthew A. Evangelista, "Stalin's Postwar Army Reappraised," *International Security* 7, no. 3 (Winter 1982–1983):111. Moreover, it is now clear that after World War II Moscow initially encouraged new governments in Eastern Europe to seek U.S. aid, Western investments, and World Bank lending; it was Washington's policy to isolate Eastern Europe.

19. Richard K. Betts, *Nuclear Blackmail and Nuclear Balance* (Washington, DC: Brookings Institution, 1987). Other analysts believe the count is higher. See, e.g., Daniel Ellsberg, "Call to Mutiny," in E. P. Thompson and Dan Smith, *Protest and Survive* (London: Monthly Review Press, 1981), pp. i–xxviii.

20. Morton Halperin, *Nuclear Fallacy* (Cambridge, MA: Ballinger, 1987), p. 46.

21. Barton Bernstein, "The Day We Almost Went to War," *Bulletin of the Atomic Scientists* 32, no. 2 (February 1976):13–21.

22. "Hush-up on Accidental War," *New Scientist,* 5 June 1986, p. 21.

23. Michael H. Shuman, "Terminal Command," *Taking Off,* April 1983, pp. 10–14.

24. Alexander Dallin, *Black Box: KAL 007 and the Superpowers* (Berkeley: University of California Press, 1985), pp. 57, 62.

25. Lloyd J. Dumas, "National Security in the Nuclear Age," *Bulletin of the Atomic Scientists* 32, no. 5 (May 1976):24–35; and Lloyd J. Dumas, "Human Fallibility and Nuclear Weapons," *Bulletin of the Atomic Scientists* 36, no. 9 (November 1980):15–20.

26. Jack Anderson, "A Pentagon Lie," *San Francisco Chronicle,* 5 October 1981, p. 43.

27. Harvard Nuclear Study Group, *Living with Nuclear Weapons* (New York: Bantam New Age Books, 1983), pp. 60–61.

28. Amory B. Lovins, *Soft Energy Paths* (New York: Harper and Row, 1977), p. 192.

29. Before 1981 the government admitted to sixty. Dumas, "Human Fallibility and Nuclear Weapons," 18. Then, during 1981, the Pentagon revealed five more accidents, including two instances in which the weapons (or debris) were never recovered. Richard Halloran, "Five Nuclear Weapon Accidents Revealed," *San Francisco Chronicle*, 26 May 1981, p. 1.

30. Wendell Rawes, Jr., "Explosion Rocks a Silo for Nuclear Missiles in Arkansas," *New York Times*, 20 September 1980, p. 1.

31. Amory B. Lovins and L. Hunter Lovins, *Brittle Power: Energy Strategy for National Security* (Andover, MA: Brick House, 1982), pp. 202–204.

32. Dumas, "Human Fallibility and Nuclear Weapons," 15.

33. For a review of the treaty, see William Epstein, *The Last Chance: Nuclear Proliferation and Arms Control* (New York: Free Press, 1976).

34. Ibid., 80; Elizabeth Young, *A Farewell to Arms Control?* (Harmondsworth, England: Penguin, 1972), pp. 58–59; and R. Rama Roa, "The Non-Proliferation Treaty," *Institute of Defence Studies and Analyses Journal* 1 (July 1969):12–19.

35. An example of an implicit threat to nonnuclear nations is found in Secretary of Defense James Schlesinger's testimony to Congress in 1974: "It is even more essential that we focus on the issues that could arise if and when additional nations acquire nuclear weapons. . . . Such a development could have a considerable impact on our own plans and programs. Indeed, this prospect alone should make it evident that no single target system and no stereotyped scenario of mutual city destruction will suffice as the basis for strategic planning." Cited in Chris Paine, "The 'Shuman Plan,'" *Bulletin of the Atomic Scientists* 37, no. 4 (April 1981):59.

36. Don Cook, "Defections from Nuclear Treaty Hinted," *Los Angeles Times*, 13 August 1980, p. I-4; Paul Lewis, "Disarmament Parley Ends in Discord," *New York Times*, 27 June 1988, p. A3.

37. For a detailed critique of the Reagan administration's efforts to reinterpret the ABM Treaty, see Abram and Antonia Handler Chayes, "Testing and Development of Exotic Systems Under the ABM Treaty: The Great Reinterpretation Caper," *Harvard Law Review* 99, no. 8 (June 1986):1956–1985. Article IV of the Treaty on Principles Governing the Activities of States in the Exploration and Use of Outer Space, Including the Moon and Other Celestial Bodies, 18 U.S.T. 2410, 610 U.N.T.S. 205, prohibits the deployment of nuclear weapons in outer space. This prohibition would apply to the proposed X-ray laser for SDI, which would be powered by a nuclear explosion. Article I of the Limited Test Ban Treaty, 14 U.S.T. 1313, 489 U.N.T.S. 43, prohibits nuclear testing or explosions in outer space.

38. Leonard S. Spector, *Going Nuclear* (Cambridge, MA: Ballinger, 1987);

and Amory B. and L. Hunter Lovins, *Energy/War: Breaking the Nuclear Link* (San Francisco: Friends of the Earth, 1980). Smugglers interviewed in a documentary for the United Kingdom's *Dispatches* television series said that at least six consignments of stolen plutonium have passed through the Sudan, suggesting that a lucrative black market for plutonium already exists. "The Plutonium Black Market," *Wise News Communiqué* (Amsterdam), 22 April 1988.

39. Fred Hiatt and Rick Atkinson, "The Next Generation of Nuclear Arms," *Washington Post*, National Weekly Edition, 23 June 1986, p. 9; David Perlman, "Scientists Meet: Major Advances in Nuclear Arms," *San Francisco Chronicle*, 16 February 1988, pp. A13–A14; Jack Anderson, "New Missiles for Burial," *San Francisco Chronicle*, 30 December 1987, p. A19; Theodore B. Taylor, "Third-Generation Nuclear Weapons," *Scientific American*, April 1987, pp. 30–38; and "After INF, the Next New Arms Race," *U.S. News and World Report*, 9 May 1988, pp. 26–27.

40. Quoted in Hiatt and Atkinson, "The Next Generation," 9.

41. R. Jeffrey Smith, "The Army Is Making 'Repugnant' Weapons Again," *Washington Post*, National Weekly Edition, 3 January 1988, p. 34; R. Jeffrey Smith, "GAO Blasts Bigeye Chemical Weapon," *Science* 22, no. 4757 (20 June 1986):1493; and Tim Carrington, "Chemical-Weapons Buildup Is Forcing Pentagon to Alter Wide Range of Gear," *Wall Street Journal*, 12 June 1986, p. 20.

42. Andy Pastor, "Destruction of U.S., Soviet Stockpiles of Chemical Arms Is Many Years Away," *Wall Street Journal*, 1 June 1990, p. A12.

43. Peter Grier, "Pentagon Researching Exotic Chemical Arms," *Christian Science Monitor*, 6 February 1989, p. 1.

44. "Army Says It Could Build a Safe Germ Warfare Laboratory," *New York Times*, 7 February 1988, p. 23; and Seth Shulman, "Funding for Biological Weapons Research Grows Amidst Controversy," *BioScience* 37, no. 6 (June 1987):372.

45. "What Might Make a Biological Weapon?" *Christian Science Monitor*, 15 December 1988, p. B2.

46. Gary Thatcher, "Disease as an Agent of War," *Christian Science Monitor*, 15 December 1988, p. B3.

47. Quoted in ibid., B4.

48. Perlman, "Scientists Meet," A13.

49. Robert J. Lifton and Richard Falk, *Indefensible Weapons: The Political and Psychological Case Against Nuclearism* (New York: Basic Books, 1982), p. 153.

50. Lovins and Lovins, *Energy/War*, 13–28.

51. Daniel Charles, "DOD Sees Risks in Plutonium Trade," *Science* 238, no. 4829 (13 November 1987):886.

52. Alan Reitman, "Nuclear Arms and Civil Liberties," *Civil Liberties*, Spring 1986, p. 8.

53. Michael R. Gordon, "'Star Wars' Information Is Withheld," *New York Times,* Western Edition, 26 January 1987, p. 11.

54. Quoted in Michael Harris, "Military Use of Scientists Hurts Economy, Report Says," *San Francisco Chronicle,* 16 October 1986, p. 7.

55. Data on U.S. defense spending taken from Council of Economic Advisers, *Economic Report of the President—February 1992* (Washington, DC: USGPO, 1992). Data on Japanese and German defense spending taken from Ruth Leger Sivard, *World Military and Social Expenditures—1991,* 14th ed. (Washington, DC: World Priorities, 1991), pp. 54–56.

56. Interview with Wassily Leontief, "Big Boosts in Defense Risk 'Economic Calamity,'" *U.S. News and World Report,* 16 March 1981, p. 26.

57. For a brief review, see Michael Oden, "Military Spending Erodes Real National Security," *The Bulletin of the Atomic Scientists* 44, no. 5 (June 1988):38–39.

58. David Gold, Christopher Paine, and Gail Shields, *Misguided Expenditure* (New York: Council on Economic Priorities, 1981).

59. Barry Bluestone and John Havens, "Reducing the Federal Deficit Fair and Square," paper presented to the symposium on the fortieth anniversary of the Congressional Joint Economic Committee, Washington, DC, 16–17 January, 1985, p. 24.

60. Lloyd Dumas, "Military Spending and Economic Decay," in *Toward Nuclear Disarmament and Global Security: A Search for Alternatives,* ed. Burns Weston (Boulder: Westview Press, 1984), p. 173.

61. Caspar W. Weinberger, "Soviet Buildup Demands a Response," *San Jose Mercury News,* 8 October 1981, p. 7B.

62. Richard Halloran, *To Arm a Nation: Rebuilding America's Endangered Defenses* (New York: Macmillan, 1986). See also "No Business Like War Business," *Defense Monitor* 16, no. 3 (1987); Michael Isikoff, "Two Can Bid More Cheaply Than One, the Pentagon Learns," *Washington Post,* National Weekly Edition, 4 May 1987, p. 31; and Nicholas C. McBride, "Government Closes in on Fraud Indictments in Pentagon Scandal," *Christian Science Monitor,* 23 November 1988, p. 4.

63. Halloran, *To Arm a Nation,* 267

64. Ron P. Smith, "Military Expenditure and Capitalism," *Cambridge Journal of Economics* 1, no. 1 (March 1977); Ron P. Smith, "Military Expenditure and Investment in O.E.C.D. Countries 1954–1973," *Journal of Comparative Economics* 4, no. 1 (1980):19–32; Bruce Russett, *What Price Vigilance?* (New Haven: Yale University Press, 1970); and Paul Lewis, "Military Spending Questioned," *New York Times,* Western Edition, 11 November 1986, p. 25.

65. Marion Anderson, Jeb Brugmann, and G. Erickcek, *The Price of the Pentagon* (Lansing, MI: Employment Research Associates, 1982).

66. Michael Boretsky, "Trends in U.S. Technology: A Political Economist's View," *American Scientist,* January 1975, pp. 70–82.

67. Jay Stowsky, "Competing with the Pentagon," *World Policy Journal* 3, no. 4 (Fall 1986):700–701.

68. Joel Yudken and Michael Black, "Targeting National Need," *World Policy Journal* 7, no. 2 (Spring 1990):257.

69. Stowsky, "Competing with the Pentagon," 698.

70. Ann Markusen, "The Militarized Economy," *World Policy Journal* 3, no. 3 (Summer 1986):496–497.

71. Ibid., 505.

72. Lester Thurow, "How to Wreck the Economy," *New York Review of Books,* 14 May 1981, p. 6.

73. If SDI is ever built, for example, many of its components will be manufactured in Japan. Michael Shrage, "Star Wars: Made in Japan?" *Washington Post,* National Weekly Edition, 24 March 1986, p. 11. See also Tim Carrington, "Military's Dependence on Foreign Suppliers Causes Rising Concern," *Wall Street Journal,* 24 March 1988, p. 1.

74. Markusen, "The Militarized Economy," 507.

75. Clyde V. Prestowitz, "About the Last Thing Japan Needs Now Is a U.S. Handout," *Washington Post,* National Weekly Edition, 6–12 February 1989, p. 23.

76. Markusen, "The Militarized Economy," 512.

77. Robert B. Reich, "The Economics of Illusion and the Illusion of Economics," *Foreign Affairs* 66, no. 3 (America and the World Issue, 1987–1988):527.

78. Ibid., 523–528. See also Robert B. Reich, "The *Real* Economy," *Atlantic Monthly,* February 1991, pp. 35–52.

79. In 1992 the gross domestic product of the United States was $6 trillion. Council of Economic Advisers, *Economic Report of the President* (Washington, DC: U.S. Government Printing Office, 1993), p. 348. That same year estimated federal expenditures were $307 billion for national defense and $200 billion for interest (net) on the national debt. William J. Clinton, *Budget of the United States Government: Fiscal Year 1994* (Washington, DC: U.S. Government Printing Office, 1993), Appendix One, p. 5.

80. Sherle Schwenninger and Jerry Sanders, "The Democrats and a New Grand Strategy—Part I," *World Policy Journal* 3, no. 3 (Summer 1986):380.

81. Joseph J. Romm and Amory B. Lovins, "Fueling a Competitive Economy," *Foreign Affairs* 71, no. 5 (Winter 1992–1993):59.

82. Paul Krugman, *The Age of Diminished Expectations: U.S. Economic Policy in the 1990s* (Cambridge, MA: MIT Press, 1992), pp. 38, 40, and 96.

83. Roger Altman, "The World Bank's Growing Irrelevance," *New York Times,* 11 July 1988, p. A15.

84. "Pentagon Slashes Estimates of Strategic Defense Initiative First-Phase Deployment Costs," *Christian Science Monitor,* 7 October 1988, p. 6.

85. Rosy Nimroody, *Star Wars: The Economic Fallout* (Cambridge, MA: Ballinger, 1988), p. 26.

86. Charlotte Saikowski, "Star Wars Defense System Losing Steam with Senators," *Christian Science Monitor,* 23 May 1986, p. 3.

87. The Miyazawa plan for Third World debt relief presented at the 1988 seven-nation economic summit in Toronto is one example of increasing Japanese activism. Walter S. Mossberg, "Japanese Proposal on Third World Debt Disturbs the Peace at Economic Summit," *Wall Street Journal,* 21 June 1988, p. 3.

88. Jeffrey Sachs, "Lack of Solidarity," *New Republic,* 7–14 August 1989, p. 20. Subsequently, the Senate and the House of Representatives voted to increase the level of U.S. assistance to Poland to about $1 billion. Clyde H. Farnsworth, "International Aid Sought for Poles," *New York Times,* 28 September 1989, p. A9; and Robert Pear, "A Broad Program of Aid to Poland Is Voted by House," *New York Times,* 20 October 1989, p. 1.

89. Jeffrey D. Sachs, "Russia Needs *Real* Aid—Now," *Washington Post,* 18 December 1992, p. A31.

90. Anthony Barbieri, Jr., "Japan Will More Than Double Aid to Third World Nations," *San Francisco Chronicle,* 15 June 1988, p. A15; Paul Blustein, "Japan to Double Offer of Funds to Reduce Third World Debts," *Washington Post,* 13 July 1989, p. A31.

91. William F. Lawless, "Problems with Military Nuclear Waste," *Bulletin of the Atomic Scientists* 41, no. 10 (November 1985):38.

92. For additional documentation, see Keith Schneider, "Second Nuclear Plant Is Ordered Closed by Energy Department," *New York Times,* 11 October 1988, p. 1; and "17 Exposed to Plutonium at a Weapons Plant," *New York Times,* 5 November 1988, p. 6.

93. Robert Alvarez and Arjun Makhijani, "Radioactive Waste: Hidden Legacy of the Arms Race," *Technology Review,* August-September 1988, p. 45.

94. Lawless, "Problems with Waste," 39.

95. Ibid., 41.

96. Robin Johnston, "How Safe Are US Nuclear Weapons Sites for Workers?" *Christian Science Monitor,* 14 October 1988, pp. 3 and 6.

97. William Glaberson, "Fear Corrodes Faith at Atomic Plants," *New York Times,* 11 December 1988, p. 36.

98. Alvarez and Makhijani, "Radioactive Waste," 51.

99. Michael Weisskopf, "Defense Pollution Cleanup Could Cost $100 Billion," *Washington Post,* 11 March 1988, p. A25.

100. Matthew L. Wald, "Cleanup Estimate for A-Bomb Plants Is Called Low," *New York Times,* 14 July 1988, p. A16.

101. Fred Hiatt, "Just When You Thought You'd Never See Another Reactor," *Washington Post,* National Weekly Edition, 28 April 1986, p. 34.

102. Jonathan Tasini, "Nuclear Missions," *Atlantic Monthly,* January 1988, pp. 28–29; and Steven Aftergood, "Nuclear Space Mishaps and Star Wars," *Bulletin of the Atomic Scientists* 48, no. 8 (October 1986):40–43.

103. Tasini, "Nuclear Missions," 29.

104. Ibid.

105. Aftergood, "Nuclear Space Mishaps," 42.

106. "Safety Problems in Chemical Weapons Research," *Christian Science Monitor,* 13 May 1988, p. 4.

107. Andrew Pollack, "Plan to Mail Warfare Toxins Draws Protest Against Army," *New York Times,* 13 June 1988, p. 1.

108. Timothy Aeppel, "Chemical Weapons Disposal Not Easy," *Christian Science Monitor,* 22 February 1988, p. 1; and Dennis O'Brien, "Study Asks Delay in Plans to Burn Chemical Arms," *Baltimore Sun,* 1 February 1988, p. D1.

109. See, for example, Ron Scherer, "US Chemical-Weapon Plan Divides Pacific," *Christian Science Monitor,* 10 August 1990, p. 5.

110. James Coates, "Utah Ponders Germ Warfare Laboratory," *San Francisco Examiner,* 10 April 1988, p. A8.

111. R. Jeffrey Smith, "'Repugnant' Weapons," 34.

112. Coates, "Utah Ponders."

113. Ibid.; and Thatcher, "Disease as an Agent," pp. B7–B8.

114. Henry S. Rowen and Charles Wolf, Jr., "Gorbachev's Choice Isn't Just Guns or Butter," *Wall Street Journal,* 24 March 1988, p. 26.

115. George Perkovich, "Counting the Costs of the Arms Race," *Foreign Policy,* no. 85 (Winter 1991–1992):88–90.

Chapter 4

1. E. P. Thompson, "A Letter to America," reprinted in E. P. Thompson and Dan Smith, *Protest and Survive* (New York: Monthly Review Press, 1981), p. 42.

2. Michael Doyle, "Kant, Liberal Legacies, and Foreign Affairs," *Philosophy and Public Affairs* 12, nos. 3 and 4 (Summer-Fall 1983):205–235, 323–353.

3. Bruce Russett, "Politics and Alternative Security," in Burns H. Weston, *Alternative Security: Living Without Nuclear Deterrence* (Boulder: Westview, 1990), pp. 108–109.

4. Ibid.

5. Ibid.

6. Seyom Brown, *International Relations in a Changing Global System* (Boulder: Westview, 1992), p. 27.

7. William Bundy, "A Portentous Year," *Foreign Affairs* 62, no. 3 (America and the World issue, 1983):503.

8. Quoted in "Multiplicity of Relationships with Chinese," *Surviving Together,* October 1985, p. 6.

9. Joseph V. Montville and William D. Davidson, "Foreign Policy According to Freud," *Foreign Policy,* no. 45 (Winter 1981–1982):155.

10. Gale Warner and Michael H. Shuman, *Citizen Diplomats: Pathfinders in Soviet-American Relations* (New York: Continuum, 1987), pp. 157–188.

11. Alex Pravda, "Costs/Benefits Point Soviets to the Door," *Los Angeles Times,* 24 January 1988, p. V-5.

12. Robert Schaeffer, *Warpaths: The Politics of Partition* (New York: Hill & Wang, 1989), p. 7.

13. Ibid., 3–4.

14. Ibid., 254–255.

15. Robert Schaeffer, "To Lithuania: Stay Put," *New York Times,* 3 January 1990, p. A19.

16. John J. Mearsheimer, "Why We Will Soon Miss the Cold War," *Atlantic Monthly,* August 1990, p. 35.

17. The term "strong democracy" was coined by Benjamin Barber, but we use it here to emphasize somewhat different political goals. See Benjamin Barber, *Strong Democracy: Participatory Politics for a New Age* (Berkeley: University of California Press, 1984).

18. Alf McCreary, "Lessons in Irish Unity," *Christian Science Monitor,* 23 August 1990, p. 12.

19. Quoted in William Blum, *The CIA: A Forgotten History* (London: Zed Books, 1986), p. 235. Behind Kissinger's words, of course, stood a massive CIA covert operation that helped subvert and overthrow Allende's government.

20. Aaron Wildavsky, *Beyond Containment: Alternative American Policies Toward the Soviet Union* (San Francisco: Institute for Contemporary Studies, 1983), p. 128.

21. Robert B. Cullen, "Soviet Jewry," *Foreign Affairs* 65, no. 2 (Winter 1986–1987):252–266.

22. Thomas F. O'Boyle, "To Radio Free Europe, Glasnost Is a Challenge to Be Better, Quicker," *Wall Street Journal,* 25 March 1988, p. 1.

23. John Spicer Nichols, "Wasting the Propaganda Dollar," *Foreign Policy,* no. 56 (Fall 1984):129–140.

24. Linda Feldmann (paraphrasing Yale Richmond), "From Hand to Hand Flows . . . Trust or Manipulation," *Christian Science Monitor,* 25 February 1988, p. 5.

25. Ann Levin, "U.S., Soviet Scientists Progress in Nuclear Test-Monitoring Effort," *Christian Science Monitor,* 13 November 1986, p. 5; and Mary McGrory, "Verification Venture," *Washington Post,* 10 July 1986, p. A2.

26. Warner and Shuman, *Citizen Diplomats,* 31–67.

27. Source requested confidentiality.

28. Samuel Pisar, "A Red or Green Light for East-West Trade: Gorbachev's Pragmatic Generation," *Wall Street Journal,* 26 December 1985, p. 6.

29. Franz Schurmann, "Fast Food Outlets Symbolize Capitalist Spirit at Communist Shrines," *East-West News,* 3 December 1987, p. 7.

30. Quoted in Flora Lewis, "Soviets Buy American," *New York Times*, 10 May 1989, p. A35.

31. "Cuddly Russia?" *Economist*, 14 February 1987, pp. 13–14.

32. Kirk Johnson, "Soviets Allow U.S. Citizens to Send More Goods," *New York Times*, 4 December 1988, p. 23.

33. "All That's *Glasnost* Does Not Glitter," *U.S. News & World Report*, 4 April 1988, pp. 50–51; and Frank Tuttitia (*PC World* public-relations staff), personal communication, October 1989.

34. Bill Keller, "For Soviet Alternative Press, Used Computer Is New Tool," *New York Times*, 12 January 1988, p. 1; and Joel Bleifuss, "I. F. Stone Defends *Glasnost*," *In These Times*, 22 June–5 July 1988, p. 4.

35. The AlphaGraphics Printshop on Gorky Street, for example, is the result of a joint Soviet-Canadian venture. Richard L. Wentworth, "Soviets Open to Deals with West," *Christian Science Monitor*, 4 April 1989, p. 9.

36. Barry Newman, "The Spirit of Glasnost Has Admen in Moscow Sharpening Up Copy," *Wall Street Journal*, 8 July 1988, p. 1.

37. Edward F. Feighan, "Keep the Gates Open: Waive Jackson-Vanik," *Christian Science Monitor*, 1 May 1989, p. 19; Ari Goldman, "4,000 Soviet Jews Migrated in March," *New York Times*, 5 April 1989, p. A10; Ari L. Goldman, "A Jewish Center, Officially Approved, Will Open in Moscow," *New York Times*, 8 February 1989, p. A7; and Esther B. Fein, "Lasting Faith of Soviet Jews Moves Wiesel," *New York Times*, 13 February 1989, p. 1.

38. Richard Morin, "Greater Glasnost, Even for Pollsters," *Washington Post*, National Weekly Edition, 2–8 January 1989, p. 39.

39. David Remnick, "Soviets Allow Public to Read Banned Books," *Washington Post*, 23 March 1988, p. A21.

40. Robert Pear, "U.S. Helping Polish Underground with Money and Communications," *New York Times*, 10 July 1988, p. 1.

41. Shirley Christian, "Group Is Channeling U.S. Funds to Parties Opposing Pinochet," *New York Times*, 15 June 1988, p. 1.

42. Robert Pear, "Poll Watching Becomes a Growth Industry," *New York Times*, 7 May 1989, section 4, p. 2.

43. James M. Markham, "The East-West Flow of People and Ideas," *New York Times*, 5 February 1989, p. 5; and Jonathan Dunn, "Corporate Diplomacy: Joint Ventures in Eastern Europe," *Multinational Monitor*, November/December 1987, pp. 9–15.

44. See, for example, Douglas M. Johnston, Jr., and Paul J. Cook, Jr., "Beyond Sanctions," *Christian Science Monitor*, 13 July 1988, p. 12.

45. Many constitutions—most recently, those of the Philippines and Nicaragua—are based in part on the U.S. Constitution. Says Stanford Law Professor John Henry Merryman, "Of all American influences in the world, our strongest is probably the Constitution." Quoted in Reese Erlich, "Exporting the Constitution," *California Lawyer*, August 1987, pp. 44–48.

46. David Corn, "Foreign Aid for the Right," *Nation,* 18 December 1989, pp. 744–746.

47. Michael Schrage, "The Secret's Out: There's a New 'Sensitive' Security Classification," *Washington Post,* National Weekly Edition, 1 December 1986, p. 32.

48. Peter van Ness, "Concealed Weapon," *Nation,* 12 March 1988, p. 329.

49. Testimony in the case of *Westmoreland v. CBS* firmly established a pattern of deception, even if the issue of General Westmoreland's culpability was never decisively resolved by a jury. Ronald Dworkin, "The Press on Trial," *New York Review of Books,* 26 February 1987, pp. 27–37.

50. John Markoff and Andrew Pollack, "Computer 'Hackers' Seen as Peril to Security of the Phone System," *New York Times,* Western Edition, 22 July 1988, p. 1; John Markoff, "Top-Secret, and Vulnerable," *New York Times,* Western Edition, 25 April 1988, p. C1; and Michael Shrage, "The Soviets Are Helping Themselves to Our Computer Data Bases," *Washington Post,* National Weekly Edition, 9 June 1986, p. 31.

51. Neil Henderson, "For Sale: Aerial Close-Ups of Anything," *Washington Post,* National Weekly Edition, 19 May 1986, pp. 8–9; Eliot Marshall, "A Spy Satellite for the Press?" *Science* 238, no. 4832 (4 December 1987): 1346–1348.

52. Robert Pear, "Congress Changes Spending Rules on Secret Programs for Pentagon," *New York Times,* 31 October 1990, p. 1.

53. Quoted in Anthony Lewis, "Reagan's Obsession with Nicaragua," *San Francisco Chronicle,* 23 March 1988, p. A14.

54. Eugene V. Rostow, "Repeal the War Powers Resolution," *Wall Street Journal,* 27 June 1984, p. 26.

55. Timothy Noah, "War Powers: An Act with No Action," *San Francisco Chronicle,* 1 July 1987, p. A3.

56. "Broken Clock," *New Republic,* 10–17 September 1990, p. 12.

57. J. Brian Atwood, "Sharing War Powers," *New York Times,* 14 October 1987, p. 35 (emphasis in original).

58. "Deployment Alarms Democrats," *Washington Post,* 17 March 1988, p. A30.

59. Alan Cranston, "Revitalize the War Powers Act," *Washington Post,* National Weekly Edition, 2 November 1987, p. 28.

60. Donald L. Robinson, "National Security Needs More than New Laws," *Los Angeles Times,* 15 December 1987, p. 13.

61. Helen Dewar, "War Powers Overhaul Proposed," *Washington Post,* 20 May 1988, pp. A1, A30. The other "reform" proposed by this group—repealing automatic troop withdrawal after the sixty- or ninety-day period has ended—would be an unwarranted and dangerous concession that would

further increase presidential power. Senator George Mitchell of Maine has complained that the current law "severely undercuts the president by encouraging our enemies to simply wait for US law to remove the threat of further American military action" and by "prompting presidents to think in terms of short-term military action regardless of purpose." But this misses the entire point of the War Powers Act: Presidents can deploy force for as long as they wish and for any purposes they wish, provided they secure congressional approval *first*. Quoted in Peter Osterlund, "Senate Leaders Push War Powers Overhaul," *Christian Science Monitor*, 20 May 1988, p. 3.

62. Cranston, "Revitalize War Powers Act," 28.

63. Richard Falk, "Nuclear Weapons and the Renewal of Democracy," *Praxis International* 4, no. 2 (July 1984):120.

64. Jeremy J. Stone, "Presidential First Use Is Unlawful," *Foreign Policy*, no. 56 (Fall 1984):94–112.

65. Frank Church, "Covert Action: Swampland of American Foreign Policy," *Bulletin of the Atomic Scientists* 32, no. 2 (February 1976):11.

66. Stanley Hoffmann, "Under Cover or out of Control?" *New York Times Book Review*, 29 November 1987, p. 3.

67. Church, "Covert Action," 11.

68. Morton Halperin, "The Case Against Covert Action," *Nation*, 21 March 1987, p. 363. Gregory Treverton of the Council on Foreign Relations estimates that "of the 40 or so covert actions underway in the mid 1980s, at least half had been the subject of some press account." Gregory F. Treverton, "Covert Action and Open Society," *Foreign Affairs* 65, no. 5 (Summer 1987): 1002–1003.

69. Robert Merry, "Policy Makers Face a Trend: 'Covert' Actions Become Overt," *Wall Street Journal*, 11 February 1986, p. 38.

70. "Text of Letter on Covert Operations," *New York Times*, Western Edition, 8 August 1987, p. 5. It is important to remember that even the best reporting requirements do not put restrictions on the president's activities.

71. Halperin, "Against Covert Action," 362.

72. Quoted in F.A.O. Schwarz, Jr., "Recalling Major Lessons of the Church Committee," *New York Times*, 30 July 1987, p. 25.

73. William V. Kennedy, "'No' to Covert Action," *Christian Science Monitor*, 18 August 1987, p. 12.

74. Robert M. Gates, "The CIA and American Foreign Policy," *Foreign Affairs* 66, no. 2 (Winter 1987–1988):216.

75. Immanuel Kant, *Perpetual Peace* (Indianapolis, IN: Bobbs-Merrill Company, 1957), pp. 12–13.

76. Bruce Russett, "Politics and Alternative Security," in *Alternative Security: Living Without Nuclear Deterrence*, ed. Burns H. Weston (Boulder: Westview, 1990), p. 111.

Chapter 5

1. Quoted in Michael Renner, "Enhancing Global Security," in Worldwatch Institute, *State of the World 1989* (New York: W. W. Norton, 1989), p. 141.

2. Arthur H. Westing, *Global Resources and International Conflict—Environmental Factors in Strategic Policy and Action* (Oxford: Oxford University Press, 1986), Appendix 2, pp. 204–210.

3. Ibid., 22.

4. Ibid., 205.

5. Milton Viorst, "Iraq at War," *Foreign Affairs* 65, no. 2 (Winter 1986–1987):350.

6. Earl Ravenal, *Defining Defense: The 1985 Military Budget* (Washington, DC: Cato Institute, 1985), p. 8. The so-called rapid deployment force was upgraded to a Unified Command in 1983.

7. See Introduction, this volume, p. 9.

8. "New Negotiations in Fishing Dispute," *New York Times,* 7 August 1989, p. A13.

9. Lester R. Brown and Christopher Flavin, "The Earth's Vital Signs," in Worldwatch Institute, *State of the World 1988* (New York: W. W. Norton, 1988), Table 1-5, p. 14.

10. Ibid., Table 1-4, 13.

11. Oswald Johnston and Eleanor Randolph, "Acid Rain to Dominate U.S.-Canada Talks," *Los Angeles Times,* 16 October 1983, p. 4.

12. Tom Cochran and Frank von Hippel, "Estimating Long-Term Health Effects," *Bulletin of the Atomic Scientists* 43, no. 1 (August-September 1986): 18–24.

13. Christopher Flavin, "Reassessing Nuclear Power," in *State of the World 1987* (Washington, DC: Worldwatch Institute, 1987), p. 62.

14. Maurice Strong, "40 Chernobyls Waiting to Happen," *New York Times,* 22 March 1992, p. E15.

15. Michael Dobbs, "Fission Splits France, W. Germany," *Washington Post,* 4 August 1986, p. A15.

16. James M. Markham, "Spreading the Anti-Nuclear Gospel in Europe," *New York Times,* 3 August 1986, p. 8.

17. "Ireland vs. Sellafield," *WISE News Communiqué* (Amsterdam), 4 April 1986.

18. Lee Yee, "China's Plan for Nuclear Plant Illuminates Hong Kong Politics," *Wall Street Journal,* 29 September 1986, p. 19.

19. Sandra Postel, "Controlling Toxic Chemicals," in Worldwatch Institute, *State of the World 1988* (New York: W. W. Norton, 1988), pp. 118–136.

20. William C. Clark, "A Sadness on the Rhine" (editorial), *Environment,* December 1986, inside cover page.

21. Ibid.

22. "Key Sections of the Paris Communique by the Group of Seven," *New York Times*, 17 July 1989, p. A7; and Marshall Ingwerson, "Environment Is First on Agenda," *Christian Science Monitor*, 14 July 1989, p. 1.

23. Philip Shabecoff, "Suddenly, the World Itself Is a World Issue," *New York Times*, 25 December 1988, section 4, p. 3.

24. Amory B. and L. Hunter Lovins, *Brittle Power: Energy Strategy for National Security* (Andover, MA: Brick House Publishers, 1982); and Amory B. and L. Hunter Lovins, "The Fragility of Domestic Energy," *Atlantic*, November 1983, pp. 118–126.

25. Lovins and Lovins, *Brittle Power*, 164–165. See also S. Fetter and Kosta Tsipis, "Catastrophic Nuclear Radiation Releases," *Report #5*, September 1980, Program in Science and Technology for International Security, Department of Physics, Massachusetts Institute of Technology; S. Fetter, "Catastrophic Releases of Radioactivity," *Scientific American* 244, no. 4 (April 1981):41–47; and B. Ramberg, *The Destruction of Nuclear Energy Facilities in War* (Lexington, MA: D.C. Heath, 1980).

26. Lovins and Lovins, *Brittle Power*, 68–69.

27. Ibid., 68–84.

28. Amory B. Lovins, "Energy, People, and Industrialization," Paper for Hoover Institution Conference on "Human Demography and Natural Resources," 5 January 1989, p. 10. (Available from Rocky Mountain Institute, 1739 Snowmass Creek Rd., Old Snowmass, CO 81654-9199.)

29. Peter Wallensteen, "Food Crops as a Factor in Strategic Policy and Action," in Westing, *Global Resources*, 144.

30. Norman Myers, "Linking Environment and Security," *Bulletin of the Atomic Scientists* 43, no. 5 (June 1987):46–47.

31. Amory B. and L. Hunter Lovins, "Drill Rigs and Battleships Are the Answer! (But What Was the Question?)," chapter in *The Petroleum Market in the 1990s*, ed. Fereidun Fesharaki and Robert Reed (Boulder: Westview Press, 1989), pp. 83–138.

32. Amory B. and L. Hunter Lovins, "Make Fuel Efficiency Our Gulf Strategy," *New York Times*, 3 December 1990, p. A19.

33. Lovins, "Energy, People, and Industrialization," 10.

34. Ibid., 13.

35. Amory B. Lovins, et al., "Response to the Concept 21 Paper" (document on resources and the next thirty years), presented by L. Hunter Lovins to the Army Concept 21 Conference, February 1988. (Available from Rocky Mountain Institute.)

36. The Rocky Mountain Institute has concluded that 70 to over 90 percent of lighting energy could theoretically be saved, displacing 120 large power plants. Amory B. Lovins and Robert Sardinsky, *The State of the Art: Lighting* (Snowmass, CO: Rocky Mountain Institute/COMPETITEK,

March 1988). Actual experience suggests that 50 to 75 percent savings are more realistic.

37. Amory B. Lovins, et al., *The State of the Art: Drivepower* (Snowmass, CO: Rocky Mountain Institute/Competitek, April 1989). Additional improvements to equipment driven by the motors could probably save about one-half of the remaining electricity being used.

38. Arnold P. Fickett, Clark W. Gellings, and Amory B. Lovins, "Efficient Use of Electricity," *Scientific American* 263, no. 3 (September 1990):65–74.

39. Hal Harvey and Bill Keepin, "Energy: From Crisis to Solution" (San Francisco: The Energy Foundation, 1992) (monograph).

40. Although reactors that have been shut down would still contain enormous amounts of radioactivity—after some weeks, the equivalent of hundreds of Hiroshima bombs per thousand-megawatt plant, rather than the approximately two thousand bombs' worth contained in an operating plant—the internal energies that could contribute to a radiation release would rapidly decay.

41. For a complete treatment of this thesis, see Lovins and Lovins, *Brittle Power*.

42. Howard Geller, et al., "The Role of Federal Research and Development in Advancing Energy Efficiency: A $50 Billion Contribution to the U.S. Economy," *Annual Review of Energy* 12 (Palo Alto, CA: Annual Reviews Inc., 1987), pp. 357–395.

43. Amory B. and L. Hunter Lovins, "The Avoidable Oil Crisis," *Atlantic Monthly*, December 1987, p. 29.

44. Lovins and Lovins, "Drill Rigs and Battleships," 7.

45. Ibid.

46. H. Richard Heede and Amory B. Lovins, "Hiding the True Costs of Energy Sources," *Wall Street Journal*, 17 September 1985, p. 28. Most of this energy is from hydropower and industrial wood wastes.

47. Lovins and Lovins, "Drill Rigs and Battleships," 4–6; and Lovins and Lovins, "The Avoidable Oil Crisis," p. 22.

48. "Transcript of Talk by Reagan on South Africa and Apartheid," *New York Times*, 23 July 1986, p. A12.

49. Kim Willenson, "The Mines of South Africa," *Newsweek*, 11 August 1986, p. 30.

50. Eric D. Larson, Marc H. Ross, and Robert H. Williams, "Beyond the Era of Materials," *Scientific American*, June 1986, p. 34.

51. Malcolm W. Browne, "Plastics and Ceramics Replace Steel as the Sinews of War," *New York Times*, 18 July 1989, p. C1.

52. Office of Technology Assessment, "Strategic Materials: Technologies to Reduce U.S. Import Vulnerability," OTA-ITE-248, May 1985, pp. 332–333.

53. John P. Holdren, "Foreword," in Ronnie D. Lipschutz, *When Nations*

Clash: Raw Materials, Ideology and Foreign Policy (New York: Ballinger, 1989), p. xxvi.

54. "Excerpts from Pentagon's Plan: 'Prevent the Re-Emergence of a New Rival'," *New York Times*, 8 March 1992, p. 14.

55. See, for example, Westing, *Global Resources*, 1–2.

56. Jonathan Kwitny, *Endless Enemies: The Making of an Unfriendly World* (New York: Penguin Books, 1984), p. 109.

57. Robert Repetto, *Paying the Price: Pesticide Subsidies in Developing Countries* (Washington, DC: World Resources Institute, 1985), p. 5.

58. With funds scrounged from Europe, the program saved an estimated $149 of food for every dollar spent on pest control. Boyce Rensberger, "Africa's Using Natural Pest Control," *Washington Post*, National Weekly Edition, 27 June–3 July 1988, p. 38.

59. See, for example, Edward C. Wolf, "Beyond the Green Revolution: New Approaches for Third World Agriculture," *Worldwatch Paper #73* (Washington, DC: Worldwatch Institute, 1986).

60. World Commission on Environment and Development, *Our Common Future* (New York: Oxford University Press, 1987), pp. 43, 89.

61. Paul Lewis, "Balancing Industry with the Ecology," *New York Times*, 2 March 1992, p. A3.

Chapter 6

1. Quoted in Richard Rothstein, "Give Them a Break," *New Republic*, 1 February 1988, pp. 23–24.

2. Paul A. Samuelson, *Economics*, 9th ed. (New York: McGraw-Hill, 1973), pp. 714–720.

3. Harper's Index, *Harper's* 285, no. 1711 (December 1992), p. 17.

4. Robert Gilpin, *The Political Economy of International Relations* (Princeton, NJ: Princeton University Press, 1987), p. 192; and William R. Cline, *Trade Policy in the 1980s* (Washington, DC: Institute for International Economics, 1983), p. 5.

5. See Robert Keohane and Joseph Nye, Jr., *Power and Interdependence*, 2d ed. (Glenview, IL: Scott, Foresman, 1989).

6. Sherle R. Schwenninger and Jerry W. Sanders, "The Democrats and a New Grand Strategy—Part I," *World Policy Journal* 3, no. 3 (Summer 1986): 378.

7. Robert B. Reich, "The Economics of Illusion and the Illusion of Economics," *Foreign Affairs* 66, no. 3 (America and the World Issue, 1987–1988):521.

8. Clyde H. Farnsworth, "Bloc by Bloc, the World Is Raising Trade Barriers Again," *New York Times*, 12 June 1988, section 4, p. 2.

9. James Sterngold, "Intractable Trade Issues with Japan," *New York Times*,

4 December 1991, p. D4. Canada is the biggest U.S. foreign trading partner (but it's not overseas).

10. Francis Stewart, "Back to Keynesianism: Reforming the IMF," *World Policy Journal* 4, no. 3 (Summer 1987):467–469, 474.

11. Ibid., 470–472.

12. Schwenninger and Sanders, "The Democrats," 470.

13. James L. Rowe, Jr., "Latin America's Cash Famine," *Washington Post,* National Weekly Edition, 31 August 1987, pp. 7–8.

14. Sarah Bartlett, "A Vicious Circle Keeps Latin America in Debt," *New York Times,* 15 January 1989, section 4, p. 5. James Henry, a New York economist and lawyer, contends that "fifty percent or more of the money borrowed abroad by the most important debtor countries in the 1970s and 1980s flowed right out the back door in the form of private capital flight. In Mexico's case, the private flight share was about 51 percent; in Argentina's case, more than 70 percent." James S. Henry, "Poor Man's Debt, Rich Man's Loot," *Washington Post,* National Weekly Edition, 19–25 December 1988, p. 24.

15. Stewart, "Back to Keynesianism," 473.

16. Clyde H. Farnsworth, "Advice by World Bank on 3d World's Deficits," *New York Times,* 7 July 1988, p. D2.

17. Barber Conable, while serving as president of the World Bank, gave an occasional speech encouraging developing countries to cut their expenditures on arms, but this rhetoric has yet to be matched by the World Bank's loan practices. David R. Francis, "World Bank Urges Developing Nations to Alter Policies," *Christian Science Monitor,* 27 September 1989, p. 7.

18. Commonwealth Group of Experts, *The Debt Crisis and the World Economy* (London: Commonwealth Secretariat, 1984), p. 188. Quoted in Arjun Makhijani and Robert S. Brown, "Restructuring the International Monetary System," *World Policy Journal* 3, no. 1 (Winter 1985–1986):65.

19. Jerry W. Sanders and Sherle R. Schwenninger, "The Democrats and a New Grand Strategy—Part II," *World Policy Journal* 4, no. 1 (Winter 1986–1987):5.

20. Michael Moffitt, "Reagonomics and the Decline of U.S. Hegemony," *World Policy Journal* 4, no. 4 (Fall 1987):568–569.

21. Steven Greenhouse, "Third World Tells I.M.F. That Poverty Has Increased," *New York Times,* 29 September 1988, p. D1.

22. World Bank, *The World Bank Annual Report* (1990), p. 32. See also Clyde H. Farnsworth, "Money Loss Grows for Poorer Lands, World Bank Finds," *New York Times,* 19 December 1988, p. 1.

23. Victoria Irwin, "World Economic Woes Take Toll on Children," *Christian Science Monitor,* 20 December 1988, p. 3.

24. Frances Moore Lappé, Rachel Schurman, and Kevin Danaher, *Betraying the National Interest* (New York: Grove Press, 1987), pp. 4, 125.

25. Merrill Collett, "Debt-Related Economic Hardships Are Making Civilians, and Some Military Officers, Restless," *Christian Science Monitor*, 1 May 1989, p. 1; and, Merrill Collett, "The Week of '100 Percent Discounts' in Venezuela," *Washington Post*, National Weekly Edition, 13–19 March 1989, p. 16.

26. For discussion of the current dangers of GATT preempting local legislation in these areas, see Michael H. Shuman, "Democracy vs. GATTzilla," *Bulletin of Municipal Foreign Policy* 4, no. 4 (Autumn 1990):4–6.

27. Russell Mokhiber, "Union Carbide and the Devastation of Bhopal," *Multinational Monitor*, April 1987, pp. 6–8.

28. Bonnie Ram, "Do We Need an International Policy on Hazardous Waste Exports?" *F.A.S. Public Interest Report* 41, no. 5 (May 1988):7–8.

29. Michael Weisskopt, "World Bank Official's Irony Backfires," *Washington Post*, 10 February 1992, p. A9.

30. Ram, "Do We Need an International Policy on Hazardous Waste Exports?" 7.

31. Robert Reich, *The Next American Frontier* (New York: Times Books, 1983), pp. 124–125.

32. Ibid., 124.

33. Michael Perelman, "The Green Revolution: American Agriculture in the Third World," in *Radical Agriculture*, ed. Richard Merrill (New York: Harper Colophon Books, 1976), pp. 111–125.

34. Today, Third World nations indoctrinated in First World economics continue to overinvest in the cities and underinvest in the countryside. Clyde Haberman, "U.N. Official Criticizes Focus of Third World Development," *New York Times*, 18 October 1988, p. A17.

35. Perelman, "The Green Revolution," 120.

36. Arthur R. Kroeber, "After the Green Revolution: The Struggle to Produce Food," *In These Times*, 20–26 April 1988, p. 9.

37. Ibid.

38. "Ecologists Make Friends with Economists," *Economist*, 15 October 1988, p. 25.

39. Clyde H. Farnsworth, "World Bank and I.M.F. Approve Plan to Cut Debt of Poorer Nations," *New York Times*, 5 April 1989, p. 1.

40. Sarah Bartlett, "Plan or No Plan, Debt Relief Is Not Around the Corner," *New York Times*, 9 April 1989, section 4, p. 1. See also Christopher Whalen, "Brady's Debt Plan: Dead in the Water," *New York Times*, 4 October 1989, p. A29.

41. Peter T. Kilborn, "Bush Acts to Ease Africa Debt," *New York Times*, 7 July 1989, p. D1.

42. Jeffrey Sachs, "Making the Brady Plan Work," *Foreign Affairs* 68, no. 3 (Summer 1989):90.

43. Ibid., 90–91.

44. Eugene Robinson, "Latin Leaders Warn of Debt Threat," *Washington Post,* 30 October 1988, p. 1. See also Robert J. Samuelson, "The Mexican Connection," *Newsweek,* 12 December 1988, p. 53.

45. Jennifer Collins, "Codifying Corporate Accountability," *Multinational Monitor,* June 1990, pp. 16–18.

46. Quoted in ibid., p. 18.

47. Great Britain is the only EEC country that has not made the charter a binding part of its domestic law. Peter Lange, "The Politics of Social Dimension," in *Euro-Politics,* ed. Alberta M. Sbragia (Washington, DC: Brookings Institution, 1992), p. 230.

48. Shuman, "GATTzilla," 4.

49. Lappé, Schurman, and Danaher, *Betraying National Interest,* 87.

50. Robin Broad and John Cavanagh, "No More NICs," *Foreign Policy,* no. 72 (Fall 1988):100–110.

51. Ibid., 99.

52. A World Bank study in 1986 calculated that $10 billion spent on household and industrial conservation measures could save half the energy that the $44 billion debt-financed dams in Brazil will be producing. Bruce Rich, "Conservation Woes at the World Bank," *Nation,* 23 January 1989, p. 91.

53. Susan George, "Financing Ecocide in the Third World," *Nation,* 30 April 1988, pp. 601–606.

54. The gap between the World Bank's rhetoric and its actions, however, remains considerable. Rich, "Conservation Woes," 90.

55. Kristin Helmore, "Self-Help Empowers Poor," *Christian Science Monitor,* 8 March 1989, pp. 12–13.

56. James Tyson, "Biogas Heats Woks, Lights Homes of 30 Million Chinese," *Christian Science Monitor,* 16 March 1989, p. 4.

57. Lisa Swenarski, "Peru's Model Self-Help Town," *Christian Science Monitor,* 16 March 1989, pp. 12–13.

58. When it came to First World countries opening their markets to Third World products, however, the principles of free market did not apply.

59. Ruth Leger Sivard, *World Military and Social Expenditures—1991,* 14th ed. (Washington, DC: World Priorities, 1991), p. 11.

60. Robert Pear, "U.S. Ranked No. 1 in Weapons Sales," *New York Times,* 11 August 1992, p. 10.

Chapter 7

1. William Schneider, "Public Opinion," in *The Making of America's Soviet Policy,* ed. Joseph Nye, Jr. (New Haven: Yale University Press, 1984), pp. 11–12.

2. Sean M. Lynn-Jones and Stephen R. Rock, "From Confrontation to Cooperation: Transforming the U.S.-Soviet Relationship," in *Fateful Visions:*

Avoiding Nuclear Catastrophe, ed. Joseph S. Nye, Jr., Graham T. Allison, and Albert Carnesale (Cambridge, MA: Ballinger, 1988), pp. 125–126.

3. Philip Shabecoff, "U.S.-Soviet Accord on the Environment Approved in Geneva," *New York Times,* Western Edition, 13 December 1985, p. A1; Felicity Barringer, "Manned Mission to Mars Seen by Soviet Researchers in 2010," *New York Times,* 7 July 1988, p. A9; John Noble Wilford, "Soviet and U.S. Scientists Join in Quest to Select Sites for Mars Landing," *New York Times,* Western Edition, 5 April 1988, p. B8.

4. Elaine Sciolino, "U.S. and Soviet, in Gulf, Show Rare Cooperation," *New York Times,* 14 January 1988, p. 5.

5. Geoffrey Kemp and Augustus Richard Norton, "US-Soviet Teamwork on Terrorism," *Christian Science Monitor,* 10 March 1989, p. 18.

6. Arthur Macy Cox, "Mr. Gorbachev's Peaceful Coexistence Ploy," *New York Times,* 25 June 1988, p. 15.

7. "Spy Meets Spy," *U.S. News & World Report,* 21 November 1988, p. 21.

8. Roger Fisher and William Ury, *Getting to Yes* (New York: Penguin, 1981); and William Ury, *Getting Past No* (New York: Bantam: 1991).

9. Robert Marquand, "Soviet Diplomat Studies at Harvard," *Christian Science Monitor,* 17 February 1989, p. 14.

10. Energy efficiency is the fastest, cheapest, and perhaps the only credible way the world will be able to reduce atmospheric carbon-dioxide levels. Amory B. Lovins, L. Hunter Lovins, Florentin Krause, and Wilfred Bach, *Least-Cost Energy: Solving the CO_2 Problem* (Andover, MA: Brick House, 1982).

11. Stanley Hoffmann, *Primacy or World Order: American Foreign Policy Since the Cold War* (New York: McGraw-Hill, 1978), pp. 273–274.

12. Robert C. Cowen, "Wanted: An International Accord Banning Space Junk," *Christian Science Monitor,* 5 January 1988, p. 17.

13. James Turner Johnson, "If Qaddafi's the Enemy, Why Not Assassinate Him and Spare Others?" *Washington Post,* National Weekly Edition, 5 May 1986, p. 23.

14. Stephen D. Krasner, ed., *International Regimes* (Ithaca, NY: Cornell University Press, 1983), p. 2.

15. Ibid., 2.

16. Joseph S. Nye, Jr., "Nuclear Learning and U.S.-Soviet Security Regimes," paper to the American Political Science Association 1986 Annual Meeting, 28 August 1986 (revised 17 September 1986) (monograph).

17. Richard N. Gardner, "The Case for Practical Internationalism," *Foreign Affairs* 66, no. 4 (Spring 1988):831–834.

18. Robert O. Keohane and Joseph S. Nye, Jr., "Three Cheers for Multilateralism," *Foreign Policy,* no. 60 (Fall 1985):153–154.

19. Ibid., 153.

20. Ruth Pearson, "U.N. Cries 'Uncle,'" *Bulletin of the Atomic Scientists* 44, no. 8 (October 1988):39.

21. Gardner, "Case for Practical Internationalism," 833.

22. Ibid., 827.

23. Hoffmann, *Primacy*, 272.

24. Amory B. Lovins and L. Hunter Lovins, *Energy/War: Breaking the Nuclear Link* (San Francisco: Friends of the Earth, 1980), pp. 24–25.

25. Ernest Conine, "Is Politics Destroying Foreign Policy?" *Los Angeles Times*, 4 July 1984, p. II-5.

26. Mitchell Reiss, "GATT: Guidelines for Arms Control," *Bulletin of the Atomic Scientists* 39, no. 5 (May 1983):53–56.

27. Hoffmann, *Primacy*, 191.

28. See Table 1, note 29 in the Introduction section of the Notes.

29. UNICEF, *State of the World's Children* (Oxford: Oxford University Press, 1989), pp. 3–4.

30. Philip Revzin, "U.N.'s Health Agency Find Funds Shrinking While Work Expands," *Wall Street Journal*, 7 April 1988, p. 1.

31. Linda Feldmann, "Tiny UN Agency Implores US, Saudi Arabia for Funds," *Christian Science Monitor*, 19 April 1989, p. 7.

32. Marvine Howe, "U.N. Fund Helps Women Help Themselves," *New York Times*, 3 November 1988, p. A6.

33. Robert Johansen, "The Reagan Administration and the United Nations," *World Policy Journal* 3, no. 4 (Fall 1986):607.

34. Between 1966 and 1981, the ICJ had only six new cases and gave five other advisory opinions. Burton Yale Pines, "Hollow Chambers of the World Court," *Wall Street Journal*, 12 April 1984, p. 32. See also William Coplin and J. Martin Rochester, "The PCIJ, ICJ, the League of Nations, and the UN: A Comparative Empirical Survey," *American Political Science Review* 66, no. 2 (June 1972):529–550.

35. Keohane and Nye, "Three Cheers," 154–155.

36. United Nations Association–USA, "Directions for the UN: U.S. Public Opinion on the United Nations," September 1983 (background paper). (Available from UNA-USA, 300 East 42nd St., New York, NY 10017.)

37. Johansen, "Reagan Administration," 610–613.

38. Quoted in Seymour Maxwell Finger, "The Reagan-Kirkpatrick Policies and the United Nations," *Foreign Affairs* 62, no. 2 (Winter 1983–1984):457.

39. Quoted in Richard N. Gardner, "One Mainstream Dukakis," *New York Times*, 11 August 1988, p. A25.

40. As of 31 December 1991, the United States owed the UN $266 million for the regular budget and $141 million for peacekeeping operations. Steven Palacio, UN Information Center, personal communication, 25 March 1992.

41. "A Revived U.N. Needs U.S. Cash," *New York Times*, 22 July 1988, p. A14.

42. Gardner, "Mainstream Dukakis," 829.

43. In the case concerning *U.S. Diplomatic and Consular Staff in Teheran,* the

United States got an opinion condemning Iran that was unanimous, including the support of judges from the Soviet Union, Poland, and Syria. In the *Gulf of Maine* case, the United States won five-sixths of the disputed territory. Bill Blum and Gina Lobaco, "International Court of Justice," *California Lawyer,* February 1986, p. 40.

44. Edward Cody, "World Court Rules Against U.S. on PLO Showdown," *Washington Post,* 27 April 1988, p. A23.

45. Paul Lewis, "Rising Star for U.N.?" *New York Times,* 30 July 1988, p. 5.

46. Ibid.; Ted Morello, "'Old Hand' on Iran-Iraq Conflict Takes Over Geneva Negotiations," *Christian Science Monitor,* 8 November 1988, p. 10.

47. Quoted in Ethan Schwartz, "United Nations: Was It the Cause or the Beneficiary?" *Washington Post,* National Weekly Edition, 9–15 January 1989, p. 19.

48. Johansen, "Reagan Administration," 635–636.

49. The value of low-flying surveillance received renewed attention after President Bush called for an East-West "open skies" arrangement. See, for example, Joe Clark, "Don't Dismiss Open Skies," *New York Times,* 5 June 1989, p. A17.

50. Zachary Citron, "We Aren't the World," *New Republic,* 15 May 1989, p. 22.

51. Thomas M. Frank, "Let's Not Abandon the World Court," *New York Times,* Western Edition, 17 July 1986, p. 23.

52. Francis Fukuyama, "The End of History?" *National Interest,* no. 16 (Summer 1989):18.

53. Ibid.

Chapter 8

1. See, for example, Alternative Defence Commission (UK), *Defence Without the Bomb: Non-Nuclear Defence Policies for Britain* (London: Taylor and Francis, 1983).

2. Jonathan Dean, *Watershed in Europe: Dismantling the East-West Military Confrontation* (Lexington, MA: Lexington Books, 1987), p. xiii.

3. Dan Plesch, "NATO's New Nuclear Weapons," *Defense and Disarmament Alternatives* 1, no. 3 (May 1988):2.

4. Quoted in Dean, *Watershed,* 33.

5. Ibid., 61–78.

6. Edward N. Luttwak, *On the Meaning of Victory* (New York: Simon and Schuster, 1986), p. 168.

7. Robert Neild and Anders Boserup, "Beyond INF: A New Approach to Nonnuclear Forces," *World Policy Journal* 6, no. 4 (Fall 1987), p. 605

8. Alternative Defence Commission, *Defence Without the Bomb,* 9.

9. Dietrich Fischer, *Preventing War in the Nuclear Age* (Totowa, NJ: Rowman and Allanheld, 1984), p. 66 (emphasis removed).

10. Albrecht von Müller and Andrzej Karkoszka, "A Modified Approach to Conventional Arms Control," *Defense and Disarmament Alternatives* 1, no. 3 (May 1988):1.

11. Adam Roberts, *Nations in Arms* (New York: Praeger, 1976), p. 98.

12. Fischer, *Preventing War*, 53.

13. Ibid., 51.

14. When measured by these indices, claims that SDI is defensive are revealed as ludicrous. SDI fails each test—dramatically.

15. For a thorough discussion of this evolution, see Dean, *Watershed*, 29–59.

16. James Fallows, *National Defense* (New York: Vintage Books, 1981), p. 49.

17. Gregg Easterbrook, "Sticker Shock: The Stealth Is a Bomb," *Newsweek*, 23 January 1989, p. 20.

18. Sven Hellman, Strategic Planning Division of the Swedish Defense Department, personal communication, August 1986.

19. Roberts, *Nations in Arms*, 84.

20. Alternative Defence Commission, *Defence Without the Bomb*, 114.

21. Sven Hellman, personal communication.

22. Alternative Defence Commission, *Defence Without the Bomb*, 114.

23. Ibid., 116–117.

24. These ideas are nicely summarized in Stephen J. Flanagan, "Nonprovocative and Civilian-Based Defenses," in *Fateful Visions: Avoiding Nuclear Catastrophe*, ed. Joseph S. Nye, Jr., Graham T. Allison, and Albert Carnesale (Cambridge, MA: Ballinger, 1988), pp. 93–109.

25. Jochen Löser, "The Security Policy Options for Non-Communist Europe," *Armada International* 6, no. 2 (March-April 1982):66–75.

26. Albrecht von Müller, "Integrated Forward Defense: Outlines of a Modified Conventional Defense for Central Europe," 1985 (unpublished paper); Norbert Hannig, "Can Western Europe Be Defended by Conventional Means?" *International Defense Review* 1 (1979):27–34.

27. Horst Afheldt, *Verteidigung und Frieden* (Munich: Deutsche Taschenbuch Verlag, 1979). See also Hew Strachan, "Conventional Defence in Europe," *International Affairs* 61, no. 1 (March-April 1982):66–75.

28. Gene Sharp of Harvard University has analyzed CBD extensively in *Power and Struggle* (Boston: Horizon Books, 1973), *The Methods of Nonviolent Action* (Boston: Horizon Books, 1973), and *The Dynamics of Nonviolent Action* (Boston: Horizon Books, 1973).

29. See Gene Sharp, *Making Europe Unconquerable* (Cambridge, MA: Ballinger, 1985).

30. Fischer, *Preventing War*, 117.

31. Luttwak, *Meaning of Victory*, 73.

32. Fischer, *Preventing War*, 62.

33. Flanagan, "Nonprovocative Defenses," 105.

34. Von Müller and Karkoszka, "Modified Approach," 1.

35. Flanagan, "Nonprovocative Defenses," 105.

36. Ibid., 107.

37. See, for example, Richard Ullman, *Securing Europe* (Princeton, NJ: Princeton University Press, 1991); and Malcolm Chalmers, "Beyond the Alliance System," *World Policy Journal* 7, no. 2 (Spring 1990):216–250.

38. Of course, the small size of these Middle Eastern countries and the proximity of their cities to one another pose some major engineering challenges for NPD. Although even short-range weapons would have significant offensive potential, there would have to be greater reliance on conventional arms-control agreements, UN peacekeeping, techno-commando units, civilian-based defense, and defensive barriers throughout these nations' territories.

39. Randall Forsberg, Rob Leavitt, and Steve Lilly-Weber, "Conventional Forces Treaty Buries Cold War," *Bulletin of the Atomic Scientists* 47, no. 1 (January-February 1991):37.

40. Randall Forsberg, "Nonprovocative Defense: A New Approach to Arms Control," last updated 20 October 1988, p. 39 (monograph).

41. For two preliminary views of how this might be done, see Gene R. La Rocque, "What Is Ours to Defend?" *Harper's*, July 1988, pp. 39–50; and William S. Lind, "Strategy and a Future Navy," paper presented at the UN Naval Institute Conference on the Future of U.S. Naval Power, 27–29 July 1988 (monograph).

Chapter 9

1. William W. Bishop, Jr., *International Law: Cases and Materials*, 3d ed. (Boston: Little Brown, 1971), pp. 1059–1077.

2. Harry B. Hollins, Averill L. Powers, and Mark Sommer, *The Conquest of War: Alternative Strategies for Global Peace* (Boulder: Westview, 1989).

3. John M. Goshko and Barton Gellman, "Idea of a Potent U.N. Army Receives a Mixed Response," *Washington Post*, 29 October 1992, p. A22.

4. Richard N. Gardner, "The Case for Practical Internationalism," *Foreign Affairs* 66, no. 4 (Spring 1988):837.

5. Robert Johansen, "The Reagan Administration and the United Nations," *World Policy Journal* 3, no. 4 (Fall 1986):623.

6. Ibid. See also Kathryn Christensen, "After Long Conflict, Cyprus Now Searches for an Elusive Peace," *Wall Street Journal*, 23 August 1988, p. 1.

7. Johansen, "Reagan Administration," 620.

8. Joanne Omang, "Policing a Latin Peace Projected to Cost Millions," *Washington Post*, 11 May 1985, p. 4. See also "Honduran Seeks U.N. Patrol to Evict Neighbors' Rebels," *New York Times*, 5 October 1988, p. A8.

9. See Brian Urquhart, "Avoiding United States Unilateralism," *New York Times*, 11 July 1988, p. A15; and Alan Cowell, "Moscow Urging a U.S.-Soviet Pullout in Gulf," *New York Times*, 26 February 1989, p. 17.

10. Edward C. Luck, "Making Peace," *Foreign Policy*, no. 89 (Winter 1992–1993):150.

11. In Afghanistan, other UN organizations also sent aid and development experts to help rebuild the economy and care for returning refugees. Paul Lewis, "U.N. Teams Will Enter Afghan Areas," *New York Times*, 18 June 1988, p. 4; Paul Lewis, "The U.N.'s Gulf War Balancing Act," *New York Times*, 25 March 1989, p. 3; Marian Houk, "UN to Host Direct Iran-Iraq Talks Following Truce," *Christian Science Monitor*, 9 August 1988, p. 7; and Ted Morello, "UN Forces: Popular But Poor," *Christian Science Monitor*, 12 January 1989, pp. 1–2.

12. Zachary Citron, "We Aren't the World," *New Republic*, 15 May 1989, p. 19.

13. "U.N. Votes for Peace Force to Be Sent to Mozambique," *Washington Post*, 17 December 1992, p. A35; Paul Lewis, "No Peace for the U.N.," *New York Times*, 29 November 1992, p. 1; Lucia Mouat, "UN Role Grows in Central America," *Christian Science Monitor*, 7 January 1991, p. 3; Lucia Mouat, "UN's Post–Cold War Stature Grows," *Christian Science Monitor*, 7 September 1990, p. 3; Robert S. Greenberger and David Shribman, "U.N., Long Stymied by Cold War, Begins to Fulfill Its Promise," *Wall Street Journal*, 30 August 1990, p. 1.

14. Luck, "Making Peace," 151.

15. Robert C. Johansen, "Toward an Alternative Security System," *World Policy Working Paper #24* (New York: World Policy Institute, 1983), p. 45.

16. Each country takes responsibility for different elements of the force: Denmark trains military police; Finland trains observers; Norway provides transport and logistics; and Sweden is in charge of staff officers. Morello, "UN Forces: Popular But Poor," 2.

17. Johansen, "Reagan Administration," 631.

18. Ibid.

19. Gary C. Hufbauer and Kimberly A. Elliott, "Sanctions Will Bite—and Soon," *New York Times*, 14 January 1991, p. A17. Some argue that since the war the misbehavior of Saddam Hussein in the face of the continued UN-sponsored embargo demonstrates its limited value. It is *because* of the embargo, however, that Hussein has more or less complied with UN efforts to uncover and destroy Iraqi weapons capability. The fact that the UN has yet to lift the embargo says more about the UN's hidden objective (to oust Hussein) than about the effectiveness of the embargo for its intended purpose (to ensure Hussein's obedience to the postwar treaty obligations).

Chapter 10

1. John H. Barton and Lawrence D. Weiler, eds., *International Arms Control: Issues and Agreements* (Stanford, CA: Stanford Press, 1976), p. 47.

2. Henry W. Kendall, "Second Strike," *Bulletin of the Atomic Scientists* 35, no. 7 (September 1979):32–37; Frank Barnaby, "The Continuing Body Count at Hiroshima and Nagasaki," *Bulletin of the Atomic Scientists* 33, no. 10 (December 1977):48–53; "The Physical and Medical Effects of the Hiroshima and Nagasaki Bombs," *Bulletin of the Atomic Scientists* 33, no. 10 (December 1977):54–56.

3. Tom Wicker, "Star Wars in Decline," *New York Times*, 14 June 1988, p. A19.

4. R. Jeffrey Smith, "A Last-Ditch Effort to Keep Star Wars Alive," *Washington Post*, National Weekly Edition, 26 February–4 March 1990, p. 31.

5. Spurgeon M. Keeny, Jr., and Wolfgang K. H. Panofsky, "MAD versus NUTS: The Mutual Hostage Relationship of the Superpowers," *Foreign Affairs* 60, no. 2 (Winter 1981–1982):290–291.

6. John D. Steinbruner, "National Security and the Concept of Strategic Stability," *Journal of Conflict Resolution* 22 (September 1978):421.

7. Robert S. McNamara, "The Military Role of Nuclear Weapons," *Foreign Affairs* 62, no. 1 (Fall 1983):79 (emphasis in original).

8. Kosta Tsipis, "If Arms Were Cut 50%," *New York Times*, 11 January 1988, p. 17.

9. On September 27, Bush agreed to remove B-1B and B-52 strategic bombers from 24-hour-a-day alert, to accelerate deactivation of ballistic missiles scheduled for deactivation under START, to withdraw nuclear artillery and short-range warheads from overseas bases, and to take tactical nuclear weapons off surface ships and attack submarines. A week later Gorbachev responded by agreeing to remove Blackjack and Bear strategic bombers from alert, to retire 503 ballistic missiles, to destroy all nuclear warheads for artillery and nonstrategic missiles, and to take tactical nuclear weapons off surface ships and attack submarines. "Disarmament Race, September-October 1991," *Bulletin of the Atomic Scientists* 47, no. 10 (December 1991):49. Psychologist Charles E. Osgood called this strategy Graduated and Reciprocated Initiatives in Tension-Reduction, or GRIT. Charles E. Osgood, "The Way GRIT Works," in *Securing Our Planet*, ed. Don Carlson and Craig Comstock (Los Angeles: Jeremy P. Tarcher, 1986), pp. 24–30.

10. McGeorge Bundy, George F. Kennan, Robert S. McNamara, and Gerard Smith, "Nuclear Weapons and the Atlantic Alliance," *Foreign Affairs* 60, no. 4 (Spring 1982):757.

11. Michael R. Gordon, "Nuclear Strategy Shift?" *New York Times*, 3 July 1990, p. A11.

12. Daniel Charles, *Nuclear Planning in NATO: Pitfalls of First Use* (Cambridge, MA: Ballinger, 1987), p. 155.

13. See, for example, Richard H. Ullman, "Nuclear Arms: How Big a Cut?" *New York Times Magazine,* 16 November 1986, p. 76.

14. "Nuclear Pursuits," *Bulletin of the Atomic Scientists* 47, no. 4 (May 1991):29.

15. See Chapter 1, infra.

16. Jimmy Carter, *Keeping Faith* (New York: Bantam Books, 1982), p. 245.

17. Robert McNamara, *Blundering into Disaster: Surviving the First Century of the Nuclear Age* (New York: Pantheon Books, 1986), p. 123, note 5.

18. Michael D. Intriligator, "Before Making Deep Cuts in Nuclear Stockpiles, We Should Assess the Cost," *Los Angeles Times,* 30 November 1987, p. II-15.

19. William E. Burrows, "Why Verification Can Be Solidly Trusted," *New York Times,* Western Edition, 28 December 1987, p. 19.

20. Paul L. Leventhal and Milton M. Hoenig, "The Tritium Factor," *New York Times,* Western Edition, 4 August 1987, p. A23; and Matthew L. Wald, "Turning Point Nears in Production of Fuel for Hydrogen Bombs," *New York Times,* 17 November 1987, pp. C1, C9.

21. See Harold A. Feiveson, Christopher E. Paine, and Frank von Hippel, "A Low-Threshold Test Ban Is Feasible," *Science* 238, no. 4826 (23 October 1987):455–459; and Paul Doty, "A Nuclear Test Ban," *Foreign Affairs* 65, no. 4 (Spring 1987):750–769.

22. Matthew Bunn, "The Next Nuclear Offensive," *Technology Review,* 30 January 1988, pp. 28–36.

23. Richard L. Garwin, Kurt Gottfried, and Donald L. Hafner, "Antisatellite Weapons," *Scientific American,* June 1984, pp. 45–55.

24. David Hafemeister, Joseph J. Romm, and Kosta Tsipis, "The Verification of Compliance with Arms-Control Agreements," *Scientific American,* March 1985, pp. 39–45; Jack F. Evernden, "Politics, Technology, and the Test Ban," *Bulletin of the Atomic Scientists* 41, no. 3 (March 1985):9–11; Michael Krepon, "The START Treaty Can Be Verified, Too," *Washington Post,* National Weekly Edition, 28 March–3 April 1988, p. 29; and Burrows, "Why Verification Can Be Solidly Trusted."

25. The paradigmatic work is the Harvard Nuclear Study Group's *Living With Nuclear Weapons* (New York: Bantam New Age Books, 1983).

26. Michael Walzer, *Just and Unjust Wars* (New York: Basic Books, 1977), p. 283.

27. The Pastoral Statement of the U.S. Conference of Catholic Bishops, *The Challenge of Peace: God's Promise and Our Response* (Boston: Daughters of St. Paul, 1983), p. 8.

28. Kenneth Boulding, *Stable Peace* (Austin: University of Texas Press, 1981), pp. 64–65.

29. Amory B. Lovins and L. Hunter Lovins, *Energy/War: Breaking the Nuclear Link* (San Francisco: Friends of the Earth, 1980), pp. 29–38.

30. Ibid., 9–28.

31. Chauncey Starr and Edwin Zebroski, "Nuclear Power and Weapons Proliferation," paper to the American Power Conference, 18–20 April 1977.

32. Amory B. Lovins, *Soft Energy Paths* (Cambridge, MA: Ballinger, 1977), p. 187.

33. Starr and Zebroski, "Nuclear Power and Weapons Proliferation," 10.

34. John R. Lamarsh, "On the Construction of the Plutonium Producing Reactors by Smaller and/or Developing Nations," prepared by Congressional Research Service, 30 April 1976.

35. Theodore Taylor, personal communication, 5 January 1993.

36. Oak Ridge National Lab Memorandum on a Crude Nuclear Fuel Reprocessing Plant, 1977. See also Report of the Nonproliferation Alternative Systems Assessment Program, *Nuclear Proliferation and Civilian Nuclear Power,* vol. 1, DOE/NE-0001/1, June 1980, pp. 34–35.

37. Lovins and Lovins, *Energy/War,* 24.

38. Natural uranium typically contains only 0.7 percent of the fissionable isotope U-235; the rest is nonfissionable U-238. Enrichment is a process designed to increase the concentration of U-235 relative to U-238.

39. See, for example, Spurgeon M. Keeny, Jr., chair, Report of the Nuclear Energy Policy Study Group, *Nuclear Power Issues and Choices* (Cambridge, MA: Ballinger, 1977), p. 280.

40. James J. Glackin, "Dangerous Drift in Uranium Enrichment," *Bulletin of the Atomic Scientists* 32, no. 2 (February 1976):22–29.

41. Ibid.

42. Edwin Zebroski, lecture at Stanford University, 28 May 1978.

43. Ibid.

44. Lovins and Lovins, *Energy/War,* 23.

45. Ibid.

46. Ibid., 19–20.

47. Thomas L. Friedman, "U.S. to Offer Plan to Keep Scientists at Work in Russia," *New York Times,* 8 February 1992, p. A1.

48. William J. Broad, "Panel Calls for Wider Help for Ex-Soviet Arms Experts," *New York Times,* 14 March 1992, p. 5.

49. William J. Broad, "Iraqi Atom Effort Exposes Weakness in World Controls," *New York Times,* 15 July 1991, p. A1; Jerry Gray, "Baghdad Reveals It Had Plutonium of Weapons Grade," *New York Times,* 6 August 1991, p. A1; R. Jeffrey Smith, "On Second Thought, Maybe the Iraqis Could Make the Bomb," *Washington Post,* National Weekly Edition, 15–21 July 1991, p. 18.

50. Gary Milhollin, "Building Saddam Hussein's Bomb," *New York Times Magazine,* 8 March 1992, pp. 30–36.

51. "Iraq Tested Missile to Carry A-Bomb, a U.N. Report Says," *New York Times*, 5 October 1991, p. 2.

52. Lovins and Lovins, *Energy/War*, 30–32.

53. The United States has produced 100 tonnes of plutonium and 500 to 600 tonnes of enriched uranium. The Soviet Union has produced 115 to 145 tonnes of plutonium and 500 to 1,000 tonnes of enriched uranium. Arjun Makhijani, Institute for Energy and Environmental Research, personal communication, 27 April 1992; and Thomas Cochran, Natural Resources Defense Council, personal communication, 5 January 1993.

54. Lovins and Lovins, *Energy/War*, 36 (emphasis in original).

55. Richard Falk, "A Non-Nuclear Future: Rejecting the Faustian Bargain," *Nation*, 13 March 1976, pp. 301–305.

56. Quoted in John McPhee, *The Curve of Binding Energy* (New York: Ballantine Books, 1973), p. 163.

57. Stanley Hoffmann, *Primacy or World Order: American Foreign Policy Since the Cold War* (New York: McGraw-Hill, 1978), p. 217.

58. Michael Mandelbaum, "International Stability and Nuclear Order: The First Nuclear Regime," in David C. Gompert et al., *Nuclear Weapons and World Politics: Alternatives for the Future* (New York: McGraw Hill, 1977), p. 79.

59. Arjun Makhijani and Katherine Yih, "What to Do at Doomsday's End," *Washington Post*, 29 March 1992, Outlook Section, p. C3.

60. Ibid.

61. Kenneth Boulding, *Stable Peace* (Austin: University of Texas Press, 1978), p. 105.

Chapter 11

1. For an excellent overview, see Medea Benjamin and Andrea Freedman, *Bridging the Global Gap* (Cabin John, MD: Seven Locks Press, 1989). See also James Brooke, "Growth of Tourism Is Benefiting Fragile Environments," *New York Times*, 9 August 1989, p. C4.

2. Guy Halverson, "Helping Hand for Foreign Business," *Christian Science Monitor*, 22 February 1989, p. 9.

3. Kathleen Hendris, "Ashoka: Grants Issued for Practical Solutions," *Los Angeles Times*, 10 July 1986, p. 1.

4. Philip Shabecoff, "An Audubon Group Finds Its Interests Extend Far to South," *New York Times*, 11 July 1989, p. C4.

5. Alvaro Umana, "Costa Rica's Debt-for-Nature Swaps Come of Age," *Wall Street Journal*, 26 May 1989, p. A11.

6. John Cavanagh, Fellow at the Institute for Policy Studies, personal communication, 27 May 1993.

7. Shabecoff, "An Audubon Group Finds Its Interests."

8. Robert Gray, "A Planetful of Trees," *Christian Science Monitor*, 12 July 1989, p. 14.

9. "Rain Forest Worth More If Uncut, Study Says," *New York Times,* 4 July 1989, p. 18.

10. Michael H. Shuman, "From Charity to Justice," *Bulletin of Municipal Foreign Policy* 2, no. 4 (Autumn 1988):50–59.

11. Mauro Suttora, "Trying to Keep the Red Cross Out," *World Press Review,* October 1988, pp. 29–30 (reprinted from the Italian newsmagazine *Europeo*).

12. For a discussion of the growth of environmental activism in Central America, see Tensie Whelan, "A Tree Falls in Central America," *Amicus Journal,* 10, no. 4 (Fall 1988):28–38.

13. Robert M. Press, "Third-World Consumer Groups Chalk Up Steady Successes," *Christian Science Monitor,* 25 March 1988, p. 11.

14. Judith Wier, Witness for Peace, personal communication, 5 January 1993.

15. For a comprehensive review, see Michael H. Shuman, "Dateline Main Street: Local Foreign Policy," *Foreign Policy,* no. 65 (Winter 1986–1987): 156–174.

16. The data that follow all appear in Michael H. Shuman, "Building Municipal Foreign Policies: An Action Handbook for Citizens and Local Elected Officials" and in various issues of the *Bulletin of Municipal Foreign Policy.* (Available from the author at the Institute for Policy Studies, 1601 Connecticut Ave., NW, Washington, DC 20009.)

17. See, for example, Peter Spiro, "Taking Foreign Policy Away from the Feds," *Washington Quarterly* 11, no. 1 (Winter 1988):191–203, especially 202.

18. See, for example, *Califano v. Aznevorian,* 439 U.S. 170, 176 (1978).

19. The Logan Act forbids any American "directly or indirectly" to correspond with or meet with "any foreign government . . . with intent to influence the measures or conduct of any foreign government . . . in relation to any disputes or controversies with the United States, or to defeat the measures of the United States." 18 US Code Section 953 (1976). Despite its sweeping language, the act has never been enforced. Detlev F. Vagts, "The Logan Act: Paper Tiger or Sleeping Giant?" *American Journal of International Law* 60 (1966):268–302.

20. Michael H. Shuman, "Put Ollie in State Prison," *Bulletin of Municipal Foreign Policy* 2, no. 3 (Summer 1988):2–4.

21. Letter to Colonel Edward Carrington, 16 January 1787, in *The Life and Selected Writings of Thomas Jefferson,* ed. Adrienne Koch and William Peden (New York: Modern Library, 1944), p. 411.

Chapter 12

1. W. H. Ferry, personal communication, November 1987.

2. Fen Osler Hampson, "Escalation in Europe," in *Hawks, Doves, and Owls: An Agenda for Avoiding Nuclear War,* ed. Graham T. Allison, Albert Carnesale, and Joseph S. Nye, Jr. (New York: W. W. Norton, 1985), p. 107.

3. For a fuller discussion of these and other principles of resilient system

design, see Amory B. and L. Hunter Lovins, *Brittle Power: Energy Strategy for National Security* (Andover, MA: Brick House, 1982), Chapter 13.

4. Quoted in William L. Ury, *Beyond the Hotline: How Crisis Control Can Prevent Nuclear War* (New York: Penguin, 1986), p. 37.

5. Data collected by the Nicaraguan Institute of Statistics and Census (INEC) suggest that the war resulted in 29,270 dead, 18,012 wounded, 10,449 kidnapped and captured, and $17.8 billion in property damage. Lisa Haugaard, INEC researcher, personal communication, October 1989. See also "Nicaragua Reports 12 Killed in a Rebel Ambush," *New York Times*, 6 July 1988, p. 3.

6. Melvyn Krauss, *How NATO Weakens the West* (New York: Simon and Schuster, 1986).

7. Alternative Defence Commission, *Defence Without the Bomb: Non-Nuclear Defence Policies for Britain* (London: Taylor and Francis, 1983), p. 169.

8. This case is substantiated in Frank Barnaby, *The Automated Battlefield* (New York: Free Press, 1986).

9. Eisenhower's address to the American Society of Newspaper Editors in Washington, DC, delivered on 16 April 1953. Reprinted in *Public Papers of the Presidents of the United States* (Washington, DC: US Government Printing Office, 1960), p. 182.

10. Independent Commission on International Development Issues (Willy Brandt, chair), *North-South: A Program for Survival* (Cambridge, MA: MIT Press, 1980), p. 14.

11. Amory B. and L. Hunter Lovins, building on the Brandt Commission's proposal along these lines, suggested a steeply rising megatonnage tax on nuclear arsenals, to be paid annually in a public ritual of penance (held at Hiroshima's Peace Museum) as token compensation to nonnuclear nations for the risks that those arsenals impose on them. *Energy/War: Breaking the Nuclear Link* (San Francisco: Friends of the Earth, 1980), p. 146.

12. Richard J. Barnet, et al., "American Priorities in a New World Era," *World Policy Journal* 6, no. 2 (Spring 1989):211.

13. In 1988 the rural population of Latin America was approximately 126 million people. Inter-American Development Bank, *Economic and Social Progress in Latin America: 1989 Report* (Washington, DC: Inter-American Development Bank, 1989), Special Section on "Savings, Investment and Growth," p. 458. The average rural family in Latin America has five people. Juan Chackiel, Chief Demographer for the UN Economic Commission for Latin America and the Caribbean, personal communication, 27 May 1993.

14. "Main Street U.S.A.—Lobby or Lose It," *Global Communities*, Autumn 1991, p. 1.

15. Michael deCourcy Hinds, "Strapped, Big Cities Take Painful Cuts," *New York Times*, 6 January 1991, p. A14.

16. Bill Turque, "Cities on the Brink," *Newsweek*, 19 November 1990, p. 44.

17. Richard Lacayo, "The State of the States: Broke," *Time,* 31 December 1990, p. 15.

18. Michael deCourcy Hinds with Erik Eckholm, "'80's Leave States and Cities in Need," *New York Times,* 30 December 1990, p. 1.

19. "CIA Report Finds Decline Trend in China's Military Spending," *FPI International Report,* 6 May 1986, p. 4.

20. Kenneth L. Adelman and Norman R. Augustine, "Defense Conversion: Bulldozing the Management," *Foreign Affairs* 71, no. 2 (Spring 1992):34.

21. A similar proposal appears in Richard J. Barnet et al., "American Priorities in a New World Era," 224.

Annotated Bibliography

Many of the arguments advanced in this book build on those made by other authors. Although we cite a number of works in the endnotes, some warrant further attention and credit.

The literature of political science, hobbled by the simplistic assumptions of the "realists," contains far more books about how the world *is* than about how it *should be*. However, several important books written over the past two decades have argued for fundamentally redefining the theory and practice of international relations. The World Order Models Project (WOMP) published a series describing preferred scenarios for world politics. The most comprehensive vision is contained in Richard Falk, *Study of Future Worlds* (New York: Free Press, 1975). Also worth reading are Johan Galtung, *The True Worlds: A Transnational Perspective* (New York: Free Press, 1980), which highlights the need for building international institutions from the grassroots up, and Rajni Kothari, *Footsteps into the Future* (New York: Free Press, 1980), which poses sharp questions about global equity from a Third World perspective.

Charles Beitz, *Political Theory and International Relations* (Princeton, NJ: Princeton University Press, 1979) makes a compelling argument that international relations should not be immune from moral scrutiny. Robert C. Johansen takes up this challenge in *The National Interest and the Human Interest* (Princeton, NJ: Princeton University Press, 1980), in which he argues that U.S. foreign policy would be more effective were it built around the values of "global humanism." Subsequent efforts at describing a more desirable foreign policy include: Stanley Hoffmann, *Duties Beyond Borders: On the Limits and Possibilities of Ethical International Politics* (Syracuse, NY: Syracuse University Press, 1981); Richard A. Falk, *The End of World Order* (New York: Holmes and Meier, 1983); Louis René Beres, *Reason and Realpolitik: U.S. Foreign Policy and World Order* (Lexington, MA: D. C. Heath, 1984); John E. Mueller, *Retreat from Doomsday: The Obsolescence of Major War* (New York: Basic Books, 1989); and Seyom Brown, *International Relations in a Changing Global System: Toward a Theory of the World Polity* (Boulder: Westview, 1992).

The burgeoning field of peace studies laid the theoretical foundation for much of this book. Perhaps the two best introductory works are Dietrich Fischer, *Preventing War in the Nuclear Age* (Totowa, NJ: Rowman and Allanheld, 1984) and Mark Sommer, *Beyond the Bomb* (Washington, DC: Expro Press, 1985). Both books define national security broadly and introduce concepts like alternative security, nonprovocative defense, civilian-based defense, and economic conversion. In *Conditions of Peace* (Washington, DC: Expro Press, 1991), edited by Michael Shuman and Julia Sweig, a consortium of academics and activists called the Exploratory Project on the Conditions of Peace (Expro) suggests what a U.S. security system might look like if it adhered to the precepts of defensive defense, participatory democracy, sustainable development, economic equity, and community. A more mainstream look at these issues can be found in Joseph S. Nye, Jr., Graham T. Allison, and Albert Carnesale, *Fateful Visions: Avoiding Nuclear Catastrophe* (Cambridge, MA: Ballinger, 1986). Other good overviews are: Kenneth Boulding, *Stable Peace* (Austin: University of Texas Press, 1981); Harry B. Hollins, Averill L. Powers, and Mark Sommer, *The Conquest of War: Alternative Strategies for Global Security* (Boulder: Westview, 1989); Robert A. Irwin, *Building a Peace System* (Washington, DC: Expro Press, 1988); and Burns H. Weston, *Alternative Security: Living Without Nuclear Deterrence* (Boulder: Westview, 1990).

Good source material on the Persian Gulf War, which is critiqued in the Introduction, is available in *The Gulf War Reader* (New York: Times Books, 1991), edited by Micah L. Sifry and Christopher Cerf. A thorough if necessarily incomplete assessment of the consequences of the Persian Gulf War is presented in William M. Arkin, *Behind Enemy Lines* (forthcoming, 1993).

The litany of new threats to U.S. national security, described in Chapter 1, can be found in the official documents of the U.S. Departments of Defense and State. The dangers of proliferation are detailed in *The Series on the Spread of Nuclear Weapons* by Leonard Spector of the Carnegie Endowment for Peace and published by Random House (1984, 1985), Ballinger (1986–1987, 1987–1988), and Westview (1989–1990). The risks of foreign purchases of U.S. assets are covered in Martin Tolchin, *Selling Our Security: The Erosion of America's Assets* (New York: Knopf, 1992). The economic threats facing the United States are well documented in: Paul Kennedy, *The Rise and Fall of the Great Powers* (New York: Vintage, 1987); Robert Kuttner, *The End of Laissez Faire: National Purpose and the Global Economy After the Cold War* (New York: Knopf, 1991); and Robert B. Reich, *The Work of Nations* (New York: Vintage, 1991). Environmental threats are covered in Jessica Tuchman Matthews, "Redefining Security," *Foreign Affairs* 68, no. 2 (Spring 1989):162–177 and in the Worldwatch Institute's *State of the World* yearbooks, published by Norton (the annual essays by Lester Brown and Michael Renner are especially useful). Two other books that suggest the need for comprehensive, integrated definitions of national security are Paul Ekins, *A New World Order: Grassroots*

Movements for Global Change (London: Routledge, 1992) and Herman E. Daly and John B. Cobb, Jr., *For the Common Good* (Boston: Beacon, 1989).

The problematic history of U.S. uses of force, described in Chapter 2, is extensively examined by Richard Barnet in periodic articles in the *New Yorker* and in his numerous books, especially *Roots of War* (Middlesex, England: Penguin, 1972) and *Real Security* (New York: Simon and Schuster, 1981). The history of U.S.-sponsored covert actions is documented in: William Blum, *The CIA: A Forgotten History* (London: Zed Books, 1986); Loch K. Johnson, *America's Secret Power: The CIA in a Democratic Society* (New York: Oxford University Press, 1989); and Rhodri Jeffreys-Jones, *The CIA and American Democracy* (New Haven, CT: Yale University Press, 1989). Other good overviews include Jonathan Kwitny, *Endless Enemies: The Making of an Unfriendly World* (New York: Penguin Books, 1984); and Saul Landau, *The Dangerous Doctrine: National Security and U.S. Foreign Policy* (Boulder: Westview, 1988).

The literature on the dangers of the arms race, the topic of Chapter 3, is gigantic, swelled by proponents and critics of Ronald Reagan's rearmament program during the 1980s. Many of these texts are obsolete, but several have withstood the test of time: Elizabeth Young, *A Farewell to Arms Control?* (Middlesex, England: Penguin, 1972); Nigel Calder, *Nuclear Nightmares* (Middlesex, England: Penguin, 1979); McGeorge Bundy, *Danger and Survival* (New York: Vintage, 1988); Daniel Ford, *The Button* (New York: Simon and Schuster, 1985); and Morton Halperin, *Nuclear Fallacy* (Cambridge, MA: Ballinger, 1987). Useful yearbooks are published by Ruth Leger Sivard's World Priorities Inc. in Washington, DC, and by the Stockholm International Peace Research Institute. Probably the best way of keeping up with this fast-changing field is to subscribe to *Arms Control Today*, the *Defense Monitor*, the *Bulletin of the Atomic Scientists*, and *Foreign Policy*.

Most of the writers urging U.S. foreign policymakers to spread democracy have been conservative (or neoconservative) and believe, unlike us, that the United States should do so through the use of force. Two books with this perspective are noteworthy: Gregory A. Fossedal, *The Democratic Imperative: Exporting the American Revolution* (New York: New Republic Books, 1989); and Joshua Muravchik, *Exporting Democracy: Fulfilling America's Destiny* (Washington, DC: AEI Press, 1992). Neither of these authors seems interested in democratizing U.S. foreign policy, and in fact there is no comprehensive treatise on the subject. Robert Keohane and Joseph S. Nye, Jr., demonstrate how nonstate actors pose limits on the ability of nations to act autonomously and unilaterally in *Power and Interdependence*, 2d ed. (Glenview, IL: Scott, Foresman, 1989). Robert Dahl explores the need to interpose stronger civilian control over atomic bombs in *Controlling Nuclear Weapons* (Syracuse, NY: Syracuse University Press, 1985). A number of books call for stronger congressional control over war powers and covert actions, including: Arthur Schlesinger, Jr., *The Imperial Presidency* (Boston: Houghton Mifflin, 1973);

Michael J. Glennon, *Constitutional Diplomacy* (Princeton, NJ: Princeton University Press, 1990); Harold Hongju Koh, *The National Security Constitution* (New Haven, CT: Yale University Press, 1990); and Frances D. Wormuth and Edwin B. Firmage, *To Chain the Dog of War* (Dallas: Southern Methodist University Press, 1986).

The seminal work documenting the connections between resources and war, the subject of Chapter 5, is *Global Resources and International Conflict* (Oxford, England: Oxford University Press, 1986), edited by Arthur Westing. The specific security problems from large-scale, centralized energy systems are spelled out in Amory B. and L. Hunter Lovins, *Brittle Power: Energy Strategy for National Security* (Andover, MA: Brick House, 1982). The connections between strategic minerals and security are explored in: Ronnie D. Lipschutz, *When Nations Clash: Raw Materials, Ideology and Foreign Policy* (Cambridge, MA : Ballinger, 1989); and Stephen D. Krasner, *Defending the National Interest: Raw Materials Investments and U.S. Foreign Policy* (Princeton, NJ: Princeton University Press, 1978). A compelling, if contradictory, plea for making economic development more sustainable is the World Commission on Environment and Development (chaired by Gro Harlem Brundtland), *Our Common Future* (New York: Oxford University Press, 1987).

The material in Chapter 6, documenting the connections between economic policy and conflict, is drawn largely from articles in the *World Policy Journal* authored by, among others, John Cavanagh, Walter Russell Mead, Jerry Sanders, and Sherle Schwenninger. The best standard, up-to-date text in the field of political economy is Robert Gilpin, *The Political Economy of International Relations* (Princeton, NJ: Princeton University Press, 1987). Devastating critiques of the Bretton Woods economic system can be found in: Richard Barnet and Ronald E. Müller, *Global Reach: The Power of Multinational Corporations* (New York: Simon and Schuster, 1974); Walden Bello and Stephanie Rosenfeld, *Dragons in Distress: Asia's Miracle Economies in Crisis* (San Francisco: Institute for Food and Development Policy, 1990); *Trading Freedom: How Free Trade Affects Our Lives, Work, and Environment* (San Francisco: Institute for Food and Development Policy, 1992) edited by John Cavanagh, John Gershman, Karen Baker, and Gretchen Helmke; and Susan George, *A Fate Worse than Debt* (New York: Grove Press, 1988).

A vast literature exists on conflict resolution, the subject of Chapter 7. The most widely read book on negotiation theory is Roger Fisher and William Ury, *Getting to Yes* (New York: Penguin, 1981). The two most celebrated works on international organizations are: Inis L. Claude, *Swords into Plowshares: The Problems and Progress of International Organizations* (New York: Random House, 1959); and Ernst B. Hass, *Beyond the Nation State: Functionalism and International Organization* (Stanford, CA: Stanford University Press, 1958). Political scientists have clearcut several forests proving the obvious—that cooperation offers nations a valuable alternative to war and coercion.

Among the most recognized works are: Stanley Hoffmann, *Primacy or World Order: American Foreign Policy Since the Cold War* (New York: McGraw-Hill, 1978); *International Regimes* (Ithaca, NY: Cornell University Press, 1983), edited by Stephen D. Krasner; Robert O. Keohane, *After Hegemony: Cooperation and Discord in the World Political Economy* (Princeton, NJ: Princeton University Press, 1984); and *Cooperation Under Anarchy* (Princeton, NJ: Princeton University Press, 1986) edited by Kenneth A. Oye. A good book on the UN, though somewhat outdated, is Toby Trister Gati, *The US, the UN, and the Management of Global Change* (New York: New York University Press, 1983). Periodic articles on the UN also appear in *Foreign Affairs, Foreign Policy,* and the *New York Review of Books.*

Most of the literature on nonprovocative defense, summarized in Chapter 8, has been published in Europe. The most important works include: Horst Afheldt, *Defensive Verteidigung* (Hamburg: Rowohlt Reinbeck, 1983); German Study Group on Alternative Security (SAS), *Strukturwandel der Verteidigung—Entwürfe für eine konsequente Defensive* (Opladen: Westdeutscher Verlag, 1984); Jochen Löser, *Weder rot noch tot: Überleben ohne Atomkrieg—Eine sicherheitspolitische Alternative* (Munich: Olzog, 1981); Lutz Unterseher, "Defending Europe: Toward a Stable Conventional Deterrent," Study Group on Alternative Security Policy, Center for Philosophy and Public Policy, University of Maryland, August 1986; Alternative Defence Commission (UK), *Defence Without the Bomb: Non-Nuclear Defence Policies for Britain* (London: Taylor and Francis, 1983); and Frank Barnaby and E. Boeker, "Defence Without Offense: Non-Nuclear Defence of Europe," *Peace Studies Paper #8* (Bradford, England: Bradford University School of Peace Studies, 1982). Good summaries of the literature also can be found in the journal *Non-Offensive Defence,* published by the Center for Peace and Conflict Research, University of Copenhagen, Vandkunsten 5, DK-1467 Copenhagen K., Denmark. In the United States, the most important piece on NPD was authored by Randall Forsberg, "The Freeze and Beyond: Confining the Military to Defense as a Route to Disarmament," in the Winter 1984 issue of *World Policy Journal.* In the years since, Forsberg's Institute for Defense and Disarmament Studies in Brookline, Massachusetts, has been studying the nuts and bolts of implementing NPD. Gene Sharp's lifelong work on civilian-based defense is well summarized in *Making Europe Unconquerable* (Cambridge, MA: Ballinger, 1985).

Surprisingly few books in recent years have been written on collective security, the focus of Chapter 9. Two recent works are *The Evolution of UN Peacekeeping: Case Studies and Comparative Analysis* (New York: St. Martin's Press, 1992), edited by William J. Durch, and Michael Renner, *Critical Juncture: The Future of Peacekeeping,* Worldwatch Paper 114 (Washington, DC: Worldwatch Institute, May 1993). Robert Johansen has written on the subject periodically for the *World Policy Journal,* as has Brian Urquhart for the *New York Review of Books.*

Some of the best works on nuclear disarmament, the focus of Chapter 10, were written in the 1950s and 1960s. The classic vision of disarmament overseen by a world government is Grenville Clark and Louis B. Sohn, *World Peace Through World Law* (Cambridge, MA: Harvard University Press, 1960). Other noteworthy books on disarmament are: *Security in Disarmament* (Princeton, NJ: Princeton University Press, 1965), edited by Richard Barnet and Richard Falk; John H. Barton,"Third Nuclear Regime" in *Nuclear Weapons and World Politics* (New York: McGraw-Hill, 1977), edited by David C. Gompert; Alva Myrdal, *The Game of Disarmament* (New York: Pantheon, 1983); Jonathan Schell, *The Fate of the Earth* (New York: Avon, 1982); Jonathan Schell, *The Abolition* (New York: Avon, 1986); and Burns H. Weston, *Toward Nuclear Disarmament and Global Security* (Boulder: Westview, 1984). Several works highlight the moral imperative of disarmament: Michael Walzer, *Just and Unjust Wars* (New York: Basic Books, 1977); and Robert Jay Lifton and Richard Falk, *Indefensible Weapons: The Political and Psychological Case against Nuclearism* (New York: Basic Books, 1982). The most interesting recent work comes from a group of physicists associated with the International Pugwash Conferences: Joseph Rotblat, et al., *A Nuclear Weapon Free World: Desirable? Feasible?* (Boulder, CO: Westview Press, 1993). Among the best texts on the dangers of nuclear-weapons proliferation and connections between military and peaceful nuclear programs are: William Epstein, *The Last Change: Nuclear Proliferation and Arms Control* (New York: Free Press, 1976); and Amory B. and L. Hunter Lovins, *Energy/War: Breaking the Nuclear Link* (San Francisco: Friends of the Earth, 1980).

For further reading on the subject of Chapter 11, citizen action in international affairs, there are several books: Gale Warner and Michael Shuman, *Citizen Diplomats: Pathfinders in Soviet-American Relations* (New York: Continuum, 1987); *Citizen Summitry* (Los Angeles: Tarcher, 1986), edited by Don Carlson and Craig Comstock; and Medea Benjamin and Andrea Freedman, *Bridging the Global Gap: A Handbook to Linking Citizens of the First and Third Worlds* (Cabin John, MD: Seven Locks, 1990). For further information on municipal foreign policy, see Michael Shuman's articles on the subject in the Winter 1986–1987 and the Spring 1992 issues of *Foreign Policy*, as well as issues of the *Bulletin of Municipal Foreign Policy* (1986–1991) and *Global Communities* (1991 to the present), available from the Institute for Policy Studies (1601 Connecticut Ave., NW, Washington, DC 20009).

Many of the concepts on resiliency in Chapter 12 were drawn from *Brittle Power*. Also worth reading on crisis management are William Ury, *Beyond the Hotline: How Crisis Control Can Prevent Nuclear War* (New York: Penguin, 1986); and James G. Blight and David Welch, *On the Brink: Americans and Soviets Reexamine the Cuban Missile Crisis* (New York: Hill and Wang, 1989).

Acronyms

ABM	anti-ballistic missile
AID	Agency for International Development
ATS	Americans Talk Security
CBD	civilian-based defense
CFE	Treaty on Conventional-Armed Forces in Europe
CHIPS	Clearing House Interbank Payments System
CIA	Central Intelligence Agency
CIS	Commonwealth of Independent States
CSCE	Conference on Security and Cooperation in Europe
CTB	comprehensive test ban
EEC	European Economic Community
EPRI	Electric Power Research Institute
FAO	Food and Agricultural Organization
FOFA	follow on forces attack
GATT	General Agreement on Tariffs and Trade
GNP	gross national product
IAEA	International Atomic Energy Agency
ICBM	intercontinental ballistic missile
IDEX	International Development Exchange
IMF	International Monetary Fund
INF	intermediate-range nuclear forces
LTBT	Limited Test Ban Treaty
MIRV	multiple independent reentry vehicle
NAFTA	North American Free Trade Agreement

NASA	National Aeronautics and Space Administration
NATO	North Atlantic Treaty Organization
NED	National Endowment for Democracy
NEPA	National Environmental Policy Act
NGO	nongovernmental organization
NORAD	North American Air Defense Command
NPD	nonprovocative defense
NPT	Non-Proliferation Treaty
NSC	National Security Council
OECD	Organization for Economic Cooperation and Development
OPEC	Organization of Petroleum Exporting Countries
PAL	permissive action link
RDF	Rapid Deployment Force
RMI	Rocky Mountain Institute
SALT	Strategic Arms Limitation Treaty
SDI	Strategic Defense Initiative
START	Strategic Arms Reduction Treaty
UN	United Nations
UNCED	United Nations Conference on Environment and Development
UNCTAD	United Nations Conference on Trade and Development
UNESCO	United Nations Educational, Scientific and Cultural Organization
UNICEF	United Nations Children's Fund
UNIFEM	United Nations Development Fund for Women
UNO	National Opposition Union
USSR	Union of Soviet Socialist Republics
WHO	World Health Organization

About the Book and Authors

The Cold War may be over, but the United States is still practicing Cold War foreign policies. From the Persian Gulf to El Salvador, from Bosnia to Somalia, U.S. policymakers continue to rely on force, threats, arms, and military aid. A fundamental redefinition of national security—beyond war and militarization, beyond bilateralism, beyond sovereign states—is long overdue.

In *Security Without War*, a dynamic author team lays out new principles and policies for the United States to adopt in a post–Cold War world. Shuman and Harvey encourage Americans to take account of all threats (not just military ones), to emphasize preventing conflicts over winning wars, to enhance every nation's security (including that of its enemies), to favor multilateral approaches over bilateral ones, and to promote greater citizen participation in foreign policy. Throughout, they show how military, political, economic, and environmental security interests are all linked—and how emphasizing one over the others can undermine the nation's safety.

Security Without War brings together for the first time the major elements of post–Cold War security thought. The authors show how a new framework for U.S. international relations can enhance U.S.—and indeed, global—security at a substantially lower cost.

Michael H. Shuman is the executive director of the Institute for Policy Studies, a progressive think tank in Washington, D.C. Since graduating from Stanford Law School, he has cowritten one book (*Citizen Diplomats: Pathfinders in Soviet-American Relations*, 1987) and coedited two others (*Conditions of Peace: An Inquiry*, 1992, and *Technology for the Common Good*, 1993). He has also written articles for such periodicals as *The Bulletin of Atomic Scientists*, *Foreign Policy*, *Parade*, and the *New York Times*.

Hal Harvey is the executive director of the San Francisco–based Energy Foundation, which is a joint endeavor of the Rockefeller, Pew, and MacArthur foundations. The Energy Foundation's mission is to assist in the nation's transition to a sustainable energy future by promoting energy efficiency and renewable energy. Previously, Mr. Harvey was the executive vice-president of the International Foundation for the Survival and Development of Humanity, where he directed its energy project and GlasNet computer network project. He has bachelors and masters degrees from Stanford in engineering.

Index

Aaron, Henry: quote of, 250
ABMs. *See* Anti-ballistic missiles
Accountability, 97, 229, 231
Achille Lauro, hijacking of, 31
Acid rain, 35, 105, 107, 108, 120, 144, 148, 221, 251
Afghanistan, Soviet intervention in, 1, 4, 51, 57, 146, 159
Afheldt, Horst: quote of, 174–175
Agent Orange, impact of, 46, 139
Aggression
  costs of, 242
  deterring, 186–187, 190
  roots of, 237
Agricultural reform, 119
AIDS, controlling, 152, 158, 224
Al Atheer test facility, 209
Allende, Salvador, 83, 90, 111, 272(n19)
Alliances, manipulating, 182
American Bar Association, 94
American Committee on U.S.-Soviet Relations, 147
American Physical Society, 75
American Society of International Law, 158
Americans Talk Security (ATS), 4
Amin, Idi, 43
Amnesty International, 223
Anderson, Jack: quote of, 62
Anglo-Iranian Oil Company, 42
Angola, intervention in, 1, 52, 185
Anti-Americanism, 43, 44
Anti-Ballistic Missile Treaty, 64, 201
Anti-ballistic missiles (ABMs), 61, 84
Aquino, Corazón, 73
  land reform and, 241
Arbenz, Jacobo: overthrow of, 42
Argentina
  debt relief for, 135
  democracy in, 83
Arias, Oscar, 1
Arias Plan, 1, 241
Arms buildups, 7, 76–77
  national debt and, 32
Arms control, xiii, 55, 56, 155, 179, 201, 203, 230, 245, 246
  cheating on, 159
  conventional, 189
  deep, 194–195

Arms race, 236, 238
  controlled, 55–64, 66–68, 70, 73–76, 170–171, 195, 244
  cost of, xiv, 67–68, 76
  justifying, 25, 159
  NPD and, 242
  nuclear, 194–195
  regional, 166
  security and, 76–77
Arms trade, 7, 123
  regulating, 5, 141
Ashoka Project, 222
Atomic Energy Commission (U.S.), 207
Atoms for Peace, 209–210
ATS. *See* Americans Talk Security
Atwood, J. Brian, 99
Authoritarianism, 8, 103
Azerbaijan, 86

Baker, James, 52, 208
Balance-of-power model, 52
Ball, George, 239
Banca Nazionale del Lavoro, 5–6
Barre, Siad, 48, 49
Barseback nuclear plant, 109
Batzel, Roger, 65
Bay of Pigs invasion, secrecy of, 100–101
Begin, Menachem, 148
Belarus
  nuclear weapons for, 64, 256(n24)
  security arrangements with, 17
Bernstein, Barton, 60
Berry, Wendell, 105
Bhopal, accident at, 109, 131
Biden, Joe: quote of, 198
Biogas digesters, 139
Biological weapons, xiv, 6, 13, 214
  controlling, 247
  producing, 65–66, 75, 201
  proliferation of, 14, 27, 160, 245
  renouncing, 188, 189, 246
Blue Nile, diversion of, 37
B'nai B'rith lodge, Soviet Jews and, 93
Boeing, spin-offs for, 70
Boretsky, Michael: quote of, 70
Borosage, Robert: quote of, 18
Boserup, Anders: quote of, 168
Bosnia, 188
  civil war in, 247

Boulding, Kenneth: quote of, 205, 214, 252
Bradley, Bill: quote of, 34, 35
Brady, Nicholas: quote of, 134
Brandt Commission, 244, 294(n11)
Brazil
    debt relief for, 135
    democracy in, 83
    instability in, 130
Bretton Woods, problems with, 124–125, 126,
        128, 131, 132, 133
Brezhnev Doctrine, 52
Broad, Robin: quote of, 138–139
Brown, Harold, 193
    quote of, 72
Brown, Seyom: quote of, 82–83
Bruntland, Gro Harlem, 119
Brzezinski, Zbigniew: quote of, 12
Budget deficit, reducing, 32, 33, 72
Bunce, Valerie: quote of, 29
Bundy, McGeorge: quote of, 198
Bush, George, 157, 198
    arms control and, 179
    Desert Storm and, 9, 11
    Kuwait invasion and, 2, 3, 5, 7
    military policy and, 47, 249
    new world order and, 2, 73, 187
    security policy and, 13
    War Powers Resolution and, 98

California Energy Commission, 200
Cambodia, 185
    NPD and, 179
    occupation of, 51, 52
Camp David Accords, 148, 154, 178–179, 184
Canada, settlement with, 145
Canadian Army Journal, on arms races, 58
Carbon dioxide, threat from, 37–38, 109–110,
        120, 251
Cardenas, Cuauhtemoc, 47
Carter, Jimmy
    foreign policy of, 30, 43, 97
    grain embargo by, 84, 146
    mediation by, 148
    quote of, 200–201
Castaneda, Jorge: quote of, 35
Castro, Fidel, 38
Cattenom reactor, 108
Cavanagh, John: quote of, 138–139
CBD. *See* Civilian-based defense
Center for Democracy, elections and, 94
Center for Energy and Environmental Studies,
        118
Center for Science and Environment, 133
Centers for Disease Control, 74
Central Intelligence Agency (CIA), 147, 150, 160,
        250
    covert actions by, 42, 44, 100, 102, 103
CFE. *See* Conventional Forces in Europe
        Agreement
Chace, James: quote of, 18
Challe, Maurice, 62
Chamorro, Violeta, 44
    NED and, 94
Charles, Daniel: quote of, 198
Charter of Fundamental Social Rights, 136
Chelyabinsk-40 nuclear-weapons complex,
        accident at, 76

Chemical weapons, xiv, 6, 13, 48, 214
    accidents with, 76
    acquiring, 14, 27, 153, 182
    controlling, 247
    development of, 65, 75, 201
    proliferation of, 160, 245
    renouncing, 75, 119, 188, 246
Chernobyl disaster, impact of, 35, 108
Chevron Oil, 46
Chile
    intervention in, 104
    NED and, 94
China
    NPT and, 63
    nuclear weapons for, 26, 64, 200
    threat from, 12
CHIPS. *See* Clearing House Interbank Payments
        System
Chlorofluorocarbons, 19
    restrictions on, 154
    threat from, 37, 38, 120, 251
Christian Science Monitor, 91
Church, Frank, 100, 101. *See also* Senate Special
        Select Committee on Intelligence Activities
Churchill, Winston: quote of, 55
CIA. *See* Central Intelligence Agency
CIS. *See* Commonwealth of Independent States
Citizen diplomats, power of, 91–92, 191, 220,
        223
Citizen exchange, 91–92, 95, 229
Citron, Zachary: quote of, 160
City-based organizations, 227–228
City-to-city relationships, 223
Civilian-based defense (CBD), 175
Civil society, 93–94, 103
    ethnic violence and, 89
    strengthening, 220, 246
Civil wars, 81, 86, 87, 133, 188–189, 245
    mediation of, 159
    preventing, 246–247
    threat from, 29, 247
Clearing House Interbank Payments System
        (CHIPS), 228
Cockburn, Alexander: quote of, 49
Codex Alimentarius, 136, 137
Cold War, 55
    democracy and, 90
    intervention during, 41
    principles of, 4
    security and, 10, 183
Collective security, 22, 151, 179, 180, 182–187,
        219, 233
    defensive, 187–191
    implementing, 193, 194
    importance of, 191
    nuclear weapons and, 194
    UN and, 145, 184, 187–188, 238, 250
    See also Security
Collective security forces, 200, 246
    creation of, 243–244
Cologne Appeal, 223
Coming War with Japan, The (Friedman and Le
        Bard), 127
Commonwealth of Independent States (CIS), 86
    joint ventures with, 251
    nuclear weapons for, 26–27, 58

support for, 25, 34
See also Russia; Soviet Union
Communications, 175, 240
disruption of, 15
expanding, 97
Comprehensive test ban (CTB), 226
Concentration of value, 172, 173
Conference on Security and Cooperation in
Europe (CSCE), 178
Conflict, 152
civil, 53, 87
controlling, 60, 90, 143–144, 150, 235, 239
ethnic, 11, 29, 53, 89, 246, 247
regional, 246
resources and, 105–112
roots of, 21, 107, 118, 143, 144, 145, 165, 214,
229, 236, 241, 244
vulnerability and, 119
Conflict prevention, xiv, 10, 22, 194, 234
emphasizing, 13–16, 165
Conflict resolution, 10, 11, 21, 22, 52–53, 81, 89–
90, 145, 148, 165, 194, 214, 234, 236–238,
248
emphasizing, 13–16
failure of, 233
nonviolent, xiii, 161, 229, 240, 241–242
NPD and, 170
security planners and, 143
Congressional Joint Economic Committee, 69
Conine, Ernest, 155
Connally Reservation, 160
Conservation, 22, 114, 221
Conservation International, 222
Contracting, 226
Contradora Group, 241
Contras, 53, 101, 185, 228, 241
democracy and, 45
Reagan and, 97, 99
support for, 1, 44, 50, 227
Conventional Forces in Europe (CFE) Agreement,
57, 179, 204
Conventional war, risk of, 29–30, 59, 199
Conventional weapons, 152, 167, 189
threat from, 28–29, 51
Conversion planning, 140–142
Cooperation, 151, 152, 161, 223, 224, 242, 251
bilateral, 145–148, 165, 235, 241
multilateral, 233, 247–248
NPD and, 170
See also Multilateralism
Cooperative ventures, 145–146
Soviet-American, 146–147
women's, 156
Corporate code of conduct, xiii, 123, 135–136,
141
Cost-plus-profit contracts, 69, 71
Council on Economic Priorities, 68–69, 72
Cousins, Norman, 84
Covert actions, 41–43, 53, 90, 104, 275(n68)
damage from, 101
democracy and, 83
funding, 101–102
restrictions on, 101, 103
Cranston, Alan: War Powers Resolution and, 99
Croatia
civil war in, 247
nationalist aspirations in, 86

Cruise missiles, 166, 167
CSCE. *See* Conference on Security and
Cooperation in Europe
CTB. *See* Comprehensive test ban
Cuba, intervention by, 52
Cuban missile crisis, 14, 60
Cultural exchanges, 223, 235, 240
Soviet-American, 146
Curtis, Tom: quote of, 220

Dartmouth Conferences, 84
Davidson, William D., 84
DDT, banning, 137
Dean, Jonathan: quote of, 166
Debt, Third World, 35, 72, 123, 128–129, 134–
135, 222, 270(n87)
Debt-for-nature swaps, 222
Debt relief, 123, 133, 134–135, 249
Defense, 174
advantage of, 175
See also Nonprovocative defense; Strategic
defense
Defense Planning Guidance 1994–99, 17, 18, 29,
117
Defense Science Board, SDI and, 193
Defense spending. *See* Military spending
Defensive weapons, 169, 171–172, 179, 233, 235
buildup of, 170, 245
cost of, 243
exporting, 151
Deficit spending, 129, 243, 249
Deforestation
threat of, 36, 37, 120, 133, 139, 147, 150, 223,
224, 251
See also Reforestation
Democracy, 34, 87, 88, 94, 95, 180
cold war and, 90
covert actions and, 83
free trade and, 137
peace and, 84–85, 103
promoting, xiv, 20–21, 22, 44–45, 53, 73, 91,
104, 140, 220, 234, 240, 244, 251
security policies and, 219
war and, 82, 83–84, 85, 233
See also Strong democracy
Denuclearization, 194, 195, 205–211, 245
Department of Defense, 25, 29, 71
covert operations and, 97, 102
Department of Energy, SP-100 and, 75
Department of Justice, Neutrality Act and, 231
Department of State, 25
covert operations and, 42
municipal foreign policies and, 229
trade promotion by, 229
Dependency, threat from, 8, 129
Desert Shield. *See* Operation Desert Shield
Desert Storm. *See* Operation Desert Storm
Deterrence, 59, 124, 176, 198, 214
distrust for, 205
See also Extended deterrence; Minimal
deterrence; Nuclear deterrence
Deudney, Daniel: quote of, 57
Development
economic, 145, 241
export-driven, 140
limiting, 147
security through, 133–134

Third World, 95, 132, 223, 235
   See also Sustainable development
Development projects, 73, 134, 240
   small-scale, 221, 223, 237
   Third World, 222, 223, 224, 229, 230, 241
de Waal, Alex, 48
Disarmament, 63, 64, 191, 194, 195
   facilitating, 211–215, 246
   nuclear, xiv, 22, 205, 213–214, 215
Dominican Republic, intervention in, 46, 49
Droughts, 133, 144
Drug trafficking, 13, 31–32, 44, 46, 51, 148, 152,
   245
   intervention against, 158, 160, 248–249
Dugway Proving Ground, 65, 76
Dulles, John Foster: massive retaliation and, 56
Dumas, Lloyd: quote of, 63, 69
DuPont, 74

Eastern Europe, 34
   U.S. influence in, 92, 94
Economic assistance, 34, 151, 237–238
Economic decline, 33, 68, 73, 245, 249–250
Economics, war and, 123, 126
Economic security, 16, 21, 68–69, 144, 219
   improving, 142, 152
   national security and, 33
   threats to, 34, 112
   See also Security
Economic threats, 33–35, 38–39
Economist, on information technologies, 93
Ecotage, 49, 111
EEC. *See* European Economic Community
Efficiency
   energy, 112–115, 120, 121, 146, 147, 158, 220,
      221, 233, 244, 251, 283(n10)
   improvements in, 112, 114–115, 116, 237
   resource, 146, 180, 235, 241, 251
   water, 119
Egypt, 186
   instability in, 130
   U.S. aid for, 138
Eisenhower, Dwight, 209, 243
Electricity, 118–119
   saving, 114, 277(n36), 278(n37)
Electric Power Research Institute (EPRI), 114, 207
Eliasson, Jan: mediation by, 159
Elks Club, 222
Elliott, Kim: quote of, 190
El Salvador, 185, 188
   civil war in, 159
   U.S. aid for, 138
Embargoes, 3, 10, 190, 245, 288(n19)
Employment Research Associates, 70
Endara, Guillermo, 47
Endless Enemies (Kwitny), 118
Energy
   renewable sources of, 116
   saving, 210–211, 220–221, 234
   search for, 106
   spending on, 115
   See also Efficiency
Energy production
   alternatives in, 119, 210–211, 245
   increase in, 115
Environment
   cleaning up, 140, 146, 150, 222, 251

damage to, 13, 15, 36–37, 107, 109–110, 130–
   133, 152, 158, 256(n28)
   technology and, 139
Environmental disasters, 36, 38, 245
Environmental hazards, 35–39, 119, 251
Environmental protection, viii, 120, 130, 139–
   140, 161, 234, 240, 241
   U.S. and, 121
   unfair trade practices and, 137
EPRI. *See* Electric Power Research Institute
Escalation, 14, 195, 196
Estes, Ralph: quote of, 50, 263(n30)
Ethnic nationalism, threat of, 29
European Economic Community (EEC)
   agricultural subsidies by, 127
   trade barriers and, 136
European Parliament, 155
Extended deterrence, 59
   phase out of, 195, 199–200
   strategies of, 166, 251
   See also Deterrence
Exxon, 42

Fahd, King, 2
Falk, Richard: quote of, 66–67, 99–100, 212
Falklands/Malvinas War, 172, 243
FAO. *See* Food and Agriculture Organization
Federal Emergency Management Agency, 225
Federation of American Scientists, 131–132
Feinstein, Dianne: foreign policy by, 225, 227
Ferry, W. H.: quote of, 233
Fertilizers, 109, 132–133, 138, 139
First use, 59, 60, 61, 179
   abandoning, 195–199, 201, 202, 234
First World Conference of Mayors for Peace, 227
Fischer, Dietrich: quote of, 170, 172, 176
Flanagan, Stephen: quote of, 176, 177
FOFA. *See* Follow On Forces Attack
Follow on Forces Attack (FOFA), 167, 168
Food and Agriculture Organization (FAO), 36,
   157
Force
   foreign policy and, 41
   limits on, 53
   threat of, 104
   using, 7, 10, 12, 15, 16, 51–52, 53, 156, 236
Foreign Affairs, on first use, 198
Foreign investment, 32–33, 68, 72
Foreign policy, 4, 55–56
   criticism of, 97, 229, 230–231
   nonprovocative, 16–18
   participation in, 20–21, 96–98, 224–231
   provocative, 16–17
Forsberg, Randall: quote of, 179
Forward defense, 167
Freedom House, 30
Freedom of Information Act, 17, 97
Friedman, Alan: quote of, 5–6
Friedman, George, 127
Fujimori, Alberto, 130
Fukuyama, Francis, 1, 161
Fundación Natura, 222

Gallup organization, 94
Gardner, Richard: quote of, 153, 158, 184
GATT. *See* General Agreement on Tariffs and
   Trade

General Accounting Office, on radioactive waste
cleanup, 75
General Agreement on Tariffs and Trade (GATT),
19, 125, 127, 137, 151, 152–153
corporate code of conduct and, 135
NGOs and, 154
social charter and, 136
General Belgrano, sinking of, 172
General Dynamics
Mitsubishi and, 71
spin-offs for, 70
George, Susan: quote of, 139
Gerasimov, Gennadi, 52
Germany
international capital from, 73
NPD and, 176
Glasnost, 4, 85
Glaspie, April, 3
Global 2000 Report to the President, 36
Global warming, 105, 121, 133, 142, 144, 221,
251
conflicts over, 147
threat from, 35, 37–38
GNP. *See* Gross national product
Gorbachev, Mikhail, 1, 4, 51–52, 93, 198
arms control and, 57, 179
Brezhnev Doctrine and, 52
quote of, 110
Grameen Bank, 139
Granda Carajas iron-ore project, 139
Green Bank, 140, 141
Greenpeace, 223
Green Revolution, 132–133, 138
Grenada, invasion of, 46, 49, 102, 157
Gross national product (GNP)
energy and, 116
interest spending and, 72
military spending and, 72, 76
Gross world product, U.S. share of, 33
Group of Seven (G-7), 128
G-7. *See* Group of Seven
Guatemala, intervention in, 104, 185

Halloran, Richard: quote of, 69
Halperin, Morton: quote of, 60, 101, 102
Hamilton, Alexander: quote of, 98
Hammarskjöld, Dag, 184
Hanford, 73, 74
Hannig, Norbert: quote of, 174
Harrison, Selig: quote of, 43–44
Harvard Negotiation Project, 147
Harvard Nuclear Study Group, 62
Harvard Project on Avoiding Nuclear War, 234
Havel, Václav, 141, 244
Hawks, Doves, and Owls (Harvard Project on
Avoiding Nuclear War), 234
Heat exchangers, 114
Henderson, Hazel: quote of, 33
Hitler, Adolf, 123
HMS *Sheffield*, sinking of, 243
Hoffmann, Stanley, 212
quote of, 100–101, 149, 153–154, 155
Holdren, John P.: quote of, 67–68, 117
Hufbauer, Gary: quote of, 190
Human rights, 135, 144, 188, 234
abuse of, 28, 224, 241
promoting, 158, 220, 246

Hummel, Arthur W., Jr.: quote of, 84
Hussein, King, 28
Hussein, Saddam, 14, 19, 29, 38, 47–48, 50, 105,
189, 190, 208, 251
ecotage by, 49, 111
Kuwait invasion and, 1–2, 3, 4, 187, 236, 237,
243
nuclear weapons and, 64, 181
threat from, 5, 6, 8, 13, 15, 30, 238
U.S. policy against, 7, 8–9
weakening of, 48, 51

IAEA. *See* International Atomic Energy Agency
IDEX. *See* International Development Exchange
IDG Communications, 93
Ikenberry, John: quote of, 57
IMF. *See* International Monetary Fund
Immigration, illegal, 35, 133
Income, redistribution of, 138–139
India
civil war in, 86
NPD and, 179
NPT and, 63
Industrial accidents, concerns about, 109
Industrialization, 138
energy for, 106
limiting, 147
INF. *See* Intermediate-range Nuclear Forces (INF)
Treaty
INFACT, 223
Information technology, impact of, 93
Insecurity, 180, 211, 235
Third World, 130
threat of, 8, 16
See also Security
Inspection, 189, 204, 209, 210, 214, 215
Inter-City Solidarity, 227
Interdependence, 31, 126, 144, 154
Interest rates, 68, 72, 242
Intermediate-range Nuclear Forces (INF) Treaty,
4, 57, 152, 166–167, 204, 225
International Astronomical Union, 150
International Atomic Energy Agency (IAEA), xiv,
108, 206, 208
failure of, 210
overhauling, 248
International Bank of Reconstruction and
Development. *See* World Bank
International Convention on the Physical
Protection of Nuclear Materials, 154
International Council for Local Environmental
Initiatives, 227
International Development Exchange (IDEX),
222
International Energy Agency, 152
International Executive Service Corps, 221
International Fund for Agricultural
Development, 156
International Institute of Tropical Agriculture,
119
International institutions, 148–151, 153–154,
156–161, 180, 227, 230
promoting, 153, 156, 234, 251
International law, 156, 186, 234
agreement on, 148–151
decline of, 67
importance of, xiv, 160

International Monetary Fund (IMF), 124, 134,
        135, 138, 152, 241
    development and, 139, 140
    loans from, 126–127, 128
    NGOs and, 154
    Third World policies of, 128–129, 130
International Nuclear Free Zone Registry, 227
International Organization of Consumers
        Unions, 224
International Red Cross, 224
International Science and Technology Center,
        208
International Union for Conservation of Nature
        and Natural Resources, 224
International Union for the Conservation of
        Nature, 46
International Union of Local Authorities, 227
International Whaling Commission, 155
Intervention, 29, 88, 90, 104, 124, 158, 182
    counterintervention and, 50
    direct, 41–42, 46–49, 53
    legacy of, 49–50
    outlawing, 150–151
    overt, 53
    UN and, 2, 3, 47, 48, 50, 156, 183
Intriligator, Michael D.: quote of, 201
Iran
    arms for, 107
    intervention in, 97, 104
    threat from, 30, 48
Iran-Contra scandal, 102
Iran-Iraq War, 5, 47, 185
    nature of, 107
    NPD and, 177, 178
Iraq
    arms for, 107
    intervention in, 48, 49, 50, 208
    NPD and, 179
    NPT and, 208
    resolutions against, 187
    threat from, 30
    water for, 37
Irrigation, 119, 132
Isolationism, 25, 26, 143, 144, 246
Israel
    nuclear weapons for, 64
    offensive posture of, 181–182
    U.S. aid for, 138
    water for, 37

Japan
    international capital from, 73
    public investment by, 250
    rebuilding, 123
    Third World and, 73
    trade with, 127–128
Jefferson, Thomas, 231
Jewish Cultural Center, 93
Johansen, Robert: quote of, 159, 186
Johnson, Lyndon: Vietnam War and, 53
Johnston Atoll, incinerator on, 75–76
Joint Chiefs of Staff, SDI and, 193
Jones, David, 193
J. P. Morgan & Company, on IMF loans, 128
Just-war theory, 204

Kant, Immanuel: quote of, 103
Karkoszka, Andrzej: quote of, 171, 177
Kazakhstan
    nuclear weapons for, 64, 256(n24)
    security arrangements with, 17
Keeny, Spurgeon, Jr.: quote of, 195–196
Kendall, Donald, 93
Kennan, George F., 58
    quote of, 198
Kennedy, John F.: nuclear threats and, 56, 60
Kennedy, Paul, 33
Keohane, Robert: quote of, 156–157
Keynes, John Maynard, 123
Khmer Rouge, 1, 52
Khomeini, Ayatollah, 5, 42, 46, 95
    Iran-Iraq War and, 177
    threat from, 30
Kim Il Sung, 38
Kirkpatrick, Jeane, 102
Kissinger, Henry: quote of, 11, 12, 90
Korea
    democracy in, 83
    NPD and, 179
Korean War, 46, 49
    unilateralism in, 9
Krasner, Stephen: quote of, 151–152
Kuwait, 186, 188
    invasion of, 1–2, 47, 50
    NPD and, 179, 181
Kwitny, Jonathan: quote of, 43, 118

Labor rights, xiii, 130, 135, 139
Labor unions, 89
Lagan College, 89
Lamarsh, John R., 206
Land reform, 138–139, 140, 240, 241
Latin America
    debt of, 128
    dependence of, 129
    U.S. intervention in, 44–45
Latin American Group of Eight, 135
Launch-on-warning, 61, 100
Law of the Sea Treaty, 153
Leavitt, Rob: quote of, 179
Lebanon, intervention in, 46, 49
LeBard, Meredith, 127
Leontief, Wassily: quote of, 68
Libya
    intervention in, 47, 49
    threat from, 30
Lilly-Weber, Steve: quote of, 179
Limited Test Ban Treaty (LTBT), 57, 148, 203, 266
    environmental protection from, 56
    violation of, 64
Lindsay, Anne: quote of, 137
Loans
    guidelines for, 137–140
    Third World, 73, 126–127
Lockheed, spin-offs for, 70
Lockyear, Frank, 222
Logan Act (1799), 230, 293(n19)
Löser, Jochen: quote of, 174
Lovins, Amory, 62
Lovins, Amory and Hunter: quote of, 207, 208,
        210
Lown, Bernard, 92

LTBT. *See* Limited Test Ban Treaty
Lumumba, Patrice: overthrow of, 42
Luttwak, Edward N.
  defense spending and, 25
  quote of, 167, 176
Lynn-Jones, Sean: quote of, 145–146

MacArthur, Douglas, 123, 187
  quote of, vii
MacLeod, Scott: quote of, 48
Maechling, Charles, Jr.: quote of, 47
Majorities
  democracy and, 88
  tyranny of, 82
Makhijani, Arjun: quote of, 213, 214
Malnutrition, 128, 240
Mandelbaum, Michael, 212
Markusen, Ann: quote of, 71
Marshall Plan, 34, 123, 133, 260(n44)
Massachusetts Audubon Society, 222
Massive retaliation, 56, 59
Mayaguez incident, 111
McDonald's, 93
McDonnell Douglas, spin-offs for, 70
McNamara, Robert S., 124
  quote of, 59, 196, 198, 201
Mearsheimer, John: quote of, 87
Mediation, 147–148, 247
Mexico
  debt relief for, 135
  trading with, 35
Middle East
  arms for, 7
  military balance in, 27
  security threats in, 12–13, 182
  U.S. aid for, 8
Migration, 144, 244
Military security, 16, 26, 34, 120, 144
  elements of, 224
  threats to, 148
  See also Security
Military spending, 16, 45, 194–195, 257(n29)
  cutting, 19, 71–72, 129, 140–141, 171, 243–
    244, 250
  impact of, 72, 230
  increases in, 33, 69–70, 250
  justifying, 25, 159
  reallocating, 69, 244–245
  waste and fraud in, 69
Military Staff Committee, 183
Military threats, 38–39, 237
  defining, 5–6, 26–30
Milosevic, Slobodan: threat from, 30
Minimal deterrence, 195, 200–203, 211
  establishing, 202–203, 213, 243
  See also Deterrence
Minorities
  democracy and, 88
  rights of, 85, 86, 88, 89, 90, 103, 228, 248
  tyranny of, 82, 87
MIRVs. *See* Multiple independent reentry
    vehicles
Mitsubishi Heavy Industries, General Dynamics
    and, 71
Mobutu, Sese Seko, 42
Modernization, halting, 203–204

Montville, Joseph V., 84
Mossadegh, Mohammed, 42
Mozambique, 185
  NPD and, 179
Multilateralism, 9, 233, 235, 248
  support for, 18–20, 22
  See also Cooperation
Multinational corporations, 131, 132
  code of conduct for, 134, 135–136, 141
Multinational Monitor, on Bhopal accident, 131
Multiple independent reentry vehicles (MIRVs),
    60, 197
Mutual defensive superiority, 168, 182
Mutual assured destruction, 64, 212, 234
Myers, Norman: quote of, 37

NAFTA. *See* North American Free Trade
    Agreement
Namibia, withdrawal from, 1, 185
NASA. *See* National Aeronautics and Space
    Administration
National Academy of Sciences, 208
National Aeronautics and Space Administration
    (NASA), 38
National behavior, changing, 149
National debt, military buildup and, 32,
    269(n79)
National Democratic Institute for International
    Affairs, 94
National Endowment for Democracy (NED), 44,
    94, 95
National Environmental Policy Act (NEPA), 98
National Geographic Society, 94
National Institute for Peace, 230
National League of Cities, 250
National Opposition Union (UNO), 44
National security, 98, 103, 112
  economic security and, 33
  isolationism and, 144
  Third World debt and, 35
  threats to, 13, 14, 96
  See also Security
National Security Council (NSC), 60, 99, 231, 252
NATO. *See* North Atlantic Treaty Organization
Natural Resources Defense Council, 92, 118, 221
Nature Conservancy, 222
NED. *See* National Endowment for Democracy
Negative control, 59–60
Neild, Robert: quote of, 168
NEPA. *See* National Environmental Policy Act
Neutrality Act, strengthening, 231
Neve Shalom kibbutz, 89
New world order, 2, 3, 123, 187
NGOs. *See* Nongovernmental organizations
Nicaragua, intervention in, 44–45, 49
Nixon, Richard, 125
  foreign policy of, 11
  War Powers Resolution and, 98
Nongovernmental organizations (NGOs), 140,
    154, 155, 191, 235
  NPD and, 245
  role of, 89, 90, 222, 223, 224, 225
  security and, 219
Nonmilitary sectors
  deterioration of, 71
  reinvesting in, 140

Nonproliferation, 152, 153, 206, 210, 246
  erosion of, 67
  IAEA and, 248
Non-Proliferation Treaty (NPT), 63, 153, 205, 206, 208, 211
  achieving, 189
  criticism of, 64
  renewal of, 213, 246
Nonprovocation, 91, 182, 233
  principle of, 90, 95, 165
Nonprovocative defense (NPD), 17–18, 22, 180, 188, 193, 202, 234, 235, 236–237, 252
  criticism of, 175–178, 181
  development of, 168–175, 177–179, 194, 200, 219, 242
  NGOs and, 245
  roots of, 165
  See also Defense
Nontariff barriers, 127
NORAD. See North American Air Defense Command
Noriega, Manuel, 28, 148, 251
  threat from, 30, 47
North American Air Defense Command (NORAD), 61
North American Free Trade Agreement (NAFTA), 127, 136
North Atlantic Treaty Organization (NATO), 3, 6, 151, 166, 168, 171
  conventional forces and, 167
  defense plans of, 25, 56, 152, 172–173
  NPD and, 173
  obsolescence of, 178
Norway, defensive deployments of, 174
NPD. See Nonprovocative defense
NPT. See Non-Proliferation Treaty
NPT Review Conferences, 63
NSC. See National Security Council
Nuclear accidents, 35, 63, 266(n29)
Nuclear deterrence, 22, 251
  substitutes for, 194, 195, 204–205
  terrorism and, 66
  See also Deterrence
Nuclear energy, abandoning, 115, 210–211, 215
Nuclear facilities
  abandoning, 234
  safety concerns about, 74, 108–109
Nuclear freeze, 21, 225, 226, 230
Nuclear materials
  controlling, 209, 215
  production of, 209, 210
  reprocessing, 206
Nuclear power plants, 64, 221
  proliferation of, 118, 206
  vulnerability of, 110–111, 115
Nuclear research, 208–209, 210
Nuclear testing, 56–57
  banning, 84–85, 148, 203, 226, 246
  unilateral, 91
Nuclear war
  accidental, 60, 203
  deterring, 3–10
  fighting, 59–61, 169
  limited, 64, 196, 198, 199, 213
  risks of, 15, 50, 92
Nuclear weapons
  acquiring, 14, 63, 153, 182, 205, 266(n35)

building, 25, 65, 73, 195, 201, 206–209, 230
  collective security and, 194
  controlling, xiv, 19, 193, 211, 213, 247
  NPD and, 193, 194
  proliferation of, 18, 28, 50, 51, 59, 144, 160
  renouncing, 188, 194, 205, 209, 211, 215, 219, 235
  security for, 62–63, 191
  terrorism and, 67, 248
  Third World, 13, 27
  threat from, 13, 59–60
Nunn, Sam: quote of, 167
Nye, Joseph, Jr.: quote of, 157

Oak Ridge National Laboratory
  environmental problems at, 74
  on plutonium production, 206–207
Occupational Safety and Health Administration, nuclear-weapons plants and, 74
OECD. See Organization for Economic Cooperation and Development
Offensive arms, 55, 165–168, 170–172, 179
  building, 168, 174, 178, 235
  controlling, 237, 247
  cost of, 243
  eliminating, 173, 180, 201
  threat of, 169
  vulnerability and, 181
Office of International Affairs, 227
Office of Technology Assessment, 117
Ogilvy & Mather, 93
Oil
  conflicts over, 107
  dependence on, 34, 113, 115, 126, 237
Omaar, Rakiya, 48
OPEC. See Organization of Petroleum Exporting Countries
Operation Desert Shield, 2, 107, 189, 190
Operation Desert Storm, 2, 3, 6, 126, 177, 186, 189, 190
  assessment of, 9–10, 11, 48, 53
  collective security and, 8, 187
  cost of, 9, 19, 50, 107, 113
  escalation of, 14
  intervention in, 47–51
  UN and, 183, 185, 191
Operation Just Cause, 47
Operation Restore Hope, 48–49
Organization for Economic Cooperation and Development (OECD), 82, 92
Organization of American States, 47
Organization of Petroleum Exporting Countries (OPEC), 34, 115, 116
Ortega, Daniel, 44, 94
Osirak reactor, bombing of, 111, 144, 181, 209
Outer Space Treaty, 64
Ozone layer, depletion of, 13, 19, 35, 38, 120, 144, 150, 244, 251

Pakistan
  civil war in, 86
  NPD and, 179
  U.S. aid for, 138
Pakistan Planning Commission, 132
Palestine Liberation Organization, 158, 181
Palme, Olof, 141
PALs. See Permissive Action Links

Panama
  intervention in, 47, 49
  threat from, 30
Panofsky, Wolfgang K. H.: quote of, 195–196
Parliamentarians for Global Action, 148
Participation, 81–82, 99–100, 233, 235, 252
  grassroots, 94, 219, 220–221, 222, 224–231
  increasing, 20–21, 22, 154–155, 234, 240
  value of, 85, 241
Partitions, 86–89
PC World, Russian edition of, 93
Peace
  democracy and, 82–90, 103
  working for, 22, 103–104, 142, 219–224, 231
Peace Action, 25
Peacekeeping, 205, 224
  UN and, 184–188, 235, 244, 247
Peace movement, 225, 226, 227
People-to-people ties, 84
PepsiCo, 93
Perestroika, 4, 93
Pérez de Cuéllar, Javier: mediation by, 159
Permissive Action Links (PALs), 62, 63
Persian Gulf War. *See* Operation Desert Storm
Pest control, 279(n58)
  sustainable methods for, 119
Pesticides, 132
  restrictions on, 137, 224
  subsidies for, 119
  threats from, 109
Peterson, Esther: quote of, 135–136
Philippines
  democracy in, 83
  loans for, 73
Pinochet, Augusto, 42, 43
  NED and, 94
Pisar, Samuel, 92
Pluralism, 84, 88, 90
Plutonium, 292(n53)
  producing, 73–74, 108, 202, 206–210, 245
  stealing, 67, 267(n38)
Podhoretz, Norman, 55
Poindexter, John: quote of, 102
Poland
  loans for, 73, 270(n88)
  NED and, 94
Police, 95, 226
Political threats, 31–33, 38–39
Pollution, 88, 118, 241
  air, 105, 148, 244
  minimizing, 120, 224
  threat from, 34
Popular Integral Development Plan, 140
Population growth, 107, 124, 153
  addressing, 152, 249
  impact of, 36
Positive control, 60
Poverty, 132, 133, 248
  addressing, 137–138, 221
  Third World, 36, 43, 128, 221
  threat from, 8
Powell, Colin: quote of, 12
Powers, Thomas, 58
Prestowitz, Clyde V., Jr., 71
  quote of, 43–44
Primakov, Yevgeny, 52

Proliferation, 144, 207, 245
  preventing, 152, 205, 210, 215
  realities of, 212–213
  Third World, 5
  war and, 63–65
Protectionism, 127, 129
Proxy wars, 41, 43–46

Qaddafi, Muammar, 143, 151
  threat from, 30, 202

R&D. *See* Research and development
Radio Liberty, 91
Rainforests, protecting, 147, 150, 224
Rapid Deployment Force (RDF), 113, 276(n6)
RDF. *See* Rapid Deployment Force
Reagan, Ronald, 1, 4, 6, 21,.46, 143, 153, 158
  Contras and, 44, 99, 228
  grain embargo and, 84
  Iranian arms sales and, 31, 43, 97
  military spending by, 56, 57, 68, 165–166, 249
  quote of, 55, 116
  SDI and, 61, 193, 266
  START and, 225
Reforestation, 119, 251
  See also Deforestation
Refugees, threat from, 15, 38
Regimes, 151–153, 165, 233
  participation and, 154–155
  quest for, 153–154
  subverting, 154
Reich, Robert: quote of, 71–72
Reiss, Mitchell: quote of, 155
Renewable energy, 112, 211
Reprocessing plants, 110, 207
Research and development (R&D), 118, 211
  arms race and, 70–71
Resources
  buying, 131
  competition for, 105–112
  conserving, 53, 105, 112–116, 150
  mismanagement of, 105, 106, 111–112
  redistribution of, 138–139
Rifkin, Jeremy: quote of, 66
Rise and Fall of the Great Powers, The (Kennedy), 33
Robinson, Donald, 99
Rock, Stephen: quote of, 145–146
Rocky Mountain Institute, 118, 221, 277(n36)
Rohatyn, Felix: quote of, 32
Rostow, Eugene V., 98
Rotary Club, 222
Rough parity, 195, 200–203
Rush-Bagot Agreement (1817), 145
Russett, Bruce, 103
  quote of, 69–70, 82
Russia
  aid for, 17, 73
  NPD and, 180
  nuclear weapons for, 64, 200, 256(n24)
  security arrangements with, 17
  See also Commonwealth of Independent States;
      Soviet Union

Sachs, Jeffrey: quote of, 134
Sadat, Anwar el-, 37, 148

Salgado, Joseph F.: quote of, 75
Salinas de Gortari, Carlos, 47
Samizdat, 93
Sanctions, UN, 190
Sanctuary resolutions, 226
Sandanistas, 44–45, 143, 158, 241
Sanders, Jerry: quote of, 129
SANE/Freeze. *See* Peace Action
Saudi Arabia
 NPD and, 179
 U.S. aid for, 11
Savannah River reactors, accidents at, 74
Savimbi, Jonas: U.S. support for, 45–46
Schaeffer, Robert: quote of, 87
Schlesinger, Arthur, Jr.: quote of, 45, 52
Schlesinger, James, 193, 266(n35)
Schneider, William: quote of, 143
Schurmann, Franz, 93
Schwenninger, Sherle: quote of, 129
Scientific American, on material substitution, 117
Scientific ventures, 146, 235
Scowcroft, Brent, 93
SCUD missiles, 6, 7, 14
SDI. *See* Strategic Defense Initiative
Second strike, 196, 197, 198, 243
Secrecy, 103, 159
 costs of, 96
 official, 20–21
 preserving, 100–101
 stripping away, 159
Security, 20, 148–151, 239, 246
 alternative initiatives to, 115, 166
 arms race and, 76–77
 costs of, xiv, 242, 243
 credibility of, 201–202
 economics and, 219
 energy, 112–113
 environmental, 16, 21, 73, 76, 121, 139, 144
 increasing, 17, 22, 119, 133–134, 142, 152,
   168, 202, 221, 224, 225, 234, 235, 244
 intervention and, 50
 natural resources and, 112, 116–117, 118–119
 political, 16, 66–67
 principles of, 65, 165, 224, 229, 233–234
 threats to, xiii, 4, 21, 25–26, 237, 245–252,
   258(n4)
 See also Collective security; Economic security;
   Insecurity; Military security; National
   security
Security Council. *See* United Nations Security
 Council
Security planners, 5, 10–11, 120, 161, 233, 239,
 240, 246
 conflict resolution and, 143
 conversion planning and, 141
 cooperation and, 147, 248
 democracy and, 96, 104
 NPD and, 178, 179
 nuclear weapons and, 59, 67, 205
 on Soviet military power, 38
 use of force and, 165
 vulnerability and, 168
 war and, 15, 81
Security policies, 151, 178, 238, 246, 252
 comprehensive, 16, 38–39
 democracy and, 219
 formation of, 9–10, 39

nonprovocative, 16–18
participatory, 20–21, 149
redefining, 10–21, 228, 251
unilateralism in, 4, 8–9, 20
Security system, 178, 240
 development of, 11–12, 235–236
 environmental threats and, 251
Self-reliance, 138, 139, 140, 241
Sellafield reprocessing facility, 109
Senate Special Select Committee on Intelligence
 Activities, 100, 101, 102
Serbia
 civil war in, 11, 247
 nationalist aspirations in, 86
Shiites, 7
Shining Path, 130
Shultz, George: quote of, 36
Sihanouk, Prince, 1
Sister Cities International, 227, 249
Six-Day War, 16, 111, 186
Slovenia
 civil war in, 247
 nationalist aspirations in, 86
Smith, Gerard: quote of, 198
Smith, Ian, 111
Smith, Ron P.: quote of, 69–70
Social Democratic Party, NPD and, 170
Solidarity, loans for, 73
Somalia, 188
 intervention in, 11, 47, 48–49, 50, 157
Somoza Debayle, Anastasio, 43, 45
South Africa, 94
 mineral resources of, 116
 NPD and, 179
 nuclear weapons for, 64
 sanctions on, 116
South West Africa People's Organization, 185
Soviet Academy of Sciences, 147, 221
Soviet Institute for Sociological Research, 94
Soviet Union
 collapse of, xiii, 57, 95
 democratizing, 90–93
 insecurity in, 76
 mineral resources of, 116
 threat from, 8, 25, 30, 265(n18)
 U.S. influence in, 92, 94, 146
 See also Commonwealth of Independent States;
   Russia
Space weapons, banning, 203
Spin-offs, 70, 71
Stability, xiv
 democracy and, 87
START. *See* Strategic Arms Reduction Treaties
Star Wars. *See* Strategic Defense Initiative
State departments, municipal, 227–228
Steinbruner, John: quote of, 196
Stewart, Francis: quote of, 128
Stone, Jeremy: nuclear planning committee and,
 100
Stowsky, Jay: quote of, 70
Strategic Arms Reduction Treaties (START), 26,
 56, 57, 198, 200, 203, 225, 256(n24),
 289(n9)
Strategic defense, 201, 243
 technology for, 60–61
 See also Defense

Strategic Defense Initiative (SDI), 61, 64, 193, 199, 204, 250, 286(n14)
  cost of, 72, 75, 243
  criticism of, 67
  spin-offs from, 70–71
  technology for, 75, 269(n73)
Strauss, Franz Josef, 108
Strong, Maurice, 108, 120
Strong democracy, 272(n17)
  peace and, 82–90
  promoting, 90–103, 219, 246
  See also Democracy
Strontium-90, 74, 76
Stunnenberg, Frank: quote of, 28
Subsidiarity, principle of, 20, 88–89, 103
Summers, Lawrence, 131
Sustainable agriculture, 121, 158
Sustainable development, 105, 119–121, 180, 224
  promoting, 53, 73, 133–134, 137–142, 234, 237, 244, 249
  See also Development
Sweden
  defensive deployments of, 174
  NPD and, 234
Switzerland
  CBD and, 175
  defensive deployments of, 174
  NPD and, 177, 234
Synthetic fuels, 111, 113
Synthetic Fuels Corporation, 111
Syria
  terrorism and, 48
  threat from, 30

Tariffs, 144, 153
Taylor, Theodore, 212
  quote of, 66, 206
Technology, 33–34, 60–61
  dependence on, 127, 138
  environment and, 139
  spreading, 64–65, 67, 138
  threat from, 13, 51, 61
Technology transfers, 95, 121
Tensions, reducing, 171, 174
Terrorism, 13, 75, 160, 245, 251
  addressing, 39, 147, 152, 158, 247, 248, 263(n23)
  nuclear weapons and, 28, 30, 66, 67, 148, 154, 248
  threat from, 30, 31
Test-ban treaty, 56, 57, 64, 148, 203
Thawrah Dam, controversy over, 37
Thompson, E. P.: quote of, 81
Thurow, Lester: quote of, 71
Tojo, Hideki, 16
Torture, 43, 149, 160, 228
Tourism, 146, 221
Trade, 95, 237–238, 240
  disruption of, 15
  fair, 136–140, 244
  free, 136, 137, 234
  promoting, 229
  rethinking, 134
  See also Arms trade
Trade Act of 1974, Jackson-Vanik amendment to, 90–91

Trade agreements, 235
  bilateral, 152–153
  city-to-city, 227
Trade barriers, 13, 123, 125, 127, 129, 153, 242
  eliminating, 136, 150
  See also Unfair trade practices
Trade deficit, 32, 33, 72, 112, 125, 129
Travel restrictions, lifting, 230
Truman, Harry, 41
Tucurui hydroelectric dam, 139

Ukraine
  Chernobyl disaster and, 108
  nuclear weapons for, 26–27, 64, 200, 256(n24)
  security arrangements with, 17
UNCED. *See* United Nations Conference on Environment and Development
UNCTAD. *See* United Nations Conference on Trade and Development
Underground testing, 56–57, 264(n8)
Unfair trade practices, 141
  environmental protection and, 137
  See also Trade barriers
UNICEF. *See* United Nations Children's Fund
Unilateralism, 4, 12, 22, 143, 246
  advantages and costs of, 8–9, 153
  norms against, 150–151
Union Carbine plant, chemical leak at, 131
United Fruit, 42
United Nations, 1, 241
  collective security and, 145, 184, 187–188, 238, 250
  criticism of, 156–157, 160–161
  embargo by, 3, 10, 190, 245, 288(n19)
  improving, xiv, 236
  intervention by, 2, 3, 47, 48, 50, 156, 183
  NPD and, 188
  nuclear disarmament and, 213–214
  peacekeeping by, 184–188, 235, 244, 247
  U.S. support for, 9, 155, 185–186, 284(n40)
United Nations Children's Fund (UNICEF), 156, 157
  on Third World development, 130
United Nations Conference on Environment and Development (UNCED), 108, 110
United Nations Conference on Trade and Development (UNCTAD), 157
United Nations Environment Program, 131–132
United Nations Fund for Population Activities, 153
United Nations Security Council, 189, 190, 191, 200
  collective security and, 183, 187
  Kuwait invasion and, 157, 238
  peacekeeping and, 184, 186
  U.S. support for, 158–159
United Nations Third Special Session on Disarmament, 63
United Towns Organisation, 227
Uniting for Peace Resolution, 183
UNO. *See* National Opposition Union
Uranium, 206, 291(n38), 292(n53)
  enriching, 207, 208, 209
  production of, 210, 245
  stealing, 67
Urquhart, Brian: quote of, 159
Ury, William, 239

U.S. Agency for International Development, 119, 127, 138
USA-Canada Institute, 147
U.S. Conference of Mayors, CTB resolution and, 226
U.S. Constitution, 253, 273(n45)
  commerce clause in, 137
U.S. Immigration and Naturalization Service, 226
USS *Stark*, attack on, 6, 30, 243
U.S. Supreme Court, Vietnam issue and, 20
Utilities, efficiency for, 220, 221

Velvet revolutions, 83
Verification, 202, 203, 224, 235
  establishing, 159, 214
Vietnam
  intervention by, 51, 52
  migration and, 144
  NPD and, 179
Vietnam syndrome, 11, 46, 85
Vietnam War, 46, 51
  foreign policy blunders during, 97
  political pressures against, 85
  spending during, 49–50, 69, 125
  Supreme Court and, 20
  unilateralism in, 9
Villa El Salvador, 139–140
Voluntary export limitations, 127, 144
von Clausewitz, Karl: quote of, 81
von Müller, Albrecht: quote of, 171, 174, 177
Vulnerability, 56, 110, 120, 168, 172, 173, 174, 181, 182, 194
  conflicts and, 119
  fabricating, 159
  interdependence and, 126

Wackersdorf reprocessing facility, 108
Waite, Terry: mediation by, 223
Wall Street Journal
  on Saudi Arabia, 2
  on security policy, 30
Walzer, Michael: quote of, 204
War, 133
  accidental, 61–63
  democracy and, 82, 83–84, 85, 233
  economics and, 123, 126
  environmental damage from, 15
  preventing, vii, 14, 15, 65–66, 81, 83, 87, 179, 182, 234, 244

proliferation and, 63–65
roots of, 8, 220
War Powers Act, 17
  Mitchell, George, complaints on, 274–275(n61)
War Powers Resolution, 98–100
Warsaw Pact, 6, 52, 167, 168, 169
  disbanding, 178
  NPD and, 171
  war-fighting strategy of, 172–173
Wastes, xiv, 109, 195, 251
  disposal of, 74, 75, 88, 109, 131
Water, 119, 133
  scarcity of, 105
  security and, 37
Weapons industries
  closing, 211
  economic conversion of, 124, 141
Weinberger, Caspar: quote of, 69
Western Europe
  extended deterrence and, 59
  rebuilding, 123
Western European Union, 178
WHO. *See* World Health Organization
Wildavsky, Aaron: quote of, 90
Witness for Peace, 224
Worker rights, xiii, 130, 135, 139
Working Women's Forum, 139
World Bank, 124, 134, 135, 152, 241, 280(n17)
  deforestation and, 133
  interests of, 124, 139, 140
  loans from, 126–127, 129
  NGOs and, 154
  Third World policies of, 130
World Commission on Environment and Development, 119
World Court, 238, 241
  Chernobyl disaster and, 108
  criticism of, 156–157, 236
  influence of, 145, 156, 234
  U.S. commitment to, 158, 160–161
World Development Report, 129
World Health Organization (WHO), 156, 157
World Wildlife Funds, 222

Yeltsin, Boris, 58
Yih, Katherine: quote of, 213, 214
Yugoslavia, 185
  civil war in, 86
  defensive deployments of, 174

Zebroski, Edwin: quote of, 207